SOLDIER: The Memoirs of Matthew B. Ridgway

It is a high thing, a bright honor, for a man to do battle

with the enemy for the sake of his children, and for his land

and his true wife; and death is a thing that will come when the spinning

Destinies make it come.

—*Greek lyric*

SOLDIER:

The Memoirs of Matthew B. Ridgway

By GENERAL MATTHEW B. RIDGWAY, U.S.A., Ret.

As told to Harold H. Martin

ILLUSTRATED

HARPER & BROTHERS : NEW YORK

Library of Congress catalog card number: 56-6032

To the American soldier with whom it has been my privilege to serve in peace and in war, with deep admiration for his steadfast courage and tenacity, deep respect for his sacrifices, and deep affection for his warm, human qualities and unfailing sense of humor.

Contents

16 pages of photographs follow page 116

Foreword

I FIRST KNEW GENERAL RIDGWAY as a young Captain in China, and later at the celebrated Infantry School at Fort Benning, Georgia, where I came to know him intimately. I found him on the General Staff of the Army when I was sent to Washington in 1939.

As the designated Chief of Staff in May, 1939, he was a member of my staff on a military mission to Brazil.

As our preparations to meet the threat of war increased, he became the Commander of the celebrated 82nd Airborne Division, which he led to fame in the invasion of France, as later he did his XVIII Corps, in the desperate fighting of the Battle of the Bulge.

General Ridgway has firmly established himself in history as a great battle leader. The advance of his Army Corps to the Baltic in the last phase of the war in Europe was sensational to those fully informed of the rapidly moving events of that day. His campaign in Korea will be rated as a classic of personal leadership. As Supreme Commander of the North Atlantic Treaty Organization in Europe, he did a splendid job. And he culminated his military career as Chief of Staff of the Army.

I have not read his manuscript, but I am confident of the integrity of his account.

GEORGE C. MARSHALL

SOLDIER: The Memoirs of Matthew B. Ridgway

1

★★★★

Combat Jump

IN THE last long light of the clear June day, weighted down with my battle gear, I climbed heavily up the little ladder of the plane that was to take me to France. In the doorway I turned for one last look at the sweep of the English Midlands, now grown soft and green with spring. All around me the dusty aircraft of the 52nd Troop Carrier Command were taking on their cargoes of fighting men—six thousand booted, burdened paratroopers of my 82nd Division. For many of them this was an old story, for they had jumped to battle in Sicily and in Italy. For me it was a new adventure. I was no stranger to combat nor to jumping. I had jumped in training; and, in Sicily and Italy, in battle on the ground, I had been with them when the fighting was the hottest. But I had never yet shared with them the very special dangers that are a combat paratrooper's particular lot—the quick leap out of the plane into the buffeting prop wash, the slow float down, hanging helpless in the harness, the drop into the darkness where armed enemies wait behind every bush and tree.

All this was new to me, and I had prepared myself to face it, as all men must steel their own souls to face new and unknown dangers. In the long days of training, as I readied this veteran fighting force for its greatest testing, there had been no time for introspection, for troubling thoughts of what fate might hold in store for me. But in the darkness after you have gone to bed, when you are not the commander, with stars on your shoulders, but just one man, alone with your God in the dark, your thoughts inevitably turn inward, and out of whatever resources of the spirit you possess, you prepare yourself as best you may for whatever tests may lie ahead.

I cannot speak for other men, but for me in such moments there has always been great comfort in the story of the anguish of Our Lord in the Garden of Gethsemane. And in all humbleness, without in any way seeking to compare His trials to mine, I have felt that if He could face with calmness of soul the great suffering He knew was to be His fate, then I surely could endure any lesser ordeal of the flesh or spirit that might be awaiting me.

There were other thoughts, inspired by poetry and the Scriptures, which gave me strength and comfort. Sometimes, at night, it was almost as if I could hear the assurance that God the Father gave to another soldier, named Joshua: "I will not fail thee nor forsake thee." And in my wallet was a picture, stained and faded, of a Scottish soldier's monument that stands in Edinburgh. The soldier sits, head up, rifle across his knees, as if for a moment there had come a lull in battle. Carved in the stone beneath him is an inscription which long ago, unconsciously perhaps, I wove into the fabric of my own philosophy:

"If it be Life that waits, I shall live forever unconquered; if Death, I shall die at last, strong in my pride and free."

Knowing that, indeed, it might be Death that awaited me, in the last moments before I left my quarters for the take-off fields I had sat down to say my last good-bys, to try to express something of the deep pride I felt in the men with whom I now was to go into battle. On the bottom of my own photograph, knowing that somebody would find it if I did not come back, I wrote these lines:

"To the members of the 82nd Airborne Division, with everlasting affection and appreciation of life shared with them in the service of our country. May their incomparable courage, fidelity, soldierly conduct and fighting spirit ever keep for this Division a place second to none in our Army."

It was no masterpiece of literary composition, I know. But it expressed my feelings. And as I took my place in the plane in the hard bucket seat, and buckled my seat belt tight around me, I felt a great serenity. All that I knew to do had been done, and I was ready to accept whatever was to come. From then on, there was no backward glancing to happy days gone by, no inner tremors brought on by fearful imaginings of what might lie ahead. My soul was at peace, my heart was light, my spirits almost gay.

The mood of the men around me seemed equally tranquil as we lifted up, engines roaring, to join the great sky train that was on its way to France. I looked at my watch. It was 10 P.M., June 5, 1944. D-day minus 1. For men of the 82nd Airborne Division, twelve hours before H-hour, the battle for Normandy had begun.

We flew in a V of V's, like a gigantic spearhead without a shaft. England was on double daylight saving time, and it was still full light, but eastward, over the Channel, the skies were darkening. Two hours later night had fallen, and below us we could see glints of yellow flame from the German anti-aircraft guns on the Channel Islands. We watched them curiously and without fear, as a high-flying duck may watch a hunter, knowing that we were too high and far away for their fire to reach us. In the plane the men sat quietly, deep in their own thoughts. They joked a little and broke, now and then, into ribald laughter. Nervousness and tension, and the cold that blasted through the open door, had its effect upon us all. Now and then a paratrooper would rise, lumber heavily to the little bathroom in the tail of the plane, find he could not push through the narrow doorway in his bulky gear, and come back, mumbling his profane opinion of the designers of the C-47 airplane. Soon the crew chief passed a bucket around, but this did not entirely solve our problem. A man strapped and buckled into full combat gear finds it extremely difficult to reach certain essential portions of his anatomy, and his efforts are not made easier by the fact that his comrades are watching him, jeering derisively and offering gratuitous advice.

Wing to wing, the big planes snuggled close in their tight formation, we crossed to the coast of France. I was sitting straight across the aisle from the doorless exit. Even at fifteen hundred feet I could tell the Channel was rough, for we passed over a small patrol craft—one of the check points for our navigators—and the light it displayed for us was bobbing like a cork in a millrace. No lights showed on the land, but in the pale glow of a rising moon, I could clearly see each farm and field below. And I remember thinking how peaceful the land looked, each house and hedgerow, path and little stream bathed in the silver of the moonlight. And I felt that if it were not for the noise of the engines we could hear the farm dogs baying, and the sound of the barnyard roosters crowing for midnight.

A few minutes inland we suddenly went into cloud, thick and turbulent. I had been looking out the doorway, watching with a profound sense of satisfaction the close-ordered flight of that great sky caravan that stretched as far as the eye could see. All at once they were blotted out. Not a wing light showed. The plane began to yaw and plunge, and in my mind's eye I could see the other pilots, fighting to hold course, knowing how great was the danger of a collision in the air.

You could read concern on the grim, set faces of the men in my plane as they turned to peer out the windows, looking for the wink of the little lavender lights on the wing tips of the adjoining planes. Not even our own wing lights showed in that thick murk. It was all up to the pilots now. There was nothing I could do, and I did it. I pulled my seat belt tighter and sat back and closed my eyes, taking comfort from the words of Hal Clark, Commanding General of the Troop Carrier Wing, whose planes transported us.

"Matt," he had told me before the take-off, "come hell or high wind, my boys will put you there, right on the button."

The cloud and rough air lasted only a few minutes, though it seemed far longer. As suddenly as we had entered the storm, we broke free. All at once there was the moon again, and clear skies, and the sharp outlines of the land below, the little fields and hedgerows. But nowhere in the sky, in my field of vision, could I see another plane.

It was too late now to worry about that. Beside the door, a red light glowed. Four minutes left. Down the line of bucket seats, the No. 4 man in the stick stood up. It was Captain Schouvaloff, brother-in-law of Fëdor Chaliapin, the opera singer. He was a get-rich-quick paratrooper, as I was, a man who had had no formal jump training. I was taking him along as a language officer, for he spoke both German and Russian, and we knew that in the Cotentin Peninsula, which we were to seize, the Germans were using captured Russians as combat troops.

A brilliant linguist, he was also something of a clown. Standing up, wearing a look of mock bewilderment on his face, he held up the hook on his static line—the life line of the parachutist which jerks his canopy from its pack as he dives clear of the plane.

"Pray tell me," said Schouvaloff, in his thick accent, "what does one do with this strange device?"

That broke the tension. A great roar of laughter rose from the silent men who were standing now, hooked up and ready to go.

"Are we downhearted," somebody yelled.

"HELL NO!" came back the answering roar.

A bell rang loudly, a green light glowed. The jumpmaster, crouched in the door, went out with a yell—"Let's go!" With a paratrooper, still laughing, breathing hard on my neck, I leaped out after him.

The shock of the opening was no worse than usual. I glanced up to see the most comforting of all sights, the spread of my canopy, round and bulging, full of air. Below me, off to the left, for a split second I could see the canopy of the jumpmaster hanging, seemingly motionless, in the dark. Then I was alone in the sky. I saw neither man nor parachute, though I knew that all around me troopers and bundles of heavy battle gear were floating swiftly down. In the stillness of the fall, I could hear far above me the roar of the engines as the following planes sped on to their drop zones.

All at once the ground was very near, and I flexed my knees for the shock of the landing. Weighted with his heavy battle gear, a combat paratrooper lands hard. He may strike swinging forward, or sideways, or backward, and he absorbs the shock by doing a tumbler's roll, loose jointed, with springy knees.

I was lucky. There was no wind and I came down straight, into a nice, soft, grassy field. I rolled, spilled the air from my chute, slid out of my harness, and looked around. As I hit, I grabbed for my pistol, for on the advice of the men who had jumped in Sicily, I had gotten nearly all the division equipped with .45 automatics. In your first moments on the ground, trussed in your tight harness, you are almost helpless. You can't possibly get to a rifle or a carbine, and if somebody is after your scalp in these first seconds, you are in bad shape. But in the tussle to free myself from the harness I had dropped the pistol, and as I stooped to grope for it in the grass, fussing and fuming inwardly, but trying to be as quiet as possible, out of the corner of my eye I saw something moving. I challenged, "Flash," straining to hear the countersign, "Thunder."

No answer came, and as I knelt, still fumbling in the grass, I recognized in the dim moonlight the bulky outline of a cow.

I could have kissed her. The presence of a cow in this field meant that it was not mined, nor staked with "Rommel's asparagus." In the days before the invasion our intelligence agencies had received disquieting word about these fields. They were, we had been told, studded with sharp wooden stakes that would impale a paratrooper and rip the belly out of a glider. Wires connected the stakes, rigged up to mines, and a man striking a stake would set off a chain of explosions. The presence of the cow meant that this field, at least, was free of these traps, and if this one was perhaps the adjoining fields were also clear.

I found the pistol and started creeping toward the shadows of the nearest hedgerow. Pale as the moonlight was, I felt conspicuous out there in the middle of that field, expecting at any moment to get a burst of small-arms fire. But at least if no friends were visible, neither were any foes, and I felt a great exhilaration at being here alone in the dark on this greatest of adventures.

As I moved cautiously toward the hedge, again I saw a movement in the shadows. I challenged and this time the proper response came back instantly. As I drew nearer I saw a man lying on the ground in the shadows, his back against the bank on which the tall hedge grew.

"Who are you?" I said.

"Captain Follmer," a voice came back. I could hardly believe what I heard. In the fighting in Sicily, as I had moved out through no man's land, hunting my paratroopers who had dropped inland in front of the troops that were coming in by sea over the beaches, the first man I had found was Captain Follmer. He was sitting under an olive tree, nursing an ankle he had injured badly in the jump. And here, a year later, out of six thousand men, again my first encounter was with Follmer.

"Well, Follmer," I asked, "what's wrong this time?"

"General, I think I've broken my back."

"Well," I said, "I guess you hope to god you never see *me* again."

By now, all over the countryside around us, the Germans were beginning to rouse and shoot. The finest fireworks display I ever saw was going on all around me. Rockets and tracers were streaking through the air, and big explosions were going off everywhere. Now and then, glancing up, I could see more C-47's going over, as the formation that had been scattered by the storm got back on course again. Low as they were, they were merely dark shadows against the sky, for a blacked-out plane is very difficult for a man on the ground to see. Even a paratrooper, coming down under a white canopy, is hardly visible until he hits the ground.

It might be interesting at this time to describe how an airborne division is committed to battle, compared to a standard unit in the Army. The infantry unit goes into battle with its communications and its command structure at its best. The radios are all functioning, the command chain is intact. The commander knows where all his people are, and what's happening to them, and he can exercise an excellent degree of control. The exact opposite is true of an airborne division. When its people hit the ground they are individuals, and a two-star general and a Pfc. are on exactly the same basis. You have no communications whatsoever for some little time, particularly when you have jumped at night. You don't know where you are. You don't know who's around you, friend or foe. Little by little, stage by stage, you have to assemble—to "roll up the stick," as the paratroopers say.

This is a fairly simple thing in theory. The first men out of the plane note its general heading in relation to the ground. When they hit and shuck out of their harness, they start moving along the track of the plane. The last men out back-track along the path the plane has followed. Somewhere toward the middle they come together. But this takes time. Under the best of conditions the men in one battalion will be strung out along a path one thousand yards long and three hundred yards wide. Along their route enemy gunners may block their way until they can be killed. In Normandy the assembling was further complicated by the fact that the fields were compartments, separated each from the other by the high thick hedges.

The first objective, of course, is to get a battalion together, for the battalion is the basic fighting unit. I had gone in with the 2nd Battalion of the 505th, commanded by Lieutenant Colonel Vandervoort, one of the bravest, toughest battle commanders I ever knew. He broke an ankle in the jump, but the para-medics who had jumped with us rigged him up a stirrup crutch and cut him a stick for a cane, and he led his battalion, limping but game, throughout the entire campaign.

All through the night, by twos and threes, the men in Vandervoort's battalion assembled. They came in slowly, for the clouds over the coast had scattered the formations widely. Many men had dropped in the middle of German concentrations and had been killed or captured. By daylight, though, Vandervoort had enough of his battalion together to move out, hunting the enemy, and in the adjacent fields the fragments of two regiments were assembled, so that by mid-morning we were able to put up some semblance of a division action.

My own little command group of eleven officers and men set up division headquarters in an apple orchard, on almost the exact spot we had planned to be before we left England. Hal Clark's boys had not failed us. They had put us down on the button.

The Germans were all around us, of course, sometimes within five hundred yards of my CP, but in the fierce and confused fighting that was going on all about, they did not launch the strong attack that could have wiped out our eggshell perimeter defense.

This was in large part due to the dispersion of the paratroopers. Wherever they landed, they began to cut every communication line they could find, and soon the German commanders had no more contact with their units than we had with ours. When the German commander of the 91st Division found himself cut off from the elements of his command, he did the only thing left to do. He got in a staff car and went out to see for himself what the hell had gone on in this wild night of confused shooting. He never found out. Just at daylight a patrol of paratroopers stopped his car and killed him as he reached for his pistol. The lieutenant commanding the patrol told me the story with great glee.

"Well," I said, "in our present situation, killing division commanders does not strike me as being particularly hilarious. But I congratulate you. I'm glad it was a German division commander you got."

For a while, had I thought about it, the chances were probably fair that I would suffer the same fate my German counterpart had met. We had nothing but hand weapons with which to defend ourselves, rifles, pistols, grenades, and light 2.36 bazookas. The guns we desperately needed, the 57-mm. guns that could stop a tank, were to come in with the glider serials that were to bring four thousand more men into the zone beginning with daylight. They came just as the first streaks of day began to show in the east, but the morning mist rising from the marshy land hung low over the hedgerows, and many a glider was smashed on landing. The fragmentary news that was coming in was both good and bad. By daylight the division's first objective, the town of St. Mère Église, was in our hands, and was never lost thereafter. The news from the gliders was less cheering. Twenty-four landed, and nearly all were badly smashed up. Some went into the trees that topped the hedgerows. Others went down in swampy places, where men sank armpit deep into the muck as they tried to bring out the heavy radios and the antitank guns.

Soon we learned what we had lost in the way of key personnel. My Chief of Staff, Doc Eaton, and about half the forward echelon of my staff, had come in with the gliders. The Chief of Staff was wounded, the G-4, the supply officer, was shot through the bridge of the nose and had to be evacuated. The ordnance officer and the surgeon were either hurt in glider crashes or wounded soon after they hit the ground and had to be evacuated. In the action of the night before the commander of the engineer battalion and one of the infantry regimental commanders had been taken prisoner.

In addition to our personnel losses, we were sadly handicapped in our communications. We couldn't get in touch with anybody—neither the troops that were supposed to be coming in over the beaches by now, nor with anybody back in England, nor with anybody afloat.

In short, we were in the typical situation for which you must be prepared when an airborne division goes into battle. So I shuffled the surviving staff officers about as best I could until some sort of effective command structure was set up. The G-3 Bob Weinecke took over as Acting Chief of Staff. The signal officer, Bill Moorman, took on the additional duties of the wounded G-4. In a little while—a matter of two or three hours—the CP was a going concern. For thirty-six hours, though, we had no means of knowing how well or badly we were faring. The Germans were boasting on the radio that they had destroyed the 82nd Airborne, a claim we were in no position at the moment to debate. As a matter of fact, we learned later, the 82nd had landed on top of, and had destroyed, the German 91st Division, which had been moved into this area only two weeks before in anticipation of a parachute attack.

These are merely the highlights of the happenings of the first hours. It is difficult to remember in specific detail the sequence of events. Shortly after I landed Don Faith, my aide, who had jumped in the same stick with me, loomed up out of the darkness, and with the first light Sergeant Casey, my bodyguard and "shotgun" man, found me. Dawn came gray and misty, and with it a great hunger. So I climbed up on the ten-foot bank of a high hedgerow at the edge of the field, broke out a K-ration—one of the three-day supply we carried.

As I ate I could hear, amid the general rattle and crack of small-arms fire that was going on all around, the sound of heavy firing from the direction of St. Mère Église, a quarter mile to the east. I went down there to find, to my great satisfaction, that the Germans were pulling out and the town was in our hands. Walking through the battered streets where only paratroopers were moving now, I looked at my watch. It was a few minutes before eight o'clock, on D-day morning.

There in the town I found my Artillery Commander, Andy March, slightly scratched and bruised but in good shape. His glider had landed in the top of a tree.

Throughout that first day I was constantly on the move, from the little CP in an apple orchard near the pasture where I had landed, to the points where the hottest fighting was going on. The Germans, well knowing the value of the causeway crossings that led inland across the swamps from the beachhead, were putting up scattered but fierce resistance against our stubborn advance toward the first of these, the causeway over the Merderet. There was little I could do during that first day toward exercising division control. I could only be where the fighting seemed the hottest, to exercise whatever personal influence I could on the battalion commanders as they drove on toward the causeways.

I had no transportation, of course, and back and forth, back and forth, all day I made that journey from my CP toward the Merderet. No sooner would I return to the apple orchard than a messenger from the "front" would come panting up to announce that all hell had broken loose in a new spot, and I would have to trudge back down there again.

I was in fine physical shape, but never in all my life have I been so weary as I was at the end of that first day in Normandy. Just before midnight, tottering on my feet as was many another soldier who had fought there on that day, I rolled up in a cargo chute and lay down for the first sleep I'd had in forty-eight hours. I crawled into a ditch, for the town of St. Mère Église was only a short distance away, and all that night German airplanes were overhead, dropping five hundred-pounders, and German artillery was shelling the city heavily.

Far in the night I was roused by someone shaking me. It was a messenger from one of the battalions fighting toward the river cross-ing. The Germans, he said, were counter-attacking in strength across the causeway.

I couldn't see what in the hell I could do about that, single-handed. So I sent back word that the battalion was to hold if it could. If this was impossible, then it could pull back. Then I turned over and went back to sleep. It held.

I woke with the first light, sore and stiff but refreshed, filled my helmet with hot water, and started to shave, with one of these little injector razors with a rotating head that a paratrooper likes because it is small, all in one piece, and takes up not much more room than a pencil. I had gotten a leather-cased field telephone in by this time, and when I was about half through shaving, it rang—a battalion down by the river reporting on the night's activities. When I put down my phone and reached for my razor again, it was gone. Some SOB had stolen it.

Throughout that day, as more and more men, scattered in the drop, coalesced into their fighting units, we drove hard against the Germans. Radios, dug from the wreckage of the gliders in the swamps, began to function, and the communication setup was greatly im-proved. The battle began to take on some form and organization—though it still in no way resembled what Field Marshal Montgomery liked to refer to as a "tidy" battlefield.

The tide began to turn in our favor along about dawn of the third day. Elements of the 82nd made contact with patrols of the 4th Divi-sion which had come in from the sea over Utah Beach. Not long afterward the Assistant Division Commander, Ted Roosevelt, strolled into my command post to offer to us all the help, in guns and ammu-nition, that we would need. It was almost the last time I was ever to see this gallant officer, a warm, close friend ever since his days as Governor of the Philippines when I, as a young captain, was his military adviser. A few days later he was dead—not of enemy action, though he always walked where the fire was hottest, as if the bullet that could kill him had not been made—but of a heart attack. I had one other brief, heartwarming meeting with Ted on the roadside just after Cherbourg was taken. No braver man ever lived.

An airborne outfit in the early days of its commitment to battle fights as light infantry. For heavy fire support, and often for resupply, it must depend on the conventional divisions. Once we had made contact with the 4th Division, and had the help of its artillery, we could get on apace with our basic mission. That mission was simply this—to seize and hold the causeway leading inland from Utah Beach, and the stream crossings over the Merderet and Douve rivers. With these bridges and defiles in enemy hands, our troops on the beach could be pinned down and decimated by artillery fire. As soon as the 82nd, and the 101st, its companion division which had jumped near Carentan, had cleared these routes over the marshes, and had sealed off the beach area by seizing key road junctions and communication centers, the assault troops of VII Corps, coming in over Utah Beach, could plunge inland, swing right, and clear the peninsula all the way to the great port of Cherbourg. The strongest opponent of the plan was General Eisenhower's Air Commander in Chief, Air Chief Marshal Sir Trafford Leigh-Mallory. Though a man of great personal bravery and boldness, Leigh-Mallory felt that the drop of two airborne divisions in this area would result only in the "futile slaughter" of these two great fighting units. He based his arguments, in part, on the presence of enemy night-fighter planes, which, he said, would get in among the slow-flying transport craft and knock them from the sky like hawks attacking a flight of ducks. The planes that might escape the fighters, he insisted, would be blown from the skies by automatic weapons' fire when they dropped to six hundred feet to launch their paratroopers.

Both General Bradley and I argued strongly that these were risks that we would have to take, and we were willing to take them. The drop was a great gamble, we admitted. The whole great operation was a desperate gamble. In the end General Eisenhower accepted our point of view. To the great credit of Leigh-Mallory, when it became known back in England that the two divisions had landed without great loss, he went immediately to General Eisenhower. No one could be more distressed than he about adding to the Supreme Commander's burdens in arguing against this operation before it was launched, he said, and nobody could be happier than he that his prediction had been wrong and General Eisenhower's decision right.

Though the disaster en route that had been predicted did not take place, the fighting on the ground soon proved to be as fierce and bloody as even the most pessimistic of us had anticipated. The hardest fighting took place on the causeways. These causeways were elevated roadways across the deep marshes, narrow two-track roads with an eighteen-inch shoulder on either side, sloping down to muddy water that was over a man's head. As we crossed the first of these we learned why, in the first days' fighting, many a paratrooper had never showed up to join his unit. Bodies lay in the water still in their harness. They had hit in the marshes and had drowned before they could free themselves of their chutes and their heavy combat gear.

The place of a commander is where he anticipates the crisis of action is going to be, and it was obvious to me that these causeway crossings were the spots of greatest hazard. Each time, therefore, before we attempted the crossing, I would go down, preferably at dark, by day if I had to, personally to reconnoiter each crossing before I sent any element of my division across.

There were four of these crossings and by far the toughest was the causeway across the wide and sluggish Merderet. Here the road came down and made a right angle turn through a low cut in the hills about twenty or thirty feet high. It then emerged onto a perfectly open, straight road that stretched five or six hundred yards across the swamp. The Germans naturally concentrated their fire on our end of the defile, and it was the hottest sector I saw throughout the war. We lost a lot of men there and I think the assault unquestionably would have failed if all the commanders from division to battalion had not been there in person to shove the troops across.

We weren't going after that crossing cold, of course. We had artillery support by then, from the battalions of the 4th Division. We had a battalion of 105 self-propelled howitzers, a battalion of 155 howitzers, a platoon of tanks, and every 50-caliber machine gun we could lay hands on. We massed them all there on the river lip, and for ten minutes before the crossing we poured shells into the German positions on the far side. It was a tremendous spectacle—the crash of the guns blended into one great blasting roar of terrific noise, and the smoke and dust and haze soon grew so thick you could hardly see six feet in front of you.

We really poured the fire across, and we were getting plenty in return. I lay up on the crest to the right of the crossing, alongside one of the tanks, whose gun was banging away with a noise to split the head. Off to the left the automatic weapons were going like the hammers of hell, and to the rear our heavier artillery was firing, the shells passing directly overhead.

I lay there watching, peering through the haze and smoke, as the first men came down to the crossing, shoulders hunched, leaning forward as if they were moving against a heavy wind. Some of them began to go down, and the others hesitated. Then they turned and started back, instinctively recoiling from the sheer blasting shock of the concentrated enemy fire. I jumped up and ran down there. The men were milling around in the cut. Jim Gavin, whom I had put in charge of this operation, was there, with the regimental CO Colonel Lewis, and the battalion commanders. And there in the cut at the head of the causeway we grabbed these men, turned them around, pushed, shoved, even led them by hand until we got them started across.

We got across all right in spite of fairly heavy casualties, and cleared the far end of the causeway, so that the 9th Division, which was to take up the attack on the other side, could pass through. The Division Commander, General Manton Eddy, told me a few hours later that he'd never seen so many dead Germans anywhere. I agreed with him. I hadn't either. And I think that fight was as hot a single battle as any U.S. troops had, at any time, during the war in Europe.

After that one, my aide told me, laughing, that back at headquarters they were referring to me as "The Causeway Kid." I didn't see anything particularly humorous in the title, for I saw too many fine youngsters killed at those swamp and river crossings. The fire was always hot along those exposed stretches of straight road. I remember one night I stepped out from behind a farmhouse to the edge of the macadam highway, and saw lights winking in the dark at my feet. I said to the officer with me:

"That's the first time I've seen fireflies around here. Wonder why we haven't seen them before."

"Fireflies, hell," he said. "Those aren't fireflies. They're machine-gun bullets ricocheting off the road."

For thirty-three days the division was in continuous action in the peninsula. From time to time we thought we'd have a chance to rest and lick our wounds—"lie down to bleed a while, then rise to fight again"—in Mr. Shakespeare's phrase, but these hours of inaction were brief. We were passed through once by the 90th Division, but they ran into heavy resistance and took a pretty severe mauling, so we were put back into the line immediately, to take over from the 90th and continue with the attack. Then the 8th Division passed through us, and we had a somewhat similar experience. When we were finally withdrawn, forty-six out of every hundred infantrymen had been killed or so severely wounded they had to be evacuated to England. Many others had suffered minor wounds which they ignored to keep on fighting. One thousand two hundred eighty-two men were dead, and 2,373 had suffered serious wounds. We had gone into battle with four regimental and twelve battalion commanders. In the course of the fight, fifteen of these infantry leaders had been killed, wounded or captured. I doubt very much that any major unit during the war suffered heavier casualties and kept on fighting.

Late in the campaign one of my senior officers came to me and told me that the division couldn't make another attack. If it did, he said, it would be so impaired in effectiveness that it would take us months to get ready for another major action.

It was an honest estimate by a gallant battle leader. It deserved soul-searching thought. I was well aware of the brutal punishment the division had taken. But I had spent most of every day of the campaign up with the forward battalions. I knew that, though they were weak in numbers, their fighting spirit was still unimpaired. And if we were called upon to make one more attack, we could do it. Soon the orders came, and we drove the enemy from the dominating ground overlooking the town of La Haye du Puits.

Before we had ever left England I had anticipated that our losses would be heavy, and with the approval of General Bradley, the Army Commander, I had made arrangements for replacements. Over their strong protests I had left behind in England a small, carefully selected training cadre, who would take charge of these volunteers as they came in, and fit them into regiments and separate artillery battalions bearing the numbers of the units fighting in France. My purpose was to indoctrinate each new man, not only with the proud spirit of the division as a whole, but with the spirit of each smaller unit which was then in combat.

After the battle for La Haye du Puits, the division was withdrawn to its permanent training area in the Midlands. Every man on reaching England was sent on pass immediately, to repair, in the ways that soldiers know, the inner wounds that combat inflicts upon the soul. For ten days they walked out with girls, they sang in bars, they told and retold the stories of their exploits so that all might know what manner of men they were. Then the division was reassembled, the fillers took their places in the shattered units, and the 82nd was a fighting force again. Three days after we had reassembled, General Eisenhower reviewed us. We took the field at full war strength— more than sixteen thousand men completely outfitted, trained, and ready for battle again, with our splendid battle partners, the 52nd Wing, beside us.

I suppose a prouder commander never lived than I was as I watched that magnificent division swing past the reviewing stand. For more than two years these great soldiers had been mine. I had seen them gather as raw recruits in the swamps of Louisiana. I had seen them in their training in the hills of North Carolina, and on the dusty rock-strewn deserts of Africa. I had fought by their side in Sicily and Italy, and I had jumped with them in Normandy. They had done all I had asked of them, and more. And I felt for them that deep love, respect, and admiration which a soldier feels for the comrades whose dangers he has shared—the feeling Mr. Kipling expressed so well in the lines:

> I have eaten your bread and salt,
> I have drunk your water and wine,
> The deaths ye died I watched beside,
> And the lives that ye led were mine.

2

☆☆☆☆

Farewell to the All-American

THE great pride that welled up in me as I watched the march past of the 82nd was tempered by a deep sense of sorrow and regret. For I knew what the division did not yet know—that this was good-by. Never again would this great fighting unit go into battle under my direct command. It would fight, and valiantly, under my orders again, but as one of many fine divisions, both British and American. For I was being shoved, with some inner reluctance, up the ladder to three-star rank and a corps command.

When I reported back to the Midlands of England following the withdrawal of the 82nd from Normandy, I went at once to pay my respects to my old friend of many years, General Walter Bedell Smith, General Eisenhower's Chief of Staff. He told me that the achievements of the airborne divisions in Sicily, Italy, and Normandy had made a deep impression on the High Command. In order, therefore, that the unique power of the airborne could be utilized to the fullest in the great battles still to come, an airborne army was being formed. Lieutenant General Lewis Brereton was to be its commander. I was to have command of one of its elements—the XVIII Airborne Corps —if I would take it.

It was, of course, a tremendous honor to be raised from division to corps command, and I gave no serious thought to the idea of refusal. Yet at the same time, I felt at once a great tug at my heartstrings at the thought of leaving the 82nd—a feeling that was accentuated in the next few weeks as I continued to train the division for its next great battles, before turning it over to General James M. Gavin, the brave and brilliant commander who would fight it so magnificently throughout the remainder of the war.

The challenge of a corps command was one that no professional soldier could turn down. The function of the corps in the chain of command has never been properly appreciated. The public knows of armies, and of divisions, but the intermediate headquarters, the corps, is generally less fully understood. The fact is the corps commander is the highest commander in the military hierarchy who is solely a battle leader, a tactical commander. The division commander has a great logistical responsibility; the army commander is primarily concerned with logistics and territorial matters. But the corps commander is almost exclusively concerned with battle tactics. He is responsible for a large sector of a battle area, and all he must worry about in that zone is fighting. He must be a man of great flexibility of mind, for he may be fighting six divisions one day and one division the next as the higher commanders transfer divisions to and from his corps. He must be a man of tremendous physical stamina, too, for his battle zone may cover a front of one hundred miles or more, with a depth of fifty to sixty miles, and by plane and jeep he must cover this area, day and night, anticipating where the hardest fighting is to come, and being there in person, ready to help his division commanders in any way he can.

When I took command of XVIII Corps on August 27, 1944, three fine airborne divisions came under my command; my own old 82nd, now under General Gavin, General Maxwell Taylor's 101st, scarred but triumphant from its battles in Normandy, and the 17th, newly arrived from the States under that pioneer paratrooper, General Bud Miley. I could not help but reflect as I took over my new responsibilities that this organization of specialists, trained to fight a new kind of war, though only a small segment of the great armies we had put into the field, was bigger by far than the entire force of all arms that had worn the uniform of the U.S. during most of the years of my military service.

It was a small and tidy army into which I was born, and in which my youth was spent. The Civil War had been over for only thirty years in March of 1895, when I came squalling into the world at Fort Monroe, Virginia, where my father, the late Colonel Thomas Ridgway, commanded a battalion of field artillery, and neither its tactics nor its organization had changed much since Lee laid down his arms at Appomattox. Its glamorous branch was the cavalry, whose swaggering mustached troopers had earned their laurels on the Western plains in battle with the Cheyenne, the Apache, and the Sioux. My earliest memories, therefore, are of guns and marching men, of parades and bands, of rising to the sound of the reveille gun, and lying down to sleep at night while the sweet, sad notes of "Taps" brought the day officially to an end. These things to me were the normal patterns of a boy's life, which is why, perhaps, I remember so vividly one brief interlude when I lived for a year the unregimented life of a civilian—the only time, until I retired in June of 1955, that I knew that freedom.

The year was 1900 and my father had gone out to China during the Boxer Rebellion to take over Reilly's battery "F of the 5th" whose horse-drawn guns had banged away at the walls of Peking. My mother, my sister, and I, of course, could not accompany him on this combat operation, and we awaited his return at my maternal grandmother's house at Garden City on Long Island.

He was back within a year, as I recall, full of stories of war in a far-off land that fascinated a six-year-old. I remember him less as a soldier, though, than as a man of infinite kindliness and patience, a gentle man—though with the iron in his soul that a soldier must have—who shared with my beautiful mother a love of music, and good books, and who had deep affection for the wild and beautiful Western country in which my early life was spent.

My father had the usual run of Army assignments, most of them spent at little Western posts, the old forts of Indian days. The first that I recall with any vividness was at Walla Walla, Washington, which lingers in my memory because it was there that I was allowed to have my first rifle. It wasn't a rifle, actually, but an asthmatic air-gun, which fired a little lead pellet with a sound like a muffled sneeze. Like any inexperienced soldier, I soon shot up all my ammunition, and had to cast about for more in a hurry. Unable to finance the purchase of a new supply of BB shot, I made the happy discovery that the hard winter wheat they raised in the Walla Walla area would serve just as well at short range, a fact I proved to my own satisfction by shooting a local farmer in the rump as he bent over to select some ripe tomatoes for my mother.

It was the last time I ever pointed a weapon at man or beast without fully intending to kill, a principle that my father pounded into my head, through the seat of my pants, when he came home that night. It has been my lot to shoot at men on several occasions since, but it was never done in a spirit of playfulness.

From Walla Walla we moved to Fort Snelling, Minnesota, to an ancient set of quarters that had been uninhabited, except for rodents, since Indian days. We arrived there in December, just as the hard cold set in, and I remember vividly how we spent our evenings during that freezing winter. Huddled in the only room that had a fireplace, we sang while my mother played the piano, the sound of our voices rising above the shriek of the whistling wind that blew the snow in drifts against the doorway.

We moved from the Western country to the more civilized posts of the Eastern Seaboard—to Fort Caswell, N.C., and from there back to my birthplace at Fort Monroe, which I remembered not at all. Without knowing it, though, during my life in the Western states I had absorbed from my father knowledge and skills that were to serve me well in later years as a field soldier. On hunting trips and camping trips he taught me to take care of myself in the open, to bed down like a bear wherever night found me. He taught me to love the open country in all its myriad forms—mountain and plain, prairie, desert, and the seashore, and to make myself at home in them. One of the hardships that besets a soldier, therefore—the living outdoors in cold and rain and snow—never greatly bothered me, even in the gray gloom of the Ardennes, the wet and biting cold of Holland, or the often bitter temperatures of Korea.

My love for hunting and fishing, for sleeping under the stars, for hiking over the hills, transcends the atavistic yearning that is in all of us to get away from cities into cleaner air. For me, life in the open has always been a deep spiritual experience that cleanses the soul of doubts and fears. The intangible things in life are the most real, and my most vivid memories are not of battle action, nor of hard decisions made in a time of crisis, but of moods—of deep feelings stirred by the sight of snow gleaming on a far-off mountain peak, the leap of a trout in a stream, the radiance of moonlight on white plum blossoms, the rising of a blue-white star above dark hills. One such moment came to me not many years ago during my period of service as military adviser to Mr. Baruch on the UN Atomic Energy Commission. I had gone by air from Washington to see the atomic energy plants at Hanford, University of California, Los Alamos and Oak Ridge, and had marveled, as all men must, at the magnitude of these great achievements of the human mind. During much of the trip, however, my thoughts were far away from the complex formulae of the atomic physicists. Flying over plain and mountain, looking down on the great peaks and valleys where I had camped and hunted as a boy, and in later years, as a mature man, I felt a deep nostalgic yearning to be down there with a pack on my back, a rifle in my hand. And some lines from Kipling came back to me to trouble me with a deep restlessness—"Who hath smelled woodsmoke at midnight? Who hath seen the birch log burning? Who is quick to read the noises of the night?"

At the end of my trip, though, I did have one wonderful day. Eight of us crowded into a Chevrolet pickup, with chains and compound gears, and, leaving the highway just north of the Colorado-New Mexico border, at an altitude of ten thousand feet, we climbed to the headwater meadows in the shadow of the Continental Divide. There, in the clear thin air, at an altitude of more than eleven thousand feet, with the great peaks rising around us, we spent one day of golden sunshine fishing for trout. We caught fish by the dozens—brook trout, rainbows, and German browns—cooked them over a campfire and ate them ravenously. The memory of that day and early evening, though, is dimmed by the great aerial display that came thereafter, when all the heavens were filled with shooting stars. It was early October, 1946, and the night was cloudless, with a half moon shining. For more than two hours, as we drove down from the high valleys, the meteorites arched above us—great glowing balls of fire with tails of flame that showed in the sky long after the body of the star had burned out. To me such moments are unforgettable. They uplift my soul as nothing else can do, and from them comes a renewed appreciation of Deity and of man's small place in the scheme of things.

Whatever tendency to gun shyness I might have felt as a youngster was soon trained out of me by my father. As an artilleryman, he had no objection to loud and sudden noises, and he felt that it was the inalienable right of every small boy to shake the world with loud explosions on Independence Day. Every Fourth of July, therefore, he would buy me a tremendous supply of cannon crackers, rockets, and Roman candles, and let me set them off myself. By the mercy of Providence I lost no eyes nor fingers, and I feel a mild regret that in a more careful generation my own small son, Matty, age six, is forbidden by law from knowing the joy of rising at dawn to rouse the sleeping world with a giant firecracker. For curiously, in the midst of battle, when guns were thundering around me, and enemy shells were falling near with great explosions, I have felt a strange detachment, derived, perhaps, from this early experience.

"Why, hell," I have thought to myself, "I made this much noise when I was twelve years old."

It was spurious reasoning, of course, and false comfort, but it served to fortify my spirits in moments of great crisis, when a more prudent man, perhaps, would have taken cover.

Though my father did shape and guide my interests in many ways, he never by word or overt act sought to persuade me that I should follow in his footsteps as a career soldier. This, I think, in no way reflected his own attitude toward the Army, for he was a soldier to the core, for all his kindliness and gentleness. It did reflect his belief that a boy was an individual, a new being on the earth, with his own traits of character and personality, and he should be allowed to choose his life work without interference—a procedure I hope Penny, my wife, and I will be able to follow in the rearing of our own small son.

Nor do I recall feeling any strong inner compulsion to take up the trade of arms as a career. I do think I sensed, deep down, that my father would be happy if I should choose to go to West Point, where he had graduated in 1883, and it was, I think, as much an effort to please him as it was any burning desire on my part to become a soldier that led me to make application for an appointment there in the class of 1912.

Like any other Army brat who'd been dragged from post to post across the country during his formative years, I was poorly prepared, scholastically, for the hard tests I had to pass before I could be accepted. I had begun my grammar school education in St. Paul, Minnesota, and had finished it in North Carolina. I had started high school in Virginia, and finished in Boston, where my father, who had transferred from Field to Coast Artillery, was stationed in my middle teens. Each transfer meant the loss of much time in school, a disruption that did not disturb me spiritually for my attitude toward school was the same as that of any other boy, but it did leave some wide gaps in my education.

Again I recall the infinite patience of my wonderful father. He never seemed too tired or too busy to help me, particularly in math, in which he as an artilleryman was necessarily gifted, and in which I was exceptionally ill informed.

It was obvious that if I were to be admitted to West Point these gaps in my education would have to be filled in. My parents very generously sent me down to Washington to Swavely's, a very fine school which has long since closed, but which at that time had a splendid reputation for preparing young men for West Point. I'm afraid, in my first efforts, I did little to enhance the luster of Swavely's reputation or my father's tutoring. I entered in the winter of 1911, at Christmastime, and took my West Point exams in May. To my bitter disappointment, I failed in geometry. Again, though, my wonderful parents came to my aid. They sent me back to Swavely's the following Christmas, and from then on until examination time in the spring, I never left the campus. Night and day, Saturdays, Sundays, and holidays included, I pored over my math books until I felt that Euclid himself would have been hard put to find a proposition that would stump me. My confidence was not without foundation. When the results of the tests were in, I had an average of 96 in geometry and algebra. I needed a high mark, for it was a competitive exam. I was seeking entrance under a Presidential appointment. There were seven places open, and twenty candidates competing, which made my chances about one in three.

I entered West Point on the 14th of June, 1913, and was immediately plunged into the ordeal which faces every plebe—the six weeks of rigorous mental, physical and spiritual testing known as "beast barracks." The first classmen and the yearlings drive you pretty hard during that period, and there is many a night when a man, sore and bruised both physically and emotionally, doubts the wisdom of ever having entered West Point at all. I know I did. But I managed to get through by giving myself little pep talks as I lay there in my bunk after lights out.

"Look, Ridgway," I'd say to myself, "your father endured this thing, and thousands of other men went through it without breaking down. And if they did it, you can."

Once this period of personal harassment was over, I think I enjoyed nearly every day of my life at West Point thereafter. I had some disappointments, of course. I tried out for football as a yearling and found to my annoyance that I was not worth a damn, though I did manage to make the Collum Hall squad, which played a fairly inept brand of football against neighboring high schools. My disappointment at not making the varsity was somewhat allayed, however, when I was selected as assistant manager at the end of my yearling year. This meant I might be manager in my senior year, which I was. This kept me close to the team, though my duties were primarily logistical, and I was happy merely to be around the men who played.

I dabbled around in other sports, but never was of varsity caliber in any of them. However, I had a tremendous ambition to wear a varsity "A." In those days you could earn your letter by breaking a school record in some track or field event. So I got out the record book and pored over it, seeking some field of achievement in which I thought I might be able to better the record by a fraction of a second or a quarter of an inch. To my delight I found that West Point in the past had been extremely deficient in shot putters. The school record stood at thirty-six feet, as I recall, some fifteen feet below the intercollegiate mark. I figured that here was my chance. I got a sixteen-pound shot and began to practice. I heaved and struggled with that thing until I began walking lopsided, but my longest toss was thirty-three feet. I gave up then and never did win a varsity letter.

One of my semi-athletic endeavors very nearly ended my military career before it was well under way. When I was a cadet, we had a great deal of riding, for it was considered one of the attributes of an officer and a gentleman that he be able to sit a horse well. It had a practical side, too, for the horse, both saddle and draft, was still a major means of transportation in the Army. Much of it was stunt riding, to condition the cadet to feel perfectly confident on a horse, and to eliminate any fear of the animals he might have. We rode bareback, and as the rider entered the chute, the instructor might tell him to drop his reins, or shut his eyes, or start twisting his trunk as the horse moved forward, the idea being to develop fearlessness and a sense of balance.

I wasn't particularly fearful, but my sense of balance evidently was not all it should have been. In an effort to put my horse over a low wooden box, painted to resemble a stone fence, I fell off—"policed" in the cadet phrase. Embarrassed at my inept exhibition, and humiliated by the instructor's loud and impolite remarks on my clumsiness, I caught my horse, climbed on, and put him at the hurdle again. He threw me again, and this time it really hurt. I landed back down across the wooden hurdle with a crash. I got up and walked off groggily, feeling no particular discomfort at the moment except profound embarrassment. In the next few days, though, I began to suffer intense pain in my lower spinal region, as if somebody had stabbed me there with a bayonet and had neglected to remove it. I knew then that I'd suffered some injury, and I thought it might cause me to be dismissed from West Point if I should report for medical attention. So I kept my mouth shut. The only way I could walk or sit without pain was to hold my back stiff as a ramrod, but this somewhat unnatural carriage attracted no attention in the cadet corps, where an erect posture is highly desirable. All my duties as a cadet continued, of course, including riding, and I still remember the agony I felt, climbing back on a horse with no saddle or stirrups, but just a blanket, so that I got the full impact of a bumpy trot. I would just lock my spine and straighten my back, and grit my teeth and take the jolting, for if I tried to bend with the motion of the horse, the pain was more than I could bear.

In due time the stiffness left me and the pain diminished and finally disappeared. Over the years, though, the old injury has come back to plague me. I was playing billiards once, and leaned over the table to make a shot, and the pain struck me so hard and suddenly that I went to my knees and had a hell of a time getting up. Fifteen or twenty times, over the years, the thing has hit me, on each occasion filling me with a tremendous anxiety that it was going to terminate my career.

Just before the Normandy invasion, for instance, I was out on a training inspection, and vaulted over a low fence. My foot slipped on the icy ground on the other side, and the old pain shot through me. Again in the spring, while we were on the take-off fields, sealed in, so to speak, with little to do but while away the time before we left for the Cotentin battles, I got another scare. I was playing softball with the men when, as I took a healthy swing at the ball, the thought passed through my mind that this was a fool thing to do. For I remembered very distinctly that one of the worst attacks I'd ever had came as a result of taking a healthy swipe at a baseball, thrown by Omar Bradley, in a game at Fort Benning in 1930. I missed it, and the bad back stiffened up on me, with a pain like a hot poker stabbing me in the sacroiliac region, and I was *hors de combat* for a couple of weeks. This recollection went through my brain like a knife that afternoon there in England, just five hours before we were to take off for the jump into Normandy.

"Ridgway," I said to myself, "if you pull that back loose again, you'll be absolutely incapable of going on this great adventure, the biggest operation of its kind in history. You'll never be able to live it down. You'll never be able to explain it to anybody, and you'll never forgive yourself."

So I dropped that bat and walked off the field, and by the grace of God nothing happened. Later, I was not so lucky. Just before the assault crossing of the Rhine in support of the British Second Army, I had a very severe attack, the result again of an amateur's swipe at a baseball. The pain was excruciating. I remember lying on a board in my room one evening, trying to sleep, for lying on a mattress on a saggy Army cot was agony. I was trying not to move a muscle, but even so, spasmodic and convulsive reflex actions of the muscles deep in my back sent such waves of pain shooting through me it was hard not to yell out loud. Fortunately, in my corps at the time we had a very fine surgeon, a captain named Gadek. He worked over me for about seventy-two hours, baking me, and taping me up, and finally, just before the assault, I was able to get up and move around. I moved up to our battle command post west of the Rhine, and called for a light plane, so that I could reconnoiter the stretch of river across which we were to attack the next morning. Those little L-4's are cramped for space. It takes a contortionist to get in and out of one, and I remember praying, as I doubled myself up in that thing, that the back wouldn't give way on me again. Again, by the grace of God, it didn't. But I am still thankful to Dr. Gadek, and to Divine Providence, that I didn't get laid by the heels by that thing.

Not all my troubles at West Point stemmed from my sacroiliac, of course. Some of them I brought on myself. In my yearling year, I had the extremely bad judgment to get caught by the Commandant of Cadets while hazing a plebe. I wasn't really causing him any physical discomfort. I was merely speaking to him with severity, urging him to assume a more soldierly posture by sucking in his belly and pulling in his chin. But the Commandant was a stern man, and I was caught red-handed, so I spent all my leisure hours for a month walking the area, an athletic exercise from which I derived no pleasure. For a while, it seemed, I could do nothing right. As soon as I'd walk off two or three hours "on the area" for some flaw in my actions which displeased the tactical officers, I'd get four or five demerits at Saturday inspection, each worth another hour.

Just as it began to appear that my career was about to come to an inglorious close, however, I seemed to break through whatever mental block was harassing me. And to my utter amazement, when the non-commissioned officer appointments were announced at the end of my yearling year, I was the senior "make" in my class. After that I had no disciplinary problems. In my final year I was cadet adjutant, and manager of the football team, and had a lot of other extracurricular activities which probably took more time from my studies than I could spare. Through these extra activities, though, I made a lot of warm friendships that have endured for more than thirty years. These personal relationships that are established at West Point, and in the Army schools to which a career officer is sent thereafter, are a vital factor in the cohesiveness, the team spirit of the professional Army. A career officer is going to school as long as he lives, and in the close associations of the barracks and the classroom, he unconsciously makes his estimates of the character, the integrity, and the competence of his fellows. And they make their estimates of him. In time of battle, therefore, top commanders know the characteristics of their immediate subordinates. They know which ones are by nature bold and reckless, and must be restrained a little, which ones are by temperament cautious, and must be prodded. They are aware of the traits of their opposite numbers, commanding other corps and divisions in the line, and can anticipate how their units will fight. For the battle action of any military organization, from a squad to an army group, is merely a reflection of the qualities of leadership possessed by its commander. In building a general staff it is important to have this background of knowledge of one's associates. Some men are by instinct battle commanders, great fighting leaders who are almost useless in staff and planning jobs. Others are brilliant planners and administrators who fail as battle leaders, when great decisions must be made in a hurry, and some are good both in the field and on the staff. Nor can friendship be allowed to influence one's judgment in matters such as these. It has been my unhappy duty, as I shall discuss later, to relieve from combat command officers for whom I felt warm personal respect and regard, but when the lives of men were at stake, I did it without hesitation.

In all my years in the service, I have never seen any evidence of an "Army clique," a small group within the service whose members protect each other and pass out the top jobs among themselves. There is, though, definitely, this mutual evaluation and assessment of an officer's talents and capabilities, that goes on throughout the years of his service. And many an officer does get his big opportunities because some higher commander has known him for years and has confidence in him. In my own case, certainly, that door of opportunity opened to me because two magnificent soldiers, Generals Frank R. McCoy and George C. Marshall, had come to know and have faith in me.

One of the extracurricular activities which gave me great pleasure during my cadet days was singing in the choir, a pastime I continued until I discovered that, by quitting the choir and teaching Sunday school, I could sleep an hour later on Sunday mornings. Mr. Fritz Mayer, our gifted choir leader, did not seem greatly upset by my departure.

My scholastic achievements were respectable, but nothing to indicate that another genius was appearing on the military horizon. When the class of 1917 graduated—six weeks earlier than usual because the U.S. had gone to war with Germany just fourteen days before—I stood somewhere around the top of the middle third of my class. This was fairly good, but not high enough to give me my choice of service. We named our preference in order of our class standing, and I, out of deference to my father, had put the artillery in first place. By the time they got to me, though, all the artillery assignments had been filled, and I was given my second choice, which was infantry.

I have never regretted for a moment that I ended up with the riflemen. To my mind, the highest service a man can perform is to lead other men in battle. It requires of him courage and competence of the very highest order, and it develops in him a deep and abiding love for the men whose lives are entrusted to his hands—a love that creates in him a complete willingness to sacrifice his own life for them, if need be. To my way of thinking no great battle commander in all history ever reached the heights he might have reached, if he did not feel this love for his men, and a profound respect for them, and for the jobs they had to do. On the field of battle all men's lives are equally precious, as they are in the sight of God, and each man's job, no matter what it is, is as important as another's, for it is the sum of the efforts of many men, doing their jobs, that determines the success of an army's mission.

In my opinion the commander who in the confusion and the excitement of battle forgets that he is dealing with men's lives, and who through callousness or stupidity sacrifices them needlessly, is more butcher than battle leader. He is a fool and not a guiltless one. I remember a bitter joke that went the rounds of the Army soon after World War I, a conflict which gave to history many prize examples of men's lives being thrown away against objectives which were not worth the cost. At a staff meeting before a big attack some fire-eating division commander tapped at a little dot on the map with his riding crop and said:

"I'd give ten thousand men to take that hill."

There was a moment of silence, and then from the back of the room, where stood the battalion commanders whose men would have to go against the hill, there came an ironic voice:

"Generous son-of-a-bitch, isn't he?"

I've never admired such generosity, and I shall go to my grave humbly proud of the fact that on at least four occasions I have stood up at the risk of my career and denounced what I considered to be ill-considered tactical schemes which I was convinced would result in useless slaughter. The airborne divisions were particularly vulnerable to these noble experiments, for once the airborne had been seen in action in Sicily, every higher commander figured that here was the key to success in combat. They sought to prove to the world, I suppose, that they were bold thinkers, quick to seize upon and utilize a new and dramatic weapon, and some of the plans they dreamed up were fantastic. I knew the airborne's limitations, as well as I knew its magnificent capabilities. I fought against these foolhardy schemes as stubbornly as I could, and I am convinced that on several occasions I saved the 82nd, or large elements of it, from being dropped into situations where it would have been destroyed as a fighting force.

I do not wish to convey the impression that I am an advocate of timidity on the battlefield, and I do not feel that I have that reputation among my brother officers. The timid commander, by prolonging combat unnecessarily, causes the death of as many men as does the reckless, foolhardy commander. Neither is a true combat leader, for the finest battle commander is the man who can accomplish his mission the quickest, with the least cost in blood to the men under his command.

3

☆☆☆☆

Memories of a Soldier's Son

TWO weeks after my graduation from West Point, with my new gold bars shining on my shoulders, I was on my way to war. At least I thought I was. To my great delight I had been assigned to the 3rd Infantry Regiment, down on the Mexican border. The 3rd, with a proud history going back to 1782, was at full war strength—one of the few Regular Army regiments that had not been broken up to form the cadres for the new draft regiments which were going overseas. The rumor was that it was soon to sail for France.

My first two or three weeks with the 3rd were pretty rough. I reported in to the regimental sergeant major, for the adjutant was by far too exalted a personage for a mere second lieutenant to approach upon arrival. He received me with the courtesy and the deference that regulars of that time paid to officers, no matter how young and callow they might be, and I walked out of regimental headquarters in a daze. The best I had expected was a platoon leader's job. I had been given a full war-strength rifle company. The battalion commander welcomed me with warmth, for he was so short of officers that he had not only the battalion under his command, but two companies as well, and I could take one of them off his hands.

I felt my way pretty carefully at first, leaning heavily on the advice and counsel of Walter Waite, a fine first sergeant. The responsibilities were mine, though, and I knew I could not dodge them. If I ever was going to be a leader of troops I had to begin now, though I was well aware of my shortcomings and I knew the troops were too. A second lieutenant does not fool old soldiers. They know very well how little he knows about handling men.

They test his mettle too, if they can get away with it. I remember right at first I felt a certain dissatisfaction with the response I was getting from the men. I couldn't seem to create that atmosphere of team spirit, born of mutual understanding and respect, which, youthful as I was, I knew to be the hallmark of leadership.

I did a lot of lying awake at night, trying to figure out what I was doing wrong, and I finally came to the conclusion that most of my troubles stemmed from one sergeant. Whether it was my inability to galvanize him or not, I didn't know. But I did know that whenever I gave him an order, he would drag his feet. Very respectfully, he'd offer a half-dozen plausible reasons why it couldn't be carried out as I wanted it done. Finally I went to my first sergeant and told him I'd come to the conclusion that I was going to bust this sergeant and get another one. He looked at me with a little smile and agreed, and somehow I got the impression he had just been waiting to see how long it would take me to discover this bad apple in the barrel. So I called this troublemaker in and busted him, and from then on things began to improve tremendously.

Thus I learned very early that one of the attributes of military leadership is knowing when to get rid of a sorehead, or a subordinate who is dragging his feet—the early recognition of those who can't, or won't respond, and their prompt elimination. And this same rule applies all the way up the line. When the responsibility of a command is on your shoulders, you cannot afford to play along with officers who won't give you all they've got.

Not long after this incident my first sergeant went off to Officer Candidate School, and I had to appoint a whole new series of non-commissioned officers in the company. In those days a company commander, even a newly joined second lieutenant, had only to convince his colonel that he had reasonably good judgment, and the men he selected and recommended to the colonel would be appointed to the non-commissioned posts. This gave tremendous power and authority to the company commander, which he should have. This power to make or break a man has largely been withdrawn in recent years, as a result of ill-conceived recommendations of certain boards and committees in the post-World War II period. The weakening of the power of the company commander has been, to my mind, a major factor in lowering the state of discipline in the Army of today. If an officer is fit to lead men in combat, he surely must be assumed to have the character and the judgment to discipline them in time of peace.

We have only recently made substantial progress toward correcting the evils which sprang from certain do-gooders, who sought to level off all rank distinctions in an organization where the constant, instant recognition of such distinctions, and the authority that goes with them, is a matter of fundamental importance to survival in peace or war.

The authority of the company commander to make or break a non-commissioned officer should not apply to first sergeants. These non-commissioned officers are master sergeants, and the status of the top-grade non-coms should have certain safeguards. They should not be subject to the loss of their stripes at the whim of some young commander, nor should they be promoted to this extremely important post solely on his recommendation. Below this rating, though, the company commander should be restored the full authority to make or break his men.

For a year, or thereabout, down there on the border, I absorbed the lessons that every young officer had to learn—to take any job that was handed to him, whether he knew anything about it or not; to issue orders as if he meant them and expected them to be obeyed; to temper justice with judgment in all matters of discipline; to be firm, but fair, in dealing with his men. It soon became apparent that the recurrent rumors that the regiment was to go to France had no more substance to them than the hot winds that blew the tumbleweeds along the sunbaked plains of Eagle Pass. Summer passed, with no orders to move, while the great battles raged on in France. I still had hopes, though, of seeing action, until September, when orders came that filled me with consternation.

They were blunt, and non-informative beyond the fact that I was to report to West Point for duty as an instructor. To me this was the death knell of my military career. The last great war the world would ever see was drawing to an end and there would never be another. Once the Hun was beaten, the world would live in peace throughout my lifetime. And the soldier who had had no share in this last great victory of good over evil would be ruined. I did what I could, of course, to avoid this sorry fate. Immediately I started trying to get my orders changed. There was only one person who might help me that I dared address a communication to—a lieutenant colonel in the Adjutant General's office at Washington, a former 3rd Infantryman. I wrote him a long letter, pouring out my woes, protesting my assignment to a dull and dusty teaching job while a war was on. I heard nothing for quite a while. Then a telegram came. It was signed by some officer I'd never heard of, who had taken over the duties of my friend. Its tone was curt. It told me, in effect, to comply with orders at once and to keep my mouth shut in the future.

I went up the Hudson with a heavy heart, too glum to brood over-much as to what my duties were to be. I expected to teach English, or law, since I'd done fairly well in both these subjects. Or Spanish, since that had been one of my good subjects too, and I had had opportunity to practice it during my service on the Mexican border. When I got to West Point and reported in to Colonel Willcox, the head of the department of modern languages, his instructions filled me with dismay. Spanish had been discontinued during the war, he told me. I was to teach French to a class that was already well along in its second year in that language. I bluntly told Professor Willcox I didn't know enough French to order a scrambled egg in a French restaurant. I hadn't spoken or read a word of French since my yearling year, and I hadn't been particularly good in it then. I couldn't possibly see how I could do a good job as a French instructor. Professor Willcox listened, saying nothing.

"Your classes start tomorrow," he said dryly, turning back to some papers on his desk.

I hadn't studied so hard since I prepped for my entrance exams in math. Finally, after about three weeks of sitting up half of each night, filling my head with French grammar, and bluffing and blundering my way through classroom lectures, I began to feel a little more at ease. I was catching up with, and passing, that class of bright youngsters who from the start had known more about the language than I did.

Fortunately, the war ended about three months later, Spanish was reinstated as a required subject, and I was shifted to that language. I stayed there more than a year, working hard, and finding that I had a natural bent for the musical and expressive tongue. Pretty soon I knew more Spanish grammar than I did English, and was completely at home in the language, an accomplishment which, though I didn't know it then, was to have a profound effect on my future career.

I stayed at West Point for six years, first as language instructor, then as tactical officer, and later as faculty director of athletics, a job that was given me by General MacArthur, then the Superintendent. The first months were not particularly happy. A gray gloom hung over my spirit, as well as over the spirit of the whole faculty, for each of us knew that we were going nowhere. We'd sit out the war without hearing a shot fired, without getting a chance to do the thing our hearts were set on—lead men in battle. Throughout that first war it was the burning desire of every career officer to get to France and get into the fight. This spirit was in marked contrast to the attitude of many individuals of my acquaintance in World War II. They seemed to have little, real, genuine, avid interest in getting into combat. They were perfectly satisfied to serve out the war in some stateside billet, or safe assignment outside the combat zone overseas. We shall do well to ponder this difference.

While I was teaching Spanish at West Point I was deeply concerned for fear that I might lose contact with my specialty, the infantry. For that reason I volunteered for after-hours duty, teaching tactics. I got some brother officers interested, too, and we organized volunteer classes, which were held at night for two or more hours twice a week.

This extra duty was particularly valuable to me, for it brought me into contact with some fine combat officers who had had wide experience in World War I. One of them whom I particularly remember as the ideal officer was Major Parker C. Kalloch. He had been badly shot up in a very gallant action near Vauquois, for which he had won the DSC, and he had been gassed thereafter. He was absolutely fearless, and had a wonderful capacity for leadership, which he exercised without any arrogance or swagger whatsoever. There were a graciousness and charm of manner about him that drew all men to him. To me he was Chaucer's "Verray parfit gentil knight" personified, and I worshiped at Parker Kalloch's feet, with an admiration and affection which have deepened through the years.

To my great regret he resigned his commission a year or two after the war, and went into business in New York. You can't keep an old warhorse out of harness, though, when the shooting starts. When World War II began he sacrificed a fine business career to come back into the service, and we met again in France. He was a full colonel then, in the Provost Marshal General's office. He lives now in Albuquerque, New Mexico, and I drop by there to see him every chance I get, for with the passing years my appreciation for this great and simple man continues to grow.

No duty lasts forever, even in the Army, so finally, after six years at West Point, orders came transferring me to Fort Benning, to take the company officer's course. I was fairly rusty, having been away from troops for a long time, but the extra hours I'd spent teaching tactics at West Point had kept me pretty well abreast of new developments in that field, and I managed to finish fairly high in the class—second, as I remember it now. From Benning I was sent to the 15th Infantry, then on duty in Tientsin. There for the first time I had the high privilege of serving under General Marshall, then the Lieutenant Colonel commanding the regiment, whose friendship and faith in me in later years were to have a profound effect on my career.

There was considerable tension in North China at that time. It was the era of the bandit commanders, of Chang Tso-lin, the warlord of Manchuria, and of Feng Yu-hsiang, the "Christian General," both of them in command of fairly large forces. The mission of the 15th Infantry, and of their British counterparts, was simply to keep open a corridor from Peking to the sea down which the members of our legations could escape in the event of trouble.

By the Protocol of 1901, Chinese forces were forbidden from entering an area of several square miles around the city of Tientsin, and it was our job to keep them out if they should approach the restricted zone. We had a number of alerts, of course, when the 15th went out to man the outer defenses, but there was no shooting while I was there.

I remember one such alert very well. A Chinese force of twelve thousand men, soldiers of Chang Tso-lin, were reported to be marching toward the restricted zone. I was told to take as many men as I thought I would need to go out and divert them. Since not all the forces of the 15th, and the British regiment combined, could have done much about "diverting" a force of twelve thousand if they had chosen to come in, I picked two men to go with me. This was sufficient, I felt, to carry out my instructions, which were to use "bluff, expostulation, or entreaty," but under no circumstances to fire unless I was fired upon.

It was a clear, bitterly cold day. Bundled in furs, mounted on shaggy Manchurian ponies of the breed that had carried the cavalry-men of Genghis Khan, we rode out, our feet freezing in the steel stirrups. Soon across the plain to the north we saw the dust of the marching column. To my considerable relief, I saw it was skirting the restricted zone. We shadowed that force all day, staying well away on the flanks but keeping the column in view. We were not molested, nor did we make any attempt to molest them.

I was much impressed by the march discipline of this column. There were no stragglers—even when passing through the little villages—and as every commander knows it is a difficult thing to march a body of men through a populated area without losing a few of them temporarily. Marching at route step, they moved steadily on, a tan snake threading the bare and dusty plain. Now and then a bugle would blow, the column would halt and the men would fall out for a break. Exactly ten minutes later the bugle would sound again and they would assemble quickly and move on. Later in the afternoon, when I stopped to watch the tail of the column pass, I saw why there were no stragglers. Bringing up the rear were a platoon of grim-looking MP's—armed with long beheading knives!

I went back that night to report my day's observations to Lieutenant Colonel Marshall. He merely nodded. It was a routine contact.

My whole service there was more or less routine. Our mission was to protect American lives and property in the event of trouble. We had no contact with, and exercised no control over, the government—a far different assignment from that I was to have later in the Philippines. There our mission was to keep order, of course, but in the main it was to prepare the Filipinos for their own self-government.

From China I came back to the States, to command a company in the 9th Infantry, at San Antonio. There, through the good offices of another higher commander, my military horizons were broadened, and an opportunity arose which I think marked a definite milestone in my career. As I pointed out before, I was never an outstanding athlete in any particular sport. However, through severe self-imposed physical conditioning I had become pretty good in several of the military versions, and I had what I thought was an excellent chance to make the Army pentathlon squad which was to take part in the 1928 Olympic games. I was lean and hard and tough from my field service in China and in Texas, and though I was thirty-three years old and past my prime as a competitor, I had visions of making something of a name for myself as an Olympic athlete in the military events—riding, shooting, fencing, swimming and running.

Orders had already been cut, assigning me to train with the Olympic squad at West Point when General Frank McCoy, who commanded the 3rd Brigade, of which my regiment was a part, sent for me. He was going down to Nicaragua, he said, as head of an American mission which was to supervise a free election in that strife-torn little republic, and he would be pleased if I would accompany him.

It was quite a tough decision to make. I loved competitive sports and I was positive I could make the Olympic squad. At the same time, I knew that any athletic career I might have must necessarily be very brief, for at my age a man's muscles begin to lose their spring, and his reflexes begin to slow. On the other hand, General McCoy's invitation offered unlimited opportunities for service in a field in which I had had no experience—the field of military diplomacy. And though my interests up to that time had been concerned almost solely with the trade of the soldier, with weapons and men and tactics, I was well aware that the pattern of world politics was changing. My own country was being drawn, inexorably though reluctantly, into a position of world leadership. And it seemed to me that I could not reject so bright an opportunity to prepare myself for any military-diplomatic role that the future might offer.

I have never regretted that decision. To watch the smoothness, the calm self-assurance, the absolute honesty and integrity with which General McCoy handled those delicate matters was a lesson which I have never forgotten. And I am sure that in later years, when I found myself dealing, not only as a soldier but as a diplomat, with the peoples of Europe and the Far East, I have, perhaps unconsciously, sought to model myself on him. By any standard, of any people, in any age, he was a great man.

We left for Nicaragua shortly after New Year's day in 1928, stopping off first in Panama to give the political dust a chance to settle in Nicaragua. That gallant American statesman Mr. Henry L. Stimson had already arranged a truce that was acceptable to both of the warring political factions which had turned that little country into a bloody shambles. This agreement included a clause which provided for a completely fair and free election, to be supervised by our group. While waiting in Panama, however, we learned that there was likely to be no government in Nicaragua with which to deal. The entire cabinet was threatening to resign, and the country was seemingly adrift on the political seas with no hand whatever at the helm. Our orders were to proceed to Nicaragua by the fastest available transportation. The fastest available transportation turned out to be a venerable Navy ammunition ship, which trudged along at about nine knots, or slower, but it gave us ample time to figure out what we should do when we first arrived on Nicaraguan soil.

Our party consisted of General McCoy and his personal aide, Lieutenant Hasbrouck; Mr. Walter Bruce Howe, a very distinguished Washington lawyer; Coloned F. Le J. Parker, another soldier-diplomat; and myself. Aboard ship, General McCoy called us together to talk over the situation. His question was simple: What do we do, now that there is apt to be no government with which to deal? I, being the junior, was asked my opinion first.

I didn't have any more idea than the man in the moon what we should do, but I answered the best I could. We had been sent down by our government to supervise an election. We should do whatever we possibly could to set up the proper machinery, hold the election, and guarantee its fairness.

I have never forgotten General McCoy's great courtesy and consideration, in asking me, a very junior officer in the group, to express my views along with the older, and wiser, men. Nor have I forgotten the consummate skill with which he handled this explosive situation. With infinite patience, fairness and tact, he brought deadly enemies together at a time when their hot Latin tempers were still running high. We rewrote the election laws, translated them from English into Spanish, and distributed them throughout the country. Some ten months later, the election was held. There was no rioting, no disorder, and I am positive that no election was ever held in any land that was fairer or more impartial.

My duties as secretary of the electoral board did not prevent my getting away now and then to see some of that beautiful country, and to observe my fellow practitioners of the arts of war, the U.S. Marines, in action. The bandit Sandino was still causing much trouble in the mountains of the North, and the Marines had their hands full trying to chase him down and wipe out his rebel "armies."

At every possible opportunity, I visited the Marines in their jungle outposts, and gained an abiding respect for their fighting qualities. Three of the young Marines I met there, Captains Schilt, Lamson-

Scribner, and Chesty Puller, I was to serve with again when I commanded the Eighth Army in Korea. They had become generals then, but they had lost none of the fire and drive they had in Nicaraguan days.

To reach the scattered Marine outposts I went by air, a mildly hazardous form of transportation. Aircraft maintenance was none too dependable under these primitive conditions, and occasionally one of the small single-engined scouting planes would fall into the jungle. This was likely to mean death for the pilot and the observer, for even if they survived the crash, they would be hunted down and hacked to pieces by the machete-armed rebels.

Some of the hunts we had in Nicaragua were potentially about as hazardous as the jungle flights I took with the Marines. The Nicaraguan lakes are full of monster crocodiles, wary creatures, but dangerous to a man alone. I hunted them by creeping up on them, crawling on my belly through the slime. I would shoot them just between those little knobs in which their eyes are set, which is all you can see sticking up when they are in the water. It was a fine test of marksmanship, for it was all offhand shooting at unknown ranges, at a very small target, and you had to get in a brain shot to kill. I used a 30-06, with an unusually wide iron-post front sight, and a big peep sight, for much of the shooting was done late in the day when the light was dim. I have killed as many as seven in a day—fourteen-footers, with big wide bellies on them, weighing up to a thousand pounds each, I would guess.

If you missed the brain, you lost the crocodile. If you hit it, he would flop over on his back with his two little stubby front legs sticking up out of the water, floating there for about a minute before he sank. We used to have big arguments about how long it took one to die, if you hit him just right. I said they died instantly, and once, to prove my point, when I had shot a fourteen-footer on land, I ran up and sat on him within ten seconds after the shot. There wasn't a flicker out of him, but looking back on it now, I think it was a damn-fool thing to do. Some of the places I crawled through, wearing nothing but shorts and shoes, I wouldn't wade through now wearing armor plate and hip boots, for a thousand dollars. It was a lot of fun then, though it did cost me one treasured memento. My loosely fitting West Point ring slipped off my finger while I was stalking one big old bull and it's still there somewhere, buried in the jungle muck. Perhaps in some far distant day some patient seeker for science's secrets may turn up that bit of imperishable metal and try to guess from the indecipherable markings what manner of Mayan or Mixtec fashioned and wore that bauble.

When that tour ended, late in 1928, I asked General McCoy's permission to come home overland. Unlike most general officers, who can find a dozen reasons why young subordinates cannot be spared for off-beat adventures of their own, he agreed immediately and even wrote our embassies along the route, asking them to give me what aid and comfort I might need. In the congenial company of a young brother officer of the 9th Infantry, a lieutenant named Irvin Alexander, I set out. By bull cart, canoe, mule back, bus and train we made our way through El Salvador, Guatemala, and Mexico, a three-month journey. Alex survived the Bataan death march later.

That was a memorable trip. We left about mid-December of 1928, and took a boat from Corinto, on the west coast of Nicaragua, to La Libertad on the Pacific coast of El Salvador. We went overland from there, leaving the traveled highways now and then to move up into the hills to visit some little village that clung like a bird's nest to the heights. Some of our travel was by jitney bus, antique automobiles driven by good-natured maniacs, who took the hairpin mountain curves on screaming wheels, while we, and the barefoot peasants who were our fellow passengers, surged about inside in a welter of chickens, fruit, and small goats. These buses were supposed to run on schedule, but in that, as in all other aspects of Central American life, the *mañana* spirit prevailed. On the beautiful drive to Guatemala City, I remember, every forty miles or so the driver would pull over to the side of the road alongside a little house and go in, leaving us sitting there twiddling our thumbs for half an hour. When he came out, we'd catch a glimpse of a bright skirt at the doorway, and a pair of dark eyes shining. This happened two or three times, with none of the passengers making any protest. Finally, though, after an exceptionally prolonged halt, I asked him just what all this stopping was about. With disarming charm he explained that he was calling on his sisters, who lived in these quiet little houses along our route. Surely *el señor* would not object to his paying these little social visits to his female relatives? He had more sisters than any man I've ever known, all of them fairly pretty and all of them, strangely, about the same age.

That journey through Central America taught me one thing that stood me in good stead later, when I served as Chairman of the Inter-American Defense Board. I learned that you should not expect the Latins to adapt themselves to the swift pace of life to which the North Americans are accustomed. It may appear to you that what you wish to accomplish may be achieved in six hours, or six days. If, instead, it takes six months, you must contain your soul; you must have patience. It is their way, and they will not change. And to be perfectly honest, I am not at all sure that their way is not the better.

Much of the enduring affection and admiration I have always felt for our neighbors to the south stemmed from that trip. Once in Mexico, we broke our journey by spending three weeks with a Mexican family, eating what they ate, living not as guests but as members of the family circle—even to the extent of bathing in our rooms from pottery jars heated over open fires, while owl-eyed children peeped in the doorways at these strange gringos whose faces and hands were brown as theirs, but whose bodies were so strangely white.

From this experience in living I gained a profound respect for the simplicity, the gentleness, the graciousness, the basic goodness and humanity of the Latin American of the poorer class—the little man who lives out his life in hardship and believes implicitly that the Good Lord will give him ease and happiness in the hereafter.

At Mexico City, I got a message to report to our Ambassador. I went with some misgivings, searching my mind for anything I might have done to jeopardize our good relations with our neighbors below the border. I could think of nothing, except, possibly, the mild rebuke to the bus driver who had so frequently visited his kin.

My fears were groundless. The Ambassador had a message for me from my revered chief, General McCoy. It said: "I shall require your services in early March with the Bolivian-Paraguayan conciliation commission. Will you come?"

It wasn't hard to decide what answer to give to that. He was a general. I was a captain. He had said, "I require your services." I went.

I joined him in Washington in March and served with the commission until September, when I left to take the advanced course—the field officers' course—at Fort Benning.

By now I had learned what every soldier eventually learns—not to fight the problem. Simplicity is the basic factor in any tactical plan.

So in our field exercises I would come up with what seemed to me to be the simplest workable solution, and I made out pretty well, finishing as I remember it now, at the top of the class. Here again I came under the influence of General Marshall—who in my opinion will occupy a place second only to George Washington in the military history of this country. Under his leadership—he was Assistant Commandant—the Infantry School had been made into one of the finest and most thorough advanced military courses in the world, with that crusty genius, Vinegar Joe Stilwell, in charge of its tactical department.

After that tour, I was sent down to Nicaragua again, briefly, for further duty with the American Electoral Commission, getting in a little more crocodile shooting, and from there I went to Panama, for duty with the 33rd Infantry in the Canal Zone. This lasted until the spring of 1932, when I was assigned to the Philippines as technical adviser on military matters to the Governor General, Theodore Roosevelt, Jr. There began the warm friendship which lasted until Ted died of a heart attack in Normandy, after winning the Congressional Medal of Honor for his intrepid actions on D-day, when to hearten his men he walked on Utah Beach under heavy fire as casually as if he strolled in a garden.

He came of hardy and resolute stock. I remember once, in 1933, he asked me to take his mother, the widow of the late President, on a visit to Corregidor. We were doing a great deal of construction on "The Rock" then, getting ready as best we could for the war which we felt would someday surely come. Part of this work consisted of blasting out a big tunnel in the rock, and piles of loose stones strewed the place. We went by destroyer across the bay, a very pleasant cruise, and then by motor around Corregidor. I had expected that Mrs. Roosevelt, who was in her middle or early seventies at the time, would be content to see everything from the comfort of the car. To my surprise, when we reached the Malinta Tunnel—where the Japs, years later, made their last stand on Corregidor—she insisted I stop the car.

"I want to see that, Captain," she said. So she got out of the car, spry as a cricket, and scrambled in her nice black suede shoes over the high pile of loose stones that still partially blocked the tunnel entrance. She went into the tunnel and gave the place a thorough inspection. Every time thereafter, when I saw Ted strolling about on a battlefield as calmly as if he were playing croquet on the lawn at Oyster Bay, I remembered that incident.

One of my most vivid recollections of my Philippine duty is of a most distressing case of dysentery I contracted there from an unwise indulgence in the native food. One of Ted's jobs as Governor General was to stimulate industry, and he was much concerned by the fact that of the seventy-odd fishing trawlers operating in Manila Bay, all but two were Japanese owned and Japanese manned. The Filipinos depended almost entirely on the Japanese for the fresh fish taken right out of their own front yard, so to speak. So Ted asked me to look into the situation and make some recommendations that might lead to the setting up of a Filipino fishing industry. I went out with one of the Filipino trawlers, ate what they ate, and came back to be knocked off my feet by an attack which the doctors first diagnosed as cholera. They hauled me off to the hospital and gave me a massive injection of horse serum, from a needle and syringe so huge that even the nurse, when she saw it, turned white and clenched her teeth. The injection made matters worse. I proved to be allergic to horse serum. My head swelled up to the size of a pumpkin, and my feet and hands were so swollen they looked like basketballs. The doctor bore my suffering with fortitude. As I began to recover enough to be recognized as a human being, he came in to see me.

"You know," he said, cheerfully, "a thing like that can kill a man."

"Yes," I said, not so cheerfully, "and you damn near did."

Later on an inspection trip with Ted down in the southern islands, I was knocked out again. I had given specific instructions to my house boy to prepare some sandwiches out of cheese or fried eggs, or anything but meat. Naturally, he made meat sandwiches, for it was not uncommon for Filipino house boys, particularly those serving their novitiate, to do, with the utmost amiability, exactly the opposite of what you told them. We decided to mix a little pleasure with our labors and spent the better part of the day fishing. Along toward dark, for you don't fish in those waters after sunset because of the dangerous reefs, we decided to eat. And very foolishly, I ate those meat sandwiches. Pretty soon I began to feel sick, and I got progressively sicker and sicker until I told Ted:

"You've got to put me ashore. This isn't sea sickness. This is something else."

So we felt our way in through the surf and I staggered ashore there and lay down on the sand. And I don't think, in battle or anywhere else, I have ever been closer to departing this earth. Ted told me later that when he felt my wrist he could find no pulse at all. I do remember, though, feeling some misgivings about Ted's safety. We were in the islands controlled by the Sultan of Jolo, a tough old Moro chieftain, whose men not long before had caught a patrol of Philippine constabulary in the jungle and butchered half of them. It would have been a great triumph for men of that metal if they could have ambushed the Governor General and let his head roll down the hill, as they had done with other heads. We built a fire there on the beach, and I posted a couple of members of the crew, armed with rifles, outside the circle of the firelight. Sick as I was, I had no intention of letting some Moro decapitate me with a barong. The night passed quietly, however, and by the time we got to Manila I was in fair shape, though weak and hollow-eyed.

With the election of Franklin D. Roosevelt in 1932, Ted's service as Governor came to an end, and my job ended with his. There was no great warmth of feeling between the two great branches of the Roosevelt family—or rather there was great warmth of feeling, all of it tartly acrimonious, between them—and when Ted tendered his resignation to the new President, which is routine in such matters, it was accepted with alacrity.

Ted came home via the Far East, and I did too, moving from Manila to Hong Kong, and ending up at Hamburg. I came home across the Atlantic, arriving in time to start a two-year course at Leavenworth, in the Command and General Staff School.

I finished there in 1935, and again joined my old mentor, General McCoy. His headquarters were at Chicago, where he commanded what is now called a continental army, but was then designated a corps area. We had four of those armies then, each responsible for one of our four frontiers. His was the Second Army, responsible for our northern frontier, which included the entire Great Lakes region.

He very generously offered me my choice of either of two vacancies on his staff—G-4, which was supply and logistics, or G-3, which was operations and training. This was closer to troops and tactics, and had the most appeal to me, so I became the Three, not only of Second Army, but of the Sixth Corps Area.

War was in the wind in 1935 as I took over my duties at Chicago. Japan had widened her military aggressions in Manchuria, Mussolini was off on his Ethiopian adventure, the Storm Troopers were marching in Germany, and Hitler, scrapping the Versailles Treaty, was conscripting the German youth who later were to die in Africa, France, and Holland. In this atmosphere of growing tension, our own armies were taking the field on maneuvers and in command post exercises.

My first assignment was to plan a big maneuver for the summer of 1936. Looking back on it now, it was one of the toughest jobs ever handed me, and at no time in my entire career was I so completely used up, so near to physical collapse, as I was at the end of that operation. Most of the other section chiefs were old enough to be my father. Years of peace had dimmed their enthusiasm for war games, and many duties fell on my shoulders which properly should have been carried out elsewhere.

My greatest concern was with the cramped zone in which we had to operate. Four divisions, plus the 7th Cavalry Brigade, mechanized, the daddy of our great armored force of World War II, and the only modern element we had to work with, were to take part in the maneuver. And it had to be carried out in a part of the country where nearly every foot of land was in cultivation and at a time when the fields would be green with growing crops.

I started planning in the winter of 1935, first picking out on a map what looked to be suitable areas. Then in February, I went up in a little two-seater open plane and nearly froze to death in zero temperatures, reconnoitering from the air. After that, I rode and walked over the ground. Even after we were so far committed that it would be impossible to change the plans, I would wake up at night in a cold sweat, visualizing hosts of angry farmers chasing me with pitchforks because their cornfields had been ruined. I had proved to be a pretty good school soldier, but this thing wasn't on paper. It was real. And I knew that if I fouled it up and it turned out to be a colossal flop, I might as well turn in my suit and start looking for a civilian job. My military career would be over.

It worked out all right, thank God, but at the end of it I was just about ready for the hospital. I remember General Marshall, who had commanded a brigade during the maneuver, coming to me at the end, and saying a few kind words that gave me a tremendous lift. He said he knew how exhausted I was, for he had watched me throughout the whole period of preparation, and the conduct of the exercise itself, and it reminded him of a similar experience he had had, years ago, when he was a young officer. But he thought I had done a fine job. His kindliness boosted my spirits more than if he had pinned a medal on my chest.

Once it had ended, I had little time for rest, for I had already been assigned to the Army War College at Washington, which was then the most advanced school in the Army.

I finished there in 1937, and reported to the Presidio of San Francisco, as G-3 for the Fourth Army. The caldron of war was bubbling hotly then, all around the world. The civil war in Spain was roaring to a bloody crescendo; in China the Japanese were moving on Nanking, Canton and Shanghai, and on the Yangtze the U.S. gunboat, the *Panay,* had been sunk by Japanese bombs. Almost every day, from the windows of our offices overlooking San Francisco Bay, we watched the Jap tankers and cargo ships headed westward through the Golden Gate, loaded with aviation gasoline and scrap steel. We knew what that meant, and were powerless to stop it, just as we knew that in Europe the big explosion was soon to come. It came in September, 1939. I received word that a message of highest priority was in the decoding room and I stood around for half an hour, in nervous anticipation, trying to figure what this top-secret transmission might contain. Finally, a code clerk rushed in with a slip of paper. "Hitler has invaded Poland," it said. "Take all necessary measures."

That caused some sardonic laughter, for we didn't know what the hell measures we could take in San Francisco which would have any effect on a war in Poland.

We had already taken some steps, though, that were of great value to us later, when we poured an army across the continent to fight the war in the Pacific. As G-3, in the summer of 1939 I laid on a huge command post exercise, which had as its basic assumption the fact that the Pacific fleet had been neutralized, and three invading armies were storming ashore at scattered points on the West Coast. The problem was to ascertain how quickly we could concentrate on the Western seaboard sufficient forces to turn back the invaders.

I well remember the loud criticism that broke around me when the scenario of the exercise was first announced. The assumption that the fleet had been neutralized or destroyed was fantastic, I was told. It was a possibility so improbable it did not constitute a proper basis for a maneuver. Nevertheless, with the approval of higher authority, we went ahead with it. We drew in from the Association of American Railroads the top traffic men in the business, some of them reserve officers, many of them civilians, who gave their time and labor in a spirit of pure patriotism. Every trainload of men and supplies was, theoretically, spotted and dispatched, through the great bottlenecks in our transcontinental rail system—the holding and reconsignment yards at Spokane, Ogden, and San Bernardino. We learned a lot, we spotted many weaknesses and corrected them, and thereby saved precious hours and days two years later when men and supplies were rolling westward over these same routes. The maneuver was held in June and July of '39. Two years later the Pacific fleet *had* been neutralized and all but destroyed, temporarily, and the lessons we had learned in our "fantastic" war game were being applied under conditions of grimmest reality.

What ominous undertones this lesson then learned has for us today. When I hear men in posts of great authority in our government, both in and out of uniform, blandly utter pontifical pronouncements as to how the next war, if it comes, will be fought, I shudder. The graveyard of history is dotted with the tombstones of nations whose leaders "knew" their enemy's intention in war and, neglecting his "capabilities," built their defense on that base of sand.

Shortly after this maneuver ended I was ordered to report to the War Plans Division in Washington. At that time there were five sections of the War Department General Staff, Personnel, Intelligence, Operations and Supply, plus the War Plans Division, which was concerned exclusively with figuring out what we would do in the event a potential enemy, either Germany or Japan in this case, did thus and so. There were fourteen officers, including me, engaged in this fascinating pastime—fascinating to me, at least, for it was the first time I had had any opportunity to participate in any planning on a global scale. For a man who had never actually commanded a unit larger than a rifle company, and, for a brief period, an infantry battalion, it was an exhilarating experience to shift armies about, even if they were only on paper. Before I settled down to these labors, though, I had one more venture into the area of military diplomacy. General Marshall had been sent to Brazil on a special confidential mission and he asked me to go along. Our job was simply to lay the groundwork for closer collaboration between us and our oldest, best, and strongest South American ally, in the event we should become involved in war. We were gravely concerned over the infiltration of German colonists into South America, and particularly over the degree to which Avianca, a German airline which operated in northern Brazil, Colombia and Venezuela, had established itself in those countries. In the event of war, we knew that a neutral Brazil would handicap us greatly, for we would need the full co-operation of that government in providing us airfields and seaports from which we could jump off to Europe and to Africa, and from which our ships and planes could operate against German submarines preying on shipping in the South Atlantic.

The President, Mr. Vargas, and the Brazilian Army Chief of Staff, General Goes-Monteiro, greeted us warmly, and in the short space of a month General Marshall's group had arranged for the use of the airfields on the northern bulge of Brazil, which served us so well throughout the African campaign. When war did come, by prior agreement with us, the Brazilians put their German and Japanese nationals under strictest surveillance for the duration.

Other than the challenge the problems presented, there was nothing of great significance about my service with the War Plans Division. We clearly foresaw the development of the Japanese attack in the Far East. We plotted each step in the southward advance of the Japanese convoys toward Malaya. But, though we had all the military information that was available, we were no more clairvoyant than anyone else with respect to the attack on Pearl Harbor. We did not foresee it and did not expect it, and were taken as much by surprise as were the officers and men of the ships that were attacked on December 7.

I was particularly surprised, for I was away from my desk and my regular job. Along with a brother officer, Colonel, later Lieutenant General, Ralph Huebner, I had gone down to Benning for a brief refresher course at the Infantry School, for I had high hopes of getting away from my paper-shuffling planning job and returning to troops. I had been given a week's leave to take a quick brush-up, after which I sincerely hoped I would be given a regiment. We arrived at Benning about noon that Sunday and were waiting for luncheon to be announced, when somebody—I don't remember who now, but I still remember the look on his face—told us that Pearl Harbor had been bombed.

All thoughts of school went out of our minds then, naturally, for a war was on and we were in it. And I remember thinking how glad I was that I was already slated for troop duty. Here at last was my chance to wipe out that blot on my record—or rather, fill in that blank on my record where it said, "Combat service—None"—a lack that had always made me vaguely uncomfortable in the presence of officers who had seen action in World War I.

But that happy day was to be delayed for a while. By mid-afternoon a phone call came from Washington, and by morning I was back at my desk in the shabby old Munitions Building.

It was not a leisurely life, though it was all paper work. One of my extra duties—bestowed on me because of our personal relationship by General Marshall, who now was Chief of Staff—was to prepare a summary, with little maps and sketches, of the battle action of the previous twenty-four hours. To do this I would get up at five o'clock, be in the office by six, read all the operations reports that had come in during the night from all over the world, and boil them down to a few paragraphs containing only the absolute essentials. This had to be on the desks of President Roosevelt, Mr. Stimson, and General Marshall by eight o'clock every morning. After that I could go ahead with my regular duties until ten or eleven at night, a routine that left me a little hollow-eyed.

Throughout my service in War Plans I had been pulling every string I knew, trying to get out of there and get with troops. Shortly before Pearl Harbor the Chief of Infantry called me in. He had a job for me, he said—in the Philippines, commanding a regiment.

I thought that one over fast. The Philippine Scouts were great soldiers, beautifully trained, and I would be happy to command a regiment of the Scouts. But I knew that we were forming some units of raw recruits out there, and as I suspected it was a regiment of these new levies that I was being offered. I declined it, with thanks. I have been forever grateful to Providence that I did, for if I had accepted, I would almost certainly have been killed or captured on Bataan or Corregidor. And I have always felt that it was Divine guidance that told me to wait awhile.

As that waiting grew longer, though, my impatience increased. General Marshall was well aware of my eagerness for a troop command, and had indicated that he would see to it I got one. Every day, therefore, I would go into Bedell Smith, General Marshall's Staff

Secretary, and ask him if he had any word for me. Bedell was sympathetic, but not too sympathetic, for he also had his mind fixed, I think, on breaking away and getting into the war.

Finally, one day when I stuck my head in Bedell's door and asked, "Any word?" he nodded.

"Yes," he said. "This morning General Marshall said, and I quote, 'Tell Ridgway I'm tired of seeing him hanging around out there every time my door opens. When I have something for him, I'll send for him.' "

That cooled me down considerably and I went back to my paper work, crestfallen. Finally, late in January, I got a call to General Marshall's office. He told me that the famous 82nd Division of World War I was being reactivated. General Bradley was to be its commander. I was to be its second in command. That put life in the old man again. Those orders meant combat. They meant a first star, even if it was only temporary. They meant everything I had ever dreamed of since I first stepped out before my company as a scared shavetail down on the Mexican border.

Two hours later I was high-tailing it across Memorial Bridge bound for Camp Claiborne, Louisiana, where the 82nd's cadre was assembling. After twenty-five years in the Army, I was off to war at last. War enough to last a reasonable man for a lifetime and of a form of which I'd never dreamed.

4

Rebirth of the 82nd

THE 82nd had been one of the great fighting divisions of World War I, with a record of having spent more consecutive days in the line than any other American division in that conflict. Its battle streamers bore the names of fierce engagements that glow in the pages of military history—Lorraine, Saint-Mihiel, and the Meuse-Argonne. A major named Jonathan Wainwright, later to earn the Medal of Honor as the defender of Corregidor, was one of its commanders, and its greatest hero was the sharp-shooting Presbyterian elder from Tennessee, Sergeant Alvin York, whose feat of arms in single-handedly breaking up an entire German battalion has never been duplicated in modern war.

It was a proud division, but it was a name, a legend, a memory only in February of 1942, when General Bradley and I reported to Camp Claiborne, Louisiana. It had been deactivated in 1918, and had gone out of existence. Now the German was on the march again, and it was our job to recreate it, from a cadre of professionals picked from the best units of the Regular Army.

We had nothing on which to build, except this fine nucleus of trained regulars and the bright legend of the old 82nd. To both General Bradley and me it seemed vitally important to indoctrinate each new recruit with the proud spirit of the old division—to plant in each man's mind the idea that valor endured from generation to generation; that the great deeds their fathers had performed could be repeated by the sons.

One of the first things we did, therefore, was to invite the grand old soldier York down from his home in Tennessee to tell the massed division about that great fight in which he, one lone man armed only with a rifle and a pistol, had killed 20 Germans, captured 132, destroyed 35 machine guns and wrecked an enemy battalion that was massing for attack. The old sergeant did a fine job. A quiet, simple, unpretentious man, he made a forthright speech that was highly effective.

We made quite a show of his visit, with an honor guard and a band, and a big review. Most of the men were draftees so new to the Army that they didn't know which foot to step off on when the drill instructor gave them "Forward, March." But a few days' drill under the tough old non-coms of the training cadre soon had them marching with the snap and swing of a veteran outfit.

One of the by-products of the sergeant's visit was that fine piece of music that later was to become the battle song of the 82nd. We didn't have a band, but about three days before his arrival, I scrambled around and found about forty or fifty men who had had some experience blowing horns and beating drums in civilian life. Then I told the band leader to pick out two or three simple marches, and let me hear how they sounded, so I could choose the one to practice on. He picked three. One of them, called "The American Soldier," seemed to me to have a particularly good swing to it. They played it at the review, and it sounded fine. The old 82nd had been made up of men from all the states and had become known as the "All-American" division, so I wrote the publishers of this song and asked permission to rename it the "All-American Soldier." Permission was granted, and that is what it is officially called today, though most band leaders refer to it as the "Airborne March." It is a grand piece of music. Whenever I hear it played, it causes my scalp to tingle and what little hair I have left to stand on end. And the words put to it by Master Sergeant Carl Sigman fully express the paratrooper's and glider man's conviction that he can whip any soldier in the world.

I am convinced that Sergeant York's visit had a great deal to do with the early inculcation of that supreme confidence, that magnificent *esprit,* which later was to be the hallmark of the airborne. He created in the minds of farm boys and clerks, youngsters of every station and class, the conviction that an aggressive soldier, well trained and well armed, can fight his way out of any situation. The airborne trooper not only believed in himself, he believed in his comrades. And he was determined that, come what may, he was not going to show up as a man less bold and valiant than they.

The rigorous program of physical conditioning we put the men through also had a great deal to do with the development of their fighting spirit, too. Though neither General Bradley nor myself had ever been in battle, we both knew that to survive the weariness, the long marches, the loss of sleep, the tremendous exertion that men in combat must undergo, each of them had to be as finely trained as a champion boxer. Many a battle has been lost merely because the fighting men have burned themselves out physically, have come up to the last attack too tired to fight. The early days of the Korean War, in which garrison troops, half comatose from sheer physical weariness, were slaughtered in their foxholes, provided many examples of that tragic exhaustion.

An extremely difficult obstacle course, made up of deep ditches, log barriers, high walls, and culverts, was one excellent device we used for hardening the men physically. It was both mine and General Bradley's idea that every officer in the division, no matter whether he had a staff job or a field command, should be required to go through the same toughening process as the men. That applied to us as well as to the others, and I will never forget the great roar of laughter that went up when Brad and I demonstrated our own skill at traversing the course. The last obstacle was a fairly wide creek, which, unfortunately, served as the drainage ditch from the reservation's sewage plant. This was traversed by running full tilt to the bank, grabbing a knotted rope, and swinging across in the manner of Tarzan of the apes. General Bradley and I ran the course together, with me, as the younger man and his junior in rank, keeping about a half stride behind him as we leaped ditches, scrambled over walls, and crawled through culverts. We reached the last obstacle still going strong, but in mid-air General Bradley's hands slipped off the rope and he fell with a tremendous splash into that malodorous stream. The sight of a two-star general in such a predicament seemed to be a source of vast delight to all ranks, and the incident became one of the memorable high lights of the training period. My first impulse, of course, on seeing my senior in such a fix, was to turn loose and fall in with him, but my decision, made in mid-swing, was that this would be carrying military courtesy too far.

Once the 82nd's training had gotten well under way, General Bradley was sent to Camp Beauregard to take over the 28th Division of the Pennsylvania National Guard, which was having trouble getting ready for combat and was badly in need of a new commander. It was my good fortune to be given the top command of the 82nd, and shortly afterward I got my second temporary star.

This change took place on the 26th of June, in 1942. A little over a month later, we got the word that the 82nd was to be converted to a motorized division, and we began to receive the hundreds of trucks and vehicles that would change us over from a foot-slogging infantry to troops that rode to battle on wheels.

We had just begun to function as a motorized outfit when my old friend Floyd Parks, a two-star general from the Training Division of GHQ, came down to visit me, wearing an air of mystery. He came into my office, shut the door, looked about him cautiously, and then in a voice that was almost a whisper asked me how I'd like to command an airborne division. I told him I didn't know what an airborne division was. He said that nobody else knew much about it either. But as we all knew the Germans had used paratroopers and glider men with great success against the British garrisons on Crete. Obviously, a new form of warfare was coming into being and the 82nd, as the best of the divisions then in training, had been chosen to develop its tactics.

My knowledge of airborne operations at that moment was exactly nil. I didn't have the faintest idea what the table of organization of an airborne unit would be, how it would be armed, or what its tactical employment would be. I knew that we were training paratroopers in small experimental units, and I had assumed that sooner or later infantry commanders would have parachute troops under their control. For that reason I had resolved that, as soon as I could get around to it, I would make a jump or two, for I didn't want to order somebody to do something that I knew nothing about, and had never done myself. When I was at Benning in February I had asked for and received permission to jump. But the only plane they had down there that was rigged for jumping had been grounded because of mechanical defects or bad weather and I'd never gotten around to jumping.

This new development made it imperative that I go up in an airplane as soon as possible and jump out of it, to find out what this airborne business was all about. So, with my artillery commander, General Joe Swing, I slipped off down to Benning on the pretext of looking at some new infantry tactics they had developed down there. I looked up an old friend, General Bud Miley, and told him what was coming up for the 82nd. If anybody in my division was going to have to jump, I told him, I wanted to be the first to do it. Miley had been a champion gymnast at West Point and was one of the two or three pioneer figures in the airborne business, commanding one of the first two platoons of paratroopers we had trained.

He told me it would give him great pleasure to check me out as a jumper. We'd do it first thing the next morning. When Joe Swing got wind of what was going on, he demanded permission to jump too. I told Joe that was exactly what I'd expected him to do, and of course I approved. Bud said sure, come along, the more the merrier.

That was fairly late at night, when a man, after a couple of highballs and a good dinner, feels capable of most anything. When I woke up about daylight the next morning, I began to have some doubt about the wisdom of this adventure. It occurred to me that this was an idiotic enterprise that might well get me a broken leg, or worse, and that I was a damn fool to be such an eager beaver, breaking the first rule of an old soldier—which is never to volunteer for anything.

It was too late to back out now, though. Miley met me at breakfast, cheerful and matter of fact, as if jumping out of an airplane was something a man ought to do every day, just to keep the muscles limber. He stowed away a hearty breakfast, and I did too, not wishing him to notice that I was a little nervous. After breakfast we went over to the gymnasium, where a sergeant gave me about ten minutes' instruction. He trussed me up in a parachute harness, made me jump out of the door of a mock-up plane about ten feet off the ground, showed me how to roll to absorb the shock, and how to slip out of the harness so I wouldn't be dragged if there was a wind blowing.

Then we went out to the plane and took off. Bud said there was nothing to it. He would jump first. I was to watch him all the way down, then as the plane swung over the field again, I was to jump out and do exactly what he had done. Joe Swing was to jump on the third pass.

I followed instructions to the letter. Bud went out the door—and I stared at him, fascinated, as he disappeared into the tops of some of the tallest pine trees on the Benning reservation. I knew this was definitely not in the script, but I was in for it now. The pilot was circling back over the field. The buzzer buzzed, the green light flashed, and out the door I went.

Many men have described the wonderful sensation of a parachute drop—the leap into the roaring wind, the hard shock of the opening that is like the blow of a club across the shoulders, and after that the wonderful silence, the motionless hanging in the sky while the earth swims up beneath you—trees and rocks growing bigger and nearer. And then—Wham!—the tumbling, bruising roll of the landing. Whatever the sergeant had told me about guiding my body straight down, stopping oscillation by pulling on the risers, I had forgotten. I hit going backward and went over on my head with a tooth-rattling crash. I made quite a speech to my officers later, about the beautiful feeling of serenity and peace you feel while going down. I didn't mention that the landing was about like jumping off the top of a freight car, traveling at thirty-five miles an hour, onto a hard clay roadbed.

Swing came down behind me to a good landing, and pretty soon Bud Miley, scratched and bruised by his tree-top landing, came up grinning a little sheepishly, to congratulate us both. I felt fine. I was now a parachutist, of sorts. But my activities as a guinea pig were not over. An airborne regiment was made up of one regiment of paratroops and two glider regiments. Next I had to get myself checked out in a glider. I went out to Wright Field for that experiment, went up in one of the big kites with Colonel Fred Dent, an experienced pilot, and soared around for about twenty minutes. Everything worked fine until we started to land. This glider was an experimental model, equipped with both wheels and skids. You rolled on the wheels until the tug plane lifted you in the air. Once you were airborne, you cut the wheels loose and let them fall away. Then you landed on the skids. But when we tried to drop the wheels, the mechanism fouled, some way, and the wheels wouldn't drop. The result was we hit the runway on these wheels that had no brakes on them. We were rolling fast, straight down the runway, when all of a sudden Fred Dent yelled, "Jump!" and I looked and there, dead ahead of us, was a four-engine bomber, propellers whirling, waiting at the end of the runway to take off. Having no desire to be chopped into bits by the bomber's props, I dived out the doorway onto the hard concrete, doing my best to land on top of Joe Swing, who was diving out just ahead of me. We were going about thirty miles an hour, though, so I overshot Joe and made the damnedest two-point landing you ever saw. I ripped all the skin off my left ankle, and off the right cheek of my behind, and I have never yet figured out what position I was in when I hit. Our dry dive onto the concrete proved to have been premature. Some quick-thinking airmen, at considerable risk to themselves, grabbed the wing of the glider as it whizzed past them and diverted it from the runway well short of the bomber.

I limped back to the division, which by now had moved up to Fort Bragg, N.C., and gave them a glowing report on the beauties of glider transportation. I told them it was the thing men had been searching for since Icarus soared too close to the sun on homemade wings—free flight, lifting and swooping like a big bird, with no engine noise and no vibration. They listened, but they looked dubious.

I sensed that the men weren't too keen about this glider business. The paratroopers wanted no part of it, naturally. They were volunteers. But they volunteered to jump, not to ride down to a crash landing in one of these flimsy contraptions of steel tubing and thin canvas. The others were not volunteers. They were being put into gliders willy-nilly, and most of them didn't like it.

I figured I had to do something to boost their confidence, so I asked General Hap Arnold to send a glider down, piloted by a top pilot, so the division could see what a fine, airworthy vehicle it was. He sent Mike Murphy, an old stunt flyer, a magnificent pilot, with all the daring and dash in the world. We lined up the whole division for this demonstration that was to convert the skeptics. I felt the division commander should go along on this first flight, so I went out and crawled in beside Mike. As soon as I was well strapped in, he asked me how I felt about doing a few loops. I told him I didn't see any sense in doing a few loops. Well, he said, if I wanted the boys to see what a glider could do, he ought to really wring it out for them. So I told him if he could stand it, I guess I could.

We went up to about four thousand feet and cut loose and he did everything with that glider that a powered plane could do. It was a big ship, nearly as long and wide as a C-47, and he did a vertical bank with it, and a slow roll or two, and then he looped it three times, and when we came out of the last one the ground looked awful close to me. Then he landed it, pulling it up short just about three feet from a man he'd stationed on the runway, just to demonstrate how completely the thing could be controlled.

That demonstration convinced a lot of doubters that the glider wasn't the death trap they had heard it was, but there were plenty of men left who still wanted no part of it. They looked at the thing and said the hell with that. There's no future in that for me.

I had the authority to wash out anybody who had any qualms about this airborne business, and in the next few months we got rid of thousands on the grounds that they were not temperamentally suited for airborne training. But thousands of others stayed, and when we finally got ready to go overseas the division had shaken down to some twelve thousand hardy characters who weren't afraid to jump, or duck in over tree tops and hedges to crash in a rocky field in a glider. And that went for the non-combatants as well as the fighting men, for we had medics and chaplains who jumped and glided into battle with us without turning a hair.

Not long after Mike's demonstration, General Marshall called me up to Washington and told me he wanted me to take a quick trip over to Africa with two or three members of my staff, to start the preliminary planning for an airborne drop on Sicily. We flew the South Atlantic route, by way of Ascension Island, and Accra on the Gold Coast, and then all the way up that tremendous bulge of Africa and across to Tunis. Although we flew in a four-engine ship, the old C-54, as we set out across the tremendous expanse of ocean that lay between Brazil and our first landfall, I remembered that old, simple prayer of the Breton fishermen:

"Oh, Lord, be good to me, for Thy sea is so wide, and my ship is so small."

And I remembered, with a wry chuckle, a sarcastic briefer's answer to our navigator when he asked how we were going to locate the pinpoint Ascension Island.

"Hell, man, you can't miss it. There's nothing else there."

In Africa, for the first time I saw the loneliest and most ominous of all landscapes, a battlefield. And I knew for the first time that strange exhilaration that grips a man when he knows that somewhere out there in the distance, hostile eyes are watching him and that at any moment a bullet he may never hear, fired by an enemy he cannot see, may strike him.

General Patton's II Corps was in action then, and General Bradley was there, understudying Patton, so that he could take over command of the corps when Patton moved up to command of Seventh Army. The Kasserine Pass battle, in which we had taken a pretty severe mauling, was over not long since, and we had put out a battalion as bait, on the plains near Sbeitla, hoping we could lure the Germans into an ambush. But they were wary and didn't fall into the trap. There wasn't much hard fighting going on at the moment, but plenty of patrol action, and Brad and I went up with the forward elements of Terry Allen's 1st Division, and Manton Eddy's 9th, and went on patrol with them.

German air was very active in those days, and there was one long straight stretch of road they called Messerschmidt Alley where the German planes would strike like hawks at anything that moved, even a single jeep. I got my first sight of the enemy there. We were rolling along in a jeep with somebody out of the 9th Division when we saw this Messerschmidt coming, his wing guns blinking red. He wasn't after us though; he was after bigger game—a signal truck that was rumbling along a few hundred yards ahead of us. He got the truck all right, but his strafing dive put him right over the 9th Division trains area, and every riflemen cut loose. Somebody got him, for there was a great roar and a geyser of dust and fire and smoke as the plane went down. Strangely enough, the pilot survived. That was my first experience with enemy air and it taught me a lesson I remembered later. During the fighting in Sicily, I never allowed vehicles to bunch up on the roads.

After a few days of drinking delight of battle with my peers far on the ringing plains of windy Tunisia—to torture Mr. Tennyson's phrase somewhat—I returned to Bragg to find that General Marshall, General Arnold, and Sir Anthony Eden were arriving at noon to inspect the division. All arrangements for their reception had been made, and a little tactical exercise had been laid on involving the use of gliders. We loaded them up and took them off, and then landed them again, and the men piled out and set up their machine guns and got their communications working as they would normally do.

Mr. Eden politely made no comment, but General Marshall and General Arnold were sharply critical. We were putting these gliders down on those nice smooth runways, they said, and that wasn't very realistic. We ought to be putting them down on small fields, onto rough ground. That observation irked me a little, but I naturally didn't show it. I was well aware that what we were doing bore little resemblance to what we'd have to do in war. But, as I pointed out to these gentlemen, when you've got only four gliders with which to train a whole division, you're pretty darned careful about breaking them up. If they'd just give us the gliders, and plenty of replacements for the ones we'd wreck, we'd use them realistically all right.

That seemed to make sense to them, and shortly after that, through the help of Generals Marshall and Arnold, we began to get plenty of gliders. We used them then as they should be used. We'd bring them in just at tree-top height and duck them down into plowed fields and pastures and onto rough terrain. We found out what we could really do with a glider, and from that time on the confidence of the division went up enormously. They saw that you did have a chance to get in without being shot out of the sky if you cut loose low and ducked in fast. And we learned that a glider could absorb a lot of punishment. You could smash them up pretty badly, but the men inside would come out all right. They'd get jarred and shaken up a little, but they could pile out of the wreck ready to fight.

We had a little problem getting pilots for a while. All the Air Corps's bright youngsters wanted to fly fighters and bombers. They didn't want to get assigned to these big, slow-moving kites that flew only at the mercy of the wind and the rising air currents. There was, at first, a feeling on the part of the men that the Air Corps was putting all its screwballs into the Troop Carrier Command that flew the tug planes, and the gliders, and the air drop C-47's. Personally, I never subscribed to this theory. To my mind General Hal Clark's 52nd Troop Carrier pilots were as skilled as any aviators I ever knew, and God knows they were brave men, both in the air and on the ground. In the run to the drop zone, they flew formations tighter and more precise than any the bombers ever flew, and they did it at night. They couldn't take any evasive action either, no matter how hot the fire from the ground might be. Once on the ground, the glider pilots fought as infantry. We used them for security guards around command posts, until we could send them back to get ready for the next mission.

They had the skill and the guts all right. All they needed was training. Throughout the war, the 82nd and the 52nd were handicapped by the fact that they didn't get much chance to train together. As soon as a combat operation was over, everybody from Supreme Headquarters on down started grabbing these troop carrier wings for other purposes. They'd put them on a milk run somewhere, hauling cargo, and they never got sufficient practice in the precise formation flying that was so essential to the success of an airborne operation. But these youngsters did a great job for us, despite these handicaps, and I have the highest admiration for them. They'd hold those planes in there tight in a V of V's, only 150 feet from wing tip to wing tip, with no lights to guide them at night except little lavender lights that you could hardly see. With only a thousand feet from one flight of nine aircraft to the next, and with as many as five hundred aircraft flying on the same track, it was extremely easy to overrun the plane ahead of you, in the dark or in rough weather, and the fact that mid-air crashes were so few is a great tribute to their skill.

Once our training was pretty well under way, we got orders to split the 82nd in two, so that another airborne division, the 101st, could be built around the cadre from the 82nd. This created a problem in morale, for already there was a great unit spirit in the 82nd, and nobody wanted to go into the new division, even under such a magnificent soldier as General William C. Lee, who was to command the 101st. Usually, in a situation such as this, when you are ordered to furnish a cadre, you pick out all your goof-offs and screwballs and send them along to the new command. I wouldn't even consider doing this to my old friend Bill Lee. So I proposed that we take all the ranks and skills in the division and divide them into as nearly two equal halves as we could. Then we'd flip a coin, and the man who won could pick the half he wanted. Bill said nothing could be fairer, and we did it that way. I don't remember now who won, but I do know that the 82nd lost some fine soldiers to its offspring, the 101st.

After this split, the 82nd was given another parachute regiment, the 504th, which turned out to be one of the finest fighting outfits in the airborne, as General Mark Clark, who took them from me in Italy, and kept them, fighting hard, until Normandy, will well remember.

About a month before we were to sail for overseas, I got word that the organization of the division would be changed. Instead of one parachute regiment and two glider regiments, the order would be reversed, and we'd go into battle with two parachute regiments and one glider. I had two fine glider regiments, the 325th and the 326th, and it was a hard decision to make. I finally decided to drop the 326th, keeping the 325th. In return, I was given the 505th Parachute Regiment, commanded by Colonel James Gavin. That was a tremendous break for the division. The 505th proved to be a magnificent fighting outfit all the way, from Sicily to the Elbe, and Jim Gavin, who is now a lieutenant general, developed into one of the finest battle leaders, and one of the most brilliant thinkers, the Army has produced.

These organizational changes inevitably threw our training schedule off stride, and on the eve of our departure overseas other basic structural changes were made. I was directed to organize a battalion of parachute artillery, men who would jump into combat with their 75-mm. pack howitzers floating down with them. No such unit was in training anywhere, and we had to take a test battery from the airborne center, and expand it into a battalion almost overnight.

So, in this state of confusion, which I presumed at the time, was normal, we sailed for Africa and the war. Looking back on it now, I am convinced that no division that left the States for battle, either in Europe or the Pacific, had been torn up and put back together again so frequently or so drastically as had the 82nd. We sailed from Camp Miles Standish, up in the Cape Cod area, with about a third the amount of training that the infantry divisions had had.

Whatever the division may have lacked in training it made up in spirit, in hell-for-leather dash. The men were proud of their special status as paratroopers, and were fiercely jealous of all their prerogatives. The first night we got in to Camp Miles Standish there was a near riot at the PX. Some of my men had gone in there to find some amphibious engineers wearing jump boots, the paratroopers' sacred symbol. They rolled these engineers on the floor and yanked their boots off. This was not easily accomplished, for an amphibious engineer is a pretty tough man himself and some minor damage to the premises was done. The night before we left Fort Bragg for Standish their spirits had also boiled over. With no other troops present with whom to engage in violent horseplay, they had started throwing beer bottles at each other. An amiable hostess, a lady of middle years, had stepped into the path of a flying bottle and had suffered a scalp wound. I apologized, of course, to the camp commander, and spoke sternly to those involved.

My concern over the division's state of readiness was in no degree allayed by my experiences on the journey to Africa. Three transports ferried the division over, and the one I was on, the *George Washington,* kept breaking down in the middle of the ocean. When we were only a few hundred miles off the coast of Africa, I woke up in the middle of the night to discover that the old tub had stopped again, and that the convoy had already disappeared over the horizon. This disturbed me, for I was damned if I was going to let my division land over there without me. So I sent a message to Admiral Pfeiffer, the convoy commander, and told him if we weren't under way by morning, I was going to jump overboard. Then they'd have to send a destroyer to pick me up and I'd arrive with the rest of the convoy. That message seemed to provide all hands with some amusement, but I wasn't joking. Fortunately, I never had to carry out my threat. Well before daylight we got under way again, and caught up with the convoy. On the morning of May 10, far on the blue horizon, we saw the domes and minarets of Casablanca shining white in the morning sun.

5

☆☆☆☆

Sicily, Test for Men
and Tactics

AFTER twelve days at sea, the men of the 82nd, humped under their huge airborne packs, filed down the gangplank at Casablanca. Around them in the harbor, they got their first sight of the wreckage war leaves in its wake. Here, in 1942, American troops had begun their drive against Axis Africa, had taken their first long stride on the blood-drenched road to Rome and Berlin. In the harbor the rusting hulks of sunken ships could still be seen. Soldiers of many nations strolled the wide streets between the chalk-white houses, and red-fezzed Moroccans stood on guard at wharfs and warehouses. The streets were a jumble of strange traffic—big Army trucks, horse-drawn autos without engines, cars powered by charcoal that left a biting stench upon the air, donkey carts and bicycles. Arab peddlers with the faces of starved hawks clutched at the sleeves of the troopers with bony hands like talons, offering worthless trinkets for sale. And everywhere the veiled women, swathed from head to foot in their long robes, moved swiftly, hugging the walls of the houses, ignoring the marching men who stared at them curiously, trying to see in them some resemblance to the harem beauties they had seen in the movies.

The stay in Casablanca was brief. Soon the division was on its way northeastward, by plane, truck and train, to Oujda, in French Morocco, where the paratroops dropped off. The glider men moved on to Mahrnia near the Algerian border. It was a two-day ride by train from Casablanca to Oujda, in rattling boxcars that resembled those the Legion rides in the annual convocations of the 40 and 8. They fought off boredom as best they could, sleeping on the hard benches, shooting dice, washing down their C-rations with gulps of astringent *vino,* bought from vendors along the route who flocked to the cars crying like seagulls whenever the train would stop.

I personally had selected the training sites on my previous quick trip to Africa, and I was astonished to read, in the 82nd's history, *Saga of the Airborne,* published after the war, that my judgment of real estate was brought severely into question.

"The site of the camp," some nameless scribe reports, "was chosen with the care so typical of sites chosen for American training camps. On one side of the town were the beautiful rolling plains—ankle-high grass which looked like a soft green carpet flowing gently over the hills and blending into the beauties of the colorful mountains on the left and the blue Mediterranean on the right. So naturally the camp was located in the other side of town, in the middle of the worst dust bowl in Africa, where every day exactly at chow time, a hurricane wind blew sand and dust through the camp."

There was some justice in this observation, for we had picked, on purpose, land that was not in use for grazing or agricultural purposes. And the observation about the wind and the sand was also accurate. We trained in a fiery furnace, where the hot wind carried a fine dust that clogged the nostrils, burned the eyes, and cut into the throat like an abrasive. We trained at first by day, until the men became lean and gaunt from their hard work in the sun. Then we trained at night, when it was cooler, but the troopers found it impossible to sleep in the savage heat of the African day. Dysentery that struck every man plagued us, but the wind and the terrain were our worst enemies. Even on the rare calm days, jumping was a hazard, for the ground was hard, and covered with loose boulders, from the size of a man's fist to the size of his head. Fatalities were few, but serious sprains, fractures and concussions were common. In one battalion jump, we had fifty-four severe injuries. Finally, we were losing so many key men, we had to cut down on the jumping. We trained the pilots to find the drop zones, and only the jumpmasters and one other jumper went out the door.

After six weeks in this dusty, wind-swept hell hole, we moved up to Kairouan, in central Tunisia, the jump-off point for Sicily. We arrived there with a strange collection of mascots—dogs and goats, mainly, and one lone jackass that the members of the 505th were trying to convert into the only para-mule in existence. His career was short lived. On the first jump he broke a leg and had to be destroyed. We arrived also with two British paratroopers who had joined the train somewhere en route, formed a deep and vinous affection for the 82nd, and would have gone into battle with us if their MP's had not come and taken them away.

In Tunisia the men got a closer look at war, for here the desert was strewn with the wrecked trucks and tanks of Rommel's once proud Afrika Korps, beaten and destroyed by the armies of Anderson, Alexander, Patton, and Montgomery. In Tunisia, too, the sun blazed even hotter than it had in Morocco and Algeria. In the shade of the pear and almond trees, we took what refuge we could from the searing heat, but for those who had to work in the Quonset huts there was no escape. It was like living and working inside a stove. There was always a wind, at times the hot sirocco, blowing off the desert like the breath of hell, and at midday the thermometer sometimes stood at 126 degrees. For the first time our supply system broke down, and for one long stretch we lived almost exclusively on marmalade and Spam. By take-off time for Sicily, the men were so lean and tough, so mean and mad, that they would have jumped into the fires of torment just to get out of Africa.

At this time I was feeling considerable heat under my own collar, that did not originate solely with the sun. One of those seemingly trivial situations had arisen, which I relate here only as an illustration of what serious effects little things can have on relations between forces of allies. The British airborne at that time had a very distinguished soldier. Lieutenant General "Boy" Browning, serving on General Eisenhower's staff as his adviser on airborne matters. He was a pioneer in the airborne business who, through his initiative, daring, and imaginative thinking, had taken the lead in the development of British jumping tactics. He was recognized, in his own service at least, as the senior authority in all matters pertaining to the use of airborne troops.

It was only natural, I suppose, that he should seem to some of us to be a bit patronizing in his manner toward those who had had considerably less airborne experience than he. I noticed it, for I had studied the history of World War I very carefully, had listened to many of our experienced officers, and I well remembered their stories of how the veteran commanders of the French and British armies had looked with some derision, at first, on their American allies. They had no great respect for their soldierly qualities, and even less for their knowledge of modern warfare on the grand scale.

Some of that feeling, unfortunately, was carried over to World War II. Some British officers, when we first began working together, made little effort to conceal the fact that they held no high opinion of the state of readiness of the American units, and of their combat know-how. Naturally this made the hackles rise on the necks of the American commanders, who had great confidence in themselves and their military schooling, and who felt a great pride in their units.

Such small matters coming up during the planning period could be as irritating as grains of sand in the eye. Practically all the troop carrier aircraft were United States, and we didn't have enough C-47 aircraft to fill the minimum combat needs of both the U.S. and British airborne forces who were to jump into Sicily. Every plane allotted the British, therefore, meant less combat strength my men could take into battle. A running argument developed with General Browning as to how these planes were to be allotted between my division and the British 1st Airborne Division. I also began to feel that General Browning, from his post at Supreme Headquarters, was in a position to exert an undue influence, both on the allocation of aircraft to American airborne troops and on their actual tactical employment.

On one occasion, for example, one of my battalion commanders received a note that General Browning was arriving to inspect his unit the following day. Naturally, I disliked that, for I had had no notice of such a visit. The note should not have gone to the subordinate commander in the first place. It should have come to me, in the form of a request, asking whether or not a visit to that particular commander at that particular time would be convenient. On another occasion I received a message from General Browning telling me that he would be down to see my plans for the Sicily invasion. I sent back a rather blunt note to the effect that there were no plans for the Sicily invasion until such time as they had been approved by General Patton, my commander. Until then they would not be available for inspection by anybody, except on General Patton's orders.

Patton liked this answer, and approved my sending it. Higher up the chain of command, though, it received quite a different reception. A few days later I was at General Eisenhower's headquarters, in Algiers, and Bedell Smith, the Chief of Staff, read me a stern lecture, which I felt sure he had been directed to deliver by General Eisenhower himself. The tenor of it was that the Supreme Commander had directed that there be the utmost co-operation between the British and American forces, and that any senior U.S. officer who in the slightest way transgressed that rule might as well start packing up, for he was going home.

That disturbed me a little, for the issue as I saw it at the time was between standing up and fighting for the needs of my command, or allowing myself to be put upon in the name of harmony. I probably would have been sent home, or at least sternly rebuked, if General Patton had not articulately and wholeheartedly approved my actions.

These very minor differences should not be exaggerated, however. Once we had the chance to prove in battle what we could do, all the doubts either held about the other's capabilities seemed to fade away, and that indispensable ingredient of teamwork—an atmosphere of sincere and mutual respect—was firmly established. "Boy" Browning and I became, and still are, staunch friends. When I was Supreme Commander in Europe after the war, and he was supervisor of the household of Her Majesty the Queen, we had occasion to meet and talk over old battles and to bask in the warmth of mutually genuine respect. I have the greatest admiration and warmest regard for him, and I think this feeling is reciprocated.

Because of the shortage of aircraft mentioned above, the division was committed piecemeal into Sicily. There were only enough planes to mount one regimental combat team from the 82nd, which was to drop in front of the U.S. 1st Division in western Sicily, and one from the British 1st Airborne, which was assaulting ahead of the British troops going in over the beaches on the eastern shore. I chose Gavin's 505th to make the first drop, with Reuben Tucker's 504th to come in on the second night. Gavin had done a prodigious job preparing for that attack, and we were ready right down to the last round of ammunition. Just after midnight on the morning of July 10, Gavin's 505th, plus the 3rd battalion of the 504th, spilled out of the night skies over western Sicily.

It was the first big-scale mass parachute drop in history, the testing and the proving of a bold new form of warfare which German operations against Crete had so dramatically and brilliantly inaugurated. It was the assault from the skies which men had dreamed of for generations. For the idea of the airborne attack was not born with the airplane. As early as 1763, in Paris, Benjamin Franklin had witnessed the second ascension in history of a free balloon carrying passengers, and the implications of this "magnificent experiment" had not been lost on him. A few weeks later he had written to a friend: "It appears to be a discovery of great importance, and what may possibly give a new turn to human affairs . . . [for] where is the prince who can so afford to cover his country with troops for its defense as that ten thousand men descending from the clouds might not in many places do an infinite deal of mischief before a force could be brought together to repel them?"

Mr. Franklin was also shrewd enough to notice that the balloon he had witnessed in flight had "met with contrary currents of air—an observation that may be of use to future aerial voyagers."

Contrary currents of air were certainly of interest to the aerial voyagers of the 505th as they crossed the coastline of Sicily. There winds of thirty-five knots velocity sprang up unexpectedly, driving them far off course and scattering their formations. Paratroopers were supposed to be dropped, en masse, in a small area near the little town of Gela, between the enemy and the beaches where General Bradley's II Corps troops were landing. Instead, they were scattered for sixty miles over Sicily.

We had, in a sense, anticipated some dispersion, for orders to all commanders were firm: There would be no return of loaded planes. Pilots and troopers were told that every jumper and every piece of equipment would be dropped. If the pilot and the jumpmaster could not locate their drop zone in the moonlight the troops would go out the door anyway, and fight their way overland to their objectives.

As so often happens in war, what sometimes appears to be a disastrous error yields unexpected dividends. Paratroopers in little groups were plunging from the skies over hundreds of square miles, and the German and Italian commanders were thrown into tremendous confusion. With riflemen firing on them from every ridge top, they suffered the natural delusion that they were under attack by one or more divisions, instead of a reinforced regiment, and they milled about uncertainly for several hours. Their disquiet was understandable, for wherever a plane load of paratroopers dropped, they began to shoot, fighting their way down roads and trails, hunting for their fellows. Some dropped in the British zone to the east and fought with them until action slowed and they could return to their own battalions. Others fell in with Terry Allen's men and fought gallantly with the 1st Division until we could get them back.

In such a situation the matter of identifying friend and foe is extremely difficult. Not all the units in the area had the same password. Ours was the password of the 1st Division—I cannot recall it now—but the British password, of course, was different and so were the challenge and reply of the other U.S. divisions in the area. We profited by our experience though. In operations thereafter, where paratroopers were involved, all the divisions in the corps had the same password. This did not solve the dilemma of the paratrooper who was not able to join up with some unit quickly, for passwords changed every twenty-four hours. In Normandy, to help in identification, I put orange armbands on nearly all our men. This worked well—until the Germans started taking these little strips of cloth from our dead and wearing them themselves.

The drop into Sicily has been called by some "the best-executed snafu in the history of military operations." I prefer General Gavin's description. He called it a safu—a "self-adjusting foul up." I also believe he has evaluated it correctly in his excellent book *Airborne Warfare,* published in 1947 by the Infantry Journal Press.

Sicily [he writes], was a sobering experiment for all the troops and staffs of the 82nd. A night parachute operation had never been attempted before by any army, so organization and training for it offered many new problems. [We had believed that a trooper could not safely jump in winds blowing in excess of eighteen knots, for example, but in Sicily we jumped in a thirty-five-knot gale.] The intangible and indefinable difficulties of fighting at night in hostile territory when every object appears to be, and often is, the enemy, had to be overcome. Rapid assembling seemed to be the greatest problem. Lacking combat experience, it was difficult to determine just how much security to sacrifice for speed. The actual combat taught us that assembling and reorganization were conducted too cautiously. It taught us what paratroopers should carry into combat. It was decided, after the loss of many heavy equipment containers, that more weapons would have to be jumped on the person, so they would be readily available on the ground. In particular, the troopers would jump with more grenades and less food, and would use simple passwords instead of mechanical aids, such as lights, in night challenging.

After Sicily, the troopers of the 82nd knew what it meant to leap from the door of a plane into the inky black night. They knew full well that whether they lived or died depended entirely upon their physical and mental resources and what they carried out the door with them. Only God came along with you, was the feeling after Sicily.

So much for our errors and for what we learned. How effective we were is perhaps best described by an expert on the subject, General Karl Student, Germany's foremost authority on airborne operations. In 1945, in a British POW camp, he told an interrogator: "The Allied airborne operation in Sicily was decisive. . . . It is my opinion if it had not been for Allied airborne forces blocking the Hermann Goering Armored Division from reaching the beachhead, that division would have driven the initial seaborne forces back into the sea. I attribute the entire success of the Allied Sicilian operation to the delaying of German reserves until sufficient forces had been landed by sea to resist the counter-attacks by our defending forces."

From this testimony it seems pretty clear that in the domain of these particular princes, Messrs. Hitler and Mussolini, the troopers of the 82nd had indeed done "an infinite deal of mischief," as the prophetic Mr. Franklin had foreseen.

With two-thirds of my command still back in Africa, I did not make the drop with Gavin's men, but went in, according to plan, on General Patton's command ship on D-day morning. We landed soon after daylight, and I went ashore immediately, hunting for Terry Allen's command post, hoping there to get some news of my paratroopers. I found Terry some two hundred yards inland from the beach, grinning and chipper despite the fact that he was limping about with his feet bandaged from a severe case of athlete's foot. He had no news of the paratroop units, he said. Hadn't seen hide nor hair of them, and hadn't heard a peep out of them on the radio. One thing he was sure of, though, they weren't out in front of him.

Wherever they were, it was my job to find them. So I borrowed a sergeant from Terry, to go along as shotgun man, and with my aide, Don Faith, a gallant young officer who later won the Congressional Medal of Honor, posthumously, in Korea, I set out on as lonely a walk as ever I hope to take. We soon passed through Terry's forward positions, and for a few hundred yards beyond we saw evidence that patrols had passed that way, for somebody had robbed a watermelon patch. But on beyond, the land was ominously still and empty, as silent and forbidding as the surface of the moon. We felt pretty lonely out there by ourselves, at least I know I did. But we kept on, climbing up out of heavy cover to a bare grassy knoll. I crawled up there to take a look around. The sergeant was off to the left, covering me with his M-1, and Don was back of me and to the right, where I had stationed him, so that he could act as getaway man in case I walked into a trap, or got lights-out from a sniper. Out ahead, the land still looked empty, and I was just getting up to move forward, when there was a tremendous blast of noise and dead ahead, coming straight at me, was a Messerschmidt, streaking along about 150 feet off the ground. I hit the dirt, feeling very conspicuous, and expecting to get a burst from his guns, but he didn't fire.

So we moved on until we came to a main road—still with nothing in sight, not a soldier or a civilian, or even a cow—and stopped there a minute, off the road, to figure out what to do next. Then we saw a vehicle coming, far down the road, and we ducked back into the cactus bushes. Then I saw it was one of our own jeeps, and in it, bless my soul, was my old friend, Ted Roosevelt. So I stepped out and hailed him and we exchanged pleasant insults, as good friends will when they meet unexpectedly under unusual circumstances. I inquired what the hell he, the Assistant Division Commander of the 1st Division, was doing wandering around out there all by himself, unarmed except for a walking stick. He asked the same question of me, though I was carrying a rifle.

He hadn't seen the first sign of a paratrooper either, so, after a pleasant chat, I moved on, still looking for some element of the 505th. Finally we came into a fig orchard, and ahead of me, sitting under a tree, I saw a soldier, with captains bars on his shoulders. I walked up close enough for him to recognize me, and he still remained seated, which I thought curious.

"Who are you?" I asked.

"Captain Follmer," he said.

"What's the matter?"

"I think I broke my ankle in the jump last night," he said.

"Well," I said, "is there anything I can do to help you?"

And that was the precursor of that strange incident which I have related previously—how, in the night, in Normandy, after the drop there, I had challenged at the sign of movement in the darkness and had found this same Captain Follmer.

Shortly after the meeting with Follmer, I began to come upon other groups of paratroopers gathering after the widely scattered drop of the night before. I moved back then to Terry Allen's CP, to report their presence out in front of him and to make radio contact with Tunisia, where the 504th was waiting on the landing fields, ready to come in on that night's operation.

That drop, as everyone knows by now, developed into one of the tragic errors of World War II. The planes bearing the 504th came in over the invasion fleet just as a German air attack was ending. The guns of our fleet turned on the slow, low-flying aircraft, and the shore batteries took up the fire. We lost twenty-three planes that night and ninety-seven men, though many men jumped and saved themselves as the planes went down. There will always be great debate as to who was to blame for that tragic mistake. It has been charged that the Air Corps failed to notify the fleet of the routes the planes would fly, but that is not the case. The Fleet Commander had been notified, but whether the word reached the gun crews of all the ships or not is doubtful. These were not all naval ships, but transports manned, in many cases, by merchant seamen, and the transmission of orders might not have been carried out as they should have been. The probable best answer is that nervous and excited gunners, who had just been under heavy attack, forgot that friendly planes were to be in the air at that hour, and continued firing in the belief that our transports were enemy bombers making another pass at them.

It was a sad and bitter lesson, but one that perhaps could not have been driven home in any other way. The same error was not repeated. Thereafter, in every drop, all firing was prohibited along the approach routes of the troop carrier planes during the hours the sky train would be passing over. Along these corridors, during these periods, ground and sea units were not permitted to shoot even to defend themselves against enemy bombing attack.

Little by little, as the days passed, we got most of the division together—the two parachute regiments, and our 75-mm. pack howitzer outfit, to which was added some reinforcing artillery from the 9th Division. We were now in shape to fight as light infantry. Our first assignment was to clear the area west of the 1st Division, and then to attack westward and clear that end of the island. This was the first time the units of the division had been committed to action and many rough spots immediately became apparent. The one that was the most noticeable to me, as Division Commander, was the caution of the advanced elements. As soon as they came under fire, they would stop and ponder the situation, and I finally found out that the best way to keep them moving was to be right up there with them, moving with the point of the advanced guard, and that's where I spent my daylight hours during that drive to the west.

Once I was told that General Patton, looking at an overlay map, told one of his staff, "That damned Ridgway has got his CP up where his outposts ought to be. Tell him to get it back."

Coming from George Patton, who was not much of a man to hang back when there was shooting going on, I considered this to be more of a compliment than a rebuke.

There was no strong resistance to the division in its drive to the west. We were running into Italians, not Germans, and we had a fairly easy time of it, for they would stand for a while and fight a brief, delaying action, then pull out, though they did cause us some casualties. Day after day, the spirit and confidence of the troopers increased, and pretty soon I didn't have to do much urging to get them to drive through the rough places.

Little incidents come to mind that illustrate the spirit of the division. Once, I remember, when an element of the leading battalion was passing along on a hard-surfaced road through a narrow defile, a mortar shell burst right among us. Several men went down, killed or seriously wounded. I ran to the nearest and knelt down beside him. He turned his face toward me, and I could see at once that his eyes had been shot out.

"Who's that?" he said.

"General Ridgway," I told him.

"Oh," he said, "I'm glad to see you, General."

Each passing day the division grew more battle wise, more confident. Lead elements weren't stopping now when they got a little fire. They fanned out, flanked the pockets of resistance, overcame them and moved on. A few miles out of the city of Trapani, resistance began to stiffen. Artillery fire, fairly heavy, began to fall in fields on either side of the road along which we were moving. I was up with the advance guard, expecting momentarily to get a salvo on the road, when I looked around to see General Maxwell Taylor, my Division Artillery Commander, standing by my side, watching the shell bursts casually, with an artillery man's appraising eye. Max was also serving as Assistant Division Commander, for the original ADC, General Keerans, had been lost on D-day night, when friendly fire brought down the twenty-three planes of the 504th. It distressed me to see Max up there, for one shell could easily have gotten us both, leaving the division without a top command.

So I told Max, by God, he was to get back and stay back until I sent for him. I didn't want the Division Commander and the second in command wiped out at once. I talked pretty strongly to Max, for I knew he had all the courage in the world, and would be right up there with the point, with the first rifleman, if I'd let him. But somebody had to stay back at the CP and I knew it wasn't going to be me. That's one of the privileges of rank—you can go where you think you can do the most good. I always felt my place was up where the heaviest action was—not interfering with the commander who was actually doing the fighting, but looking over the situation and helping him all I could. In this particular action, I felt the best thing I could do to help was to get some guns up there. So Max, with his fine spirit, went back and borrowed a battery of 155 howitzers from the 9th Division, and shoved them up there, and we soon blasted the Italians out of their nests and went on into Trapani.

An Italian admiral named Manfredi was in command, and he surrendered the city and five thousand prisoners to me without too much fuss. I also took his sword and fieldglasses, a fine pair, which I later gave to Mark Clark. I returned the Admiral's sword later, a gesture which he seemed to appreciate.

The city of Trapani is on a high rock cliff overlooking the sea, and there is a lighthouse there which had been guiding mariners on the Mediterranean since the days of Homer. Trapani was a Greek outpost long before the time of Christ, and before the Greeks came it was a Phoenecian trading center. It was also an extremely valuable prize for us, for by opening up the harbor, we could bring in supplies by sea. The port was reportedly heavily mined, though, and Admiral Manfredi very firmly, and very properly, of course, refused to give us his mine defense plan. We never did get it, and I don't know what trouble the Navy had later, when they came in to clear the place of mines.

The interludes after combat linger in the minds of soldiers longer than the memory of battle, and all the troopers of the 82nd, I think, will remember Trapani with nostalgia. They swam in the blue sea, cleaned their bodies, clothes and weapons, and went out by boat to surrounding islands to accept the surrender of the small Italian garrisons which had been posted there.

In its drive to the west the division moved 150 miles in six days, capturing fifteen thousand prisoners. We moved on foot, at a pace which astonished even General Patton. Late in the campaign, I remember, one little incident occurred which vastly amused the whole division. As we moved on Palermo, we received orders to get the hell off the roads and let the 2nd Armored through so they could administer the *coup de grâce* to this big town on the north shore. So we got off the roads with none too good grace, and the 2nd Armored came tearing through and went roaring into the center of Palermo— to find troopers of the 82nd applauding them derisively from the sidewalks, where they had been for hours, cutting the dust from their throats with wine. The 2nd Armored wasn't very happy about that, and some harsh words were passed.

The whole campaign had been brief, and for the 82nd more like a maneuver than a shooting war, though, Manton Eddy's 9th Division and General Truscott's 3rd had run into some very heavy fighting in the northeast. As the Americans reached the north shore in the west, the British and the Canadians were clearing the eastern part of the island. Toward the end of the month all resistance collapsed. The Italians were tranquilly peering at their conquerors from behind barbed-wire stockades, and the remnants of the German forces were scrambling to safety across the narrow Straits of Messina. The battle for Sicily was over. In the words of Winston Churchill, we had seen, in this war, "not the beginning of the end, but the end of the beginning."

6

★★★★

Catastrophe Averted

MANY memories of the Sicilian campaign come back to me, some of them having little to do with the actual combat. In my files I find a letter dated July 22, 1944, addressed to Mrs. Raymond Clapper, which brings to my mind one of the calmest, happiest, most tranquil evenings I ever spent. I know of no better way to express my feelings than to quote here the letter I wrote to Mrs. Clapper, telling her of that evening, and expressing my deep regard for her brave and brilliant husband, whose great career as a correspondent had ended tragically not long before in the Pacific. This is the letter I wrote:

Dear Mrs. Clapper:

One year ago this evening Ray came to my command post in Sicily. It was evening, the sun was down. Sounds of battle had ceased. The soft Italian night filtered through the olive grove in which we camped and the peace and quiet which in war, as in peace, always succeeds turmoil, fell about us like a mantle.

Your husband, Ernie Pyle and Jack Thompson began to talk; first of the progress of the fight, then our estimates of the outcome, and finally the way in which we might improve this "sorry scheme of things" absorbed our thoughts and conversation.

I had not known Ray before, except, of course, as all Americans knew him, by his splendid reputation. But little by little the magnetism of his nature, the quiet strength of his mind and the greatness of his spirit revealed the man. I felt I had come to know him well in that one evening. He left at daylight.

Weeks later from back home came a clipping of a description Ray wrote of that evening. In it he quoted a verse of Kipling which I had given him and which he said he had not known before. It will now forever be associated in my mind with him, and because it touches upon the things we felt and of which we spoke, I thought you might care to have it.

> "I have eaten your bread and salt,
> And I've drunk your water and wine.
> The deaths ye died I watched beside,
> And the lives ye led were mine."

This note comes to you with sincerity and deep feeling.

M. B. Ridgway
Major General, U.S. Army
Commanding

From Mrs. Clapper there came in reply one of the most beautiful letters I have ever received, and one which I will treasure always.

The column that Ray Clapper wrote about that visit with us I record here, for it expresses better than I could the mood of that evening which indeed, as Mrs. Clapper said in her letter, "seemed to have a magic in it":

There was one evening in Sicily that I shall never forget. We were following Lt. Gen. Patton's 7th Army into Palermo, Ernie Pyle of Scripps-Howard, Jack Thompson of the Chicago *Tribune,* and I.

We overtook the 82nd Airborne Division and as Thompson had jumped with their paratroopers on the invasion, we decided to stop overnight. This was no imposition because everybody was sleeping in the open on the ground. We just rode in, picked out trees with low branches so we could hang mosquito nets over our bedrolls, borrowed some water to fill our helmets—which were the only washbasins available in the field—and were soon at home.

A major we knew gave us some heated C-rations. It was dusk when we walked over to call on the Commanding General. He was sitting at a small table under an olive tree. With him was a Colonel who was playing solitaire. The General was reading a book of Stephen Vincent Benet, but he said Kipling was his real favorite because he wrote of soldiers of all kinds. The General quoted some favorite passages. I remember one. . . . [This is the passage that I quoted above.] That, the

General said, was why Kipling wrote of the soldier as he was; he lived with him and knew him.

The moon was coming up, the Colonel folded up his cards. It was that quiet pause which comes so often at sundown when men say little and you know their thoughts are far away. It is not good to talk about home.

And so the General got to talking about courage. Three of the group had done parachute jumping. The General said the night before a jump was the hardest time for him. The Colonel said the worst part of it was standing at the open door of the plane looking down and waiting for the signal to jump. Then seconds seem like frightful hours. Those long pauses had now been eliminated and men jump out a second apart, one almost pushing the man ahead of him. Thompson said the trouble with his jump was that he was the last man out of the plane and there was nobody to push him. He just had to step out by sheer will power. The Colonel said courage was a combination of factors. He said that all volunteer outfits like the paratroopers had a naturally high average of courage, but he said individuals varied and the weaker ones were brought along by group courage, built up over a long period, so that although a man may be frightened out of his boots, he'll go ahead to keep up with his group and prove himself as good as the others. The Colonel thought that was the strongest force in soldiering.

It became quite cool and peaceful and quiet. Tired soldiers were sleeping under olive trees all around. The General said: "What a wasteful thing all of this is. Look at all those vehicles around here—all that is being used up in war." But I suspect that he must have been thinking of his men, some of whom were sleeping back along the road, and who will never wake up. The camp was still now. The General said: "Will you excuse me? I think I'll take a bath."

We picked our way over to our bedrolls. We had to be careful not to step on those rumpled blankets scattered around on the ground or to trip over the heavy field shoes protruding from them.

No war was ever fought, I think, in more ideal weather than was the Sicilian campaign. The soft spring lay upon the land like a benediction; the days were warm, the nights cool, and there was no rain. After the frying pan of Africa, the balmy weather was like heaven to the troopers who had suffered through Morocco and Tunisia. There were no insects, except mosquitoes, and these were no problem. All you had to do was unroll your sleeping bag beneath the olive trees, string up a mosquito bar, and go to sleep, lulled by the sound of the breeze in the ancient grove.

From the excitement and high adventure of pursuing a running enemy the division turned, at the end of the campaign, to the challenges, and the headaches, of planning for the next campaign. The drop into Sicily, dispersed as it was, had stirred the imagination of every higher commander, and all up the line corps and army commanders were dreaming up grandiose schemes for our employment.

One in particular which I strongly opposed was a planned drop in the area of Rome. On the highest levels a scheme had been worked out whereby we would try to woo the Italians away from Mussolini and the Germans, and employ them as our allies in the fighting up the boot. Part of this plan called for dropping an airborne division into the Rome area, to be followed by a quick advance overland by other Allied forces to join up with the airborne force. And the only airborne division available was my 82nd.

I took an extremely dim view of this plan for it seemed to me to be exceptionally unsound. In the first place, Rome was completely out of range of supporting fighters, flying either from Africa, or from take-off fields in Sicily, and we would have to go in without fighter support, which meant we'd be at the mercy of the enemy air. It also meant that we'd have to depend entirely on our own light, parachute artillery, and on bomber support, but would not have the help of the dive bombers who could pinpoint a target and serve as our heavy artillery. Also, I knew, as did everybody else, that the Germans had about six good divisions in the Rome area, and I felt sure that the ground forces couldn't get to us in time to save us from being chewed up by these divisions. Nor did I have any confidence at all that the Italians would be able to furnish us the trucks, the gas and oil and the ammunition and supplies we'd have to have to sustain ourselves in battle while help was fighting its way to us.

I remember sitting up all night, in an olive grove in Sicily, with Bedell Smith, the Chief of Staff, talking with the Italian military representatives. And I could read in their faces their fear of the Germans, and I knew in my heart they could not, or would not, meet the commitments they were making.

Despite my misgivings, which I expressed vehemently, plans for the drop continued. This left me in a most unhappy situation. I could either acquiesce in a tactical plan which I knew to be unsound, and which I truly believed would result in the sacrifice of my division; or I could carry my protests right up to the top, and argue my point with the higher authorities who evidently believed firmly that this thing would work.

In my troubled state of mind I sought out my old friend Bedell Smith, and asked for a private talk with him. We sat down together under an olive tree, out of earshot of anybody else, and I unburdened my soul to him. He was wonderfully receptive, very quiet and very grave, and he heard me out. Finally, he said:

"Well, Matt, if that's the way you feel about it, I think the only thing for you to do is request an appointment with General Alexander, and tell him personally how you feel. I'll arrange it for you if you wish."

So I told him please to do this, and he did, and I went and made my little speech, as sincerely and earnestly as I could, to Field Marshal Alexander, who was Supreme Commander in the Mediterranean.

General Sir Harold R. L. G. Alexander is one of the great soldiers of this generation, a man of proven gallantry in World War I and World War II. He is purported to have been the last man off the beaches at Dunkirk, and his physical and moral courage are of the highest order. In addition to that he is a brilliant soldier and a wonderful personality—a talented, versatile gentleman. But I was shocked at the reception he gave my presentation of what I believed sincerely to be the facts about this abortive plan. He brushed me off in a cavalier manner, hardly listening to what I had to say. I recall very clearly his last words as he dismissed me.

"Don't give this another thought, Ridgway. Contact will be made with your division in three days—five at the most."

I went back, discouraged, to do some more hard thinking. I called Max Taylor, my artillery commander, and told him all that was on my mind. To me it seemed essential, I told him, that we should send some responsible officer secretly into Rome, to visit with Marshal Badoglio and learn from his own lips whether or not the Italians were willing and able to give us the help they promised. Max agreed, and we went to Bedell Smith with this plan, and he carried it up to Alexander. It was rejected. Too dangerous, too risky, Sir Harold said.

Risking the lives of one or two officers on a clandestine mission did not seem unreasonable to me in view of the fact that we were about to risk the lives of a whole division on a shot-in-the-dark.

So long as the high command insisted on going through with the operation, there was nothing the 82nd could do but get ready for it, and preparations were carried forward intensively, as the time grew shorter and shorter. Despite the rebuffs I'd had, though, I couldn't give up without another effort. After about twenty-four hours of brooding, in which I did a lot of searching of my own soul, and asking for guidance from on high, I went to Bedell again and asked him if there wasn't some way we could get this thing reconsidered. Max Taylor agreed with me, and very gallantly volunteered to make the dangerous trip to Italy. So Bedell went to Alexander again, and I think added strong arguments of his own. The result was it was agreed, by the Supreme Commander himself, to let Taylor and an Air Corps officer, a Colonel Gardner, make the trip to Rome. They went in in the guise of captured airmen, were taken to a secret rendezvous with Badoglio, and there got a first-hand appraisal of the situation. From the information he received it was clear to Taylor that the operation could not succeed, and he so notified higher authority in a radio message containing the agreed code word "innocuous."

Word that the operation had been postponed, and then that it had been called off entirely, reached us just in time. All preparations had been made. The loaded planes were on their take-off fields. Nothing remained but the flight, the drop and the fighting. I was playing cribbage with my Chief of Staff, Doc Eaton, trying to keep my mind off the fact that in a few minutes I would be flying with the bulk of my division to a rendezvous which I felt almost sure would mean death or capture for most of us, when the word came. I felt a tremendous relief.

That was how close we came to executing this operation. In the light of history, I think it is interesting, to add this footnote. We had been assured that ground troops would fight their way to us in five days. Actually, it was nearly seven months before the advanced elements of the ground forces, in spite of every possible effort on their part, finally took Rome. And when the time comes that I must meet my Maker, the source of most humble pride to me will not be accomplishments in battle, but the fact that I was guided to make the decision to oppose this thing, at the risk of my career, right up to the top. There were other operations which I opposed, on similar grounds, but this was the one of greatest magnitude, and I deeply and sincerely believe that by taking the stand I took we saved the lives of thousands of brave men.

And it seems to me, too, that the hard decisions are not the ones you make in the heat of battle. Far harder to make are those involved in speaking your mind about some hare-brained scheme which proposes to commit troops to action under conditions where failure is almost certain, and the only results will be the needless sacrifice of priceless lives. When all is said and done, the most precious asset any nation has is its youth, and for a battle commander ever to condone the needless sacrifice of his men is absolutely inexcusable. In any action, you must balance the inevitable cost in lives against the objectives you seek to attain. Unless, beyond any reasonable doubt, the results reasonably to be expected can justify the estimated loss of life the action involves, then for my part I want none of it.

On the other hand, there are occasions in which daring and risky operations, boldly executed, can pay great dividends. One such plan, hastily conceived and carried out with great daring, probably turned the tide in the early days of the Battle of Italy. With only the briefest preparation the 82nd was sent in as a fire brigade and stopped a German drive that was threatening to split the Allied beachhead and drive our attacking forces into the sea.

☆☆☆☆
To Naples from the Sea

SHORTLY after the abortive drop on Rome had been called off, Mark Clark's Fifth Army hit the beaches at Salerno, drove inland against fierce opposition, and by nightfall were clinging by teeth and fingernails to a dominating ridge line overlooking the beachhead area. The Germans struck hard in counter-attack, hitting the left flank of the VI Corps, driving it back to the Albanella River. Several days later it began to appear that the German onslaught might drive clear through to the beach, split our forces there, and push us into the sea.

I knew none of this at the moment. At scattered airfields in Sicily, the 82nd, rested and refitted, was waiting for whatever mission might be assigned us. No plans for future operations were at that moment on the books. At noon on September 12, I left the airfield at Licata to make an inspection swing over the 82nd's bivouac areas. About fifteen minutes out, the navigator of my C-47 came back and told me that there was an urgent message for me back at Licata. He had no information as to who the sender was, nor what the nature of the message might be. This presented quite a problem of decision, for I was on fairly urgent business of my own. However, some sixth sense must have told me that this thing was important, for I gave orders to return. We landed at Licata about two o'clock, and there I found a tired, begrimed P-38 pilot, bearing a personal letter from Mark Clark.

Even through the formal official phrases I could read my old friend's deep concern. The gist of the message was that unless we could get help to him and get it there fast, the landing in Italy might be turned into another Dunkirk. It was absolutely essential, he wrote, that we drop strong forces within the beachhead area that night.

Word was sent at once to Troop Carrier Command, and I took off immediately for south central Sicily, where Reuben Tucker's fine 504th was in bivouac. To Tucker and his staff I quickly outlined the plan. Within two hours the men were assembling at their aircraft in full combat gear. Maps were spread over the tail surfaces of the C-47, and there on the field the units of the regiments were given their missions. Plans for lighting the drop zone came with Clark's letter. The troops on the ground were to fill oil cans with sand soaked in gasoline, arrange these cans in a big T, and as the first drop plane drew near, the T would be lighted. Every plane would spill its stick to fall on this flaming beacon. We also had Clark's assurance that along the corridor we would fly not a gun on the ground would fire.

Eight hours after the pilot had handed me General Clark's letter—he would let nobody else see its contents—planes of the 52nd Troop Carrier were lifting from the Sicilian fields, carrying the 504th Regiment, plus Company B of the 307th Airborne Engineers. Shortly after midnight the first plane, guided by the incandescent glow of the volcano, Stromboli, which made a magnificent check point on their course, was over the drop zone. No beacon showed, but in the moonlight the terrain features identifying the area showed up perfectly. Out the door went the first stick, and as their parachutes bloomed, the huge T flamed up below. Back at Licata, Gavin was readying his 505th to drop in the same area on the following night.

I went in by LST, over the beach, the next day, and set out immediately to find Tucker's men. I reached his advance battalion just after a fierce fire fight. They were in rough mountainous country, heavily forested, with a low cover of berry bushes about eighteen inches high. The fighting had been heavy, almost hand to hand, for the German infantry had aggressively pushed their attack up to within twenty-five yards of the forward elements of the lead battalion. The troops were in fine fettle, though, vastly amused by a thing that had occurred during the fight. The enemy had been so close that the men could hear a German officer profanely exhorting his men, calling them cowardly bastards and all sorts of other uncomplimentary things as he drove them into the fight.

One platoon of the 504th had a German youngster in it who understood every word that was being said. So he imitated this company commander's voice, and in fluent German would call out: "Hans, you coward, where the hell are you? Why don't you move?"

So poor old Hans would jump up to move forward and a paratrooper would shoot him between the eyes.

"Carl," our youngster would yell, "get going, you bastard. Are you afraid?" And Carl would stick his head up above the berry bushes, and our people would knock him off. They killed six or eight of them that way before the Germans caught on to what was happening. The next night Colonel Gavin brought in his 505th Regiment. They came down in the same drop zone in a perfect landing, reassembled quickly, and stood ready to back up their comrades of the 504th. The divisions that had come in over the beaches made available to us all the heavy artillery that we needed. Backed up by these guns, the paratroopers broke the back of the Germans' fierce assault and the beachhead was never in danger thereafter. As Colonel Gavin said in his book, *Airborne Warfare*: "At a moment when the scales of defeat and victory were in balance, the weight of the airborne reserve tipped them to the side of victory."

In contrast to the success of the two beachhead drops was the tragic miscarriage of the third airborne operation which General Clark had requested. On the night of September 14, the 2nd Battalion of the 509th Parachute Infantry was dropped upon the little town of Avellino, which lay in the high mountains twenty miles inland from the beaches. It looked like any other little mountain town. Roads and rivers, which would have provided excellent check points, were obscured by battle haze. Many of the planes of the 64th Troop Carrier group missed their drop zones, and 640 troopers were scattered over a hundred square miles. Individuals and small groups wandered through the hills for days, lost and confused, but blowing bridges, cutting communications, ambushing German searching parties, and raising all the hell they could. Eventually, 510 men filtered back to Allied lines. They caused the Germans vast annoyance, but whether they had any real effect on the Salerno operation is a matter for military historians to debate.

With the whole 82nd in the Salerno beachhead, General Clark committed us as a division, giving us the mission of moving westward, close to the coast, and seizing the dominating high ground that overlooked the Naples plain. German resistance was spotty, but the terrain was an implacable enemy. The hills rose to four thousand feet. The only routes were footpaths. It was a terrific task to get ammunition and water up to the fighting men, and to bring down a wounded man took six able-bodied troopers out of the fight. The supply problem became so difficult I told the regimental commander that I was going to scour the countryside for pack animals. I told him to canvass his command for men who had had experience handling mules and horses, and I would do the same thing throughout the division. Then we would organize a pack train.

The idea was probably sound, but it didn't work out worth a damn. We got the animals all right, and rigged up some improvised pack saddles for them. But most of the animals were big, clumsy, heavy-footed horses, and they were no good at all on those steep, winding, twisting mountain trails. They'd slip and fall, and go rolling off down the slopes, and there were many places they just couldn't climb. So we abandoned this plan and recruited a few hundred native mountaineers who could carry heavy loads on their backs.

I don't remember now how many days it took us, but we finally fought our way to the top of the ridge line, and looked down on the Naples plain. From there on we moved with good speed, rooting out small German delaying detachments who put up a sporadic resistance now and then. Finally we got down to Castellammare, and started working up the main road toward Naples, fighting our way through that string of towns and villages surrounding the Bay of Naples. We pushed on fast, against dwindling resistance, but as we neared the city we found our progress slowed by the populace. In every little village they thronged the streets, shouting and throwing flowers, overwhelmed with joy to see the Germans running and the Americans coming in. We were happy to receive such a welcome, of course, but they made it difficult to progress. You can't just run a truck over a delegation that wants to make a speech, or present you with some flowers, and I know of no soldier who won't pause for a moment when a pretty girl throws her arms around his neck and offers him a glass of wine.

It soon was obvious that I must take some action or we would fall far behind schedule. So I halted the whole division some five or six miles from Naples and sent for the Chief of Police. He arrived within a couple of hours, and I gave him explicit instructions. I told him I wanted the streets of Naples cleared completely, because when we came in we were coming fast, and anybody in our path, either German or Italian, was going to get hurt. We gave him time to get back to town and carry out this order, and then we went in. General Clark had come up by now, and we rode into Naples standing up in the turret of the same tank. I rode shotgun for him, carrying a Springfield, for it would have been the easiest thing in the world for a sniper to have killed the Army Commander. While he surveyed the scene, I kept an eye on the windows and the rooftops, figuring that with the Springfield I could knock off anybody who tried to draw a bead on him.

It was quite an experience, riding into the heart of that great dead city of over a million people. The Chief of Police had done a good job. Every door and window was shuttered, and not a living soul moved in the streets except our own men. As we came to the center of the city, a great deal of small-arms fire broke out, most of it coming from rooftops. I soon found out it was not directed at us. The Italians were settling some old scores among themselves, evening up old grudges that had grown up during the German occupation. Colonel Gavin, who was now serving as Assistant Division Commander as well as Commander of the 505th, came up and I told him to pass the word that the city was to be divided into three zones. Each regiment was to be responsible for keeping order in its zone. And the shooting must be stopped at once. The regimental commanders were to get in touch with the city authorities and tell them that if those people kept on firing, we would kill them. It took all night and most of the next day to bring this private vengeance shooting to an end, but we finally got it under control, with no casualties to our own troops.

By this time we were beginning to realize what tremendous damage the retreating Germans had done to this old and beautiful city. The harbor area had been subjected to the most complete destruction I have ever seen in war. Every big crane was down, damaged beyond use. Ships of all sizes, from a twenty thousand-ton passenger vessel, which lay on its side, half submerged, down to little launches, clogged the harbor, holed and wrecked by explosives. Cruisers and destroyers had been sunk at their anchorage, with nothing but their top masts showing. The water had a thick scum of oil over it.

The rail lines had suffered equal destruction. Most of the trains in that part of Italy are electrified, and the Germans had cut all the catenaries and knocked down most of the poles. They had put a charge of TNT into every switch, and every frog, and the rails were twisted like spaghetti. There was no water in the town. They had gone into the hills to the reservoirs and jammed the valves, and had blown up aqueducts which had been bringing water into the city since Roman times.

We put the engineers to work immediately to restore the water supply, but for the first two or three days we had to put the townsfolk on a strict rationing of a liter of water per day per person. When finally we got a trickle of water through the pipes, we let the people come out of their homes. The queues would form at the water points at 4:30 in the morning, and all day the long lines would be waiting there, with every kind of container imaginable, from Chianti bottles to chamber pots. The sewage-disposal system had to be restored, too, for the Germans had done a thorough job of destroying it.

The Germans not only had wrecked the town, they had left it so thoroughly booby-trapped that it was dangerous to move about. Time bombs, delicate clockwork mechanisms that could be set to go off from five minutes to seventy-two hours after they were placed, were found in public buildings which the Germans thought we might utilize.

All of the waterfront hotels in the center of the city had been burned or blown up. I slept the first night on the marble floor of the Questura, old headquarters of the secret police, expecting that at any moment the place might blow up under me. The next day we found one beautiful hotel on a high hill back from the waterfront that was suspiciously untouched. It would make excellent quarters for our forces, but I thought a thorough search of the building would be in order first. It is well this search was made. In the basement we found enough TNT to blow the whole building off the face of the earth, seventeen hundred pounds of it, all rigged up, fused and ready to go. A very brave and skillful lieutenant of engineers disarmed this thing minutes before it was due to blow up and we used the building thereafter.

On Sunday morning, I went with General Clark to services at the Cathedral, and while we were there we heard a tremendous dull explosion. We left at once, to find that the barracks where the engineer battalion had been quartered had blown up. I will never forget the tragic sight. Arms and legs of American soldiers, killed in their sleep, were sticking pitifully out of the rubble of the second floor. Twenty men were killed, and many more were wounded. We were never able to establish definitely whether the explosion was the result of a time device left by the Germans, or whether some of the engineers' own demolitions went off by accident. I still believe, though, that it was the result of a German booby trap.

Later, while I was with a regiment of the division that had moved out of Naples and was fighting on toward the north, another tremendous explosion occurred in the central post office, a beautiful marble building. While this caused no casualties to our people, it did kill many Italians, women and children among them.

We did everything we could to find and capture the German colonel who had been in command at Naples, but he had moved on by the time we entered the city. We learned later he was killed in battle, which, for the peace of his soul, is a good thing. If we had caught him, he would have been tried by court-martial for the useless, senseless, needless slaughter that he caused.

My own closest brush with death came not from these planted explosions, but from the normal hazards of war against which no soldier can properly complain. I had set up my headquarters in a small villa in the western hills, overlooking the city. Just at twilight one evening, I heard the sound of airplane engines overhead and stepped out through a French window onto a little balcony to see whose planes they were. I soon found out. About ninety yards away from my window the British had set up a heavy AA gun, a 90-millimeter. The planes swept over low, and just as I stepped out, a 250-kilo bomb fell right on top of that big gun. It tore the seven-ton tube off this gun and hurled it fifty feet, burying it halfway in a hard clay bank. I ducked, of course, as I heard the whistle of the bombs. The blast blew the French window, just behind me, completely out of its frame, blew all my things off my bureau, and left my room a wreck. Yet, I didn't feel a thing. It was one of those freakish tricks that bomb or shell concussion sometimes plays. The artillerymen and the engineers probably understand it, but I don't.

I remember thinking that we might be subjected to one explosion greater than anything the Germans could lay on. My window looked straight across the bay to Vesuvius, which smoked and rumbled a little now and then, and I wondered if we were going to get to see a real show of fireworks. Nothing happened while we were there, but it did blow later on, knocking several hundred feet off the cone.

Our occupation duty continued until mid-November. It was, by and large, a fairly pleasant experience. It was the first time since the 82nd had sailed from the States that the troopers had been able to sleep in a bed, bathe when they wanted to, know again the little pleasures of life as it is lived by civilians. They had lived hard in Africa, and in Sicily, and had endured miserable hardships in the drive through the mountains toward Naples. Now they were tasting the "fleshpots of Egypt," so to speak, and I was extremely proud of the way they behaved. Of 156 court-martial offenses committed by Allied troops during the Naples occupation, troopers of the 82nd were involved in only two. They had proved again, as American soldiers demonstrate in every war, that they can be the gentlest of conquerors.

For Reuben Tucker's 504th the Naples stay was brief. As Mark Clark's armies moved on in the cold and rain of a miserable Italian winter, the 82nd was called on to supply a regimental combat team to assist in the crossing of the Volturno. The 504th drew that assignment. They were still under Clark's command when I received orders to take the 82nd back to England to prepare for the biggest fight of all —the drop into Normandy.

I begged for their return, for I had no desire to leave that magnificent regiment—one-third of my fighting strength behind, particularly when I knew what ordeals lay ahead. I wrote General Clark the strongest letter I could devise, asking for their return.

Dear Wayne [I wrote]:

I leave in your hands another part of me—that portion of the Division remaining temporarily under your command. These officers and men, like all the other members of the Division, have given without reserve of all they have to the Fifth Army. When you appealed to me, personally, on the afternoon of September 13, 1943, for immediate help, the Division instantly and whole-heartedly responded, accepting without thought of self the unusual hazards involved.

Now this Division sees a major part of itself about to be left behind when it moves to another theater. Its officers and men view this separation—temporary as it is promised to be—with live concern. Eighteen months and an untold amount of devoted effort have gone into the building of this team. It has been tested in and out of battle. It has worthily met all those tests. It has developed a spirit and a soul of its own and no member of the Division could view its partition without a sense of personal hurt.

I therefore bespeak earnestly your personal attention in safeguarding the interest of these units and helping to bring about their early return to their own Division.

Clark's answer was brief and to the point. "Dear Matt," he wrote, "I need them."

I could not blame him. No commander would willingly give up troops who fought with the skill and dash and fire of the 504th. But I needed them, too, for reasons not only of military necessity, but for sentimental reasons. They had been part of the 82nd from its earliest days. They were, as I told Clark, part of me. Finally, I appealed directly to General Marshall. Through his intervention I got them back.

They arrived in England a month before the Normandy drop. They were so badly battered, so riddled with casualties from their battles in Italy, they could not be made ready for combat in time to jump with us. To my deep regret, and theirs, as the planes took off for Normandy, they were left behind, licking the wounds they had suffered in their last great fight at Anzio.

8

☆☆☆☆

England, the Eagles' Nest

BEFORE I close the book on Italy and Sicily, I would like to mention several operations, other than the proposed Rome drop, which I strongly opposed in the firm belief that they would result in the destruction of my division. As I have pointed out before, the use of airborne troops presented a tremendous temptation to all higher tactical commanders. It was a brand-new toy—somewhat as the thermo-nuclear weapon is now a brand-new toy. With the exception of the German assault from the air on Crete, it had never been tried prior to the Sicilian campaign. It intrigued men's imaginations. It was the vertical envelopment, long dreamed of, but never before tried in warfare in mass.

It was not unnatural, therefore, to find senior commanders reaching for this magic key which would open many tactical doors, whenever an assault operation was planned. It was human nature for them to want to appear completely modern and imaginative and bold in their thinking, so the first thing they thought of, when pondering how to overcome some enemy strongpoint, was to drop some airborne troops on top of it. Unfortunately, though they might have a fairly good grasp of what airborne troops could do when properly employed, they had little idea of the complexity of the operation, of the split-second timing, the high degree of co-ordination between ground, air, airborne and seaborne elements, which a properly executed drop required.

They also had only a faint conception of the limitations of an airborne division once it was in action on the ground. An airborne division, at the time of the Italian battles, did not have the capability of dropping heavy loads. Even the dropping of a jeep was beyond our technique then. The heaviest load we could drop effectively could weigh no more than three hundred pounds, and in the field of heavy weapons—artillery that could stop a tank—the best we could take in with us was a 75-mm. pack howitzer. This gun is a little peashooter, when you are fighting tanks, as you can tell by looking at it. We did, of course, have the 2.36 bazooka, which was the best available at the time, but it was none too effective against thick armor plate.

Thus handicapped in weight of artillery, an assaulting airborne force had to rely solely on fighter-bomber support. The dive bomber had to take the place of friendly artillery, and when you contemplated putting an airborne unit down beyond the range of these planes, to face strong and balanced enemy forces that included armor, you were consigning them to almost sure destruction.

Despite these limitations, which I and all my staff understood clearly, but which higher authority seemed to comprehend not at all, the 82nd was fair game. In preparing for Italy, no tactical plan of which I heard failed to include some scheme for employing at least a major part of this gallant division. The first of these abortive ideas was a plan for dropping the 82nd near Capua, Italy, where the Germans were in strong force in an area that lay far beyond the range of our fighter bombers.

My analysis of this plan convinced me that it was tactically unsound and that it represented an unreasonable risk to the elements of the 82nd, which would be committed there. I said so, strongly, to the proper superiors. I didn't seem to have much effect at first. Later, though, at a luncheon at Mostaganem, on the Algerian coast, where all the top commanders had gathered to hear General Eisenhower outline the plan for Italy, I got a chance to talk to Air Chief Marshal Tedder. He was the top air man in General Eisenhower's organization at that time, a very reasonable, open-minded gentleman. Standing there with a plate in my hand at this buffet luncheon, I caught his ear long enough to pour out my arguments. To my surprise, he agreed with me instantly.

"I think you're right," he said. "Why don't you tell Clark what you told me?"

So I sought out Mark Clark and told him my views. The result was that this operation was drastically modified, so far as employment of the airborne elements was concerned, and later was canceled altogether.

The next was the proposed Rome drop, which I have already described, which still seems like a nightmare to me. Before any combat operation, no matter how hazardous, I have always been able to compose my soul, to come to a final acceptance of whatever ordeal Fate might hold in store for me, by taking a long, quiet walk, alone or with a good friend. But I will not soon forget the doubts I felt as I walked in a little olive grove with George Riddle, my Division Chaplain, trying to reconcile myself to that operation in which I felt most of them would inevitably be killed or captured.

With George's understanding help, I did finally find the peace of mind, the acceptance which I sought, and as I sat down the next day to play with Doc Eaton the last game of cribbage I thought we'd ever play together, my mind was at rest. And I well remember my bitter disappointment when the first word came, as we waited the planes, telling me that Brigadier General Dunn, Commander of the troop carrier planes that were to take us in, had received a flash message saying the operation had been delayed for twenty-four hours.

Cancellation would have been welcome, but this delay left me profoundly disturbed. In the hours before battle a tremendous nervous tension is built up, which translates itself into valiant action when combat is begun. Once a unit has reached this keyed-up state, its spirit cannot be deflated and then built up again in the space of twenty-four hours. Each man, in his own way, had made his own decision, had made his peace with himself. Now that their thoughts had been diverted, each would have to reopen the whole question, in his own soul. Each of us, myself included, would have to go through again the agonizing hours of spiritual travail we had undergone before.

This period of inward turmoil did not last long. Soon the word came that the operation was not postponed. It was off, completely.

The third plan which I opposed did not require an air drop. It came in the roughest days of the Italian campaign when Clark's Fifth Army was stopped at the Volturno River by strong German forces well dug in on rough terrain. My whole division was concentrated at that time in the Salerno and Naples area, and, of course, the availability of that splendid unit could not be overlooked by so skillful a commander as General Clark. I got orders one day to contact General Lucas of VI Corps, whose troops were deployed along the Volturno. He told me of a planned operation which had been outlined to him—I don't know by whom—which would use the 82nd in an assault crossing of the river to seize the high hills on the far side.

I knew that Fifth Army had been hammering at this particular nut for quite a while without being able to crack it. The high ground on the German side was a rough semicircle of hills, with a lot of flat open ground toward the river which the German guns on the heights could dominate completely. It was about as mean a place to try a river crossing as any I saw during the whole war. So as soon as I got wind of what was afoot, I went up to reconnoiter the ground in person. I took my G-3 and 2, and one or two others and we looked over the whole thing from a forward position where we could look down on the nearer part of the German ground organization. We couldn't see any Germans, of course, but there were many signs of their presence, and I knew this place would be a hornets' nest.

We were pounding the place pretty hard, naturally, with 155's firing from the low ground behind us, and as we lay on the ridge peering across the river, the shells were rustling like dead leaves close over our heads. I remember my G-2 stuck his hand up as one salvo went over. If they came any closer, he said, he was going to field one and pitch it back.

After sizing this thing up I went back down the hill to see Lucian Truscott, a top-flight battle commander, who had his 3rd Division facing this particular bit of ground. I told him what was afoot and asked him what he thought of the plan. But first I told him what I thought.

"To me," I said, "this thing is fantastic. I wouldn't put a full-strength, first-class infantry division up against that thing alone, much less a little airborne division with less than half the fire power."

"Matt," Lucian said, "I wouldn't tackle this with the 3rd Division."

So I went back and told the corps commander what I thought about it, and I didn't mince any words. And then I went and told Mark Clark the same thing. That was the last I heard about it, thank God, for if that plan had been forced through, I haven't the slightest doubt what the result would have been. We'd have lost much of the 82nd.

The next thing of a similar nature that I felt obligated to oppose came nearly ten years later, in the spring of 1954, when there was strong support for a proposal that we should send ground forces to Indo-China. I fought that plan, too, but the story of that argument is out of context here, and I will go into the details of it later on.

Now, I don't want to give the impression that I, as a senior U.S. Army Commander, was thinking solely in terms of saving the lives of my men. That isn't the point I am trying to convey at all. I don't think any commander, during this period of hostilities, was any more willing or eager to employ offensive action than I was or used it more often. But I had to be convinced that the scheme of maneuver was sound, and that there was a reasonable chance of success. I was not going to see my men butchered for nothing.

My views in these matters, I will admit, had been conditioned by what I had read of the battle actions in World War I, and the stories I had heard from veterans of those battles. That conflict, to my mind, frequently reached the peak of stupidity in military operation. It never seemed to have dawned on the military leaders of that day that the machine gun was a lethal weapon and that bullets did kill men. The senseless slaughter of hundreds of thousands of men for the gain of a few yards of muddy trench stands out in my mind as a monument, for all time, to the inflexibility of military thinking in that period. I have spoken before of the commander who tapped a little dot on the map and said:

"I'd give ten thousand men to take that hill."

That frame of mind is by no means rare among troop commanders even today. Certain individuals, because of their personal traits, their upbringing, their whole outlook on life, including the spiritual, lose whatever balance they might have had when they are faced with a tough combat situation. For personal glory, for prestige, in an effort to prove that they are bold and imaginative leaders with iron in their souls, they are willing to sacrifice men needlessly. To my mind, the ultimate goal is to attain your objectives which first must be sound and proper ones, at a minimum cost in human life. If that thought is not in a field commander's mind at all times, then there is something lacking in his make-up which unfits him for top command.

A commander must have far more concern for the welfare of his men than he has for his own safety. After all, the same dignity attaches to the mission given a single soldier as to the duties of the commanding general. The execution of the soldier's mission is just as vitally important, because it is the sum total of all these small individual missions, properly executed, which produces the results of the big unit. All lives are equal on the battlefield, and a dead rifleman is as great a loss, in the sight of God, as a dead general. The dignity which attaches to the individual is the basis of Western civilization, and that fact should be remembered by every commander, platoon or army.

With Fifth Army still grinding slowly northward toward Rome and the capitulation of Italy, the 82nd Division moved by sea from Naples to ports in the United Kingdom. I waited until the last units had cleared, and then went by air. We flew by way of North Africa, taking off from Casablanca at night for the last leg of the flight. We had been sending four-engine planes direct from Casablanca to southern England, flying a course which took them close to the coast of France, and three or four of them had never been heard from since. We never knew why. The surmise was that German long-range fighters, flying from France, had intercepted them and shot them down. So they had started diverting these flights, turning them far out over the Atlantic and taking them almost up to Iceland before they were permitted to turn east for Ireland. It was a long and wearying flight. The plane I was on was a bucket-seat job, jammed full of people. I sat until my bottom was paralyzed, and then I slid off onto the floor and tried to sleep. It wasn't easy, for all during the night men were making their way aft to the toilet, and none, as I recall, failed to kick me in the head or step on my face as he passed. Just at dawn one of the Frenchmen who had been sleeping near me woke and proceeded to make a typically French toilet. He got out a bottle of cheap cologne and doused it on his hands and wiped his face with it, and from then on the place smelled like hell. Fortunately, the air was smooth, and nobody was sick, but fresh air never smelled sweeter to me than it did as we landed on the field at Prestwick, Scotland. I went at once to Belfast.

As soon as the division came in by sea, we started active training which went on until mid-February. Nothing of great consequence happened during this period, though I will always remember with affection the gay, witty, and charming people who, with typical Irish hospitality, made us welcome there. I also remember one delightful old biddy—the Irish called them shawlies, as I recall—who showed great fleetness of foot in pursuit of a shilling. My aide, Don Faith, and I had gone up to inspect an anti-aircraft battery that was in position

near the Giants Causeway, and while we were there, we thought we
might as well give way to a tourist impulse and inspect that great
natural phenomenon. Where we were, the approach to the causeway
was blocked by a barred iron gate and cyclone fence, but we climbed
the fence and walked out on the causeway and took a good look
around. Down below us, two hundred feet or more, was an old lady
gathering clams along the shore. She looked up and saw us, and
dropped her bucket and started up the cliff. We left and were just
about at the top of the fence when she came puffing up to demand
thrupence from each of us for looking at the causeway. We paid
gladly, with great admiration for the old lady's stamina. She would
have made an excellent paratrooper.

I recall one other moment of embarrassment during our brief stay
in Ireland. The lakes of north Ireland were heavily populated with
tremendous wild swans, and every time I saw one of these big birds
it made my mouth water. I made inquiry about the game laws, and
found that these big birds belonged to the Crown of England, and
anyone molesting them would be fined. I was tipped off, though, that
if the Division Commander were to slip off discreetly some morning
and shoot one, nothing would be said. So Doc Eaton and I borrowed
shotguns from some of our Irish friends and went out and banged
away. The swans didn't even flinch. The shot bounced off their thick
feathers like hail off a tin roof. So I sent back for a carbine and shot
one, sitting, at about two hundred yards, and bore him back in
triumph to the mess. He looked wonderful when plucked and drawn—
twenty-six pounds of nice firm, pink flesh. Unfortunately, the day we
were to serve roast swan, I was called to London unexpectedly. I got
back to find the staff looking slightly ill. The swan looked fine, but
he had tasted so horribly of fish no one could eat him. After that, His
Majesty's swans needed no protection from the hunters of the 82nd.

We trained hard in Ireland, using every hour of the all too short
winter days. In mid-February, we moved to the Midlands of England, in the general area of Leicester, Nottingham, and Market Har-
borough. I had been there earlier, to look over the ground, and what
I found had disturbed me a little. The only other U.S. troops in the
area were service troops, most of them Negro units. They had been
there for some little time, and had established themselves socially with
the friendly folk of England. Many of them had made pleasant liaisons
with some of the young women of the towns, and I could foresee that

I was really going to have a rough time when I brought my paratroopers into the area.

My fears were justified. The first night one of our combat units got in there, one of my men was stabbed in a fight with one of these service troops. He didn't die, but the rumor spread through the division that he had, and I knew the situation called for instant and energetic measures to prevent a serious outbreak. Immediately, I visited every unit bivouacked in the area. I called the officers together, and laid down the law to them. I told them that the troops who were there when we arrived were wearing the same uniform we were wearing, they were there under orders of competent authority. They were performing tasks just as essential to the war as the tasks we were performing. And though this matter of color might be one of the great problems that plagued our people at home, it was not our responsibility to try to settle it three thousand miles from home in the middle of a war. Then I called a meeting with the officials of those towns and told them that we would do everything in our power to keep peace and order throughout our stay. To give weight to these pledges, I doubled our MP patrols and personally spent the early hours of the next few evenings riding and walking through the streets to see that my orders were being carried out.

There were no more incidents of violence. And when we came back there to refit and refill after Normandy, the people gave me two beautiful little antique salvers of Irish silver, and presented the division with a silver tray in appreciation of the good relations between the troops and the citizens of Leicester and Nottingham.

There were four trained parachute regiments in England at that time, non-divisional and awaiting assignment. I drew two of them, the 507th and the 508th. The 501st and the 502nd went to the south of England, to the 101st Division, then commanded by General Bill Lee. This gave me four parachute regiments, one of which, the 504th, was still in Italy, and one glider outfit. This was considerably more than our authorized strength.

As I had spent much time and energy in Italy and Sicily arguing against the employment of my division on tactical operations I believed unsound, I spent my time in England fighting for their use. Right up until the the last hours before the take-off, Sir Trafford Leigh-Mallory clung to his view that both the 82nd and the 101st would be annihilated before and during the drop. And right up to the last,

General Bradley and I argued that despite the hazards, which we recognized clearly, the divisions could carry out the missions assigned to them.

We hoped for the best. We were prepared for the worst. While the units trained with the troop carrier planes, airborne staff officers gathered at Bristol with the commanders of the troops who were to go in by sea. There we went through a war game in anticipation of the major situations we thought would arise. They were worked out from two points of view—one, that everything would go as well as or better than we expected—the other that everything would go to pot. The various commanders then had to state what their actions would be under the conditions stated. I remember expressing my confidence that, given the element of surprise, the 52nd Troop Carrier could get us there without disastrous loss either to enemy fighters or ground fire. And once on the ground, we could take care of ourselves. If, of course, we lost great numbers of planes before we ever reached the drop zone, there was little those who survived to reach their objectives could do but fight until they were killed or captured. But I didn't believe that we would suffer these great losses in the air—the point which Leigh-Mallory had stressed.

After this meeting, Field Marshal Montgomery called all Allied commanders to London for one last conference, a kind of graduation ride. All three arms of the service, Army, Navy, and Air, participated in this conference, the final topping-off exercise before we started moving to the ports and take-off fields. I came away feeling confident of success. I had been assured that during the hours of our flight over there would be no danger from friendly fire, and the tragedy of the 504th in Sicily would not be repeated. I also felt that our security measures were effective. In our own units, for example, not even the lower unit commanders had been told our destination until the division had been "sealed" in its take-off areas. There, in the last few hours, sand tables were set up, maps were pulled out, and the platoon commanders assembled their men, told them exactly where they were going, what objectives they should strike for the minute they hit the ground, and what the objectives of adjacent units would be. It was the biggest and most complicated air-drop operation ever attempted, but I don't believe German intelligence had the slightest inkling of where or when it was coming off until the first paratrooper hit the ground.

The flight, the drop, and the fighting that the 82nd saw in Normandy I have already described in some detail, but there are two or three small unrelated things that happened there which I would like to recall. In Normandy, as soon as we got some sort of staff organization functioning, I told my Chief of Staff to pass the word to every single unit that the buddies of the men who had been wounded and evacuated should write to them whenever a lull in the fighting gave them an opportunity. To know that the men with whom they shared battle's dangers remember them and are thinking of them has an enormous effect on the *esprit* of the men in the hospital. It builds up in their minds an intense desire to get back with their pals. And every man of that type you do get back is worth two or three new men who come in cold and have to learn not only how to handle themselves in combat, but must absorb the spirit of the fighting team.

I tried the same thing in Korea, and it worked there, too. Every time I visited a hospital I called the nurses and doctors together and told them how important it was to keep alive that pride of outfit which makes a good soldier.

"When you go around talking to these men," I told the nurses, "I want you to give them a minimum of sympathy and a maximum of bucking up. Don't encourage them to feel sorry for themselves. Build up in their minds the idea that they've got to get out of here and get back to their units as soon as the doctors will let them go."

That, along with letters from the men still in combat, had a great effect on these youngsters. Even men who had been wounded two or three times were doing their best to get back to join their old commands.

That loyalty to the unit must start at the top. I treasure in my memory one remark by a GI made in the midst of battle in Normandy. He was lying on a stretcher on the floor of a farmhouse when I stopped by to visit with my G-4, who had been shot through the bridge of the nose. I was talking to him when the soldier on the stretcher beside him spoke.

"Still sticking your neck out, huh, General?" he said.

The remark has stuck in my mind for years. There was nothing disrespectful in it. I like to think that in spirit it represented the affection one combat soldier feels for another who has endured the same trials he has endured. For men who have shared combat together forever afterward have a common bond, no matter what their difference in rank may be.

While I am on the subject of this brotherhood that exists between fighting men, I would like to speak briefly on two types of noncombatants who are wholeheartedly accepted into that brotherhood—the medics and the chaplains. The pages of World War II history are bright with the deeds of doctors and their enlisted assistants who went unarmed into the hottest fire to administer to our wounded. The chaplains in many cases braved equal dangers, and their influence was profound.

In Normandy, the first Sunday we were there, George Riddle, the Division Chaplain, held services in an apple orchard. Our chairs were our steel helmets and we sat in rows, beneath the trees, to hide ourselves from enemy air. No more devout congregation was ever assembled in the great cathedrals of the world. For the great truths of the Christian faith have meaning real and deep to a man who knows that he himself within the hour may go into the shadows where legions of his comrades have gone before.

They were brave men, these chaplains. They jumped with the paratroopers and rode the gliders down, and on the ground they shared without complaint all the dangers that the troopers shared. They tell the story of one chaplain of the 505th who jumped into battle carrying with him his little field organ, on which, as he floated down, he played "Nearer My God to Thee." I somehow doubt that, but I would not have been surprised.

Somewhere in the back of my mind there lurks a fragment of a half-forgotten poem that contained these lines, as I remember them now:

> The bravest are the tenderest,
> The loving are the daring.

In thinking back over the days in Normandy, I am reminded of these lines as I recall the bravery of the men of the 82nd in battle, and of their infinite kindliness to the people of France once the battles were over. Some of that gentleness and compassion was conveyed in a letter from the Mayor of Cretteville, France, to General de Gaulle, which came into my hands.

During the night of 5 and 6 June [the Mayor wrote], the wings of salvation brought to our Norman countryside the proud parachutists, first messengers of the Allied Army for which our old France, all murdered but so proud, so long had prayed. In the night of June 12 and 13, after an artillery barrage which reminded this old soldier of the epic fights of the other war, at the first daylight, we discovered the heroes who had just finished clearing out the Germans. Since then, the great soldiers of the 82nd Airborne Division proved to be the best men, the most understanding brothers, of which one can think.

They give freely their rations to the people, cigarettes to the men and candy and chocolate to the children, who had forgotten the sweetness of sugar. The civilian casualties were wonderfully cared for by the first-aid men, by the doctors and surgeons, and they still are treating them with all the most advanced methods.

As great as was the pain of the Kingdom of France, so great is the joy of our Norman people to see the tricolored flags wave on our town halls again. We have only one wish—to see all of France liberated as our Cotentin Peninsula; to see all Frenchmen free, in a Free France.

Proud of having done its part in restoring freedom to a captive land, the 82nd went back to England. Ahead of us, to the hospitals, more than two thousand wounded had already gone. Behind us, among the hedgerows, white crosses marked the graves of one thousand dead

9

★★★★

War Comes to Captive Holland

BACK in the Midlands, which seemed like home to us by now, I found my work cut out for me before I moved up from division to take over corps command. Combat mutually shared draws men together, but it sets them apart from other men who have not seen battle, or who have known war of a different kind. The paratrooper has little enough respect for other soldiers—infantrymen, tankers, and artillerymen—who have not experienced the peculiar joys and trials of jumping into battle. He has even less regard for men who have seen no combat at all. As was the case when we trained in the Midlands for Normandy, we found the area still full of service troops when we came back there. By stern lectures and sterner discipline, we had solved that situation before, convincing each of our tough, cocky paratroopers that no matter how valiant a soldier he might be, he had no God-given right to go around punching other soldiers in the nose. Also, as so often happens with troops who know their battle records shine with particular luster, we found a strong tendency to ignore those details of dress and behavior that are the mark of good discipline in garrison. They got a little sloppy in their dress, they ignored road discipline when they drove out in military vehicles, and they walked with a chip on their shoulder that caused the MP's of other units in the area so much anxiety that they stopped patrolling in pairs and started patrolling in quartets.

A cartoon by Bill Mauldin illustrates the spirit of the division at that time. It shows Mauldin's famous character, Willie, hat askew, face unshaven, boots unlaced, leaning against a lamppost staring dully into space while two officers of rear-echelon units walk by.

"It's best not to speak to paratroopers about saluting," one colonel, a well-fed man, is saying. "They always ask you where you got your jump boots."

I was well aware of the combat soldier's natural desire to kick up his heels a little, to relax, to forget stern discipline and live as he pleased for a while. I also knew that such relaxation, if carried too far, could destroy the morale of the division. Very quickly we began to tighten the reins. I got out a directive dealing with such matters as smartness of dress, courtesy, saluting, and road discipline while in uniform, and with their general conduct while off duty.

"No amount of gallantry and success in combat will cause derelictions in these essentials to be condoned indefinitely," I told them. "You know your battle record and can be justly proud of what you have done. But other things—your dress, manner and soldierly conduct—are the yardsticks by which you now will be judged. I am just as anxious as I know you are that your records in battle, of which you are so justly proud, are guarded out of action by every member of the command. No man of this division should ever forget that the honors which come to him, who survived, are in great measure due to those who did not survive."

They responded like the fine soldiers that they were. When I left them to move up to corps command, they were as smart and soldierly an outfit as any in the Army.

I left feeling a tremendous pride in, and affection for, the men of the division, and a sense of satisfaction over some things I had been able to accomplish during the two years they had been under my command. Throughout the war I had fought for equal pay for the glidermen, a small thing on the surface, but of tremendous importance to the division's morale. Through General Marshall's intervention, that unfair and foolish discrepancy had been eliminated. Throughout the war I had fought for the proper use of airborne troops, as divisions, in situations they could handle with their light weapons, and I believed my views in that regard had been accepted. The formation of an airborne army itself was recognition that the airborne divisions were an integral part of the combat team, to be fought as units, and not to be frittered away piecemeal in gallant but futile "lost battalion" stands.

One of our besetting difficulties, up to the time of the formation of the First Allied Airborne Army, was the fact that airborne units functioned under two parallel commands. There had been no one lower than the Supreme Commander, General Eisenhower himself, who could exercise command control over the troop carrier units of the Army Air Corps, and the divisions the troop carriers hauled into battle. The creation of the Airborne Army under General Brereton solved that problem. Now the troop carrier planes and the paratroopers of my XVIII U.S. Corps, of the British Airborne Corps, and the French and Polish parachute elements, all could fight under a single command.

I am convinced that no man was ever given finer troops to lead than I was. Twenty-two divisions, all told, were under my command at one time or another during the remainder of the war. They included some of the most valiant outfits in the U.S. and British service—units like the 1st Infantry Division, the 82nd Airborne and the 3rd Armored of the U.S. Armies, and the British 6th Airborne, the Commando Brigade, and the 6th Guards Armored Brigade.

As the First Airborne Army came into being, we began to get tentative directions to draw plans for various operations that would assist General Bradley's 12th Army Group and General Montgomery's 21st Army Group, as they stormed across the continent of Europe toward the German heartland. It was a frustrating business. After the breakout at St.-Lô and the turning loose of Patton's Third Army, the advance became so rapid that we could scarcely complete a plan for dropping in front of these forces before they overran that ground.

Finally, deep in Belgium, these racing armies began to slow down. A daring plan was laid down that called for the British armies to drive across the neck of Holland to the Zuider Zee, trap the Germans in Holland with their backs to the sea, and seal them off there while the main drive rolled on into Germany. To expedite this plan, First Airborne Army would lay a carpet of airborne forces in front of the ground armies. Their job would be to seize and hold the major crossings of the great rivers that lay across the path of the British advance.

There were two major elements in First Allied Airborne Army then—my own XVIII Corps, made up of my old 82nd, the 101st, now commanded by Max Taylor, and the 17th commanded by Bud

Miley; and the British Airborne Corps, commanded by my old spar-ring partner, General Browning, which had only one division.

I well remember my bitter disappointment when General Brereton announced that he was giving command of this operation to General Browning. I had not anticipated this. We had two divisions committed to the operation. The British had one. We had won our spurs in three battles already—in Sicily, Italy, and France. I felt in my heart that we could do a better job of commanding that operation than could anyone else, and I imagine I expressed these views, in private, with some fervor. I made no official protest, however, for I could not justify such an action. General Browning was a brave and widely experienced soldier, and it was entirely Brereton's prerogative to appoint any commander he pleased.

The plan of the carpet drop was bold and brilliant in conception, but there was a large measure of uncertainty about it. Those airborne divisions, the British, the U.S. 82nd and the U.S. 101st, were to be dropped in that order, from east to west. The British were to be dropped the farthest in, to seize the crossings over the Rhine. The 82nd was to drop in the middle, to take the crossings of the Waal and the Maas, and the 101st was to be dropped closest to friendly troops. With these bridgeheads in our possession, it was expected that the British armies could swiftly slash across the neck of Holland and seal the Germans in the pocket.

There was no doubt in anybody's mind that the airborne elements could take and hold the bridgeheads. But the trapping of the German forces in Holland depended entirely upon the speed with which the ground forces could move. As it worked out, they did not move fast enough.

The serials took off from their fields in England on a Sunday morning, and as I went down to the 82nd's marshaling areas to watch them go, I felt a great sense of loss—a deep regret that for the first time this gallant division was going into battle without me. There was nothing to prevent my going along, though, just to watch, for aside from my sentimental interest in anything that might happen to these men, this operation was of great technical interest to a professional paratrooper. It was to be the biggest single air drop up to that time, and the first big daylight drop, made possible by the fact that the German air force had been practically wiped out.

I flew in a borrowed B-17 that hovered some two hundred feet above the transport planes below, and I remember thinking how big a target we must make up there, and how slow we were flying. Over Holland, in the clear light of that sunny Sunday, the flak began to come up heavily, and planes began to go down. My pilot was also well aware of the hazards of our situation. One of those brave, light-hearted men who, like Ulysses' mariners, "ever with a frolic welcome take the thunder and the sunshine," I could hear him talking to his crew over the inter-com.

"Boy, did you ever see anything like that?" he was saying. "I never saw the stuff coming up like this before. I'm going to tell my grand-children about this."

His uneasiness was understandable, for he was used to flying up-stairs, at twenty thousand feet or so, and this slow, wobbly flight eight hundred feet above the ground was new to him. I remember hoping fervently that he did survive to tell his grandchildren about that ride.

The drop was beautiful, the best we'd ever done. Despite the fact that planes were being lost to AA fire, those magnificent pilots of the 52nd Troop Carrier held formation perfectly, and hit their drop zones on the nose. As we circled wide, watching the skies fill with thousands of colored chutes, we could look down into the streets of the little villages. The people were all out in their Sunday best, look-ing up, as the great sky train, five hundred miles long, went past. The little houses were all intact, and I felt a great pang of regret, knowing that these fine Hollanders were all unaware of the tragedy that was soon to strike. Up to this time the German occupation had brought little of war's devastation to that peaceful countryside, but I knew the German reaction would be quick and violent.

I flew back to England to sleep that night, and early the next morning flew in a C-47 to Antwerp, to move up by jeep to join the parachute divisions on the ground. The weather was zero-zero and we could not get down, but the next day we dropped in there, though the field was under German artillery fire. With General Brereton, I moved out by jeep through the countryside to Eindhoven, a city of considerable size, so far untouched by war. It was jammed full of British motor transports, moving up, and just at dusk we worked our way to the center of town. The square was jammed with vehicles of all kinds—gasoline trucks, ammunition trucks, and troop transports. In the deepening light a single plane flashed over and dropped two flares, and I said to General Brereton: "Lewis, I don't like the looks of this. Let's get the hell out of here."

So we jumped in the jeeps and started off. We'd gone about two blocks when the whole world exploded. A German bomber formation, guided by those flares, was tearing that town apart. We leaped from the jeeps and hit the ground in a little park, Lewis in his nice uniform scrambling for the pistol he had dropped. Somehow we got separated there in the dark, and later, in a lull in the bombing, when I got in my jeep and tried to move on, I couldn't find him. I never did find out what happened to him, nor how he got back to England.

I soon found myself blocked on every road. Great fires were burning everywhere, ammo trucks were exploding, gasoline trucks were on fire, and debris from wrecked houses clogged the streets. Trapped on every side, I pulled up beside a ditch, got out my sleeping bag, crawled into it and went to sleep.

The next morning early, with Captain Don Faith, my aide, Sergeant Farmer, my jeep driver, and Sergeant Casey, my personal bodyguard, we set out again. In the light of dawn we could pick our way around the rubble and the burned-out hulks of the trucks, and soon were out of town.

A few miles up the road we came up with the advance elements of British armor. There a junior officer stopped me and told me I could go no further because the road in front was swept with small-arms fire. So we stopped a minute to watch how our good British comrades would take out this resistance. They had the muzzles of their tank guns pointing down the road toward where the enemy was supposed to be, but not a shot was being fired. It was a demonstration of caution that was most unusual among the British veterans, who in the main were bold, hard-charging troops. But I had seen it, and dealt with it, many times before when my own paratroopers were getting their first taste of battle in Sicily.

Having no command responsibility for this operation, however, I couldn't order this tank commander to move on down the road. So, after waiting about forty minutes, and seeing no visible effort being made to outflank this resistance, I told Farmer to stay where he was until he heard from me. I then took Don Faith and Casey, and put Don on one side of the road, and Casey and I took the other, and we started walking down the ditch along the side of the road. We went a mile and a half, perhaps, with every sense alert, but not a shot was fired at us. This was a good thing in my case, for if I had had to hit the ground I couldn't have gotten up again. Diving out of the jeep the night before, and sleeping on the cold, damp ground, had aggravated the old sacroiliac injury I'd had since West Point days, and my back was stiff as a board.

We moved on until we found General Max Taylor, at the CP of the 101st Division. I then sent back for Farmer and my jeep, and went on for another couple of miles until I found General Gavin and the 82nd. They were in fine shape at that moment, as was the 101st, but there was much hard fighting ahead of them before the ground elements came up.

I have always felt, and I still feel, that the sluggish actions of the ground armies in that campaign were inexcusable. A more vigorous command supervision from the top could have driven that armored force on through. As a result of this failure, the British 1st Airborne that dropped out beyond the Rhine was almost destroyed. Its stand at Arnhem was a monument to British valor, but a monument, too, to human weakness, to the failure to strike hard and boldly. The major objectives of that operation were not attained. The main German forces in Holland were not cut off, and the front became stabilized. The 82nd and the 101st stayed in the line until late November, when they were withdrawn and came back under my command. They had been 58 days in the line and had lost 658 killed, 1,796 wounded, and 80 missing in action. They came back to rest, refit and train replacements in the Champagne area of France, and around Mourmelon-le-Grand, Suippes, and Rheims.

I then had a split headquarters. My advanced CP was in France with the 82nd and 101st, and the main command post was back in England, where the 17th Airborne was in training.

We were thus divided when, at two o'clock in the morning on the 18th of December, at my headquarters in the Midlands, I got word by phone from France that the Germans were smashing in great force through the Ardennes. The Battle of the Bulge had begun.

10

☆☆☆☆
Panzers in the Ardennes

THE message from the continent came from General Hodges's First Army CP. It told us little beyond the fact that General Eisenhower had released XVIII Corps from theater reserve, and that the 82nd and 101st were to move with utmost speed to the general area of Bastogne. There they would receive further orders.

As soon as this message was received, I got hold of Troop Carrier Command and got them to line up every C-47 they had available. We took off for France at dawn, in fifty-five planes, carrying the entire UK-based staff. With a fight like this going on, I wanted everybody over there. We'd been watching this thing build up, and I knew this was no local flare-up or diversion. This was something big. Behind me in England I left Bud Miley's 17th Airborne, with orders to follow as soon as it could.

We were lucky that we moved so fast. As the last planes bearing the staff took off, a pea-soup fog rolled in from the Channel and we were the last planes to leave England for forty-eight hours. We flew in that soup across France to Rheims. Fortunately, my own personal pilot, Colonel J. G. Brown, a magnificent airman, was at the controls. By a miracle of navigation, or sixth sense or something, for we had no ground contact, and no radio aids to speak of, he hit Rheims on the nose. It lay under a blanket of low-hanging cloud, and as we broke through the cloud cover, I looked out the window to see the spire of a church steeple flash by. It was considerably higher than we were.

We landed on a deserted strip and I immediately made my way by car to my advanced CP. I found evidence of considerable apprehension there, due mainly, I think, to the flood of urgent messages that were pouring in from higher headquarters, beseeching us to hurry the movement of the two airborne divisions into the great gap that had been torn in our lines. As I stepped into the CP, Doc Eaton, my Chief of Staff, handed me a telephone. General Kean, First Army Chief of Staff, was on the line with oral instructions from Hodges for me personally to do everything in my power to get these divisions out of their bivouacs and into combat fast.

I issued a few simple orders then. But the main thing that sticks in my mind is this: In all this flurry of excitement about the German offensive, and the defensive measures we had to take to stop it, it seemed most important to plan an *attack* the moment the German penetration was checked. I don't believe that many others were thinking of the offensive at that particular time. But my reasoning was simple. If a man hits you a surprise blow and knocks you sprawling, you've got to get up off the ground at once, and flatten him, or you are beaten.

As soon as these orders had been dispatched, I set out for the bivouac areas of the 101st and the 82nd. The 82nd had already moved out and the last elements of the 101st were clearing their area as I arrived. I waited until the last battalion had cleared, and moved on up the road myself. It was not a pleasant ride. The only transportation available was some ancient GI sedans. We couldn't see out of these things. The fog was thick as heavy smoke, a cold, drizzling rain was falling, and the chances were good that a German patrol might loom suddenly out of the murk to take us by surprise.

The danger of crashing into the heavy trucks of the divisions moving on this same road was greater than the danger from the Germans. I am not usually a nervous man in an automobile, but when we had narrowly missed ramming the tailgate of a stopped truck about a half-dozen times, I got pretty jumpy.

"What's the matter, sonny?" I asked the driver. "Can't you see?"

"Not too good, I can't, sir," he said.

So I moved him over and took the wheel, and we crawled on through the fog and the rain. Just about dark, we found the command post of General Troy Middleton's VIII Corps. The gloom inside that headquarters was thicker than the fog outside. This atmosphere of uncertainty was in no way the fault of General Middleton, a magnificent soldier with a wonderful combat record in two wars. But the most disquieting thing in any war is to be in a completely unknown situation. General Middleton knew that some of his units had been overrun. He knew the German attack had opened a great gap in his lines. But nearly all his communications with his forward elements were out, and he had no knowledge of where his forces were, nor where the Germans were, nor where they might strike next.

It was pitch-black night before we finished our conversation, and with the woods full of Germans there was no point in trying to move on until daylight. So I spread my bed roll on the floor in the blacked-out CP, crawled in and went to sleep. Along toward daylight, I woke up to go to the latrine and in the dark hallway I brushed against a little group and heard for the first time in this war a conversation the like of which I had not heard before. One man said, and you could detect the anxiety in his voice:

"We'd better get the hell out of here."

And the other fellow said: "We can't. They've got us surrounded."

The tone of those voices, full of anxiety and alarm, spoke volumes. But I didn't feel that way. Paratroopers were accustomed to fight surrounded. So I brushed my teeth and shaved, and felt confident that we could handle whatever dangers the cold, gray day might bring.

I got my little group together and we set out as soon as possible, still flying blind, so to speak, in those confounded sedans. As we were leaving, a message came for me. It told me to have the 101st drop off at Bastogne. The 82nd would continue on to Werbomont. I passed this order on to General Tony McAuliffe, commanding the 101st in the absence of General Max Taylor, who had gone to the States, at my request, to confer with General Marshall on certain matters pertaining to the airborne. I felt a keen regret, and I think Tony did, too, as I read this message. For the 82nd and the 101st were brothers in the blood. They had fought side by side in Normandy, and they knew and trusted each other. Now they were to be separated—the 101st going into that immortal fight that held Bastogne, the 82nd into battles less publicized, but equally as severe.

We moved on, to find our road blocked by a great log jam of trucks —ten-ton trailers stopped to unload the 101st in its objective area. Casting about for an alternate route, we found we had the choice of two secondary roads that would take us on to Werbomont. I picked the one that went by Marche. It was God's guidance that I did. The Germans lay in strength across the other road, and if we had continued along it, we'd have found our caravan of two sedans trying to make a penetration of two German divisions.

I found Gavin at Werbomont, which was no town at all, but a forlorn little crossroads with a small two-story farmhouse as its only habitation. Only one battalion of the 82nd had come up. The rest of the division was grinding over the roads, moving as fast as the fog and the muddy roads would permit. With his usual fine initiative, Gavin had put out patrols, making a strong reconnaissance to find the enemy we knew was moving around, somewhere, out there in the snow and the fog. As other elements of the division began to come in, I set up my advanced CP in the farmhouse and we operated out of there for the next five or six days. I doubt that a corps battle CP ever functioned out of such a constricted area before, but there was nothing else to do.

The 82nd arrived, battalion by battalion, and each element as it arrived was pushed forward to make contact with the enemy. But we had more than twenty-five thousand yards to cover with that one division, and to my great delight a magnificent fighting outfit, the 3rd Armored Division, was assigned to Corps to help us plug up that gap. The 3rd Armored was far away and was coming piecemeal, and in my anxiety to make contact with its leading elements and hurry them along, I started out long after dark one night to find it. I soon found myself in Thieux, a Belgian town of considerable size, but completely dark and deserted, and while I wandered the dark streets, trying to find somebody I could ask about the roads, by purest luck I saw a beam of light shining through a crack in a door. I reconnoitered cautiously, not knowing but what I might be walking into a German bivouac, and to my great pleasure saw that the half-dozen men in the room were GI's wearing the triangular patch of the 3rd Armored.

They were members of a recon platoon who themselves were lost and trying to locate their whereabouts on a map. But they did know the road their division was moving over, and they guided me until I found the combat command.

General Maurice Rose, one of the most gallant soldiers I have ever known, was in command. He was later killed in action, riding his jeep far out in front, like the brave officer he was. He ran into a German tank column, and the story we first got was that he was killed in cold blood. The Germans later claimed that when they told him to put up his hands and he started to obey a tank driver thought he was reaching for his pistol and shot him.

Little by little, we got units to plug in there on that wide front, and slowly the desperate German drive began to lose its momentum. It was a bitter battle all the way, in temperatures down around ten to fifteen degrees Fahrenheit. The story of those battles is history now, and I won't try to go into details about them here. There was heavy fighting for six weeks, and at one time I had as many as six divisions in my command, with a combat strength of ninety-seven thousand men.

A few personal things stand out in my mind about the fighting there, and I would like to recall them here. On one occasion, I was with the 30th Division, up in the Malmédy area, in wooded, hilly country, where the snow lay knee-deep on flat ground, and waist-deep in the hollows. The division was attacking but was meeting heavy resistance, and one of its battalions had bogged down. It had come to a dead halt, and I was on my way up there to see what I could do about getting it going again. I was moving along through the woods, headed for one of the assault platoons, where I had been told I could find the battalion commander. All of a sudden I heard a tremendous clatter and saw something that looked like a light tank, with a big black swastika on its side, coming at me from my left rear. It was only about fifteen yards away. I was alone then—I had lost my orderly somewhere, and I knew that unless I did something pretty drastic, I'd be dead there in that snow in another two seconds. So I swung around, firing my Springfield, and I got five shots in, fast, at the swastika. The tank moved along, veering crazily, for another fifteen yards or so, and then came to a halt. Then I saw what it was—no tank, but a German armored self-propelled gun. I dropped in the snow then and crawled away fast, thanking God for my old Springfield, and for the fact I had loaded a clip with armor-piercing cartridges. I am just old-fashioned enough to love the Springfield. I was brought up with it, and I always carried one. For I knew that I would react automatically with the Springfield, whereas with the newer M-1 I wasn't sure of myself. But I can take a Springfield apart in the dark and put it together again. I am completely at home with it.

I crawled on until I found the assault platoon I had been looking for, and looked along the line until I found a bazooka man. That soldier was a typical American GI. He was taking shelter up under a

iting combat orders that never came. While the final great battles of World
ar I raged in Europe, as a young second lieutenant just out of West Point I com-
nded Company F, 3rd U.S. Infantry, at Eagle Pass, Texas. From here I was
sent back to the Academy as an instructor in French and Spanish.

During training at Fort Be
in 1942, I posed for a pre
picture. (U.S. Army photog

Lieutenant General Patton and Major General Omar Bradley visit the 82nd Airborne as we train for the invasion of Sicily. The training area was a wind-swept, sun-baked plain at Oujda, French Morocco. (U.S. Army photograph)

...e Division was committed piecemeal into Sicily. I did not jump, but went in at ...wn on D-day in General Patton's command ship. Here, in the landing craft ...aded for shore, I had no idea how the drop had gone. I did not know that high ...nds had scattered the troops for 60 miles over Sicily—nor that I would have to ...owl for hours through no man's land before I found the first of the scattered units.
(U.S. Army photograph)

...e Sicilian campaign was brief, and for the 82nd not particularly bloody. Once ...regiments assembled, we pushed on foot through the open fields and olive ...ves. Within a month the Italians had surrendered and the remnants of the ...rman forces were fleeing across the Straits of Messina. Here, to M/Sgt. Frank ...rang, I point out the route of the advancing troops. By radio from the jeep I ...t contact with the forward elements, moving up to help however I could when resistance stiffened and the advance slowed. (U.S. Army photograph)

In England, paratroopers of the 82nd are given a final inspection by their jump master before they board the plane which will take them to Holland. I was spectator on this drop. I had been moved up to command of XVIII Corps (A borne) and though the Corps participated, the overall operation was under Brit command. (U.S. Army photograph)

Burdened with their heavy combat gear, officers and men of the 82nd Airbo await the take-off for Holland. Veterans by now, they know what dangers ahe and each man, in his own heart, has prepared himself to face them. (U.S. Ar photograph)

Friendly wings over England. Paratroopers of the 82nd spill out of gray skies in a practice jump over the English Midlands. We were severely handicapped by lack of planes for training. (U.S. Army photograph)

ward for valor. As Corps Commander I am proud to pin a Silver Star on rporal Carroll F. Gott, of Jonesboro, Ark., for gallant action in Normandy, ere the 82nd and 101st dropped before dawn on D-day. At left is General Max lor, now Chief of Staff, then the Commander of Gott's division, the 101st Airborne. (U.S. Army photograph)

In the fog and gloom of the Ardennes, men of the 325th Glider Regiment of the 82nd Airborne move up to fight Von Rundstedt's panzers during the Battle of the Bulge. (U.S. Army photograph)

Bearded, hollow-eyed, cold and gaunt, the paratroopers and glidermen fought in the snows of December. Here Pfc. Vernon L. Haught, a bazooka man of the 325th Glider Regiment, moves back for warmth and rest after three hours of night guard. (U.S. Army photograph)

A 75-mm. pack howitzer s
shells across the Salm
in Belgium. The gun c
men are members of B
tery of the 376th Parac
Field Artillery. (U.S. A
photograph)

now the tide of battle had turned. The German assault had been contained. ᵔove, near Born, Belgium, I look over a Nazi strong point overrun by infantry-꜆n of XVIII Corps. The body in the snow is that of a German soldier. (U.S. Army photograph)

꜆ops of the 82nd Airborne move cautiously out of the woods, through knee-deep ⱽdrifts, as they hunt down scattered German remnants during the last days of the Bulge. (U.S. Army photograph)

Monty—Sir Bernard L. Montgomery—and I, check a situation map at my impr
vised headquarters near Harze, Belgium. The great British commander was rare
found in such comfortable surroundings. He preferred to be tucked away son
where close to the fighting, with a small command group housed in trailers. At t
time my XVIII Corps was part of his 21st Army Group. Later he was to be
deputy at SHAPE. (U.S. Army photograph)

bove are a few of the thousands of Germans caught in the trap when the Ruhr ocket was cleared. When the situation became hopeless for the Germans, I begged eir commander, General Model, to surrender and save further bloodshed. He refused. (U.S. Army photograph)

a fine old castle at Ludwigslust, Germany, Russian and American commanders et and lay out a buffer zone between our troops and theirs. The big fellow at left Major General Dzinet, who never spoke, but merely glowered. The short officer General Smirnov, more friendly and agreeable, but nursing a hand badly bruised a jeep accident. At center is General James M. Gavin, gallant commander of 82nd. The officer beneath the painting of the lady is Brigadier General Eaton. (U.S. Army photograph)

My first day at the Korean front, December 27, 1950. Here I am shown leaving
I Corps headquarters near Seoul with Major General Frank W. Milburn. I hadn't
had time to get a grenade. (U.S. Army photograph)

etting ready for our attack across the Han. In Korea in March of 1951, I toured
e front-line positions, getting from commanders on the ground their estimate of
e situation. The officer with the map is Lieutenant Colonel Gilbert J. Check,
rave and seasoned battle commander of the 27th Infantry—the famous Wolf-
hound Regiment. (U.S. Army photograph)

At Suwon airport in Korea, I get a
warm greeting from an old and
respected friend—General Douglas
MacArthur. Later, when I reported
to Tokyo to take over command in
the Far East, his greeting was just
as warm. He showed no signs of
bitterness at his abrupt dismissal by
President Truman. (U.S. Army
photograph)

One of the great human tragedies of all time—the pitiful flight of the South Koreans before the onrush of the Red Chinese. (U.S. Army photograph)

Riding the line in Korea. Up the road only a little way, Lieutenant Colonel John H. Chiles' 23rd Regimental Combat Team is engaged in a hot fight with dug-in Chinese blocking the UN advance to the north. No matter how cold the weather, I always traveled in an open jeep. A jeep with the top up is a death trap. (U.S. Army photograph)

me people thought I wore the grenades as a gesture of showmanship. This was
t correct. They were purely utilitarian. Many a time, in Europe and in Korea,
en in tight spots blasted their way out with grenades. The pocket on the left
shoulder is a first-aid kit. (U.S. Army photograph)

President Truman was in a jo
mood as he greeted me and G
eral Bradley as I paused in W
ington en route from the
East to Europe. He asked n
questions about the POW r
and then proudly showed
over the remodeled White Ho
(U.S. Army photograph)

After the meeting with President Truman, I reported to a Joint Session of Congre
my views on the state of defenses in the Far East. A few days later I succeede
General Eisenhower as Supreme Commander, Europe. (Wide World)

At a breakfast meeting at the White House, President Eisenhower asked the new Chiefs of Staff to analyze our foreign policy, and to recommend the military establishment which could support our many commitments overseas. (Wide World)

...tary of the Army Robert Stevens, a man I came to admire ...ly, greets Mrs. Ridgway and me as we arrive in Washington ... Europe. I had returned to take over my duties as Chief of ...of the Army—the toughest, most frustrating job of my whole career. (Wide World)

This picture of my wife Penny and my little son Matty was taken in Garmisc
Bavaria, in 1953 while I was on vacation. (J. E. Kovacs)

little bank, with his bazooka beside him, and I said, "Come on. Get up here. Here's what you're looking for. Here's your meat." And I told him about the German gun so close, back in the woods.

He looked at his bazooka.

"I can't," he said. "This ———— thing is full of snow."

"Get a stick and poke the ———— snow out," I said.

But he just sat there, cold and blank-eyed, and I didn't have any more time to spend on this little personal adventure. It was just as well. The next day, back up there, I found the German gun in the same place. Our men had found it and pulled the dead crewmen out of it. The old Springfield had served me well.

In that same fight, not long afterward, I came upon another war-wise, war-weary GI. He was a mortar man, down in a hole, with his weapon. He wasn't firing.

"Here," I said. "Get going with that mortar. Those people are right over there. Pour some fire on 'em. Let's blast 'em out of there." He looked at me glumly.

"General," he said, "every time we shoot them SOB's shoot right back."

"The hell with that," I said. "Get that mortar working."

He took a sight on the opposite ridge top, dropped a shell down the tube, and the mortar belched with a bang and a smoke. Hardly had our shell exploded on the ridge opposite than there was a tremendous explosion a few yards to our left, and shell fragments screeched through the trees. Deafened by the explosion and shaken by the blast, I picked myself up off the ground. The mortar man peered warily out of his hole.

"See whadda mean?" he said.

Some men and units in the Ardennes battle reached heights of gallantry rarely matched in the annals of war. Other men, and other units, found the strain of fighting in that fluid, confused situation, and in that dreadful cold, more than they could bear. These individuals I found it necessary to relieve, and my reasons for doing so I would like to discuss here, for they embody my whole philosophy of combat command.

The first occasion on which I had to ask for the relief of a higher commander came within the first forty-eight hours of the Ardennes battle. My Corps Chief of Artillery had been one year behind me at West Point, where I had known him well. He had had a very superior record throughout his entire service, and I not only had a warm personal regard for him, I felt toward him a great admiration and respect. He was with the Corps in the States, before it was shipped to England. When I was first apprised of my assignment to command of that Corps, I asked at once for a list of the officers then heading the various staff jobs. I made many changes. I took with me from the 82nd my Chief of Staff, Doc Eaton; my G-1, Colonel Schellhammer; my G-2, Colonel Jack, and my signal officer Colonel Moorman. I sent word back to Washington that I would appreciate it if the officers in these corresponding posts could be relieved before the Corps left the States, so that there could be no possible inference that they were relieved for cause. I pointed out that I had plenty of seasoned officers available who were thoroughly experienced in airborne, and the stakes were too high to risk committing the Corps to battle in this specialized field with all green personnel in the top staff jobs.

I left the Corps Artillery Commander in his post, however, because I had nobody in a comparable position in the 82nd, and I had the greatest respect for his reputation. But after some weeks in England, where we were planning a great many operations, I began to feel that there was little meeting of the minds between him and me. Perhaps it was due to my own working methods, but I just couldn't seem to get from this officer that degree of conspicuously superior and instant response, in the planning field, that I regarded as essential. Reluctant to take any drastic action, I did nothing about this until the Corps was committed to battle in the Ardennes. Then it became clear to me that I had to have an immediate replacement for him, or I would lose the optimum potential of this extremely powerful combat element, the Corps artillery. His replacement was General L. Mathewson, then serving as Deputy Chief of Corps Artillery in VII Corps, under General Joe Collins. Mathewson came to me on a few hours' notice, and the change in that Corps artillery was almost incredible. It changed in a twinkling. I had my Fire Control Center in the hayloft of a barn adjoining my own farmhouse headquarters at Werbomont. Within twenty-four hours after Mathewson took over, the smooth efficiency, the alert response of that fire control center were perfectly manifest. Its whole character of operations changed, and from then on was conspicuously superior. At one time, during the Ardennes battle, it was handling up to nineteen battalions of corps artillery, firing along a front of forty miles.

Twice again in the Ardennes battle I was forced to relieve high-ranking officers. In the first rush of the Germans, the 106th and the 28th Divisions had been badly mauled and scattered. In the area surrounding St. Vith, the 7th Armored Division, commanded by General Hasbrouck, had put up a very gallant fight. He had gathered around him the remnants of the division which the Germans had broken and dispersed. He had his whole division, the 7th Armored, intact, and with it a combat command of the 9th Armored under General Hoge, a most gallant officer commanding a most gallant unit. He had also practically all of the artillery of the 28th Division, one infantry regiment of the 28th, and a regiment of the 106th.

Surrounded on three sides, subjected to heavy pressure, hard hit by casualties, these troops fought stubbornly for five days until, back at Werbomont and Thieux, the 82nd and the 3rd Armored gathered enough strength to move out and make contact with them down the one narrow corridor that had not yet been cut by the Germans. On the afternoon of December 22, I made my way into that surrounded area, along with General Hasbrouck, and contacted the principal commanders of those beleaguered units. By hearing their voices and looking into their faces there on the battlefield, it was my purpose to get from them, on the ground, their own sensing of what they were up against. It was a gloomy picture. On the outer periphery was Combat Command B of the 9th Armored under General Hoge. He stood at the point of greatest pressure, the point of greatest danger. And in the event of a withdrawal, his force would have to bear the savage attrition of fighting the rear-guard action.

I had known Bill Hoge since our cadet days at West Point. I knew what a calm, courageous, imperturbable fellow he was. I knew that nothing could ever flurry him, and so above all I wanted to talk to him, to get his "feel" of the situation.

I made my first contact with him by radio. Knowing the Germans had our code, I talked in the clear—but double-talked, making allusions to West Point football days, until I was sure he knew who I was. Then I gave him the grid co-ordinates of the farmhouse where I wanted us to meet. He got in there that evening, just at last light. I took him aside for a little personal talk, alone, out of hearing of any of the other commanders present.

"Bill," I said, "we've made contact with you now. This position is too exposed to try to hold it any longer. We're not going to leave you in here to be chopped to pieces, little by little. I'm going to extricate all the forces of the 7th Armored, and the attached troops, including your own. I plan to start that withdrawal tonight. We're going to get you out of here."

"How can you?" he said. That one sentence revealed more to me than anything any commander out there had said, or any amount of reports I could have gotten, because here was a man in whom I had absolute, implicit confidence—in his personal courage, in his professional competence, and in his stability of character.

"Bill," I said, "we can and we will."

Then I left him to get this withdrawal started. I went by jeep, in the dark, through the snow and the bitter cold, to the CP of the 106th Infantry Division. It was many miles to the rear. The division commander was there. True, his division had been overrun and scattered, and much of it was missing. But a good fraction of it was up there in that surrounded pocket, fighting, and that's where he should have been. I went in to see him in his room. His attitude seemed strange to me. He appeared to be casual, almost indifferent, little interested in the fact that that night we were going to bring his people out of the trap.

After talking to him a few minutes, I sent everyone from the room except the general officers and Colonel Quill, my Deputy Chief of Staff. On a scrap of paper Colonel Quill at my direction wrote down in longhand my orders relieving this officer of his command. Then I put all his troops under command of General Hasbrouck, of the 7th Armored, though Hasbrouck was junior to the relieved officer.

That night Hasbrouck began the withdrawal of that entire force. We brought them out without the loss of a man, with all their equipment. In fact, we hauled out with us several eight-inch howitzers which had been abandoned by units not then present in the encircled area.

Not long afterward, while we still were fighting in the Ardennes, I found it necessary to relieve another top commander. I had gone to the headquarters of his division, which was heavily engaged, and had had a fairly satisfactory talk with him. As I started to leave, I asked him what we, meaning the Corps, could do to help him.

"Just pray for me," he said. Now, I believe in the power of prayer as deeply as any man, but the tenor of this reply, made in the presence of his officers, shocked me. It indicated an attitude of mind totally lacking in self-confidence, in the aggressive spirit that dangerous moment called for. I called him outside, explained to him the implications of his statement, and the disastrous effect it could not help but have on the spirit of his subordinates. Then, with deepest regret, for he was a good friend whom I deeply admired, I ordered his relief.

I want to make it clear that none of these changes were lightly made. During World War I, senior officers frequently were relieved for what seemed to me to be trivial reasons, based on hasty judgments. And early in my career I resolved that if the responsibility of high command ever fell on my shoulders, I would never be guilty of such a procedure. It deeply affects the unit concerned, and it may blast the entire career of a fine officer, for very transient reasons. But your first consideration must be not for the welfare of the officer in question, but for the lives of the men who are under his command. In the cases cited above, there was no question in my mind that the men in the units concerned were not receiving the leadership they deserved.

In time of battle, when victory hangs in the balance, it is necessary to put down any sign of weakness, indecision, lack of aggressiveness, or panic, whether the man wears stars on his shoulders or chevrons on his sleeve, for one frightened soldier can infect his whole unit.

I remember once standing beside a road leading through a pine wood, down a slope to the road junction of Manhay, where a hot fight was going on. That whole Ardennes fight was a battle for road junctions, because in that wooded country, in the deep snows, armies could not move off the roads. This particular crossroads was one of many that the Germans had to take if they were to keep up the momentum of their offensive, and we were fighting desperately to hold it. I had gone up to this point, which lay not far forward of my command post, to be of what help I could in this critical spot. As I was standing there, a lieutenant, with perhaps a dozen men, came out of the woods from the fighting, headed toward the rear. I stopped him and asked him where he was going and what his mission was. He told me that he and his men had been sent out to develop the strength of the German units that had reached Manhay, and that they had run into some machine-gun fire that was too hot for them, so they had come back.

I relieved him of his command there on the spot. I told him that he was a disgrace to his country and his uniform and that I was ashamed of him, and I knew the members of his patrol were equally ashamed.

Then I asked if any other member of the patrol was willing to lead that patrol back into the fight. A sergeant stepped up and said he would lead it back and see to it that it carried out its mission.

In another hour, on that same spot, another incident occurred which I remember with regret. In the fierce fighting, the town changed hands several times. The Germans had brought up some flat trajectory guns, and they started shelling our little group. Fragments whizzed everywhere. One struck an artillery observer, who was standing by me, in the leg, and another punctured the tank of his jeep. As this shell exploded, an infantry sergeant standing nearby became hysterical. He threw himself into the ditch by the side of the road, crying and raving. I walked over and tried to talk to him, trying to help him get hold of himself. But it had no effect. He was just crouched there in the ditch, cringing in utter terror. So I called my jeep driver, Sergeant Farmer, and told him to take his carbine and march this man back to the nearest MP, and if he started to escape to shoot him without hesitation. He was an object of abject cowardice, and the sight of him would have a terrible effect on any American soldier who might see him. I got his name, rank, and organization and made a report to his commander, but I never had the opportunity to follow up and see what action was taken in his case.

That's the sort of thing you see sometimes. It is an appalling thing to witness—to see a man break completely like that, in battle. It is worse than watching a death—for you are seeing something more important than the body die. You are witnessing the death of a man's spirit, of his pride, of all that gives meaning and purpose to life. I saw two or three paratroopers do the same thing when they came under intensive fire in Normandy. They just lost control completely and gave way to sheer physical terror. But I've only seen it happen three or four times, and that is a small percentage of the hundreds of thousands of men I have seen in battle.

That a few men break is understandable. But I prefer to remember the others who did not break, the men who stood and fought and died. What quality in them sustained and strengthened them I do not know. Surely it was not fearlessness, for in battle no normal man is entirely free from fear. I think perhaps Housman gave one answer in his lines:

> Here dead we lie because we did not choose
> To live and shame the land from which we sprung.

Nor did they choose to shame their comrades, or themselves.

11

☆☆☆☆

"The Beast We Must Slay"

PROFESSIONAL soldiers will long debate certain aspects of the Battle of the Bulge. One of the points of greatest controversy centers around the simple question: Did Von Rundstedt's sudden slash through the Ardennes take the American high command by surprise?

The only proper answer to that question is an equivocal "Yes" and "No." We were well aware the Germans possessed the capability for a major offensive action, and we expected it to come soon. We did not anticipate exactly where it would strike. We did not expect it would come through the Ardennes. We thought it far more likely that it would come across the Cologne plain, north of the Ardennes, between the Roer dams and the point where the Roer River flows into the Maas—an area that was deep in General Montgomery's sector.

In my own case, I had no doubt that, as the German forces drew nearer to their own homeland, they would lash out in one final, massive counter-offensive. On the 9th of December, when I was still at my main command post in England, I dictated the draft of a memorandum that was to be distributed as a Christmas message to the men of the corps. In paragraph 5 of that message appeared this sentence:

"They will shortly make one more desperate major effort with all the strength they still possess."

This message probably was never distributed to the troops. It went out of headquarters under the date of December 16. By that time, the divisions of the corps were moving into battle with Von Rund-stedt's panzers.

I would like to put down here the text of that message, exactly as it was issued, for I think that it illustrates, perhaps better than I can express them now, my thoughts and feelings at that time.

To the members of the 18th Corps Airborne:

In other years we have been accustomed at this time to send light-hearted greetings to our friends, wishing them a Merry Christmas and a Happy New Year. In the face of grim reality, there is this year little place for such sentiment. The fleeting optimism of a few months ago of war's end by Christmas has vanished. Looming large across our path is the beast we must slay, and we see now that the slaying will not be easy.

In our homeland there has evolved through three centuries a concept of human liberties and human dignity and a form of government designed to preserve them both—a concept in tangible form, unequalled elsewhere on this earth. Upon several past occasions our people have been called upon to defend this concept and with great sacrifice. The call now comes again. Our answer will follow.

We perceive these truths a little more clearly today than formerly. Back in the days of our national youth the great men who against sloth and ignorance and cowardice and greed, and all manner of weakness, put our nation on its feet, and started it forward on the path that it has since followed, saw and spoke those truths in language that lives today. More than a hundred years ago, speaking of the United States of America, Thomas Jefferson wrote, and I quote: "I shall not die without a hope that light and liberty are on a steady advance. Even should the cloud of barbarism and despotism again obscure the science and the liberties of Europe, this country remains to preserve and restore light and liberty to them. In short, the flames kindled on the 4th of July in 1776 have spread over too much of the globe to be extinguished by the feeble engines of despotism. On the contrary they will consume these and all who work them."

I quoted here from a book called *Journey into America,* by Donald C. Peattie, published by Houghton Mifflin Co., in 1943. I then continued:

For four years the German people, by every conceivable means, have sought to extinguish these flames. They continue to seek this end. They will shortly make at least one more desperate major effort with all the strength they still possess, and once more, as Jefferson wrote, the flames they seek to extinguish will consume them and their works.

For the year ahead I wish the members of this Corps a deeper insight into those elemental principles for which our nation fights, rekindled faith in their ultimate triumph, and renewed determination to contribute our utmost to the upward climb of the United States of America.

Signed: M. B. Ridgway
Major General, U.S. Army
Commanding

Before I leave the subject of the Ardennes fight, and move on to the great battles that lay ahead of us as the Corps drove on into the Siegfried Line, I would like to speak in some detail of the visit of General Max Taylor to Washington, a trip from which he returned with all speed to rejoin his division in battle at Bastogne. As I have said, that journey was made at my request, and it was a mission of supreme importance to the airborne.

Even in the early days when the airborne divisions were being created, I became increasingly convinced of the serious inadequacy of the authorized organization of this new fighting force, and the Sicily operation had completely confirmed my views.

In simple terms, the idea had evolved in Headquarters, Ground Forces, back in Washington, that the airborne division should be organized within a ceiling strength of 8,800 men. It struck me at the time, and with increasing force thereafter, as we actually started working with the tool that we were able to make out of such a strength, that it was somewhat comparable to calling in a very large man and saying, "Here are two yards of cloth. Go make yourself a suit of clothes." In other words, the jobs which an airborne division was to be called upon to execute could not possibly be accomplished by such a strength. You could not build a division into the combat strength required with any such ceiling as 8,800 men.

Obviously, the only thing to do was to ignore these limitations. This we did. We built far beyond our authorized strength. In the Normandy operation, both the 82nd and Max Taylor's 101st had a strength of nearly 15,000 by the time the glider regiments and the tail which came in by sea had joined up for battle on the ground.

As we repeatedly pointed out to the high command, once these divisions are committed to battle, they can only be relieved over the dead body of the army or corps commander. He knows he has no finer troops at his disposal, and regardless of the tactical situation, and the ease or difficulty of extricating them at any particular moment in the battle, he is never willing to give them up. He is going to keep them just as long as he possibly can. That means that they have got to

---

have the sustaining power to stay in there and slug. And that could only be made possible by an authorized—not an unauthorized—major increase in division strength.

I had been repeatedly turned down in my efforts to get this authorization. I had sent officers back. They had talked to officers in the Operations Division of the War Department General Staff, then headed by General McNarney, and I had been able to get nowhere. The answer every time was an inflexible "No."

Early in December, there in England, I decided to make one more effort, because I felt that if I could get this matter to the personal attention of General Marshall, who was then Chief of Staff, the answers might be different. Finally, working through channels, I got approval from Bedell Smith to send a specially selected senior officer back with one more request. I know of no one better qualified to evaluate a tool than the man who has had to use it in actual battle. Accordingly I chose Taylor for this mission. General Marshall knew him well and regarded him highly, and I knew he would be received and given an attentive audience.

The result is now history. General Marshall received General Taylor, listened to our presentation—and granted a very material increase in the strength of the airborne divisions. From that time on, we had no more trouble with this problem.

By a quirk of fate, Taylor was in Washington when his gallant 101st was thrown into the path of the German attack, and it fought its epic battle at Bastogne under General McAuliffe, the Assistant Division Commander. Taylor flew from Washington as soon as news of the break-through reached him, and returned to his division at the earliest possible moment. The details of his visit to Washington, the reasons for it, the high importance attached to it, have not been told before, so far as I know, outside of classified documents. But these are the facts. As a fighting soldier, I know Taylor felt a tremendous sense of frustration when his Eagles went into battle without him. But his mission to Washington was of incalculable value to the airborne.

Parenthetically, I would like to say that if General Marshall had adopted any other attitude than the one he did I would have been profoundly surprised. The combat soldier never had a better and more understanding friend than George C. Marshall. With the burdens of a global war upon his shoulders, he never forgot the man with the rifle, the man whose task it was to kill and be killed.

12

☆☆☆☆

Smashing the Siegfried Line

IN SIX weeks of savage fighting the German attack had been contained. Von Rundstedt had made his great gamble and had lost; the time had come for the counter-blow, the drive that would wipe out the last vestiges of German strength in the Bulge, and carry on to breach the Siegfried Line.

The opening phase of that operation was a massive offensive with General Gerow's V Corps on our left, and General Collins's VII Corps on our right. I then had four divisions in my XVIII Corps. All were infantry. I had been asked by the Army Commander if I wanted armor other than the separate tank battalions already attached to my infantry divisions, and I had refused it. The snows were deep up there—waist deep in the hollows—and roads were few, and I thought that armor could do little under such conditions.

The formation with which I decided to attack was with two infantry divisions up and two back, and when the two forward divisions were stopped, I proposed to leapfrog the two in the rear through them and continue the assault. I led off with the 1st Division and the 82nd, and I don't think any commander ever had such a magnificent experience as to see those two splendid divisions, both veteran outfits at their highest state of combat effectiveness, attacking side by side. It was a joy to see. It was like watching two great racehorses, driving head and head to the finish line. All I had to do was give them their head, and then help them with all means at the Corps's disposal, and with everything that I could get from Army. This was the sort of thing that would happen:

The 82nd was having a very difficult time at one stage of the attack. They were getting very heavy fire from a village on the edge of their zone of attack, within their zone but very near the boundary of the 1st Division. So the 1st Division swung over there and cleaned out that village and made a present of it to the 82nd. Naturally, that burned up the 82nd just a little. They didn't like to feel that anybody had to come into their own bailiwick to help them out. So the next day, without being asked, they swung over into the zone of the 1st Division and took a village and presented it to the 1st. That way everybody's pride was satisfied.

I had anticipated extremely heavy going and in my own estimate of the situation I had figured these two assault divisions would run out of steam just about the time they hit the first bunkers of the Siegfried Line. The Siegfried in our zone of advance was a double line of tremendous obstacles—concrete pillboxes, wire, and dragons teeth to break up an armored assault—and I had planned to stop the 82nd and the 1st as they came up against the first of these zones. Then I would pass the 30th Division, under General Hobbs, and General Bolling's 84th, on through to breach the Siegfried's outer defenses. But it didn't work out that way. General Andrus's 1st and Gavin's 82nd were going with such momentum they smashed through the first zone and moved well inside. And there they were stopped, not by the enemy, but by orders from First Army.

About the time we made the first penetration of the Siegfried, General Eisenhower, General Bradley, and General Hodges all came up to see me. They told me that my corps was to be pulled out very promptly, and sent northeastward some sixty miles, to help Ninth Army in a big offensive against the Roer dams. Could we do it?

I told them, of course, we could do it. But I doubt that any major unit was ever faced with such a situation. Here we were in the middle of a major offensive against one of the most heavily fortified zones in all Europe, with another major operation—to help the British Second Army get across the lower Rhine—already on our books for late March. Now we were to move north to attack the Roer. But we wouldn't be there very long, they told me. Once the dams were taken, we'd be pulled out to help General Patton's Third Army in its assault across the Rhine. So here we were, planning two major offensives while we were still in the middle of a hard fight. I don't think any unit the size of a corps ever was given so many missions in such widely separated areas in so brief a time. And I don't believe any other corps but the XVIII could have executed them. I guess that's just a manifestation of an old soldier's pride in his unit, but that's the way I feel.

So ended for me the Battle of the Bulge and the break-out thereafter. It began in darkness and confusion, under a pall of gloom born of the threat of dreadful defeat. It ended in triumph, due, in the main, to the mobility of the American Army, and the courage and resolution of the American soldier. None of us who were there will ever forget those days of battle in the snow, and the nights when the German armor was rumbling all around us in the darkness. Strangely, though, one of my most vivid memories is not of battle, but of a little thing of no importance which happened during a lull. I remember it perhaps because a good laugh is a rare thing in combat, and this was one of the funniest incidents I remember from the war.

It came early in the Bulge, when the Germans still were everywhere, and no man could be sure that the next patch of woods might not conceal a nest of them. I had been up forward on reconnaissance, visiting one of the advance infantry elements, a platoon, which was digging in in the snow. I was on my way back by jeep, with Sergeant Farmer at the wheel, with an armored car coming along behind to protect us if we got in trouble.

We were traveling along at a fair rate of speed, over a narrow, twisting, hard-surfaced road, when I noticed a masonry bridge ahead, a narrow bridge with steel railings. We slowed down to cross, and I saw on the sides of the bridge a row of our own anti-tank mines. Their safety forks had been pulled and they were ready to blow at the first touch.

Just across the bridge there was a company of our engineers, standing around their little campfires, drinking coffee. Just as we drew abreast of them there was a terrific explosion, and it flashed through my mind immediately that the armored car had skidded and hit those mines.

But it flashed through the minds of those engineers that the Germans were upon them, and they left for the hills. Coffee cans were suspended in mid-air as the men who were holding them fled. They had their overcoats on, but unbuttoned, and as they took off, their coattails stood out behind them flat as planks. I have never seen men achieve such speed from a standing start.

Miraculously, not a soul had been badly hurt. The armored car had been blown off the bridge, but had landed upright fifteen feet below in the shallow river bed. Fragments of stone had torn the windshield out of our jeep, and one sharp piece had slashed through Farmer's heavy winter clothing to break the skin on his back. Not a single engineer had suffered any wound, except to his pride. A hundred yards away, up in the hills, they were peering from behind rocks and trees, and it was quite a while before they came shambling back, shamefaced and grinning sheepishly. But Farmer and I weren't grinning. We were laughing. For I never saw anything funnier in my life than the sight of those engineers, tearing through the woods like low-flying birds, with those overcoats standing out in the breeze.

13

☆☆☆☆

The Drop Across the Rhine

WITH deep regret, on First Army's orders I broke off action against the Siegfried Line. We had penetrated the outer zone of defenses. We felt a supreme confidence that the momentum of the Corps attack would take it on through the last organized resistance there on the ground. And beyond this inner rampart lay the Rhine and the heartland of Germany.

But the ways of the Lord are inscrutable at times—and so are the ways of high strategy. The decision of Supreme Headquarters was to halt that offensive and shift the weight of the attack up north. So, feeling much like a pack of bear dogs who have been pulled off just as they brought the bear to bay, the Corps moved north and reported to General Simpson's Ninth Army.

We were to join with VII Corps in an attack abreast against the Roer dams. It was the Allies' second assault against these great reservoirs, which posed a deadly threat to our operations. Flood waters, loosed by the Germans, catching us astride the Roer, could have been disastrous. Recognizing this fact, in the late fall of 1944 we had first attacked the great Schmidt dam, one of the largest of the mammoth concrete structures. The 28th Infantry Division had been assigned the task of taking it, which they had, most gallantly. Then they had fallen into the error that all but the most seasoned troops are prone to make. Once the assault was over and the Germans had been driven back, they let their guard down. They forgot about reconnaissance, and they failed to consolidate their defensive positions as they should. When the Germans counter-attacked quickly, in great strength, the 28th was caught off balance, suffered heavy casualties, and lost their positions. That ground had not been recovered.

Immediately upon arrival there in the northern sector, I made a personal reconnaissance into these deep wooded valleys where the 28th had been attacked and overwhelmed. It was a graveyard of war, a no man's land populated by ghosts. We found the remnants of the 28th Division's equipment. Tanks and trucks had been abandoned in country so precipitous and rugged they should never have been employed there in the first place. The winter snows were melting in the first warm days of spring, and from beneath the snow the bodies of the 28th Division's dead were beginning to appear. They littered the ground, in various stages of decomposition, lying singly and in little groups and clusters, just as they had fallen months before.

I remember that as I came back through this forest of the unburied dead, one of my most seasoned commanders suggested to me that during our attack we should make certain that the new units assigned to the Corps should not be required to attack across this sector. It should be given to seasoned veterans who had seen much of death on the battlefield, and would not recoil from these macabre surroundings. A green unit, he felt, might be strongly affected by the sight of so many American dead, in such a condition, and should not have to undergo such an experience the first time they were committed to battle.

It was a thoughtful suggestion, but I never had to act upon it. Heavy spring rains flooded the rivers, and the floods, combined with the threat that the Germans might blow the dams at any moment, caused Ninth Army's attack to be delayed. The Corps was withdrawn by the High Command and sent back to the Champagne country to get ready for the operation to which we were already committed—to help the British Second Army in its drive across the Rhine at Wesel.

This was to be a small but a complex operation, involving a great deal of co-ordination. The Corps was to be made up of two airborne divisions—the 6th British, under General Bols, flying from airfields on the continent, and the 17th U.S. Airborne, flying from England under command of my old friend Bud Miley, who had checked me out as a jumper in my first drop back at Benning two years before.

At ten o'clock in the morning of the 24th of March we dropped these two divisions across the Rhine. We put them down right on top of the German artillery positions that commanded the river crossings, and for a while they had a pretty rough time, for from the moment they hit the ground they were under the aimed fire of the German guns.

It was sunny above but a misty morning in the woods and valleys as I stood there on the river bank, watching those serials come over, flying low. There was no enemy air interference at all, and behind me, to our rear, not a gun was firing. We had shut off all the British Second Army's guns for the time being to ensure that the planes would not fly into the trajectory of our own artillery shells.

Across the river, the German guns were responding angrily, however, and we had some losses from ground fire, particularly in the case of the 513th Parachute Infantry, commanded by Colonel Coutts. We did not have enough of the old workhorses, the C-47's that we had been using for paradrops, and we had to put the 513th and its supporting engineers and parachute artillery into seventy-two C-46's, a twin-engine plane capable of carrying a tremendous load. Out of those seventy-two planes we lost twenty-two from ground fire, and of these twenty-two, fourteen were flamers that caught fire in the air as soon as they were hit.

This was the greatest single aircraft loss we had in any operation during the war. Most of the paratroopers got out, thank God, for in every parachute aircraft there is an abandon-ship bell. When it rings, the sticks go out regardless of where they are and they stand not on the order of their going. They pile out the door in a pell-mell rush, and so far as I know, not a single paratrooper went down with the falling planes. We did lose a number of combat crews, though, for those brave youngsters stayed with the flaming ships until the paratroopers had cleared, and in many cases they stayed too late to save themselves.

After that tragedy, I gave orders that under no circumstances would we ever use C-46's as paradrop planes again. The ship was a fire trap. If a wing tank was punctured, the fuel ran down along the fuselage, and an incendiary shell would set the whole aircraft aflame in a second.

We had a resupply mission coming on the heels of the paradrop. These planes were B-24's, the big four-engine Liberators. They came over low, and we lost quite a few of them, too. They were down so low the AA guns could not come on target, but rifle fire, and fire from light automatic weapons riddled many of them. So we didn't try that again, either. As a matter of fact, that trans-Rhine crossing was the last big airborne assault of the war. We learned a lot from it, but the knowledge cost us dearly.

I crossed the Rhine in an Alligator, an amphibious tracked vehicle, manned by a British crew. It had a 50-caliber gun on it, and as we waddled down the bank on the near side, we turned this gun loose at every patch of grass or bushes on the opposite bank that looked as if it might hide a German. We didn't have any idea what was over there. As it turned out, nothing was, for we drew no answering fire.

As was my custom, I had my own little personal patrol group with me, three men and an officer aide, and we said good-by to our British friends and started off, the five of us, through this heavy forest—the Dierforterswald—looking for Bud Miley and his troopers. We had gone only a little way into the woods when I came around a little bend in the path, and there, just fifteen yards ahead of me was a German soldier, his head and shoulders sticking up out of a foxhole. He had me cold, and I stopped stock-still, just staring at him, and he stared back. Then I saw that his eyes, though open, were seeing nothing. He was stone dead. Why his head had not slumped onto his chest, I do not understand, but it hadn't.

Breathing a little heavily after that encounter, we moved on. Then I caught a flicker of motion in the woods ahead, and heard the thump of heavy feet. I motioned with my hand, and we all took cover. Peering out of the bushes, I saw one of the strangest sights I ever observed in war. Down that little trail came a big, heavy-footed farm horse. On his back was an American paratrooper. On the paratrooper's head was a high silk hat. He had his rifle slung on his back and a look of smug contentment on his face. I stepped out from hiding and he saw the two stars on my shoulders and he damn near fell off the horse. He didn't know whether to salute from the horse's back, wearing that hat, or dismount and present arms, or what in the hell to do. He thrashed around up there on top of that horse for about a minute. Then he saw I was doubled up laughing and didn't do anything. He just sat there, grinning. He told me he found the horse in a barn, and the hat in a farmhouse.

To me that incident was typical of the American soldier. I don't think the combat soldier of any other army would have pulled a stunt like that. I know the German soldier wouldn't, for he'd have been shot for showing disrespect to the uniform of the fatherland. But this man was a typical paratrooper—tough and brave, with a certain what-the-hell dash about him. If I had been a German there'd have been nothing ludicrous about him. He'd have been off that horse in a flash, silk hat and all, with his M-1 blazing.

Not long afterward, I found General Miley's CP. He was having plenty of trouble. The 513th Parachute Infantry, under Colonel Coutts, a most gallant and competent commander, not only had taken a bad mauling in the air, they had landed in a hornets' nest on the ground. One of their battalions had landed right in a German artillery position, and the Germans had turned a howitzer on them at a range of about one hundred yards. They had many dead in that field that morning—men who had been killed before they could even get out of their harness.

Darkness came on, and we still had no report from the other airborne division, General Bols's 6th British. So along about twilight, General Miley and I moved out with my patrol, in a jeep, with a second jeep, armed with a 50-caliber machine gun, coming along behind. We were moving along a dirt road through the forest when we came upon a big German truck that had been burned. It completely blocked the road, so we had to turn out, making a little detour through the woods.

It took a long time to find Bols's CP. There was a lot of sporadic firing going on all about, and confused tactical situation, which is normal in an airborne drop. We didn't know where our own people were, much less the enemy, so we had to move with a moderate degree of caution. Finally, about eleven o'clock that night, I found Bols's CP, and we had a very satisfactory talk. He seemed glad to see the Corps commander, and his brother division commander, General Miley. So the two of them got together there over maps, evaluated the situation as best they could, and laid plans for concerting their action thereafter, with me helping at Corps in any way I could.

It was around midnight when we left, a clear night, with a half moon shining, lighting up the woods so that you could see for perhaps one hundred yards all around. There was a tremendous amount of firing going on, most of it machine-gun fire, and the bulk of it heavy stuff—50-caliber. Pretty soon, looming up in the moonlight we saw the hulk of the burned-out truck. My jeep was in the lead, and just as we reached the truck and turned out over the same little detour we had traveled before—suddenly there was a scurrying of men in the road some twenty yards ahead. We had bumped into a German patrol. I jumped from the jeep, firing my Springfield from the hip, and I heard the first man squeal and saw him fall. Then they all hit the ground, firing, and so did we, and there was a great deal of cursing and swearing in German and English there for a while. Every gun was shooting except my jeep-mounted 50-caliber, which never fired a shot, and I wondered why the hell it didn't. I found out later they were afraid to fire. We were so mixed up there on the ground that they couldn't tell friend from foe, so they didn't cut loose with the 50. Which I guess was just as well, in that situation.

I fired all five shots in my Springfield, shooting from the hip because the range was so close. Then I hit the ground to reload, rolled to get another clip out of my belt, and this threw my head right beside the right front wheel of my jeep. There was quite an explosion then, very close to me, and I felt the heat and sting of a fragment in my shoulder. Some German had thrown a grenade and it had gone off under the front of the jeep, about three feet from my head. But, by the grace of God, the wheel was between me and the blast, and all I got was one small chunk that hit me in the shoulder. It wrecked the jeep, though, broke the crankcase and all the oil spilled out on the ground.

After that explosion there was complete silence. I could hear men breathing around me in the dark, but nobody was quite sure where anybody else was, so we held our fire. Then I caught sight of a little movement to my right rear, across the ditch in a little bunch of willows, and I could vaguely see the head and shoulders of a man. I couldn't tell whether it was one of us, or a German, so I eased around until I got him covered, then I called out:

"Put up your hands, you son of a bitch!"

I got a very friendly answer back in good American. "Aaah, go sit in your hat," he said. So I eased my finger off the trigger.

There was no more firing. The Germans had melted away into the shadows—we hoped—and we went on back, pushing my crippled jeep.

The little incident illustrates one thing I think is important—the paratroopers' habit of holding his fire until he knows exactly what he's shooting at. The man in the willows could have killed me easily, and I could have killed him, if we hadn't taken the trouble to identify each other. But the paratrooper is not trigger-happy. He's so used to being alone and surrounded, not knowing where his friends are, nor the enemy, that he's very, very careful about firing until he's sure he knows whom he's shooting at. It has to be that way, otherwise a parachute battalion in a night drop would destroy itself. Wars are full of incidents, since the beginning of time, of units getting in a hot fight and then finding at the end that they've been shooting at friendly forces. It's easy to do, but I think there are fewer incidents of that kind between paratroop elements than in any other units in the field army.

14

☆☆☆☆

Cleaning Out the Ruhr Pocket

THE battle of the Corps in the Wesel area was short but sharp. By nightfall of D-day, four thousand prisoners had been taken, the German artillery positions were overrun, and the ground elements, moving up fast from the river, had made contact with the paratroopers who had dropped deep in. We were in action for six days, the two airborne divisions driving eastward abreast. On the third day, the British 6th Guards Armored brigade was attached to the Corps. Troopers of the 513th Parachute Infantry climbed on the British tanks, and the advance moved forward relentlessly, with the 6th British and the 17th Airborne keeping pace on foot to the left. Five days after the drop we seized the defiles at Haltern and Dülmen, and held them open while the 2nd Armored roared through, swinging in a great arc to the north and east to encircle the Ruhr. At the same time, the 3rd Armored, to the south and east, executed an encircling movement to join up with the 2nd Armored and form the famous Ruhr Pocket.

On the sixth day, Corps Headquarters was pulled out, leaving the two airborne divisions to carry on. It had been a small operation and a short one, but it had given to the British Second Army's drive across the Rhine a momentum that was to carry it, practically without pause, to the Baltic and the join-up with the Russians and the end of the war in Western Europe.

Back in our old bivouac area near Épernay, in France, the Corps was given its next assignment—to drive into the Ruhr trap and clean it out while the two great armored divisions held that tremendous industrial area in an iron clamp. It was to be a three-pronged drive— XVIII Corps moving in from the south, Van Fleet's III Corps driving from the east, and Ninth Army squeezing from the north.

I was given four divisions for this drive—the 86th, the 8th, the 78th and the 97th. It was a meat-grinder operation. The Germans were trapped and doomed, but they fought with great skill and stubbornness.

The battle, for me, began as usual, with a preliminary look at the ground. I'd been in my headquarters at Épernay for only a few hours when I received orders to report at once to General Hodges, commanding First Army, far up the Rhine. I flew first to Hodges's rear CP, to find him gone, displacing forward. I set out from there in a borrowed jeep, along with Don Faith, my aide. For nine hours, we drove up and down the valley of the Rhine, hunting Hodges. Night came on, and a heavy fog, and my driver had not been taking his carrot juice as he should have been. Time and again, groping through the woods in the dark and the fog, he narrowly missed striking trees, until finally I moved him over and took the wheel. Now and then an MP would loom up out of the fog at a crossroads, and we would ask our way. The MP's were apologetic, but they had no remote idea where General Hodges could be found. I thought the people who should be apologetic were the members of the staff back at First Army rear. It is a serious thing to lose your own advanced CP—especially when the Army Commander is in it.

About one o'clock in the morning, by the grace of God and a few lucky breaks, I found General Hodges's CP, and he gave me the mission described above.

After the first few days, it became perfectly clear that the Germans were folding fast. Less than two miles ahead of us was the headquarters of General Model, Commander of German Army Group B. His situation was hopeless, and I knew that so shrewd a soldier as Model was well aware that he didn't have a chance. It seemed to me that here was an excellent opportunity to save many thousands of precious lives. I called in one of my personal aides, Captain Brandstetter, who spoke fluent German, gave him my instructions, and sent him to Model under a flag of truce. My message was simple. I merely told Model that he was in a hopeless situation and that further resistance could only cause needless slaughter.

Brandstetter came back with one of Model's staff officers—and Model's answer. It was to the effect that he could not consider any surrender proposal. He was bound by a personal oath to Hitler to fight to the end, and it would do violence to his sense of honor even to consider my message.

I decided to make one more try. I sat down and composed a personal letter to General Model, and I think that part of the text of it might be of interest here. The date was April, 15, 1945:

Neither history nor the military profession [I wrote] records any nobler character, any more brilliant master of warfare, any more dutiful subordinate of the state, than the American General, Robert E. Lee. Eighty years ago this month, his loyal command reduced in numbers, stripped of its means of effective fighting and completely surrounded by overwhelming forces, he chose an honorable capitulation.

This same choice is now yours. In the light of a soldier's honor, for the reputation of the German Officer Corps, for the sake of your nation's future, lay down your arms at once. The German lives you will save are sorely needed to restore your people to their proper place in society. The German cities you will preserve are irreplaceable necessities for your people's welfare.

Brandstetter delivered this letter. He came back with Model's Chief of Staff. It was no use, they said. Model would not consider any plea whatever. That was that. I could do no more. From now on the blood was upon Model's head. His Chief of Staff was a wiser man. I told him he could go back under a flag of truce and take his chances in the disaster that was sure to come. Or he could remain in our custody as a prisoner of war. He did not debate this option long. He chose to stay. Model found a way out that satisfied, I suppose, his stubborn sense of honor. He committed suicide.

The attack ground on. We had been told that there were probably 150,000 Germans in the pocket. Allied forces captured more than 300,000. Of this number, the XVIII Corps took 160,000, including 25 generals. We overran 5,000 square miles of German soil, liberated 200,000 DP's from German slavery, and freed 5,639 Allied prisoners of war. Our drive began on April 10, with the 13th Armored recently given me, spearheading the assault of the infantry. It ended at daylight April 18, when the last organized resistance in the Ruhr pocket collapsed.

I hoped that we'd get a breather after this. In the space of three months the Corps had been almost constantly in battle—sixty days in the Ardennes, a week in the assault crossing of the Rhine in support of Second Army, ten days in the Ruhr pocket. A corps command post is a pretty high one, and normally operates in fairly decent accommodations. But for all this time we had been moving so fast and shifting around so much that my personal shelter had nearly always been in dirty, filthy places. I had slept in barns and abandoned houses, and several nights I'd spent curled up in my sleeping bag. Now I was eager for a dry, clean, decent place to live in for a while, so I could rest, and relax a little, before the next big row began.

I sent Don Faith up in a cub plane to hunt for a house somewhere in that beautiful Westphalian countryside that lies south of the industrial Ruhr. He flew over that beautiful rolling country, covered by forests and laced by streams, until he finally found an ideal spot. It was a handsome, relatively modern home, built about thirty years before, I'd say, and elegantly furnished. The owner, a small manufacturer, and his wife were still in residence.

We moved them out, into quarters over their garage, after first going over with them the list of furnishings so that all could be returned to them intact when we moved on. Then I moved in with my staff, and for about two days we really luxuriated there in that fine, clean house, among those beautiful hills. It had one of the most beautiful dining rooms I have ever seen, perfectly proportioned and handsomely paneled. The library was also a delightful room, and the first night there I noticed over the divan one of the most magnificent Oriental rugs I have ever seen. It was deep red, a Bokhara, and I remember thinking that, despite the ban on looting, this rug was going to be a sore temptation.

Forty-eight hours after I moved into this fine house, I got orders to report to General Montgomery, 250 miles away up toward the Danish peninsula. It was as wearying a journey as I ever made. I was gone only twenty-six hours but traveled 500 miles in a jeep in that time. When I got back, the rug was gone, and never seen again.

We were moving again, this time to the north, to protect the right flank of the British Second Army as it drove to the Baltic to cut off the Danish peninsula. Four divisions were placed under my command—my old 82nd; the 6th British Airborne, that had jumped under Corps command in the crossing of the Rhine; Hasbrouck's 7th Armored, which had fought under me in the Ardennes; and Bryant

Moore's 8th U.S. Infantry, which I had had before, when we were cleaning out the Ruhr pocket.

We picked up and moved out at once, northward to the Elbe. I hated to leave my comfortable little eyrie in Westphalia, but I was looking forward to the operation to which I had been assigned. After my long jeep ride I had found Montgomery hidden away in some deep woods. He had the habit of operating like this, leaving his main command post to be run by his Chief of Staff and hiding himself away, with just a handful of officers, at an advanced CP where he could do his planning without distraction. We had met before, in the days preceding the Normandy invasion, and again in the Ardennes, when my Corps was for a time under his command, so he knew me pretty well.

He had great confidence in me, apparently, for he gave me the kind of directive that a field commander most hopes to get. He merely outlined the task he had in mind for me.

Then he said: "You'll find Dempsey down the road. You two have worked together before. Go down there and fix it up between you. Then come on back here and I'll put you up for the night."

So I went down to see my old friend, General Dempsey, whose Second Army I had supported in the Rhine crossing, and we laid our tentative plans for my mission of protecting his flanks as he drove toward the Baltic to slice off the Danish peninsula.

I left him with some regret, for I was fairly sure that at Dempsey's mess there would be a little touch of something to warm and cheer me after my sleety ride. And I knew Monty was a teetotaler who eschewed alcohol in any form.

To my great surprise, however, as I sat down at General Montgomery's table in his little field tent, that evening, he asked if I would like some wine. I told him I would, indeed. His offering it marked no real break in his teetotalitarian armor, however, for he took none himself. It was good wine, too.

We assembled in the north as rapidly as possible, for all of us had the feeling that the end was near, that this onslaught might be our last combat action of the war. I went up early, by air, with my little planning group, and then went on by jeep to find and look over on the ground the zone of advance assigned to the Corps. We were on the south bank of the Elbe. Across the river lay the Germans, bruised and battered from years of hard pounding, but still full of fight. I went down to the river bank in the afternoon to take a look. I exposed myself as much as I thought necessary, but drew no fire. Across the wide river all was silent.

In a vacant farmhouse by the river, we found a tremendous basket of what appeared to be fresh eggs. I took them with some misgivings, for I remembered how, back in Holland, the good, frugal Dutch had kicked up a tremendous fuss about some activities of the 82nd Division, accusing the paratroopers of looting and pillaging. I investigated their charges and found what they boiled down to was that some hungry paratroopers had raided a few Dutch hen houses, taking chickens and eggs. They had also found that they could pursue fleeing Germans faster on bicycles than they could on foot, so they had commandeered a few bicycles, too. This had caused a tremendous to-do, and I wanted to stir up no similar ruckus about these eggs. But I hadn't tasted a fresh egg since I left England, and to my mind an egg is legitimate spoils of war. If kept too long uneaten, it is no good to anybody anyway, except perhaps as a missile. So we ate those eggs with gusto.

After that reconnaissance, during which we exposed ourselves without drawing any fire, I did some hard, fast thinking. It seemed to me we had an opportunity here to get the jump on the German, to seize a bridgehead across that twelve-hundred-foot river before he had a chance to organize. We had no combat troops up at the moment, but I knew that one battalion of Gavin's fast-moving 82nd should be pulling into the area soon. They would arrive shortly after dark. We'd let them rest until daylight. Then we'd shoot them across there in assault boats, just at dawn, and we'd have a toehold in enemy territory across the Elbe. And that we did. That battalion crossed without opposition, fanned out on the other side, and we started bridging that same morning, laying the pontoons on which the following elements would cross.

It was absolutely necessary we get that bridge down fast, for one battalion alone across the river could not long hold out against a powerful counter-attack in case the Germans should throw one at us.

I had two rather inexperienced engineer units building that bridge. One of them, I think, was going into combat for the first time. They made a good start, though, and the work was moving right along, when from across the river the Germans started shelling the bridgehead area. It was light and sporadic at first, then it got heavier and heavier, until we were getting quite a shelling there. These men who had never been under fire before didn't like that. They left the river and took shelter and all work came to a halt.

That disappointed me a little. So I walked out on the portion of the bridge they had finished, and stood there, and I noticed that when these shells hit in the water they burst deep down, and there were no fragments flying around. So it seemed to me there was a lot of noise, but not too much danger. So I went back and got hold of the engineering group commander and some of the engineer battalion commanders and gave them a pretty good talking-to.

"I don't see any reason why an engineer shouldn't get killed the same as a doughboy," I told them. "And a lot of doughboys are going to be killed here unless you get those bridges built. Now you get your people out from behind those trees and out of those ditches and let's get on with our mutton here. Let's get this bridge built in record time."

Well, that seemed to work. They got their men together and they pushed an 1,180-foot bridge across that river in fifteen hours, as fine a performance under fire as I've ever seen.

Under the original arrangement, my Corps was to cross further north, in the British zone. Once across I was to sideslip south, into my own sector, and drive on from there. Now, with my own bridge in, I didn't see any sense in that, so I sent a polite note to General Barker, commanding VIII Corps, telling him we'd use our own bridges and not bother him.

We had one little amusing incident there. The 6th British, an airborne division, was part of my Corps that did cross in the British zone. When the British corps commander got his bridge in, he assigned a crossing priority. He wanted his armor over first, so he impounded the airborne people and would not let them approach the bridgehead until the armor had crossed. This left the airborne troopers champing at the bit. Then some bright trooper figured out a ruse. The airborne wore a red beret, with a black lining, and the armored people wore a black beret. So the airborne troopers turned their berets inside out and went across under the noses of the MP's, disguised as armored elements. Then they came on down the bank to the south and joined us. It was a damned smart stunt.

A corps is a big outfit. With all sorts of support elements—armor, artillery, communications people and engineers—added to its infantry divisions, it may number 150,000 men, and you don't just shift it around like a pawn on a chessboard. In this operation the XVIII Airborne must have established some sort of record for rapidity of movement. In less than a week we had moved, by truck and jeep, nearly three hundred miles from the Ruhr to the south bank of the Elbe, had crossed that broad and formidable stream, and had driven sixty miles eastward against disorganized German forces to make contact with the Russians, forty-eight hours earlier than the plans called for. Never, to my mind, has the all-important element of time been exploited so effectively in a military action, and at no other time, to my knowledge, in the war, did U.S. and British elements work together in so closely co-ordinated a team effort.

One example of that teamwork came at the very beginning, when we were pushing our lead patrols across in assault boats, ahead of the single battalion of the 82nd. General Dempsey, as well aware as I that this was to be the last big smash that would crush the Germans between our armies and those of the Russians advancing from the East, called on me. He said it would mean a great deal to British prestige if I would arrange my plan of attack so that the British elements of the Corps—the 6th Airborne—could be the first to make contact with the Russians.

I felt a deep admiration and respect for Dempsey, a magnificent soldier under whom I had served before. But this request would throw my attack off stride. I had already laid my plans to shoot Hasbrouck's 7th Armored eastward as fast as possible. On the south, the 82nd, which was accustomed to move fast, was going in at almost equal speed. To permit the 6th Airborne to make the first contact meant that I would have to cut them diagonally across the zone of attack of the 7th Armored, which could cause all sorts of trouble on the roads.

I explained all this to Dempsey and he understood my position perfectly.

"That's quite all right," he said. "I understand. You do it your own way."

But back in my Corps CP I started thinking. I remembered the great fight the British had made throughout the war, the disaster of Dunkirk, the quiet valor of the people of England under the German bombings. So I changed my scheme of attack a little and turned Bols's 6th British Airborne loose. They got up there with amazing rapidity to make the contact with the Russians only an hour or so after the

82nd had met the first Red patrols farther south. Dempsey, I think, deeply appreciated that gesture, for I later had a very nice note from him, thanking me for what I had done.

I remember well one canny British directive which set the pattern for the conduct of the British soldier when in the presence of the Russians. Our Russian allies should be treated with civility, the directive said, but there must be no excessive overture of friendship. Such efforts on the part of the British, it was pointed out, would be taken by the Russians as a tribute to their superiority as soldiers. And neither the British nor the American soldier, at that time, had any reason to look up to any other fighting man that walked the earth.

The achievements of the Corps in that drive to final victory are a matter of pride to all of us who took part in that action. We drove against the Germans for 60 miles, conquering 1,200 square miles of territory. We took 359,796 prisoners, including 50 German generals, and destroyed or captured great numbers of tanks and guns and miscellaneous implements of war. We moved at least 30 miles eastward of the line which originally had been set as the point where Allied and Russian forces would meet—and on Montgomery's orders, I clung to that "Wismar cushion," so that it could be used for negotiating purposes. We took it by force of arms, but we gave it up to the Russians later, as the diplomats and politicians came in to take over from the soldiers. There were good reasons for it, I suppose, but I always considered it unfortunate that we had to give up that much of that beautiful Mecklenburg countryside. A soldier always hates to give up land he has conquered, even to an ally.

We made contact with the Russians on the Baltic on the 2nd of May. I saw my first one, a Russian general, a day later. I was interested to note that, in coming to make a formal call on an ally, he brought along a platoon-sized body guard, armed with tommy guns. General Gavin's headquarters, where the meeting took place, was in a great palace, still untouched by war, and it made an incongruous picture to see the armed Russians scowling suspiciously about them in the great halls where the counts of Mecklenburg-Schwerin once held grand balls and feasts.

Five days afterward, the war in Europe was over, the killing and the dying were done. The beast that had brought so much blood and tears and anguish to the world at last had been slain.

15

☆☆☆☆

Meeting with the Russians

WE had known the German soldier in battle, and however we might have despised the ideology which motivated him, we respected him as a fighting man. As the war ended we got an insight into the mind and soul of the German civilian, and we felt as all men must a sense of horror and revulsion at the dreadful things these people had tolerated and condoned without protest.

I had my headquarters in the little town called Hagenau, in the province of Mecklenburg. There had been a concentration camp there, small compared to Dachau and Buchenwald, but equal to them in ghastliness. The horror of these camps has been too often described for me to repeat here what we found. I do want to say this, however— no scenes of death on the battlefield can prepare a soldier for such sights, and no human can look on those piles of pitiful dead, those ranks of living skeletons, without feeling the profoundest emotions of compassion and despair—compassion for the victims, and despair that men, made in the image of God, could inflict such evil on their fellows.

Two days after VE Day, we assembled all the authorities of this town, and all the citizens we could round up, and took them to the place where we had laid out the bodies of some two hundred poor creatures, prepared for decent burial.

We brought them into the cemetery and paraded them past the

graves, so that they could look upon their handiwork. Then Colonel Harry Cain, my civil affairs and military government officer, later Senator from the state of Washington, addressed the German populace. His speech, I think, was one of the most effective I have ever heard, and I would like to set down here the highlights of what he said to those stolid, impassive Germans as they stood beside the open graves of the Dutchmen, Poles, Czechs, Belgians, and Frenchmen whom they had murdered.

These dead who lie here [Colonel Cain told them], were driven and starved and beaten to slake the unholy thirst of your German war machine. When possessed no longer of the will or ability to work, or fight back, or live, they were either tortured to death or permitted to slowly die. The Allies shudder because they never dreamed or visualized that human leadership, supported by the masses, could so debase itself as to be responsible for results like those who lie in these open graves. The civilized world shudders on finding that a part of its society has fallen so low. The world isn't content to believe that this thing which fills our hearts with horror was the work of any small group of German gangsters, maniacs and fanatics. That world must, as it does, hold the German people responsible for what has taken place within the confines of this nation.

Time will prove to what extent the German people recognize the enormity of their crimes and to what extent they will shoulder a full national responsibility for making amends. That any future conduct can eradicate the knowledge and memories of a service like this is a matter in high dispute. If there be a soul within the German nation it will rise now to make impossible the doing of such future wrong. If there be not a soul in this German nation, its future is forlorn and totally lacking in hope.

The bodies are being buried here under the sight of God, and true words consecrated by the Protestant, Catholic and Jewish faiths are being spoken over them. In death these bodies are receiving from Allied, Christian hands the decent, humanitarian and spiritual treatment they didn't receive in life from German hands. As we listen, Allies and Germans alike, let us pray for that rebirth of the soul which Germany must find if there is to be a future life for her.

In a service last Sunday held in the German cathedral in Wismar, 2,000 Allied soldiers [this was at the 6th British Airborne Thanksgiving service] —the same who had helped beat down and crush your military machine, spoke a prayer aloud that drifted into your German skies—God's skies— "Pray," they said, "for the German people, that they may be rid of the burden of false teaching and one day take their place again among honorable peoples." Each German ear should hear that.

Today, ten years afterward, we still are seeking a means by which a united Germany may take its place among the honorable peoples of the world—a quest made more difficult, of course, by the intransigence of the Russians.

That suspicious, stubborn, ill-mannered nature was manifested by the Russians fairly early in our contacts with them. As the war ended, commanders of the Allied and Russian forces made the usual courtesy calls upon each other. In the organization of the Russian armies, what they call a corps is more nearly the size of one of our divisions. There were three Russian corps, therefore, along the front of my single Corps, which meant that I had to entertain, and be entertained by, three Russian commanders. The first was a man named Smirnov, a short, stocky fellow. He brought with him a great hulking giant of an officer, a mountain of a man about six feet four inches high and broad in proportion, whose only social function, so far as I could tell, was to try to intimidate me. He never smiled, never shook hands, but stood by the side of his commander, glowering at me—one of the most formidable-looking creatures physically I have ever seen. I could not help but think what an excellent target he would make, seen over the sights of my Springfield, though, of course, I was careful not to let this feeling be reflected in my manner.

Smirnov himself was much more agreeable. He had suffered an injury to his hand in an automobile accident, and was obviously in some pain at our first meeting. I noticed this and asked his permission to let our Corps surgeon look at it. The surgeon gave him something to relieve the pain and gave him some sort of analgesic tablets to take back with him. Our next visit, therefore, was very cordial, and without his scowling friend, whom I never saw again.

The Russians were fairly crude in their efforts to take the Americans off guard. When we dined with them, I noticed that Smirnov would drink a toast in vodka with me, then he'd slip to one side and bring up one of his other officers to drink with me. But Smirnov wasn't drinking every toast. So I got my arm through his and told him, through an interpreter, "O.K. If we are going to drink toasts, let's drink 'em. But let's do it together. Let's have no more of this ganging up." Thereafter, every time a toast was proposed I'd look him in the eye and he had to drink. So we both ended up in good condition—but in the same condition.

Then we gave a dinner for Smirnov and his officers in return, and

I don't think there have been many better dinners served anywhere. I sent my personal patrol out to one of those wonderful Mecklenburg preserves, one of the great North German refuges where the game has been protected for centuries. They came back with deer and geese and duck and fish, and we really put on a magnificent dinner. We didn't have any vodka. We served Bourbon whiskey, which is a little stronger than vodka, and it was funny to watch those Russians handle that Bourbon. They were very suspicious of it, and of us, too, I think, but we never tried to take advantage of them. We forced no toasts on them, as they had tried to do on us.

At the end of the evening, we showed them some combat films, battle actions of the airborne troops, and they seemed to be pretty impressed—so much so I heard later that one young Russian officer jumped out a second-story window just to prove that Russians were so tough they didn't need parachutes.

We established a wary but fairly pleasant official and social relationship with the Russians during the few days I was there. I had no trouble at all arranging the military details with them. We set up a buffer zone which we both would police, but neither of us would occupy, and the plan worked without a hitch. The troubles came later, when the political commissars came in to take over from the combat soldiers.

But I had gone by then, back to Supreme Headquarters. There I asked General Eisenhower if I might have about five days back home, a request which he very graciously granted. When word that I was going on stateside leave reached my personal pilot, Bill Williams, a wonderful youngster from Hillsboro, Texas, he wouldn't hear of my flying back in one of those big four-engine planes. He rigged up some extra tanks in the C-47 which I had used a great deal during the war, and we made the journey back in that.

At that time I was expecting to return to Europe shortly, for word had reached me that I was to be in command of the U.S. Zone of Berlin, a job I didn't look forward to with any great eagerness.

However, when I got back to Washington and called to pay my respects to General Marshall, he gave me a far happier, and to my mind more challenging, assignment. We were marshaling our forces for the last great drive on the home islands of Japan, he said. And my Corps was one of five that was being redeployed to the Pacific.

So I went home to Washington. When Corps headquarters came in to Boston by ship, I met them there, and we went down to Camp Campbell, Kentucky, to reorganize. Finally orders came to move again, and we headed west, to a new and different war, against a new but equally savage enemy. My plane was over the Golden Gate when word came on the radio that Japan had surrendered. I sent a message to the pilot, suggesting he turn around and take me home. Quite properly, he refused. I didn't greatly care. The fighting was over. The world was at last at peace. I leaned back in my seat and went to sleep.

16

☆☆☆☆

The Pacific, and Back to Italy

I TOOK a busman's holiday there in the Pacific—visiting the sites of famous battles, particularly those in which airborne units had taken part. On arrival in Manila, I had reported first to General MacArthur, running into him by accident in the hall, as I was on my way to his office. He greeted me with great warmth and cordiality, calling me by my first name. We had a pleasant talk, recalling the days I had spent at West Point as faculty director of athletics, when he was Superintendent. He looked as young and vigorous as when I had last seen him ten years before, when he was Chief of Staff. The long years of war seemed to have left no mark upon him. Placing his hand on my shoulder, he smiled past the pipe clenched in his teeth, excused himself and then bounded up the stairs to his office to work on the myriad details of the forthcoming occupation of Japan. Later, at a long luncheon, he asked me a thousand questions about the war in Europe.

When I got around to suggesting, though, that since the war in the Pacific was over I might as well take my Corps staff and go home, he turned me down. The occupation of Japan might involve many difficulties, he said, and he wanted the Corps to be ready and available if needed.

He gave me command of the Luzon area, which was not too great a task, and I spent a lot of time in happy meetings with old comrades who had fought the war out there while I was busy in Europe. I was pleased to get around again, over that country I had known so well when I had served in the Philippines, but I must confess that much of it, particularly the city of Manila, had been so devastated by the war that I had difficulty orienting myself.

I went out to Corregidor to see the place where the 503rd Parachute Infantry, under command of Colonel Jones, had made their gallant drop in the late days of the war. Two motives drew me to this spot. One was sentimental. The 11th Airborne, to which the 503rd belonged, was commanded by my old friend and one-time artillery commander, Joe Swing, who had made his maiden jump with me at Benning. The other was a matter of professional curiosity. Of all the airborne assaults made by U.S. troops in either theater of war, this was perhaps the most hazardous, and mechanically the most difficult. The Rock stands some six hundred feet above the level of Manila Bay, and the drop was made in February, when the winds are always blowing hard. The drop zone was small and rugged and heavily infested by Japs. Even a practice jump into such an area would have been difficult under such conditions. A few of the men, I learned, were swept over the six-hundred-foot cliffs to fall in the South China Sea.

After going over the shell-pocked land on top of the Rock, I went down to the entrance to the Malinta Tunnel—where I had taken Ted Roosevelt's mother so many years before. Even so resolute a spirit as Mrs. Roosevelt would not have entered this place now. The Japs had holed up there for their last stand on Corregidor. They had been killed in there like rats, and even now, months after the battle, there was a choking stench from the tunnel.

I visited the ridge line where the 38th U.S. Division had seen a very hard bit of combat. General Fred Irving, a classmate of mine at West Point, had commanded the division in this fight, and went along to show me the ground and describe the action. We were in a jeep, stopped on a muddy trail, and Fred was pointing out some of the terrain features that had figured in the fight, when about fifty yards from us two Jap soldiers jumped up out of a trench and started scuttling for the shelter of the cogon grass, which stood some seven feet high on that ridge. I sent a soldier after them, and he had no trouble running them down. They were two of the most emaciated creatures I have ever seen. The fight there had been over for at least two weeks, and I don't think they'd had a bite to eat in all that time.

Fred kidded me about coming over from Europe and capturing a couple of Jap prisoners right off the bat, but actually I didn't take them. The sergeant just ran them down like rabbits and brought them back. They were unarmed, which was lucky for us.

Pretty soon, as plans for the formal surrender went forward, I found myself with nothing to do. I was invited to go up to Tokyo, to witness the surrender ceremonies aboard the battleship *Missouri,* and I wanted to go merely to be present at this historic ceremony. But the space on the *Missouri* was extremely limited, and there were hundreds of officers who had fought the Pacific war all the way who could not witness the signing for lack of deck space. Every one of them, I felt, deserved to be there more than I did, so I declined the invitation.

Since there was no job at the moment which required a lieutenant general to run it, I asked General MacArthur's permission to come home on leave. This was granted, and I went out to the airport there at Manila to hitchhike my way across the Pacific. It was pretty hard to get passage, for there were far more passengers with stateside orders than there were seats. The planes were all bucket-seat jobs, too, and I didn't particularly relish the idea of that long flight across the Pacific in one of those. But there was nothing else flying, so I finally got passage on a battered old B-24 bomber. When I got aboard I went up to talk to the pilot and crew and found that they had no lifesaving equipment at all on the ship—not even a raft. So I said thank you very much, I'll wait.

The next one that had a seat available was a C-54, a worn-out old relic that was being flown back to the States for overhaul after extremely arduous service in the China-Burma theater. The pilot said his engines were in pretty bad shape, and his radio wasn't working as well as it should, but he thought the old wreck could make it all right.

Well, I wasn't in that much of a hurry either, so I thanked *him* and climbed down again, lugging my gear. I finally made it in a B-24, a chair job, packed full of people. We made it to Hawaii all right, though worn to a frazzle.

We arrived in Honolulu just ahead of six or seven general officers who had been freed from Japanese prison camps, and I later dined with them. I knew many of them from the old days before the war, and I marveled, as I looked at each of them, how their long captivity seemed to have affected their personalities. Some seemed little changed. They laughed and joked and told stories as they always had. One or two of the others were very, very different. They sat quietly, scarcely speaking a word. Many of the cheerful ones seemed to be in worse shape, physically, than the silent men who wore their scars upon their spirits.

And I remember again feeling a deep sense of gratitude to whatever Power had guided me years before, when I had turned down the command of a regiment in the Philippines. If I had accepted, I would have been dead, or one among these gaunt, sick men who sat at table with me.

On arrival in Washington, I called on General Marshall. We hadn't been talking very long when he asked a question that left me thunderstruck.

"How would you like to be an ambassador?" he said.

I told him I'd never given a moment's thought to such an assignment but the idea sounded interesting.

He then went on to explain that the government was planning to use some of the senior battle commanders in top diplomatic jobs around the world, and my name was on the list of those who had been recommended. He was thinking of me for the post in Argentina.

He sent me over to see Dean Acheson and some of the assistant secretaries, among them Spruille Braden, the Assistant Secretary for Latin Affairs. We had a long discussion and I remember particularly bringing up the subject of remuneration, for I knew an ambassadorship was an expensive post, and its financial responsibilities were far more than I could bear on an Army officer's pay.

Acheson told me that he was well aware of this but that from one fund or another he thought that I could count on special allowances which would provide nearly $40,000 a year. To a soldier that seemed to be a fabulous sum so that part seemed solved. We then went over to call on President Truman, and I spoke my mind frankly.

"I want to make it clear, Mr. President, that I am not flying under any false colors. I am trained only as a soldier, and I make no pretense at being a diplomat."

The President laughed.

"General," he said, "I don't imagine you got your three stars without being something of a diplomat. Anyway, what we want is a man with common sense. When it comes to the complex things, like economics and so on, you'll have to count on your advisers. And

I'm confident that you'll do a good job in choosing the people to advise you."

Doubts still gnawed at my mind, however, for in my talks with Mr. Acheson and Mr. Spruille Braden I had discovered that their ideas of how diplomatic relations with Argentina should be maintained were diametrically opposed to mine. My feeling was that in the Latin American countries, where the influence of the military on the government is profound, we should maintain the closest relationship with their armies, navies and air forces. We should provide the equipment they used, and the personnel to teach them how to use it, and to train their armies. But we should scrupulously refrain from meddling in their internal politics. Otherwise our relations would worsen and these nations would be drawn inevitably into the orbit of some other nation, possibly a potential enemy—as Argentina before the war turned her face toward Germany, who trained her army. The gentlemen in the State Department, who were far more experienced than I, disagreed. Such a policy, they said, would entrench dictators in power and give them a trained force to use against their neighbors.

The pleasant talk with Mr. Truman, though encouraging, had disturbed me, for I feared that I had gone too far—that I had in effect committed myself.

I brooded over the problem overnight and then went back to the one man whose advice I valued above all others. I asked General Marshall to tell me frankly how he felt. Was it his wish that I take this job? If so, I would accept at once despite my misgivings. If on the other hand I was completely free to make my own decision, I would decline. He told me to do exactly what my judgment dictated. I was completely free to choose.

So I never became an ambassador, and I am forever grateful that I made the choice I did. In that particular time, I am sure, I would have been at cross purposes with certain key officers of the State Department, for their attitude toward the Argentine problem was exactly opposite to mine, as I have pointed out previously. I would have been unable to render the service so urgently required—the bettering of U.S.-Argentine relations—a service I think I could have performed. My whole subsequent career then would have taken a different course.

That decision left me at loose ends for a few days, until General

Marshall, in his usual thoughtful and considerate way, called me in again.

"Well," he said, "you turned that down. Here's another proposition for you to consider. How would you like to go back to Europe—as Commander in the Mediterranean theater?"

"General," I said, "I don't even have to think that one over. That is a troop command. Nothing could please me more."

I flew to Italy in solitary splendor, the only passenger on a newly renovated B-17 that General McNarney, whom I was to replace, had ordered for his headquarters. We went the southern route, by Bermuda, the Azores, and Casablanca, and it was only after we landed that I learned that on one leg of our flight we had caused great concern to the people on the ground. Our radio had gone out and we could make no periodic position reports. So, for a short while, we were listed as missing, and rescue aircraft were on the fields, ready to begin a search.

The headquarters was at Caserta, north of Naples, where it had been since shortly after my 82nd Airborne had marched into that silent city. General Sir William Morgan, of the British Service, was Supreme Commander, Allied Forces, Mediterranean, and in addition to being Commander in Chief, Mediterranean Theater of Operations, which was a U.S. command, I was his Deputy Supreme Commander. That was a very happy relationship, for I soon came to admire Bill Morgan greatly, and we struck up a warm friendship.

During that particular tour of duty, I had the unhappy responsibility of tearing down a great military establishment. The cry of "Bring the boys home," was ringing from the United States, and we were plunging headlong into the shameful demobilization of one of the greatest military organizations the world has ever seen, the magnificent U.S. Army that had done its full share in beating the German, Italian and Japanese armies to their knees. We have paid dearly for that disgraceful demobilization in the years since the war, and we will suffer from the consequences of that unwise act for years to come.

It was done, of course, on the point system. If a man had enough points—for overseas service, for battle participation, for decorations, for dependents—by direct order from Washington he was to be sent home. No matter how desperately he was needed, the field commander had no choice but to take him off his assignment and put him on a boat.

One result of this was that we lost literally hundreds of millions of dollars' worth of equipment and supplies, through sheer inability to guard them with U.S. personnel. Every item had value to the impoverished Italians, and it was impossible to control their thieving. They would even steal the powder bags for the heavier calibers of artillery, break them open and scatter the powder, and take the silk bags to make clothes.

My greatest problem during this time was not only to protect government property, but to create and maintain a more intangible thing—the discipline and spirit of these organizations which day by day were being decimated through the withdrawal of their key personnel. The problems of leadership and command were very difficult. The fighting soldiers—the old battle commanders—were going home. The few replacements who were being sent over were men of a different stripe. They had come into the war late. They had no "points," and they were shipped overseas to serve out their time. They, too, wanted to get out of uniform and go back to civilian life, and they had little interest in their jobs.

I found on my inspection trips that as a result of the actions of these subordinate commanders enlisted men were living under shocking conditions of filth and dirt, mess facilities were miserable, bathing facilities were inadequate, a complete degradation of the high standards which the U.S. Army takes pride in maintaining. There were not enough hours in a day for me to get around all over Italy, visiting these installations, jacking up these commanders, firing the totally incompetent ones and replacing them with leaders who were going to be there long enough to take these units in hand and put them on their feet again.

One of my great problems had to do with the Army nurses in my theater. There were some 320 of them serving in our hospitals. All were urgently needed. However, they were under the point system, too, and were entitled to go home, for most of them had served most devotedly throughout the years of war. Obviously I could not permit these nurses just to walk off the job, so, on my own authority, taking full responsibility, I refused to release them until their replacements had arrived. However, I was well aware of the basic unfairness of this action, so I got in touch with my old friend, Major General Norman Kirk, the Surgeon General of the Army, and got from him a promise that replacements would reach me at the soonest possible moment. If things worked out as I hoped, the new nurses would arrive in early December, and the nurses then on duty could be sent home in time for Christmas.

I was very anxious that this be done, but at first it seemed almost impossible, for no shipping was available. Fortunately, I had a splendid commander of the naval component in my theater, Vice Admiral Bill Glassford, and there was an aircraft carrier then at Naples, under command of a most co-operative captain, named Pirie, now a Rear Admiral. Between the two of them they discovered some vague discretionary reference in Naval Regulations which could tortuously be interpreted to mean that females might be transported on naval combat vessels. So the officers of the carrier very gallantly turned over their staterooms to these young ladies.

The whole thing took some doing, though, and I remember one brief moment of irritation. I went down to the carrier, which lay at a pier in the harbor at Naples, just after the nurses had gone aboard. I got in touch with the chief nurse and told her to see that the girls were in a proper state of dress, so that I could inspect the accommodations in which they were quartered. This was done, and I walked into one of these rooms in which there were four or five girls.

"Well, how do you like these accommodations?" I asked.

One young woman spoke up. "Oh, they are all right."

"All right!" I exploded. "You remind me of a schoolboy who had made a perfect recitation, and when he finished his teacher said, 'Sit down, Johnny. That was very good.' And he said, 'Very good, hell! It's perfect.'"

Then I told these young ladies that these accommodations they were enjoying through the exceptional courtesy of Captain Pirie were so far superior to those I had known as a junior officer, traveling on Army transports, that there was utterly no comparison. And I hoped they would fully appreciate what had been done for them in an effort to get them home on time.

I think they did. The carrier reached Norfolk two or three days before Christmas, which gave them all a chance to reach their homes in time for the holidays.

One other vexing situation arose there in the harbor at Naples. On an inspection trip I discovered one of our largest aircraft carriers lying alongside that famous Pier #1 which Mussolini had built, with numerous other naval vessels at anchor nearby. Just across the pier lay a Victory ship, out-loading ammunition, the bulk of which was high-explosive aircraft bombs of large size. I got hold of the harbor master as soon as possible and told him to get that ammunition ship out of there immediately. He said it couldn't be done. She didn't have steam up.

"Steam up, hell!" I told him. "Get the tugs in here and pull her out right now and don't you ever bring an ammunition ship into an area like this again."

If that thing had blown up there, we'd have lost that carrier and all of those other naval ships, and hundreds, perhaps thousands, of men would have been killed.

Sundry problems of a political nature rose from time to time. The British were having their troubles in Greece, and approaches were made to me, through British sources, indicating that the British government would be very happy indeed to have U.S. troops sent into Greece to take over some of the burden there. This happened several times, and on each occasion I made it quite clear that I would not recommend that U.S. forces be sent to Greece. The Greek islands were outside my zone of responsibility, and I had plenty of hot spots of my own to worry about. One was Trieste, an exceedingly troublesome spot, where violent political feeling was liable at any moment to flare into rioting. I needed a commander for the U.S. forces in that area on whom I could place absolute reliance. He had to be an officer of character, integrity, and outstanding competence. At the same time he had to be imperturbable under conditions of heavy pressure suddenly applied.

I was offered several commanders, none of whom, to my mind, met these qualifications. Finally, I sent to the War Department a message to the effect that I wanted the best division commander in the U.S. Army. I accompanied this request with a list of nominations, at the top of which was the name of Major General Bryant E. Moore. He had commanded the 8th Infantry Division in my XVIII Corps while we were cleaning out the Ruhr pocket, and in the final advance from the Elbe to the Baltic. I knew him well and regarded him as being particularly suited, temperamentally, to handle this job. I got him, and thereafter I stopped worrying about Trieste. His service was conspicuously superior in every respect.

Later, General Moore became Superintendent of the Military Academy at West Point, where he did an outstanding job. Afterward, when I needed a top-flight commander in Korea, I requested General Moore again. He came out to take over IX Corps and was doing his usual fine job, when death brought an end to his career. He had flown up to the Han River by helicopter, to personally look over some bridging operations there, when the machine in which he was riding became entangled in an overhead cable which the pilot apparently did not see. The helicopter fell into the icy river, and though General Moore extricated himself, apparently uninjured, the shock of the fall and the cold brought on a heart attack. He died within thirty minutes of getting ashore.

So died, in harness, a great soldier and my friend. The number of top commanders who suffered heart attacks shortly after the war indicated that perhaps the years of combat had done inner damage to many of us—damage of which we were unaware.

I know that when this same grim killer knocked gently at my door, I was taken completely by surprise. I had gone up to Trieste to inspect the garrison there, and had spent the night in the command post of the British Commander, Sir John Harding. His headquarters were in the ancient palace of Miramar, the castle from which Carlota and Maximilian had set out on their ill-fated adventure to Mexico. We had a very pleasant dinner there in that history-haunted palace, and I left early next morning to inspect the U.S. troops in the city of Trieste.

I wanted to look at the harbor first, and they had a launch fixed up for my trip. As I stepped down from the dock into the launch, my vision began to blur. The next thing I knew, I was lying on the deck of the launch, still conscious, but feeling very weak and ill. Then all grew dark, and when I came to, I was in a British field hospital. They told me that I had had a heart attack and that a cardiologist, Dr. Dupuy, was on his way from Naples to attend me. He arrived next day by air—a very wonderful gentleman, who now is a noted heart specialist in New Orleans.

He looked me over carefully, made a lot of tests, then told me it was the heart, all right.

"There's only one thing for you to do," he said. "You must ask to be relieved from duty, and return to the United States. And in my opinion you must retire."

"I'll do nothing of the kind," I told him. "I won't even request return to the U.S. for examination. If I did, it would mean the termination of my service. It would set in train a whole set of circumstances which never could be arrested, much less reversed. I'm going to stay here and do my job."

He didn't like that much, but in a few days he let me go back to my command post at Naples, and pretty soon I felt all right again. I was still attracting a lot of attention from doctors, though. They kept checking me, but they couldn't find a thing wrong with my heart. I don't think they ever did agree on what happened, but I think the consensus was that some little capillary had burst, and I had blacked out temporarily. Anyway, that was in the fall of 1945, and there hasn't been the slightest recurrence, and I've had very arduous duty since.

It's very interesting to see how prone the doctors are to commit a man to a course of action from which there is no return. If I had taken the doctors' advice, I'd have retired ten years ago and would have missed all that was to come—the Korean War, Supreme Command in the Far East and Europe, and the two-year period as Chief of Staff, which were among the most interesting, as well as the most arduous, periods of service in my whole career.

I would not recommend that any other person who has suffered a similar collapse should follow this same course. But I ignored my heart attack—if that is what it was—and nothing bad happened.

The near approach of death, or invalidism, did cause my thoughts to dwell, at times, on the unexpected blows that fate strikes so suddenly, to end, or alter, the pattern of men's lives. It was during my Mediterranean service that I received word of the tragic death of General Patton in a collision with a truck in Germany. His death was a great shock to me. George Patton was a controversial figure to many, but I knew him well, and to know him well was to admire him greatly. He was a magnificent battle commander—an inspired leader of the highest caliber. He had been the soul of consideration to me during the times I served under his command, and the knowledge of his death, particularly in what seemed to be such an unnecessary manner, filled me with deep sorrow.

Men's lives are precious to society, as well as to themselves, and one of the hardest tasks that faced me during my time as theater commander had to do with a case in which the decision of life or death rested on my shoulders. A German lieutenant general, Anton Dostler, a corps commander, had been tried by a military court after the war and convicted on charges of shooting Allied prisoners without proper justification. He had been sentenced to death. The case was under review when I arrived there, and it came to me for final action. If I had met General Dostler in battle, I would have killed him without hesitation, as he would have killed me. But this thing was different. It was the kind of problem to which you must give your utmost consideration and prayerful study. This I did for a number of days, while General Dostler's counsel, and the General himself, made various appeals to me. My decision was that the verdict of the court should stand and the execution should be carried out. Twenty-four hours before Dostler was to be shot, he addressed through me a personal appeal to His Holiness, Pope Pius XII. I sent this to the Vatican by officer messenger, with instructions that I be informed of its delivery to His Holiness without delay. A few hours before the execution, I received the Pope's reply. It was to the effect that he was confident the case was in proper hands, and that he did not seek to intervene. General Dostler died before a firing squad.

On New Year's Day, 1946, I received word that I was to be assigned as the representative of General Eisenhower, then Chief of Staff, to the Military Committee of the United Nations, which was to meet and organize a month later in London. This came as a complete but welcome surprise to me, though it gave me little time to turn over command to Lieutenant General J. C. H. Lee, my successor. Short as the time was, it gave me an opportunity to familiarize myself, a little, with our forces in Europe. I had not had the chance to see Berlin after VE Day, so enroute to London I flew there and spent a very educational night and day with our brilliant proconsul General Lucius Clay and that old master of diplomacy, Bob Murphy, his adviser. I went on to London then to find Secretary of State Stettinius and the American delegation already on the ground. My military associates, General George Kenney of the Air Force and Admiral Kelly Turner of the Navy, and I found ourselves traveling in distinguished company as members of the American delegation, which included Senators Vandenberg and Connally, John Foster Dulles, Adlai Stevenson, Mrs. Roosevelt, and Ralph Bunche.

It was a privilege to serve with Americans of such stature in such a cause as that for which we existed as a group—to find a way whereby, through strength, we could keep peace in the world. I still remember how, as the three senior military officers arrived for the first meeting there in London, the people gathered in the streets cheered and applauded. In their faces you could read their bright hope that here, in these councils, a war-sick world could find a formula for peace. I too felt that hope in my own heart. And I remember well how swiftly that hope died as in later sessions the U.S.S.R. representatives, when stubborn questions arose, picked up their brief cases and stalked like pouting children from the room.

17

☆☆☆☆

Peacetime Soldiers

IT HAS been said of the Military Staff Committee that very little was known of its work because "it did practically nothing under conditions of absolute secrecy." This criticism is in large degree true, but before I move on to a discussion of my service with that committee and my own comments on the reasons for its failures, I would like to digress for a moment. I would like to discuss further that shameful dissolution of the American military forces which took place in the years immediately after the war—the precipitous demobilization which robbed us of the strength that would have added power and meaning to our voice in the councils of the UN.

In September of 1945, Secretary of War Stimson made the following statement:

The United States is now not only at the peak of its military strength but it has attained an influence and leadership among all nations that is unprecedented. Now that we have arrived at that position, we must make sure that we conserve it and use it in the cause of justice and peace throughout the world.

In my opinion the maintenance of this preeminent position will depend on two factors. One of these is the acceptance by our people of the military and naval strength that necessarily go with leadership in the world of today. The State Department will have increasing difficulty in making our voice effective in the councils of nations unless our people and our

Government show their readiness to carry the inconveniences and burdens, and sometimes the sacrifices, which accompany such leadership, under the present unstable conditions.

The state of our military establishment in the future must be the constant concern, not only of our Government, but of our people. In particular we must be alert that no system is established, however palatable it may seen, which fails to provide the power we need at this state of the world's development.

We chose to ignore the words of this wise and able statesman, whose vision and rocklike integrity had served us so well throughout the years of war.

I well remember the anger and disgust I felt when I arrived in London to take up my duties with the Military Staff Committee. There I witnessed for the first time those disgraceful exhibitions by United States military personnel who, while wearing the uniform of their country, met in public squares openly to protest their further retention in service and the extension of their overseas duty. And I am sure I felt no greater chagrin and inner shame than did thousands of other loyal members of our military establishment.

No such disgraceful exhibitions had occurred in the Mediterranean theater up to the time I had left, and I remember thinking that, if I were in command of this theater, I would put a stop to such shameful acts immediately.

I felt so strongly that something must be done that I sat down and wrote a letter to my Chief of Staff, General Eisenhower:

As a recent theatre commander [I wrote] I anticipated this problem and sought to prevent it from arising in the area of my responsibility. I have now been an observer of some of these demonstrations in London. The problem has, I believe, passed beyond the sphere in which a military commander can reasonably be expected to take final action.

So basic and so vital does the problem seem to me that I want to suggest for consideration that the matter be viewed as a fundamental military-sociological one, and that some civilian agency, perhaps some great American university, be asked by the President to examine into every phase of this problem—including searching investigations on the spot in our principal theatres at once.

This letter was answered by General Eisenhower on March 15, 1946. In his reply he kindly informed me that the Secretary of War and he were contemplating the appointment of a board composed of two former enlisted men, two former company or field-grade officers, and two general officers, none of whom was then on active duty. The board would focus primarily on the relationship between officers and enlisted men, but in the opinion of General Eisenhower, it could well accomplish the matters discussed in my letter to him.

I think that this was the genesis of the so-called Doolittle Board. And I think personally, as I thought when I first read the report of that board, that, however well intentioned, it dangerously undermined that priceless element—the officer-enlisted man relationship based on mutual respect—that had been built up over generations of service together. In the intervening years a great part of that report has been repudiated and its trend of thinking has been reversed, after efforts to carry out its recommendations proved them to be unsound. The purpose of the report, of course, was to create a more "democratic" Army. Its effect was to undermine discipline.

18

☆☆☆☆

Slow Hound on a Cold Trail

I TOOK over my duties on the Military Staff Committee in January of 1946. In late October of that year I found myself writing a letter to General Marshall in which I expressed my views that the committee had accomplished next to nothing.

We have dogged along [I wrote] like a hound on a dusty country lane, snuffling about under every bush, trying to find some trail that would lead us to mutual understanding and agreement. In the nine months of our existence, we have laid a firm and potentially useful basis of cordial personal relationships on which to build for the future. This is a material accomplishment, but beyond that, the results have been pitifully meagre. The blame lies neither in the committee nor, in our opinion, even in the Russian military members. They are, we are sure, acting under explicit orders which permit them no latitude. They can only have recourse to delaying tactics.

For the past three months the bulk of our work has been in our capacity as advisors to the U.S. member of the U.N. Atomic Energy Commission, Mr. Baruch. The questions they have posed to us have been numerous and in a completely uncharted field. The resulting stimulation to our intellectual processes has been most healthy. While we feel some answers have eluded us to date, and we have no monopoly in the wisdom of those we have offered, we are convinced of the general soundness of our reasoning, and are unshakeably optimistic as to the possibilities of success, granted only we can create an equal willingness on the part of the Russians to find a solution.

After the organization meeting in London, the Military Staff Committee transferred its activities to United Nations headquarters in New York. Its members were Army, Air Force, and Naval representatives of the five great powers—the United States, Great Britain, France, China, and Soviet Russia.

In general, our task was to advise and assist the Security Council on all questions relating to the Security Council's military requirements for the maintenance of international peace and security; the employment and command of forces placed at the disposal of the Council; the regulation of armaments; and possible disarmament.

The basic problem was to determine the number and the nature of the armed forces which each of the Big Five would make available to the Security Council for its use in carrying out its missions under the UN charter. Our deliberations soon shattered upon that rock. We debated that point throughout the two and a half years I served with the Military Staff Committee, and today, nearly ten years later, it is still on the agenda, and is about as near solution now, so far as I know, as it was then.

The chief obstacle to agreement was the question of composition of forces. The view of the Western nations was that the forces provided by each nation should be roughly comparable in strength and composition. In other words, the Russians and the Chinese obviously could not supply contingents including long-range bombing planes and aircraft carriers. On the other hand the Western powers could not begin to match in manpower any contributions which the Soviet Union and the Republic of China might make.

Therefore, we never varied from the position that these forces must be roughly comparable. The Russians, on the other hand, from the outset insisted that these forces be equal—that is, gun for gun, ship for ship, plane for plane. This meant that UN forces allocated would be made up, in the main, of ground forces, in which field the Soviet Union held the dominant position. Thus the pattern of the overall Soviet objectives in the military field began to unfold—a point which I will discuss in more detail later.

Very early in our discussion, the U.S. Air Force, through its representative, General George Kenney, suggested that the U.S. contribution be exclusively air. In fact, he suggested that the entire contribution of the Big Five should be in air power and that control of this first international air force should be vested in a U.S. commander. I heartily disagreed with the philosophy behind this proposal. I protested vigorously at the time, and on my next trip to Washington I presented my views to General Eisenhower and his staff and got their complete concurrence. I also got his assurance that, though General Kenney was a four-star general, and I was a three-star, and therefore subordinate in rank, as the personal representative of the Army Chief of Staff I held equal status on the committee with the Air Corps representative. I went back to New York and continued vigorous opposition to this proposal, and ultimately, of course, it failed to be adopted.

I recall that in my discussions with General Eisenhower I made the point that, in view of Russia's great manpower advantage, I thought the control of the ground force component was of first priority. In reply, General Eisenhower said that he had not envisioned a situation requiring an overall commander for each of the three air, sea, and ground force pools as contributed by the Big Five. He had been thinking more in terms of regional arrangements, with the world divided up into areas, and a nation, or nations, designated to keep the peace within each area. Of course, a commander would have to be selected for the combined forces contributed by the Big Five. And he recognized the need for the advance appointment of such a commander, the selection of his staff, and the preparation of plans for the employment of forces under the Security Council. Also, he clearly foresaw that difficulties might arise when a commander asked for the privilege of inspecting the forces of the other nations which were placed under his control.

I pointed out that it was unthinkable that U.S. ground forces should ever be placed under Russian command—because of their widely different attitudes toward human life. Under Russian command, I said, U.S. troops might be called upon to sustain such losses, or be ordered to carry out such reprisals against non-combatant civil populations, that the natural repugnance of the American people would bring about a dissolution of the UN force.

While I struggled on the Military Staff Committee with the seemingly insoluble problem of the forces that each nation should contribute to an international military organization, as adviser to Mr. Bernard Baruch on the United Nations Atomic Energy Committee I was observing the Russian strategy unfold in another field. Here a problem just as thorny occupied our minds—the control of the atomic explosive.

The first meetings of the committee were held in an atmosphere of hope as bright as that which had marked the first meetings of the Military Staff Committee. But from the moment the Russians gave their answer to Mr. Baruch's dramatic plan for world-wide supervision and control of atomic energy installations, it was clear that we had quickly reached another impasse. What the Russians demanded from the outset was a complete ban on the manufacture of atomic weapons, and the destruction of all those already in existence.

The pattern of the Soviet military objectives became starkly clear then. That objective was simply this—to destroy all the capacity the Western world and particularly the United States, possessed for attack or reprisal against Russia; to reduce the military establishment of the Western world to a position completely subordinate to the Russian military.

My observations of the Russians, on both the Military Staff Committee and the UN Atomic Energy Commission, led me to certain conclusions as to Russian aims and objectives which I wished to set down in written form. With General Eisenhower's approval, I then wished to make these views available to my superiors on the policy-making levels who might find them useful in evaluating the Russian goals.

The essential facts with which I dealt were three: (1) That the Russians were adamant in their insistence on an international convention designed to prohibit the employment of atomic energy for military purposes, and the destruction of all existing atomic weapons, while at the same time refusing to accept U.S. proposals for effective supervision of atomic energy production facilities; (2) that the U.S.S.R. had introduced a disarmament resolution and had pressed for United Nations action thereon; (3) that the U.S.S.R. had effectively prevented any agreement on the armed forces to be made available to the Security Council by insisting on their absurd plane-for-plane, gun-for-gun, man-for-man contribution.

Now, as to the evaluation of these basic facts. First, and obviously, Russia was making a co-ordinated effort: (1) to force the U.S. to agree to the prohibition of all use of atomic weapons for military purposes; (2) to prohibit the use of all other weapons of mass destruction, including strategic air forces, guided missiles, and certain naval categories; (3) to reduce the forces available to the UN to the level of those Russia herself could contribute, and finally to reduce all the world's armaments to those assigned to the United Nations; (4) to use the pressure of world opinion and the U.S. national conscience to bring agreement to these objectives—while at the same time Russia clandestinely created her own atomic energy installations and sustained strong army and air forces.

My conclusions derived from the above facts and their evaluations were simply these: If we should accede to Russian demands we should have deprived ourselves of atomic weapons at no cost to the U.S.S.R. We should have abandoned our complex weapons systems and vastly enhanced the relative value of manpower as the determining factor in war—to the great advantage of the Russians. Once these reductions in the military fields in which we held a decided superiority had been attained, the U.S.S.R. would then turn to an attack on our superior industrial potential. By the infiltration of Soviet agents into our industrial structure they would acquire means of paralyzing our national systems of transportation, fuel production, and telecommunications. Thus handicapped, we could not restore our great technological superiority in time to halt the march of Russian armies vastly superior in numbers to our own.

In short, the Russians were sponsoring a plan for unilateral disarmament of the United States, under the guise of a plea for general regulation and reduction of armaments by all nations. It was a plan to strip us of our present technological and scientific superiority and to elevate the U.S.S.R. to the position of the dominant military power in the world.

That memorandum was written in 1947, after ten months of observation of the Russians at close hand. Nothing that has happened since—not even the widely hailed conference at Geneva—leads me to believe that they have abandoned one iota of that plan. Today, tomorrow, a decade hence, their one great motivating idea is the same —by guile or subterfuge, or force if need be, to bring this nation to its knees.

I submitted this report through channels—that is, to my next superior, General Eisenhower, the Chief of Staff. He, in turn, submitted it through his own secretary, Mr. Robert Patterson, to the Secretary of State, General Marshall, who gave it his full approval. In fact, he told me later, and this was confirmed by the then Under Secretary, Dean Acheson, this document became basic guidance in the formulation of U.S. policy, thereafter altered.

19

☆☆☆☆

Tough Talk to a
Tough Russian

IT WAS during my service on the Military Staff Committee and the U.S. Delegation to the Atomic Energy Committee of the UN that I was given additional duties in a field where I felt myself more qualified to serve. I was named as Chairman of the Inter-American Defense Board, the military agency within what then was called the Pan American Union, and which is now the Organization of American States.

The problem facing this agency at that time was the implementation of the Act of Chapultepec, an agreement between this country and our Latin-American neighbors which would provide for the common defense of the Western Hemisphere. The outline of the plan was embodied in the Act. It had no force, however, until it could be finally implemented by a treaty. The heart of this treaty would be a mutual defense pact in which this country would assist in training the land, sea, and air forces of the Latin signatories, would maintain and repair their equipment, and, under certain circumstances, would transfer to them certain arms, ammunition, and implements of war. In speaking on this subject before the House Foreign Affairs Committee in 1947, I urged the passage of the enabling legislation—HR 3836.

Passage of the bill, I testified, would greatly facilitate military co-operation between the American states, and greatly strengthen the inter-American system. We would thereby greatly contribute to the maintenance of world peace and security. Without its passage we would correspondingly weaken the inter-American system, and that factor which is still dominant in the world today—namely the ability to apply unified and adequate military force in support of integrity of purpose. We recognize today, I said, that the political, the military, and the economic are no longer separable. We must, therefore, make equally intense efforts to strengthen the military elements in this unique system into which have gone a century and a quarter of devoted effort. No single U.S. act could be more calculated to provide this military strengthening than passage of this bill. Failure to do so, in my opinion, would result in rendering a mutual defense pact, when concluded, gravely lacking in effectiveness in an emergency.

The ideas expressed above were contrary to the thinking of many Latin-American experts in the State Department at that time, who held to the views described earlier—that military aid would have the effect of sponsoring dictatorships, and increasing the risk of war among Latin-American neighbors. It was not until 1952, therefore, that a Mutual Security Agreement for Hemisphere Defense, providing for arms and economic aid, was enacted between the U.S. and Brazil, Chile, Cuba, Colombia, the Dominican Republic, Ecuador, Honduras, Nicaragua, Peru, and Uruguay. Mexico and Argentina did not sign.

In a few months after my plea before Congress, however, one great forward step was taken, when the Inter-American Treaty of Reciprocal Assistance, known informally as the Rio Pact, was signed by the U.S. and nineteen Latin-American nations. The heart of this pact was an agreement for mutual defense against external attack, but each nation had the right to withhold consent to the use of its own armed forces.

I think that, for all its limitations, the Rio Pact was, and is, one of the great milestones in the development of the inter-American defense system. As a matter of fact, it is the model on which the North Atlantic Treaty was subsequently drafted, and the language of the two documents is much the same.

One of its great achievements was to bring Argentina into agreement with her sister republics, though it looked for a time as if Argentina was going to break up the meeting. No one man, to my mind, did more to prevent that catastrophe than did the late Senator Arthur Vandenberg. His penetrating analyses of the issues, his fearless, forthright expressions of this nation's views had a tremendous influence. He never minced words. It was refreshing to see him in action, on and off the floor. He didn't believe in soft and flowery phrases. One morning, after a particularly vexing session the day before, which had lasted far into the night, one of the Latin delegates came up and asked the Senator how he was feeling.

"I feel fine," the Senator said. "You ought to feel fine too. I never heard a man talk more, and say less, than you did yesterday."

On another occasion one of the delegates was complaining bitterly that the press correspondents had been needling him cruelly.

Vandenberg spoke up in that booming voice of his and said: "Why don't you just tell them, 'I refuse to answer'? It took me twenty-five years to learn that I don't have to answer a tough question if I don't want to."

I went down to Rio in a B-29, with my colleagues of the Navy and the Air Force. We flew first to Ramey Field, Puerto Rico, took on a load of gas there, and set out, non-stop, for Rio. It was a very uncomfortable flight, for those big bombers were never meant to carry passengers. We left Puerto Rico about ten o'clock at night and flew and flew for hours, five or six of us crowded into a little compartment back in the tail. I'd been around South America by air several times, and I knew the geography of the place pretty well. At dawn, when I could see the ground, I could tell we were still a long, long way from Rio. I began to wonder then how our gas was holding out. As I suspected, we were running low, for the pilot passed the word back that we were going down, to land at Caravelas, several hundred miles short of Rio.

We had helped build Caravelas in the early days of the war, as a result of agreements made on that trip to Brazil with General Marshall I have already described. And I knew that it was a short, lightly built runway that was not designed to take the landing impact of a B-29. So we strapped in tight, and held our breath on the touchdown, expecting the ship to crunch through. Luckily it didn't. Our troubles weren't over though, for all the gas they had there was in fifty-gallon drums, and we had to wait while fifteen hundred gallons were pumped by hand into the wing tanks. Meanwhile, weather reports reached us that fog was approaching Rio, and there was a chance we couldn't get in there by B-29. So they hurried a C-47 up from Rio for us and we went on down in that. The trip back, made in the B-29, was without event except for the weariness that beset us on the five thousand-mile ride from Rio back to Washington.

I went back to my duties as a member of the Military Committee of the UN with the memory of Senator Vandenberg's blunt and forthright actions in my mind. It was a time when Mr. Vishinsky was being particularly vituperative, calling us warmongers and murderers and other opprobrious names. I finally had about all of that that I could stand. I was only a military adviser and my opinion had not been asked, but there are limits to human patience. There are times when you forget that it is inadvisable to enter into certain competitive activities with a skunk. So I stood up there in a meeting, and said that conscience compelled me—as an American citizen, not as a soldier— to denounce as vicious lies the dangerous statements that had been made there by the Russians. It was a mistake, I said, for us to try to dissociate the Russian people from their leaders. I had too vivid a recollection of those who differentiated between the kindly, goodhearted German people and the murderous Nazis, for I had seen at the dreadful camp at Hagenau the sort of thing these kindly German burghers had condoned. I saw no evidence, I said, that the Russian people had either the capacity or the desire to unseat the criminal conspirators who held them in thrall. All allegations of misconduct on the part of our government I rejected completely, also. Whatever minor errors we might have made, I said, were mere peccadilloes compared to the enormous crimes of Mr. Vishinsky and his government. It would be a tragic mistake, I said, for any American official to invite attention to any derelictions on our part, when the code of ethics and the moral standards under which we operated were infinitely higher than the Russians'. Whatever the mote in our own eye, I said, it was of infinitely less danger to the peace of the world than the bloody dagger in the hands of the Russians.

With that off my chest, I sat down, amid a stony silence. Never before, in war, or in competitive sports, or in any other situation in which the emotions are aroused, had I felt such a sense of anger and frustration. And I remember thinking that it was curious that these tides of passion could run so deep in men who had met to settle their differences over a conference table.

The emotion was one that I was to feel again, soon, in a different setting. Not long afterward, at a conference of the twenty-one America nations at Bogota, in Colombia, I found myself behind a barricaded door, prepared to defend my wife and myself with a table leg.

20

☆☆☆☆

Bogota in Riot Time

WE FLEW to Bogota in the early spring, Penny, my wife, and I. It was in the nature of a honeymoon trip for us, the first of many journeys we were to take together. It was late March, the cherry trees were in full bloom around the tidal basin as we lifted up from Washington, and we flew through blue skies and warming weather all the way to Panama, where we broke our journey briefly with a pleasant visit with General Crittenberger, Commander in Chief in the Caribbean. From there our route lay over the northern branch of the Andes, and we looked forward to the sight of those great snow-crowned peaks which would be in view by mid-morning. We saw but little of them. As our plane climbed to fifteen thousand feet, we ran into a violent thunderstorm. We were both asleep when there came a tremendous crash of sound, and a sharp jolt as if the plane had struck a tree top. I jerked bolt upright, wide awake, expecting momentarily to feel another more violent shock. But nothing happened. Later when we landed at Bogota, the pilot told me that we had been hit by lightning.

We first were quartered in the old Majestic Hotel, on the main square downtown, an unsatisfactory arrangement, for the big French windows of our living room opened directly upon the street about four feet above the ground. And the street, as is normal in Latin cities, was one bawling cacophony of sound, with passersby chattering volubly, and auto drivers, as was their custom, plunging through with great blasts upon their horns.

We moved as soon as possible to a newer and far quieter hotel up on a hill, some quarter of a mile farther from the center of the city. As it turned out, it is lucky that we did.

I had come into the hotel for lunch after our deliberations of the morning, when Cooke, my sergeant, came in to tell me, in some agitation, that Gaitan had just been assassinated. This I considered regrettable, but it so happened that I had been so wrapped up in my own duties, which had to do with military co-operation between the nations, that I hadn't paid much attention to the biographies of the local political leaders. As a result, I didn't have the faintest idea who Gaitan was.

So I finished a leisurely lunch and left by car with Sergeant Cooke driving, headed back to my office. We had some difficulty, for excited crowds were gathering in the streets. I went up to my office and began to dictate, but the noise from the street, six floors below, soon became so disturbing that Cooke couldn't hear me any longer. We went to the window and looked out upon a most fantastic scene. It brought to my mind stories I had read and pictures I had seen of the French Revolution, when the mobs came roaring up out of the gutters of St. Antoine to storm the streets of Paris. The streets below were packed with a screaming throng. I watched them as with their bare hands they tore down the iron grilles that protected the front of a hardware store, surged in, and rushed out waving every sort of weapon from rifles to kitchen knives. They next attacked the liquor stores, so it was not long before they were an armed, lawless, drunken, shooting mob. As we watched them, a fantastic spirit of wanton fury seemed to take hold of them. They overturned automobiles, slashed the tires, broke out the windows and set them afire. They went down the street, headless, leaderless, full of blind rage, smashing store windows and looting as they went.

I knew that somehow I had to get home to the hotel, where Mrs. Ridgway was alone. I was in civilian clothes, armed with no weapon except a knowledge of Spanish. I went down to the street, shouldering my way through the mob, until I came to a man who seemed to be some sort of leader—at least he was carrying a red flag. I asked him what was going on in the direction of the hotel, and how I could best get there. He told me the best thing I could do was get off the street and stay out of sight.

I pondered that advice a moment and then decided the hell with it,

I was going to go to my wife. So I set out, ignoring the shouting throngs, who bumped past me but made no effort to molest me. I found Mrs. Ridgway watching from the window of the hotel the wild scenes in the streets below. The gravity of the situation had not dawned on her. She was as fearless and unconcerned as a child but enormously interested. By now great fires were billowing up all over the center of town, and I heard the sound of firing. I knew that the city's utilities would not survive for long, so I sent a bellboy down to buy all the candles he could find. He came back with a generous supply.

All through the afternoon the mob raged in the streets. Toward dusk, the sounds seemed to be coming nearer. Suddenly, from the lobby below we heard a tremendous crash of breaking glass, shouts and curses in Spanish, and the flat crack-crack of pistols.

It seemed to me the time had come to give some thought to defensive measures. I still had no weapons, but there were some very sturdy small tables in the room. So I upturned one of these and pulled off two of the legs. I gave one to Penny and kept the other myself.

"Now," I said, "the first SOB who sticks his head in this room, we'll brain him. What we do with the body is my concern. But they can come in but one at a time, and we'll nail the first one anyway."

So we shouldered our clubs and waited, listening for the first rush of footsteps in the hall. All was quiet. I found out later what had happened. The manager, a very courageous man, had met the mob as it smashed in his door. He had led them down to his basement where his liquor stocks were stored, and there he had persuaded them to stay, getting suddenly drunk and molesting nobody while the riot raged on outside.

Naturally, we got no sleep that night, and the next morning we looked out on scenes of devastation that reminded me of World War II. Entire blocks looked as if they had been bombed. These buildings have little steel in them. They are constructed of masonry, on heavy timber framing, and when gutted by fire they collapsed in heaps.

That morning, through the unforgettable courtesy of my friend Ambassador Quintanilla of Mexico, Mrs. Ridgway and I made our way, without hindrance, to the American Embassy. Without his voluble Spanish, and his diplomatic manner, I think we would have had great difficulty. From the Embassy I made contact with the Secretary of State, General Marshall, who headed our delegation. He told me that many of the delegates and their wives had taken refuge in the barracks of the Presidential Guard Battalion. With the prior approval of the conference he instructed me to rescue these people and convey them to a place of safety. I was given four other military members of the conference as my colleagues—a Colombian, a Brazilian, an Argentinian, and a Paraguayan. I received these instructions about four o'clock in the afternoon, and I knew I had only about two hours of daylight left. I had to move as fast as possible, therefore, for it would be extremely hazardous to operate at night, in the blacked-out lawless city.

My first task was to get together an armed patrol strong enough to protect us as we went into that part of the city where shooting was still in progress. I went immediately to the senior general officer of the Colombian military establishment and asked for help. He promised such assistance as I would need. I knew that the United States had furnished the Colombian government with some light tanks, and I knew that one of these would be an ideal escort as we traveled, by bus, to the barracks where the delegates were impounded.

I had great trouble getting that tank on its way. Daylight was dwindling fast, but the tank commander kept making all sort of excuses. First, he had no crew available. Finally, though, he got a crew assembled. Then he discovered the tank's batteries were run down, and the engine would not start. Another hour passed, while darkness deepened and my impatience grew. If this tank commander had been in our army, I would have relieved him immediately, but I had no authority over a Colombian officer, and had to hold my tongue and exercise my dwindling patience.

Finally, we set out, the tank leading, the big bus, with the five of us rattling around inside, following behind. We had no radio contact with the tank. All signals were visual, and in the dark all we could see was his exhaust, fleeing down the street at a speed which indicated the tank commander would be happy to lose us if he could. We reached the barracks without a shot being fired, loaded the bus with the overjoyed inmates of the barracks, and brought them to safety in the houses in the suburbs where they were staying. It was late at night by now, and just as I was thanking my lucky stars this job was over and was about to dismiss the tank, I got a message saying that some extremely important people had missed the bus and were yelling to be brought out.

Well, my orders were to bring all of them out, so I told my colleagues and the timorous tank commander that we would have to make the five-mile journey all over again. The tank commander heard this news with no obvious elation. Then one of his enlisted men came up and spoke to him. His face lighted up.

"Ah," he said, "such a journey is now impossible. The tank is out of gas."

I think my patience would have run out then, and I might have done and said things that would have severely strained our relations with our Colombian friends, if an old axiom of command had not come to my aid. One of the basic principles of combat—and this was essentially a combat situation—is to verify a report before you take action on it. I checked the tank. It was out of gas. Then I decided to check back to see if some dignitary actually had been left. It took forty-five minutes to get the phone call through to the barracks. To my great relief, nobody had been left. We had brought them all the first time.

That ended that little adventure. I never want to go through such a thing again. I know of no more helpless feeling than to be caught, unarmed, in the middle of a drunken, rioting, hysterical mob liberally supplied with weapons and filled only with the urge to destroy. If I ever am called upon to attend a peace conference in that region again, I think I shall carry a revolver—small in size but of a caliber large enough to possess some shocking power.

The great hall where the conference sessions were held had been very badly damaged, but, very courageously, the delegates voted unanimously to move to a private home in the suburbs and continue their deliberations there. It would have been tragic in the extreme to have done otherwise, for in essence the Bogota riots, though violent, were purely local in nature. They were not directed at the conference, which brought together representatives of twenty-one American states in deliberations which take place only once every five years. So, very wisely, the meeting continued, with the result that the Pact of Bogota was signed. It greatly strengthened the inter-American system, by changing its organization into what is now the Organization of American States.

We returned in mid-April to Washington, where my old friend, General Bradley, the incoming Chief of Staff, called me in and asked what new assignment I would like. Owing to the recognized ineffectiveness of the Military Staff Committee, he said, the military representation was being down-graded, both in rank and numbers. Also, I had served my full tour with the UN, and in the normal course of things it was time to make a change. General Bradley told me I could have either a continental army, or the post as Commander in Chief of the Caribbean. I chose the latter, because for thirty years I had been closely related to and deeply interested in our relations with our friends in Latin America. It proved to be a happy choice, for in all my career, I never had a quieter, more pleasant tour of duty.

21

★★★★

Panama Idyll

THE Caribbean is one of the great strategic areas of the world, of vital importance to the safety of the United States. It is peaceful and quiet now, and has been for generations, owing largely to the measures we have taken there to work out, over 120 years of patient negotiation, a basis of understanding between us and our neighbors. What the American people must not forget is the continuing vital importance of this area to us. This hemisphere is our inner citadel. Within it, we, and the twenty-one Latin republics and the Dominion of Canada, can live in peace together, and can defend ourselves against outside enemies as long as we remain united in purpose. If, however, in the event of global war, even some of these other American republics were opposed to us, or neutral in attitude, we would find ourselves in a position of gravest danger. It is hard to exaggerate the importance of harmonious co-operation between us and these twenty-one republics, based on mutual trust, mutual understanding, and mutual confidence.

The Caribbean command is a small one. Neither the Navy nor the Air Force maintains any permanent combat forces there. The Army itself has only a small force—one regiment of infantry, a little anti-aircraft artillery in the Canal Zone, and a small garrison in the Antilles, stationed in Puerto Rico. But the importance of the command is out of all proportion to its size, and the Commander in Chief of the Caribbean, and his component service commanders, exercise a tremendous influence on the military establishments and, therefore, on the political regimes of the Latin-American republics. Our military establishment is their model, and the U.S. Army, particularly, is the model for the armies of most of the Latin-American republics. And it is their armies which exercise the controlling influence over their governments.

The months I spent in Panama as Commander in Chief, Caribbean, were an idyllic interlude which will long linger in my memory. After the physical and mental strain of the war, and the intellectual and spiritual tensions of my service on the Military Staff Committee, I needed a few months of rest. In the early months of 1946 I came home to find that my earlier marriage could no longer survive the long years of separation. The only answer lay in divorce. In December of 1947 I had married again, and no event in my whole life has ever brought me more inspiration, more thankfulness to God, and more of all the true richness of life than this marriage to my beloved Penny. Nor can I ever forget the great spiritual comfort I derived from my association with the Rev. Dr. Paull Sargent, Rector of St. Bartholomew's Church in New York, who gave our marriage his blessing. I was highly honored to be asked to join the vestry of St. Bartholomew's, where I had the great privilege of knowing, from the vantage point of the church's inner councils, the inspiring qualities of that fine Christian gentleman and patriot.

We had only been married seven months when we went down to Panama to take up residence in lovely old Quarters One on Quarry Heights. It had been the official residence of the senior officer of the U.S. forces in the Canal Zone for many years, and it was a cool and comfortable, sprawling old house, surrounded by a huge U-shaped screened porch, 130 feet long on the longer side. It was almost a shell when we arrived, due to the ravages of the climate and the rapacity of the termites. Later, when I was Chief of Staff, I finally got authorization to replace its heavier wooden members with steel, and it should now survive many more decades of tropic weather. Penny met magnificently the challenge that faces all Army wives at frequent intervals—that of furnishing a new house—just as she was to meet the far greater challenges which were to come in following years. She did a beautiful job, particularly with this huge screened porch, which was our living room. She covered all the chairs and sofas with cool cotton fabrics in gay colors and brightened the place with the jungle plants and flowers which grew so luxuriantly there. To me it was a little Paradise, a delight both to the eye and to the spirit. Penny, too, with her fine artistic sense, responded to the beauty of the land about her. She first took up painting in a serious way there and her first canvases were of Panamanian scenes.

The greatest event of all down there was the arrival of our little son, Matty. Old soldiers and young babies both wake up very early in the morning, and when he was only a tiny fellow, just a few days home from the hospital, I would get up just at dawn, while his mother was still asleep, and take him from his crib and walk on the porch, holding him in my arms. It was the time of morning when the parrots were flying, with raucous cries, and I would point them out to him, and he would look with his little unseeing eyes as if he were aware of all the bright world around him. I think that in all my life I have never known greater happiness than I did there. I just can't imagine a man more blessed than I, there among those friendly people, in a climate like morning in Paradise, with a fine new son to bear my name, and a noble, wonderful woman for my wife.

Good friends were with us there, too—my own splendid Chief of Staff, General Bryan, Governor Newcomer, head of the Canal Zone administration, Major General Porter, commanding the Army units, Vice Admiral Dan Barbey, commander of the Caribbean Sea Frontier, and Major General Willis Hale, an old comrade with whom I had had many years' service. Mr. Monnett B. Davis was the Ambassador, a gracious and charming man, and Penny and I had many pleasant social evenings with these distinguished gentlemen and their wives.

There was many a fine day spent in the open, too. "Panama" in the aboriginal speech means "place where the fish abound," and Penny, who shared my love for fishing for salt-water game fish, soon found that this was no misnomer. We fished for marlin and big sail in the Pearl Islands, eighty miles west of Balboa, and for fine tarpon in the Chagres River, which empties out of Gatun Lake.

Fishing in the Bay of Panama, she took a fine sail, weighing 126 pounds, and I boated a big fellow that weighed 165. By way of comparison, the biggest sails taken off the coast of Florida rarely go over 100 pounds. In Panama, if you pull in a 100-pounder, you throw him back.

The finest fishing we found, as well as the most amazing scenery, was in the Galapagos Islands. We had flown to Ecuador to attend the inauguration of President Galo Plaza, a distinguished gentleman who had been a star football player at the University of California. After the inauguration, we had flown to the Galapagos, where our government still maintained a small Air Force unit on a field built there for use of the planes that flew the sea patrols guarding the western approaches of the Panama Canal during the war.

I don't know of any place I have ever visited on this earth's surface which gave me more of the feeling that I had suddenly entered a by-gone geological era. The bird life and the marine life in those islands are fantastic, both in kind and number. The great dry cones of the ancient dead volcanoes lurch upward from the sea in rocky crags, covered with a scrawny and shriveled vegetation, where birds in myriads live, so unaccustomed to the sight of man they have no fear of him.

We were there for fifty-two hours. We must have fished for forty-five of them. We fished for tuna, on light tackle, for an eighty-pound tuna on a six-ounce rod and a twenty-four-pound test line gives you a wonderful battle, yet it does not take so long to boat him that you spoil the fishing for the others. There were great sailfish in these waters, too. Fishermen there a week before we arrived had taken one weighing 211 pounds. We did not try for sail, but we took many beautifully colored dolphin, one of the fastest fish that swims, a spectacular fighter, with a wonderful flavor once you get him on the table.

The sharks were a problem in the Galapagos, as they were to Hemingway's old fisherman. Once, within fifty yards around our launch, I sighted forty-seven of them, swimming lazily, close to the surface. I had a carbine aboard, and we took turns popping away at them. They did not seem to be greatly perturbed. They would accelerate a little as the bullet struck, then slow down and continue their lazy circling.

Along the shorelines, we often saw huge sea lions and seals, the big bulls lying proudly in the midst of their harems, surveying us without fear. They added to the feeling that here, indeed, as Dr. Beebe had described it, was "World's End."

Not all my time in Panama, of course, was spent in pleasant cruising. When I took command in the Caribbean, we still had a little combat strength of all three arms on station there. We had a squadron of submarines based on Coco Solo Island, and a group of F-80's—which were then our most up-to-date operational fighters—stationed in the Zone. However, it was during the period of financial retrenchment, when Secretary of Defense Louis Johnson, was "paring the fat" from the military establishment, as he expressed it—and cutting deeply into our military muscle. So both the submarine squadron and the F-80's were withdrawn, which to my mind was a most unwise move.

Our Panama idyll ended abruptly. I had taken command there in June of 1948. Early in September of 1949 Mrs. Ridgway and I were on an official visit to Venezuela when I received a message from the Pentagon. General Bradley was moving up from Chief of Staff to Chairman of the Joint Chiefs. General Joseph Lawton Collins was to take over the duties of Chief of Staff, and General Collins would require my services as Deputy Chief of Staff for Operations and Administration.

We did not cut short our Venezuela visit, but these orders did require drastic alterations in our future plans. We had been invited to visit Brazil, which Mrs. Ridgway had never seen, and where I had many warm friends whom I was eager for her to know. This trip proved to be impossible, for on my return to Panama another message was awaiting me, to the effect that I was needed in Washington at once.

I immediately made plans to go up by air, in a B-17 bomber that had been converted to passenger service. I also took certain precautions against the possibility of accidents in the air. These things had never concerned me greatly when I was flying alone, but with Penny and the baby traveling with me, I thought it might be well to recognize the fact that, though disasters are rare, they do occur sometimes. So I had a special parachute rigged up for Penny, a standard chute cut down to size so that it would not slip off her shoulders in the air, a mishap that might prove embarrassing in the event she had to jump. Without telling her about it, I also slipped her hunting boots into my baggage, and her hunting cap with long ear tabs. A lady who jumped in high heels would certainly land shoeless on the ground. And a woman's long hair streaming out in the wind could cause a tragedy, for the risers bursting from the chute at the moment of opening might become entangled in her hair and snap her neck. Once Penny had been taken care of, I turned my attention to the best way of getting Matty down. I knew it would be impossible to jump with him in my arms, for the opening shock would tear him from my grasp. So I had a tiny harness made for him, and had special snaps fastened to the bottom of my own chest pack. I tried this harness on, with him attached, and I felt pretty sure that, barring rough air, or high winds, or an exceedingly rough landing, I could get him down without injury. I could protect him with one arm as I went out the door, with the other hand free to pull the D-ring, and on landing I could shelter him again, unless there happened to be a strong wind blowing and we were dragged.

There was only the remotest chance, of course, that we would have to jump, *en famille,* from an airplane, but there is always the possibility that it might happen. So you plan to meet it if you have to, and once you have done the best you can, your apprehensions and worries are allayed.

There were various logistical problems also that were outside my previous experience—the matter of having an ample supply of diapers on hand through the journey, for example, and the problem of how to heat the baby's bottle while in the air, and so on. Finally, all these things were worked out, and we were set to go.

Just as we finished all our final preparations, though, Colonel Eaton, the Adjutant General, called on me, wearing an expression of great dolor. I had seen that expression on Doc Eaton's face before, when he was my Chief of Staff in Europe and had an occasion to bring me unhappy news.

"Well, Doc, what is it?" I said, knowing something was wrong. He handed me a paper.

"I didn't want to bring this to you," he said. "I sat on it for several days."

It was a directive from Mr. Louis Johnson, the Secretary of Defense, flatly prohibiting the transportation by air of families of men in service.

The news was vastly disappointing, for, by flying home, I would have been able to make a quick trip out to San Diego, to see my mother and to let her meet Penny and see her new grandson for the first time. Now that was no longer possible.

So we scrapped all our plans for flying, and through the courtesy of the Zone Administration finally managed to get a stateroom on a steamer that was leaving fairly soon. The change did not make me happy, but I did not fret too much. After years in the Army, I was used to these sudden changes, for I've had my share of them both in war and peace.

Penny took it all with good grace, and I think that one of the wonderful aspects of family life in the Army is the way the wives and children of service folk take the vicissitudes they must endure. Nine times out of ten they impose more distress and dislocations on the wife than they do on the soldier concerned. Children are pulled out of school in mid-term and propelled across the country, or across the world, to another region that is totally strange to them. Furniture must be packed and shipped on a moment's notice, and new households set up in far corners of the earth. Treasured mementoes which Army families love to collect are lost and broken in transit (there is an old saying in the Army that three moves are more destructive than a fire), and there is a gypsy quality to life that requires a special philosophy. That the wives and children do take these things in stride, with great courage and lightheartedness, is one of the brightest sides, I think, of family life in the Army. The children are particularly resilient. At the age of six and a half, my son Matty, for example, has lived in a dozen different houses and hotels, in Panama, the U.S., Japan, and France. He has had nurses who taught him to chatter in Japanese, French, and German, languages he picked up quickly and just as quickly forgot. Yet he seems to have suffered but little from the sudden dislocations that have been his lot. He is, on the contrary, a little proud of the fact that he has been on the move so much. Not long ago, in a hotel in Washington, an elevator boy said to him as he came in from a walk:

"Hey, young fellow, where have you been?"

"Me?" said Matty. "Oh, I've been all over."

We arrived in New York on the 14th of September and left for Washington immediately by rail. I checked in at the Pentagon that afternoon. As has been my unfortunate lot, particularly with respect to Washington duty, I was put to work immediately. And for more than five years, until I retired last June, there was no breathing spell.

22

☆☆☆☆

War in Korea

FOR nearly nine months after my return from Panama, I worked at my Pentagon desk without a break. It was a time to give a soldier deep concern, for in that period following the end of World War II, there was a growing feeling that in the armies of the future the foot soldier would play only a very minor role. Two factors stimulated this thinking—the earnest desire of the nation to cut down on its military expenditures, and the erroneous belief that in the atomic missile, delivered by air, we had found the ultimate weapon.

That thinking was strongly reflected in our troop disposition around the world, particularly in the Far East. There our resources were extremely limited. On orders from the highest levels, we had hamstrung our Army forces. They were there purely on occupational duty, their primary mission to function, not as soldiers, but as policemen, and they were not trained for combat, for such training would have interfered with their police duties. They were not ready for battle either mentally or physically, except in the case of their few professional officers, both commissioned and non-commissioned, who are always, in their minds, ready for combat.

Under the policy of retrenchment forced upon us by Secretary Louis Johnson, we had reduced the infantry battalions in the regiments from three to two. The firing batteries in the artillery battalions had been reduced from three to two. All of the medium tanks had been taken out of both the infantry regiments and the divisions, and placed in storage—partly because they were not needed in police duty, but mainly because, when we ran them on the roads of Japan, they broke the bridges down.

We were, in short, in a state of shameful unreadiness when the Korean War broke out, and there was absolutely no excuse for it. The only reason a combat unit exists at all is to be ready to fight in case of sudden emergency, and no human being can predict when these emergencies will arise. The state of our Army in Japan at the outbreak of the Korean War was inexcusable.

It was this bitter lesson, learned through our experience in Korea at such a cost in blood and national prestige, that steeled me in my resolution later, when, as Chief of Staff, I protested with greatest vehemence against "economies" which would have placed us in the same relative state of ineffectiveness. When urged to cut combat forces in Korea below 100 per cent strength, I reported to Mr. Wilson in writing, over my signature, that any such reductions would be made only on direct orders from competent authority.

The outbreak of that war came to me as a complete surprise, as it did to all our military men—from Seoul to Washington. On the 21st of June, with Mrs. Ridgway, I had taken my first break from my desk job. It was in a sense a busman's holiday. We had gone up to Indiantown Gap, Pennsylvania, where I was to review the elements of the Pennsylvania National Guard. I'd had a very refreshing afternoon. Out in the field with the troops, I had felt as lighthearted as a schoolboy, happy to escape from the stultifying atmosphere of the Pentagon. I spent a pleasant evening with Governor Duff, and with the officers of the 28th Division of the Pennsylvania National Guard. The next morning there had been a formal review, and afterward a pleasant luncheon, and in the afternoon we had motored down to Carlisle Barracks. It was our hope to spend a quiet evening there in that sleepy little place, get up for church on Sunday morning, and then drive back to Washington in the afternoon. Our host had different ideas, though. He drove us all the way to Harrisburg for dinner. We didn't want to go, but as so often happens in such cases, it turned out to be a most pleasant and happy evening. We returned at a reasonable hour—around eleven—and turned in.

About two o'clock, or a little after, I was awakened by a violent ringing of the telephone, and an equally violent prodding by Mrs.

Ridgway. My G-2 in Washington was on the phone, with the word that the North Koreans had just attacked across the 38th Parallel. I got such details as he was able to give me, hung up the phone, and turned to my wife:

"Well," I said, "there goes our quiet, happy weekend."

There was no more sleep for us that night. We rose, packed, drank a cup of coffee, and by first light were on our way to Washington.

The thought, of course, had flashed through my mind that this was the beginning of World War III. The Sino-Soviet treaty had been signed only a few months before and here, it seemed to me, could well be the beginning of Armageddon, the last great battle between East and West.

I arrived in Washington well before noon, to find the telecoms pouring in from General MacArthur and communications from the Joint Chiefs streaming back to him. And I well remember my feelings when I realized that on the highest levels there was, for a little while at least, a feeling that only the Air and Navy forces would be needed to contain this thing. I was standing by General Bradley at the telecom when the directive went out authorizing the use of Air and Naval forces to cover the evacuation of American personnel from the Seoul and Inchon area, and I asked him whether this was deliberately intended to exclude the use of ground forces in Korea. He told me, "Yes."

That bright delusion did not last long. Soon there followed our only alternative—the commitment of those skeleton regiments in Japan—those police troops who were in no shape to fight.

This is one more thing, I think, that should go down in the recording angel's book—the book of history where men's errors are put down never to be erased. All modern military history is filled with these records of failure in which a nation places its reliance on one single arm and learns too late that that arm will not suffice. It is a tragic lesson and its message is clear, but to date we have not learned it, for we still find political leaders—and plenty in uniform too—forlornly hoping that we can defend ourselves, save ourselves, by choosing what appears to be the easiest, cheapest way.

The ebb and flow of the battle tides in the early days of the Korean conflict are still green in men's memories—the piecemeal commitment; the slow fall-back until, on the battle maps, the space we occupied on that whole peninsula could be covered by the span of a man's hand; and then the brilliant breakout and the seaborne landing that crushed the North Korean armies and hurled them back to the Yalu. My knowledge of these actions differs from that of every newspaper reader's only in depth of detail, for all the reports of battle action flowed across my desk in the Pentagon. This narrative, therefore, will begin later on, in December, when having conquered one foe we were suddenly confronted with another enemy—the Red Chinese.

My mind goes back now to a Saturday afternoon in December, 1950. It was a time of great apprehension, due to the quick and drastic change in the battle situation in Korea. I had gone to Philadelphia to the Army-Navy game, hoping, in the enjoyment of that great sporting spectacle, which has such meaning to all military and naval academy graduates, to be able to put aside for an hour or two the deep worries that beset me. Even there, though, I did not wish to be out of contact with my office—I was Deputy Chief of Staff for Operations—for across my desk would come all reports emanating from Korea. I, therefore, had had a telephone installed beneath my seat in the stadium, so that in case of emergency I could be reached immediately.

I think that for a moment, as with my wife I joined the throng moving slowly into the great bowl, I did become caught up in the spirit of that great sports pageant, to forget for a moment my own deep concern. This feeling did not last long. As I walked into the stadium, Major General A. R. Bolling, Chief of Intelligence of the Department of the Army, caught my eye. The message he had for me was the most depressing that I ever have received. It told that in Korea Major General L. B. Kaiser's 2nd Division had become combat non-effective. I had served in that division in the period between World Wars I and II. Its battle record in both conflicts had been magnificent. In World War II, it did not achieve the fame, in some respects, of the 1st Division, but in the minds of the military historians—the men who look behind the headlines to evaluate battle performance—it did, in truth, live up to its proud motto, "Second to None." In the period between the wars, it had been our only laboratory for training officers in the actual handling of a division in the field, and all of us who had learned in it the ABC's of high command were tremendously proud of our service in it.

To walk into that stadium and learn that this great organization, at the peak of its battle strength of eighteen thousand men, had been so nearly destroyed that it now was non-effective as a fighting unit was a profound shock. From my field telephone, I immediately called the Pentagon to ask for further details, but they could give me no further information, because of its classified nature, over the phone.

Now, the curious relation of pleasure and pain in life is fairly well illustrated by that incident. We lost the football game that year to a great Navy team we had confidently expected to beat. In other circumstances I would have felt a bitter disappointment. I felt none. I watched the play on the field with my eyes, but my thoughts were far away, with the remnants of a once great fighting division that were rolling southward in defeat.

So began a week of great labor and deep anxiety. Hour by hour, we followed the meager reports that told of the gallant actions of Major General Oliver Smith's 1st Marine Division as it battled its way from Chosin Reservoir to the sea. Back here, nine thousand miles from the fighting, I think perhaps our anguish of soul and our anxiety were deeper than those experienced by the men who were at the front. Back here, we could only try to anticipate their needs and get whatever they needed to them. Their concerns were of the moment. When you are in battle, you don't have time to indulge in apprehensive fears. You are too deeply engrossed in your immediate problem—the fight that is going on around you.

For days we watched that threatening situation unfold. The directive went out to regroup the forces, to evacuate the Hungnam-Hamhung area, to pull back to the south, and there prepare to start all over again from Pusan, Masan and Taegu. Finally, the danger of great losses was over, the forces had broken contact with the enemy and were withdrawing by land and sea. We had been gravely hurt, but a great catastrophe to American arms had been averted—more narrowly than our people yet know.

To me there had come no inkling of what fate held in store for me. Yet, deep inside, a small still voice kept whispering that, whatever happened, I should be ready. One gray Sunday afternoon, without telling Penny, I slipped up to the attic. And there I got together, ready to my hand, the boots and baggy battle dress, the combat gear I'd laid away, I'd hoped forever, after the war in Europe ended.

23

☆☆☆☆

"Eighth Army Is Yours"

IT was nearly midnight on Friday evening, December 22, three days before Christmas of 1950. The living room of our dear old friends, the Jaynes, was filled with the talk and happy laughter of the guests who were saying good-by. It had been a pleasant evening. I had worked for fourteen hours that day and had found in this brief social interlude a moment of surcease from my troubles. The last message I had read that day had brought good news. The withdrawal in Korea was continuing without a hitch. I felt a little easing of the tension under which all of us had labored since word first had reached us of the Chinese entry into the war.

In the pleasant hubbub around me, I hardly heard the voice that told me I was wanted on the telephone. Joe Collins, the Chief of Staff, was on the wire. He spoke quietly:

"Matt," he said, "I'm sorry to tell you that Johnny Walker has been killed in a jeep accident in Korea. I want you to get your things together and get out there just as soon as you can."

Whatever effect this message had on me personally was lost in the sorrow I felt at hearing of General Walton Walker's death. I had known Eighth Army's commander, a rugged little bulldog of a soldier, for many years, and I admired him as a fighting man.

We talked a moment longer, then I rejoined the others. Across the room I saw Penny looking at me, a question in her eyes. I smiled and shrugged and shook my head. I had already resolved that I would not trouble her sleep that night—the last night left to us together. Morning would come all too soon, and that would be time enough to break this harsh news to her.

Could those who in careless criticism impute a love of war to professional soldiers share one such experience as this, I think they never would repeat that accusation. Christmas was almost upon us. Saturday I was to go out and find a tree and dress it for our little son, now twenty months old, with the presents that in the rush of the past few weeks I had not had time to buy. And now I knew that before Christmas came I would be gone.

We had coffee the next morning in the little study upstairs, with Matty bouncing happily in his crib nearby. Talking of small, inconsequential things, I delayed as long as I could, for I dreaded to strike this blow at the heart of my dearest. Finally, I told her of Joe Collins's call.

No battlefield heroism can compare with the courage and faith of a noble woman. There were no tears, no questions, only an agonized, long-drawn-out "O—h," that stabbed at my heart.

The demands of a hundred "musts" soon brought the blessed relief of action. We began together, first to plan, then to do, the multitude of little, but important, things that had to be crowded into the next few hours.

The Pentagon was nearly empty when I arrived there well before eight o'clock, but my faithful, incomparable secretary, McCleary, was there, and so were Colonels Beishline and Moorman, both equal to any emergency in peace or war.

With their good help, all things moved rapidly. I checked my will, executed a power of attorney, arranged an allotment for my family, conferred with General Collins, General Haislip, the Vice Chief of Staff, Secretary Pace, and Admiral Sherman, the Chief of Naval Operations. Already it was nearly noon.

I had left the house with the departure date open. I knew that Penny clung to the hope that we could have Christmas Eve together—just the three of us together at Matty's first real tree. But General Collins felt that I should leave at once, and in this I concurred. We set the take-off time for eight o'clock that same evening, which should put me in Tokyo before midnight on Christmas Day. Now she must be told that there would be no happy Christmas Eve together. I picked up the phone, then put it down again. This I could not do. I asked

General Haislip, my life-long, devoted friend, if he would please tell my Penny. He looked me straight in the eye, a long, level gaze. "Yes, Matt," he said quietly, "I will." God bless him for taking that burden from me.

Now came the task of gathering clothes and equipment. Many a time, in the past, Penny had had her quiet laugh at me for my fussiness about keeping track of things—for keeping planning lists for trips of varying duration all worked up in advance, so that when the time to pack arrived, whether dress uniform and decorations for a social junket, or rough clothes for a fishing trip, we'd have a check list at hand. Now this preliminary planning paid off, for these lists showed in which box or trunk to look for what I needed, and soon I was packed and ready.

As my luggage was assembled in the hall downstairs, I thought to myself how strikingly appropriate it seemed. My eventual mission was to command an allied force made up of all arms—soldiers and Marines, with sailors and airmen in support. And here was a battered old Marine Corps seabag acquired in Nicaragua in 1928, an Army footlocker from the 9th Infantry, *circa* 1926, a steel chest picked up from the Navy when I was Commander in Chief, Caribbean, and an Air Force valpac still stained with the snows and mud of Holland and the Ardennes. Surely, I thought, this ought to bring me luck—and no field commander ever attains much success without a full measure of good fortune.

By the time I had finished packing, the news services' men were there for interviews, and the house was full of photographers. All were appreciated and accommodated, but time kept slipping away, and I began to understand that flicker of impatience I'd seen on the faces of other men when somebody said, "Please, just one more."

There was just one more that I was particularly anxious to get. Earlier I had sent for a commercial photographer to take a last-minute picture of my wife and baby that would follow me and keep me company in the days ahead. There was no time to dress Matty. We took him from his crib in his pajamas, all soft-eyed from sleep, and plunked him down between us as the photographer fired away. The pictures turned out wonderfully. Penny had them nicely mounted and sent them out to me, and a week later they illuminated my bleak room in Central Korea with the light which nothing else on earth can shed.

I took another treasured memory with me. A kind friend, Colonel Shytle, went out to find the tree that I had not had time to buy. He brought it in, set it up, strung it with lights, and I'll never forget the look in Matty's eyes as we sat down that night to early dinner in the glow of that little tree.

There were only the four of us there that evening. Penny, her sister Lucy, Matty, and me, carefully avoiding the topic that was closest to all our hearts—the fact that in an hour or so I would be gone. We sat around the tree, quiet but happy. Matty was contentedly playing—not with a toy, but a silver cigarette box that had caught his eye. Penny wanted to show me how much he had learned that day. She began:

"Jack and Jill went up the ——?"

"Hill," Matty responded.

"To get a pail of ——?"

"Water," said Matty.

"Mary had a little ——?"

"Goat," roared Matty.

It was the first good laugh we'd had that day, and the memory of it cheered me, as, an hour later, my plane lifted up from the airport, headed westward into the dark. Below me, beneath the Constellation's wings, the dome of the Capitol glowed with light. As we climbed, I caught one brief glimpse below me of my own house at Fort Myer, where Matty, his beloved cigarette box clasped close to him, already was sound asleep. Down there, too, Penny was riding home. I watched a long time from the window, wishing I knew, amid the myriad headlights that turned the streets into rivers of light, which one was hers.

Soon there was only darkness below, and the windows were turning white with frost. But there were warmth and brightness in my heart, and they came from that home below, and the good friends I was leaving. In my pocket were two messages, each from a revered chief I had served in days gone by—General Frank McCoy and General Marshall. And many an old comrade had broken his Christmas holiday to come out to the terminal to say good-by.

In the rush of getting away, I had had little time to think of the job that was facing me. Now, in the darkness as the plane droned on, I could close the door of memory on all that was past, on family and home and a job at a desk. I could think now of battle command, of the great responsibilities which would fall upon my shoulders the moment this journey ended and I stepped down on Korean soil.

My mind ranged back for a moment over all that had gone before. And it seemed to me that basically this problem that was facing me was little different, except in degree, from the problems that had confronted me throughout all my years in service, first at the Infantry School, then at Staff College, and later in combat. The whole training of an officer seeks to accomplish one purpose—to instill in him the ability to take over in battle in a time of crisis. Many a time, in Infantry School, I had been given such a problem. A map would be thrust before me. "You are here," I was told. "The enemy is here. The tactical situation is thus and so [it was always bad]. Your battalion commander has been killed. You are now in command. What do you do?"

And then I would think the thing through, as quickly as I could, working out in my own mind each concrete step I would take, in an orderly process, basing my decisions on what knowledge I possessed of the enemy's disposition, his strength and capabilities, and of the strength and capabilities of my own men.

And here, after all these years, the same situation was facing me, but real now, not a theory but a fact. The Army Commander *was* dead. The tactical situation *was* bad. I was in command, and on my answer to the question "What do you do?" depended something far more important than a grade in an instructor's book. On it hinged victory or defeat.

Quickly I ran over in my mind all that I knew of the situation. As Deputy Chief of Staff for Operations, the map of Korea had become as familiar to me as the lines in my hand. I knew our strength, and our weakness. I knew personally all the top commanders in Eighth Army, except General Oliver Smith of the 1st Marine Division, and from what I knew of him, I knew I could depend on him implicitly.

Armed with this background knowledge, what should I do? Quickly, a pattern of action took place in my mind. First, of course, I would report to General MacArthur, and receive from him his estimate of the situation and broad general directives concerning operations. Next, I would assume command—and this, I knew, must be done in one simple, brief, sincere statement which would convey to Eighth Army my supreme confidence that it could turn and face and fight and defeat the Chinese horde that had sprung so suddenly from beyond the Yalu. Once this was done, I would meet with Eighth Army staff and get from them their appraisal of the situation. After that, I would call on every commander in his battle area, look into his face and the faces of his men, and form my own opinion of his firmness and resolution—or the lack thereof. Once these things were done, then I could begin to plan, could make the big decision whether to stand and hold, or to attack.

These thoughts, which take so long in telling, went quickly through my mind. Once they had arranged themselves in logical order, a great relief came over me, and a great weariness. A long night lay ahead. The steward came back to tell me that my bed was ready. The air was smooth, the engines beat steadily with the sound of far-off surf. Soon I was asleep.

Eight hours later, I was up, dressed, refreshed, and full of ideas. The steward brought hot coffee and eggs straight up. I pitched in, first into the eggs and then into a brief case full of work. By the time we landed at Tacoma, I had a great deal done. Messages went off by wire, radio, and mail to Penny back in Washington, to the office, to the Department of the Army. I had traveled alone, for I had no heart to rip an officer from home and fireside so close to Christmas. Now, though, I sent a message back, gratefully accepting Lieutenant Colonel Walter Winton's kind offer to join me.

It was night when we left Washington, night when we landed at Tacoma, still black dark when we took off westward over Puget Sound. Dawn came in a thin, gray light, with no sight of sky or sea. There was nothing to see, nothing to do but think and work. I put down the questions I would ask General MacArthur, penciled the first rough draft of my message to the troops. Suddenly, I realized I needed a haircut. It was Sunday in Adak, our next stop, but our good Navy friends there wouldn't be going anywhere. There was nowhere to go. I radioed ahead for a barber.

An hour out of Adak the sun broke through, the undercast dissolved, and below me I could see the black crags of the Aleutians—rock-ribbed, snow-capped, and ringed on the Bering side with surf. We landed in brilliant sunshine. A strong salt-tanged wind was blowing and the thermometer was just below freezing.

Captain Hamilton, the commanding officer of the U.S. Naval Air Station, was waiting for me with a cheery smile and a barber, and I had a delightful half hour with him and his gracious wife in a lovely hillside home which she had made most charming. They told me of their archaeological researches, showed me artifacts of stone, wood, and bone, left here by primitive peoples long since gone into the mists of the past. They spoke of the lovely flowers that dot the hills in spring, and of the birds they had been able to attract to their transplanted Kodiak spruces. And I thought again of Penny, and of her wonderful capacity for making a place of beauty out of any habitation in which she might find herself. Mrs. Hamilton, too, had that touch—the genius of the serviceman's wife for making a home no matter in what far, bleak place her husband might be stationed.

We left in the full glory of that rare sun-shining day. Twelve hours later, just before midnight, we touched down at Haneda Airport, outside of Tokyo.

Old friends were there to greet me, as old friends had seen me off—Doyle Hickey, R. R. Allen, O. P. Weyland, and others. I rode in with Hickey, and got from him my first firsthand information on what was happening in Korea. With his usual consummate courtesy and thoughtfulness, General MacArthur had lodged me in the Guest House of the Embassy. I worked until after one o'clock, then went into the bedroom to find coffee and sandwiches on the dresser.

I was up at seven, to breakfast alone before an open fire. I felt that Penny should be there. And in a sense she was there, smiling, with Matty in her arms, for her picture and his have a special place in my brief case, and wherever I am this picture is the first thing I unpack.

At nine, I saw General MacArthur. In a masterly briefing, he covered all the points I had in mind to ask him. As I rose to go, I asked one question. "General," I said, "if I get over there and find the situation warrants it, do I have your permission to attack?"

A broad grin broke out on the old gentleman's face.

"Do what you think best, Matt," he said. "The Eighth Army is yours."

That is the sort of orders that puts heart into a soldier. Now the full responsibilities were mine; not to be delegated, as authority may be delegated, but indivisibly and ceaselessly mine, day and night, as every commander's responsibilities are his alone, from theater to infantry squad—from five stars to two stripes. Command responsibilities—for as long as it might please God and my superiors to keep me on the job.

24

☆☆☆☆

There to Stay

THE first message I wished Eighth Army to receive from me was one of profound respect for the indomitable heart of the great soldier whose responsibilities it had become my privilege to assume. It merited a separate identity, unmingled with the thoughts I wished to convey at the moment of taking command. Accordingly, I gave to Major General Hickey, for transmittal to the troops before I arrived, a simple message of sincere respect for the memory of Lieutenant General Walker—a dear friend and honored comrade of more than thirty years.

There now remained but a scant two hours before I would fly to Korea. I spent them soaking up information from General Hickey and his assistant chiefs of staff; from the Air Force Commander, General Stratemeyer; and from Vice Admiral Turner Joy, commanding the Naval forces in the Far East. There was still time for small personal chores—time to order an extra pair of eyeglasses, to have a wrist watch fixed, to have Eighth Army patches sewn on the shoulders of my blouse, and to find and send to Penny a belated Christmas gift.

We were airborne at noon, against a strong head wind, with the same fine crew that had brought me out taking me on the last lap of my journey. Mount Fuji swam below as I ate luncheon. Snow blanketed its southern slope, clouds shrouded it on the west to break its exquisite symmetry, and from its summit a plume of feathery cloud trailed down the wind. That blowing cloud was a portent of trouble ahead. Just as I finished my notes on the remarks I wanted to make on taking command, we hit a storm. In cloud and rain we flew on to Taegu. We landed there under gray skies, in cold that struck to the bone. I could hear, I thought, the lilt of Penny's quiet laughter. For all my boasting about my expert packing, I had come off without an overcoat.

The weather was cold, but the greeting of life-long friends was warm. Lev Allen, the Eighth Army's great Chief of Staff, was there to greet me. No fuss and feathers, though. Just a smile, a handshake, and we were off, bouncing over the pot-holed roads in the old familiar jeep. All around me were the scenes a soldier knows so well—the tents, the trucks, the men in battle dress—all the dusty trappings and accouterments of war, which look the same wherever you find them. Here amid the reek and clamor of an Oriental town it was hard to believe that just three nights before I had left a happy party back in Washington to take Joe Collins's telephone call.

Night was falling as I checked in at headquarters to find there many an old friend I had known in other days. We talked till late. Then I unpacked and laid out my battle gear—the worn and stained old combat dress I'd worn in Europe. By dawn the next morning I was on my way, by air, to the advanced CP two hundred miles north at Seoul. I flew by B-17, an old warhorse of an airplane I had known since 1936, when I flew with the late Bob Olds in the second one that was ever commissioned. I crawled through the little door, climbed over the catwalk through the bomb bay, crept on my hands and knees to the bombardier's place in the nose, and settled down there, feeling a rush of warm affection for this most rugged and graceful of all our bombers.

There is no substitute for personal reconnaissance, so on my order we flew a roundabout route, covering some sixty miles of rugged mountain country. Peering down from three thousand feet, I traced on a map the ridge lines where later on a reorganized Eighth Army could stand and fight. The sight of this terrain was of little comfort to a soldier commanding a mechanized army. The granite peaks rose to six thousand feet, the ridges were knife-edged, the slopes steep, and the narrow valleys twisted and turned like snakes. The roads were trails, and the lower hills were covered with scrub oaks and stunted pines, fine cover for a single soldier who knew how to conceal himself. It was guerrilla country, an ideal battleground for the walking Chinese rifleman, but a miserable place for our road-bound troops who moved on wheels.

Wars are fought, though, where armies face each other, and it was the will of God that here we should meet our enemy. We could only make the best of it.

I flew on to Seoul, to the advance CP, to find to my great disappointment only a handful of officers there. The others were back at Taegu, two hundred miles from the front—a situation I resolved to remedy at once. I called first on our Ambassador, Mr. Muccio, and then, with him, paid my devoirs to His Excellency, President Rhee. He welcomed me graciously.

"General," he said, "I am glad to see you."

"Mr. President," I said, "I am glad to be here. And I've come to stay."

There was no bluster in that statement. I meant it from the heart. We were faced with only two alternatives here. We could stand and fight and conquer. Or we could be driven into the sea. And to the second possibility I never gave the slightest thought.

For three days I traveled the front, talking with the commanders who faced the enemy beyond the Han. I rode in an open jeep, and would permit no jeep with the top up to operate in the combat zone. Riding in a closed vehicle in a battle area puts a man in the wrong frame of mind. It gives him an erroneous sense of warmth, of safety. His mental attitude is that of an ostrich poking his head in the sand. Also, I held to the old-fashioned idea that it helped the spirits of the men to see the Old Man up there, in the snow and the sleet and the mud, sharing the same cold, miserable existence they had to endure. As a consequence, I damn near froze. I had only a little flat-topped cloth cap I had worn in Europe. It had no ear flaps, no fur lining. I was wearing civilian gloves. Finally, some kindhearted major dug up a pile-lined cap for me and a pair of good, warm gloves. I can't remember his name now, but I'll never cease to bless him for his kindness.

I must say, in all frankness, that the spirit of the Eighth Army as I found it on my arrival there gave me deep concern. There was a definite air of nervousness, of gloomy foreboding, of uncertainty, a spirit of apprehension as to what the future held. There was much "looking over the shoulder," as the soldiers say. There was good reason for this. When I arrived, only three of the seven U.S. combat divisions were in the battle zone. The 24th and 25th, at about two-thirds of their fighting strength, were in contact with the enemy. The 1st Cavalry, also far under strength, was in a blocking position to the rear. The 2nd Division, still non-effective as a fighting unit, was reorganizing and refitting in the far south of the peninsula. The 1st Marine Division had just closed in the Masan area on the south coast, and the 3rd and 7th Divisions, which had also been mauled in the north, were still moving south by sea.

My first contacts, therefore, were with the divisions holding the line beyond the Han. And my first task was to infuse these commanders with the confidence which I felt. For I was sure, deep in my heart, that all we had to do was pull ourselves together, take stock of our capabilities, and use those capabilities to the fullest. If we did that, we could make a different war of it; we could beat these Asiatic hordes to their knees. It was clear to me that our troops had lost confidence. I could sense it the moment I came into a command post. I could read it in their eyes, in their walk. I could read it in the faces of their leaders, from sergeants right on up to the top. They were unresponsive, reluctant to talk. I had to drag information out of them. There was a complete absence of that alertness, that aggressiveness, that you find in troops whose spirit is high.

Having lost their aggressiveness, their *esprit*, their eagerness to fight, they seemed to have forgotten, too, a great many of the basic, unchanging principles of war. They were not patrolling as they should. Their knowledge of the enemy's location and his strength was pitifully inadequate. There are two kinds of information that no commander can do without—information pertaining to the enemy, which we call combat intelligence, and information on the terrain. Both are vital. I told these commanders that I had learned in my military primer, and I supposed that they had learned the same, that the first rule in war is to make contact with your enemy at the earliest possible moment. Once you get that physical contact, you never lose it. You hang on to it with a bulldog grip. Here the enemy was leaning right up against us, but we did not know his strength, and we did not have his location pinpointed on a map. All Intelligence could show me was a big red goose egg out in front of us, with "174,000" scrawled in the middle of it. I immediately ordered vigorous and aggressive patrolling all along that thinly held 135-mile line. We would find the enemy and poke and prod him until he revealed his positions and his strength. At the same time, I ordered every unit to do its utmost to kill or capture the Red patrols which every night were sneaking into our lines.

The second type of vital battle information is information of the terrain. I told these commanders I didn't want to ask any man where a trail went and have him tell me he didn't know. It was his business to know what lay in front of him, what kind of vegetation was there for cover, how the roads and streams ran, whether a tank could operate there or not. I ran into some attitudes that amazed and angered me. One infantry commander told me he couldn't make contact with the company on his right because his radio was out. I reminded him that the Indians had been able to communicate across a great many miles of open country long before the mind of man had ever conceived of a radio, and I would expect him to do the same. If a vehicle couldn't make it over those hills, then, by God, a good tough pair of legs could make it, and I wanted them used.

Another thing I stressed was the use of firepower. One of my first actions on arrival was to send a message back to the Pentagon expediting the shipment of ten new battalions of field artillery. These guns would be arriving soon, and I wanted them used. Time and again, I told them, in the service schools, and on maneuvers, and time after time in battle in Europe, I had heard commanders hollering for help when they still had from a half to a fourth of their firepower unused. I said I didn't want to hear any commander asking for help until he could show me he was using every weapon that he had, every rifle, every machine gun, every howitzer, AA gun, and tank.

Then I talked about supply. I pointed out to them that every item a soldier used up there had to come from nine thousand miles away. That took time, and it cost money. And I didn't want to hear of any more precious equipment being abandoned. Any man who lost or threw away or needlessly damaged any piece of equipment or property was going to be court-martialed.

Then I talked a little about leadership. I told them their soldier forebears would turn over in their graves if they heard some of the stories I had heard about the behavior of some of our troop leaders in combat. The job of a commander was to be up where the crisis of action was taking place. In time of battle, I wanted division commanders to be up with their forward battalions, and I wanted corps commanders up with the regiment that was in the hottest action. If they had paper work to do, they could do it at night. By day their place was up there where the shooting was going on.

The power and the prestige of America was at stake out here, I told them, and it was going to take guns and guts to save ourselves from defeat. I'd see to it they got the guns. The rest was up to them, to their character, their competence as soldiers, their calmness, their judgment, and their courage.

Exhortation would have done no good, I know, without works to back it up. Before we could put up any sort of fight we had to organize the ground. The first day there I had called upon President Rhee for thirty thousand native laborers. He provided the first ten thousand by dawn the next morning. We equipped them with picks and shovels and axes, and they began to dig and string with barbed wire the strong, deep, fortified positions from which we would meet the onslaught which I was sure was soon to come.

These were some of the things I said, and did, in my first three days in Korea. There was nothing brilliant about them. They were simple grass-roots things that any seasoned commander would have ordered in that situation.

There was still one great question that lurked in the minds of the troops, and it was basic. That question was simply this: Why do we fight at all? What the hell are we doing here, in this God-forgotten spot? Back in the States some commentator had said that in Korea we were fighting the wrong war in the wrong place against the wrong enemy, and that glib generalization had made a deep impression on the men of Eighth Army. One night in my room I sat down, and out of the depths of my own great faith in our cause, I tried to answer.

The answer to the first question, "Why are we here?" [I wrote] is simple and conclusive. We are here because of the decisions of the properly constituted authorities of our respective governments. As the Commander in Chief, United Nations Command, General of the Army Douglas MacArthur has said: "This command intends to maintain a military position in Korea just as long as the Statesmen of the United Nations decide we should do so." The answer is simple because further comment is unnecessary. It is conclusive because the loyalty we give, and expect, precludes any slightest questioning of these orders.

The second question is of much greater significance, and every member of this command is entitled to a full and reasoned answer. Mine follows.

To me the issues are clear. It is not a question of this or that Korean town or village. Real estate is, here, incidental. It is not restricted to the issue of freedom for our South Korean Allies, whose fidelity and valor under the severest stresses of battle we recognize; though that freedom is a symbol of the wider issues, and included among them.

The real issues are whether the power of Western civilization, as God has permitted it to flower in our own beloved lands, shall defy and defeat Communism; whether the rule of men who shoot their prisoners, enslave their citizens, and deride the dignity of man, shall displace the rule of those to whom the individual and his individual rights are sacred; whether we are to survive with God's hand to guide and lead us, or to perish in the dead existence of a Godless world.

If these be true, and to me they are, beyond any possibility of challenge, then this has long since ceased to be a fight for freedom for our Korean Allies alone and for their national survival. It has become, and it continues to be, a fight for our own freedom, for our own survival, in an honorable, independent national existence.

The sacrifices we have made, and those we shall yet support, are not offered vicariously for others, but in our own direct defense.

In the final analysis, the issue now joined right here in Korea is whether Communism or individual freedom shall prevail; whether the flight of fear-driven people we have witnessed here shall be checked, or shall at some future time, however distant, engulf our own loved ones in all its misery and despair.

These are the things for which we fight. Never have members of any military command had a greater challenge than we, or a finer opportunity to show ourselves and our people at their best—and thus to do honor to the profession of arms, and to those brave men who bred us.

I knew our testing was soon to come. The last of the Old Year would, I thought, bring the general attack, all along the line, that the Chinese had obviously been so long preparing. I had been in Korea a little less than a week. In this short space I had done, I felt, everything that possibly could be done in the time available to prepare the troops in contact for the onslaught. We had added depth to their disposition. We were preparing, with the native laborers, strong defensive positions both north and south of the Han. Plans for withdrawal under pressure were thoroughly co-ordinated between the several corps, particularly the I and IX Corps in the critical area. X Corps

was still assembling at Pusan after its skillful evacuation from Hungnam, and its elements were being hurried northward to the battle
zone as fast as they came ashore. The 2nd Division, still refitting and
refilling, was about to begin moving up to join the battle.

All intelligence reports clearly indicated the probable direction of
the main attack. The Chinese, we thought, would drive straight south
down the age-old invasion routes from Uijongbu to Seoul. A strong
secondary smash, by North Korean forces, would move from the
Hwachon area toward the road center at Chunchon.

It is the basic responsibility of a field commander to anticipate
where the crisis of battle will occur, and to be there when it develops.
Only in this way can he see with his own eyes what is happening, and
get a proper sensing of the reactions of his subordinates and their
troops. Accordingly, on Sunday morning, the 31st of December, I told
my chief of staff that I was moving up at once to my advanced command post at Seoul. I expected the attack might come on New Year's
Eve. If it did not develop by the 2nd of January, I would return.
Meanwhile, I directed him to push with utmost vigor the movement
to the battle zone of every available unit in the south.

I landed at Seoul airport at eleven-thirty and arrived in the city
about noon. Immediately, after a quick lunch, I moved out by jeep
to the command posts of I and IX U.S. Corps, the forces that lay
astride the axis along which we expected the attack to come. For
two hours that afternoon I rode that thin defensive line, stopping to
talk with the unit commanders. It was lovely hill country, but very
lonely and wild—rough land that soaked up infantry as a sponge
soaks up water. In the zone of the British Commonwealth Brigade,
I came upon one magnificent young British lieutenant, out with a
working party, preparing a ridge-line defensive position. He met me
with a flourishing salute and a cheerful smile. I asked him if there
was anything I could do to help him. He said there was not a thing.

"You think everything's all right up here?" I asked.

"Splendid, sir," he said. Then, as an afterthought: "It is a bit
drahfty, though."

He was right. It was drafty up there. He had a thousand yards to
cover with a handful of men. But it couldn't be helped. Every other
unit along that line was spread as thinly. The day was waning as I
left him to return to Seoul.

Two hours later, just after full dark, the Chinese struck. They came along the route we had anticipated—but in strength it was beyond our power to withstand. All night long, at my CP back in Seoul, the fragmentary reports came in of Chinese storming by thousands against our lines. We were killing them by thousands, too, but they kept coming on. By morning, on a six-mile front, they were driving deep into our lines, smashing against the 1st and 7th ROK divisions and the 19th U.S. Infantry on the left flank of the 24th. And the ROK's had broken and had begun to run.

At dawn I headed for the front by jeep, toward the ROK sector, the point of deepest penetration. Only a few miles north of Seoul, I ran head-on into that fleeing army. I'd never had such an experience before, and I pray to God I never witness such a spectacle again. They were coming down the road in trucks, the men standing, packed so close together in those big carriers another small boy could not have found space among them. They had abandoned their heavy artillery, their machine guns—all their crew-served weapons. Only a few had kept their rifles. Their only thought was to get away, to put miles between them and the fearful enemy that was at their heels.

I jumped from my jeep and stood in the middle of the road, waving them to a halt. I might as well have tried to stop the flow of the Han. I spoke no Korean, and had no interpreter with me. I could find no officer who spoke English. The only solution was to let them run— and to set up road blocks far enough back where they could be stopped, channeled into bivouac areas, calmed down, refitted, and turned to face the enemy again. I went back immediately to order these straggler posts set up.

It must be remembered that from the beginning those troops had been mauled as few armies in history have been mauled. During the early months of the Korean War they had been practically decimated. Their leaders had been killed or captured, and as they faced the Chinese in those last days of the dying year the officers commanding divisions had had no more experience than a company commander should have had, if as much.

Still, I was sure they could be made to stand and fight again. I called on Syngman Rhee for help. I asked him if he would go up to the front with me, find these troops, talk to them and try to put some heart back in them. He agreed immediately. We flew in bitter cold, in little unheated planes, the battered old canvas-covered Cubs of World War II. The temperature aloft was close to zero, and I nearly froze, though I was bundled in my heavy GI winter gear. President Rhee flew in his native dress, in a long white cotton kimono and low shoes, without even a scarf at his neck. His wrinkled, brown old face seemed to shrivel with the cold, but he never uttered a word of complaint.

We found them, as I had anticipated, where the MP road blocks had stopped them. They had been fed. They were being rearmed. Their first great panic was over. The brave old President addressed them with fiery eloquence. I could not understand what he said, but the effect of his words was obvious.

As we left them, he placed his hand upon my arm. "Do not be discouraged," he said. "They will fight again."

An army commander must be ambidextrous. With one hand he must guide and direct his corps commanders as they fight their divisions. With the other hand he must control the vast logistical complex which supplies the men in combat. For two days and nights, as we fought north of the Han, by jeep and light plane, I traveled the surging battle line, visiting each division in action. Our situation was precarious. In front of us was a fired-up, resolute enemy. At our backs was a broad, half-frozen river, its lower, tidal sections filled with floating ice that alternately froze solid and then broke under the rise and fall of the tides. And our only route of withdrawal was across the two fifty-ton floating bridges that spanned the Han at Seoul.

I had known that if the Chinese came in strength we could not hold for long. Our job, therefore, was to fight a stubborn delaying action—to kill as many of them as we could, and then under pressure to break off action quickly, and fall back swiftly across the Han to a new defensive line that had already been prepared, fifteen miles to the south.

Late in the afternoon of January 2, I made one last tour of the lines. Traveling by open jeep I found all the corps and division commanders in action there, and got their estimates. The pressure was building up. It was time to go. Reluctantly, the next morning, I gave the order to fall back south of the Han, to leave Korea's ancient capital, Seoul, once more in the hands of the enemy.

25

☆☆☆☆

Ice on the Han River

THE Han River, where it flows through the outskirts of Seoul, is as wide and deep as the Potomac where it flows past Washington. In that bitter January cold the ice was four or five inches thick, frozen solid except in the water adjacent to the floating bridges. There men in rubber boats, armed with pike poles, fought the grinding ice floes away from the pontoons, in scenes reminiscent of the painting of George Washington crossing the Delaware. On these light, floating bridges the fate of our Army depended. Beyond the Han were nearly 100,000 fighting men. Beyond it were all the heavy guns and tanks that were in the combat zone. And all of these, men and guns, had to be brought back across these bridges, or remain to be destroyed.

So vital were these bridges to I and IX Corps that I selected Brigadier General C. D. Palmer of the 1st Cavalry Division as Traffic Control Officer, gave him full authority to act in my name, and made him personally responsible for the safety of the bridges, and the flow of traffic over them.

The decision to evacuate Seoul, which I conveyed to President Rhee as soon as the orders had gone out to the troops, set off one of the greatest mass flights of a frightened people in all history. More than a million people lived in the city of Seoul. Out of the narrow alleys and byways of that great metropolis, at least a million of them poured toward those two bridges across the Han. Until three o'clock in the afternoon of January 3, we let them pass. Then, as the first elements of the withdrawing combat units approached the bridgeheads, on my orders the bridges were closed to all but military traffic.

At that hour, I left my command post in the city and drove to the river front. Already, the trucks were rolling bumper to bumper across the sagging, swaying bridges. Behind them came the heavy eight-inch howitzers and the tanks, spaced at intervals of seventy-five yards, for the bridges could bear the weight of only one of these ponderous weapons at a time.

I stood there until dark, watching the pontoons sink and rise again, praying, as I know all of us were praying, that the bridges would hold. But my thoughts did not dwell alone on our own military problems. Off to the right and left of the bridges was being enacted one of the great human tragedies of our time. In a zero wind that seared the face like a blow torch, hundreds of thousands of Koreans were running, stumbling, falling, as they fled across the ice. Women with tiny babies in their arms, men bearing their old, sick, crippled fathers and mothers on their backs, others bent under great bundles of household gear flowed down the northern bank and across the ice toward the frozen plain on the southern shore. Some pushed little two-wheeled carts piled high with goods and little children. Others prodded burdened oxen. Now and then an ox would go down, all four legs asprawl, and the river of humanity would break and flow around him, for in this terrible flight no man stopped to help his neighbor.

There was no weeping, no crying. Without a sound, except the dry whisper of their slippers on the snow, and the deep pant of their hard-drawn breath, they moved in utter silence. Until long after dark, I stood there watching that endless flow, while across the bridges men and guns, tanks and trucks, moved in an unbroken stream.

It was a sight to be remembered as long as those of us who witnessed it shall live. The next day I called the war correspondents together. I told them that what we had seen here was one of the great tragic dramas of our times, a revelation stark and unmistakable of the terror which fills the hearts of men and women when they are faced with life under Communist control. I told them I hoped they would use all their verbal powers to convey to our settled, placid, peaceful people back home this pageant of human fear and human misery which we had witnessed. There was, I felt, a great lesson for all those at home in this thing that had happened so far away upon the frozen

Han. What would happen to us, if, in the dead of winter, under the threat of atomic attack, we tried to evacuate a city of two million people? Where would our people go? How would they survive when all the roads were closed to them, and an MP with a rifle ordered them from their automobiles and sent them on foot into the hills? These fleeing Koreans were a tough but docile people, inured to hardship, accustomed to taking orders. How would Americans, physically soft, but stubbornly independent, accustomed to doing as they damn well pleased, survive such an exodus?

I stayed on the banks of the Han until I was satisfied that we had successfully brought off this trickiest and most dangerous of all military maneuvers, the withdrawal of a fighting force in the face of a pursuing enemy. We had done our best. We had fought with an icy river at our backs, we had achieved maximum delay, we had inflicted heavy casualties. A great part of our Eighth Army had been saved. As bitterly as I regretted the necessity for withdrawal, I took great comfort from this fact.

Back in my own bleak room at Seoul, I prepared to join the movement to the south. Carefully I put Penny and Matty's picture in my brief case and gathered up my meager gear. As I was putting my few personal belongings—some extra socks, a shirt or two—in my musette bag, I found that the bottom half of one pair of striped flannel pajamas had seen better days. It was split beyond repair in the upper posterior region—owing, I hasten to add, entirely to fair wear and tear in the government service.

My orderly wanted it for a shoe rag, but there was, I felt, a far better use for it than that.

We tacked it up on my office wall—the faded, torn, and worn-out seat flapping derisively in the breeze. Above it, in large block letters we left this message:

TO THE COMMANDING GENERAL
CHINESE COMMUNIST FORCES—
WITH THE COMPLIMENTS OF
THE COMMANDING GENERAL
EIGHTH ARMY.

26

☆☆☆☆

Eighth Army Finds Itself

WE came back fast, but as a fighting army, not as a running mob. We brought our dead and wounded with us, and our guns, and our will to fight. Fifteen miles south of the Han, on the ridge lines I had marked on the map in that first flight to Seoul, the two corps turned and drew abreast. Here we faced the enemy, not from shallow foxholes but from a defense in depth, a strongly fortified line of gun emplacements and log barriers which the Korean civilians, in ten days of prodigious labor, had prepared. Here, dug in and ready, we awaited an attack that did not come.

Immediately we started patrolling, back over the roads we had come, reaching out toward the enemy to take him by the throat. Steadily, on my orders, these reconnaissance detachments were increased in size and strength. First they were platoon-size—thin fingers poking out into no man's land. Then they went out in company strength. Then we began punching out with infantry battalions, reinforced with armor and artillery, and then, by January 15, with regimental combat teams moving out in front of each division. And then we struck deep with a division from each corps.

Again our great handicap was lack of information. The reconnaissance elements went out into empty hills, drew fire, came back to report a handful of enemy here, a stronger force there. The best G-2 could give me was a big goose egg on the map, with the enemy's strength still estimated at 174,000 men. It was up to me as the responsible commander to confirm or disprove this estimate. On January 24, with Lieutenant General Partridge, Commander of the Fifth Air Force, at the controls of a two-seat trainer plane, I flew twenty miles into enemy territory. For two hours we flew over that lonely, empty land, skimming the ridge tops, ducking into the valleys, circling over the little dead villages. Over all this snowy land, which covered our entire battlefront, we saw no sign of life or movement. No smoke came from the chimneys, and nothing moved either on or off the roads, neither vehicles, men nor animals. In only one little village, that lay at the head of a valley, did I see faint signs that troops were there. From this huddle of thatched houses a thin line of cart tracks led from the outskirts of the village into the dense pine woods on the hills above. It was clear that here, in this village, the enemy was taking shelter against the bitter cold by night, moving out before sun-up to hide in the woods, for with our bomber aircraft hunting targets like hungry hawks hunting mice, a village was no safe place to be by day. I flew back to my headquarters pondering what I had seen. The information I had gathered was negative. But I was satisfied in my own mind that, if I should order an attack, I would not be sending Eighth Army into a trap in which it could be destroyed.

All along the two-corps front the attack jumped off at dawn of January 25. It was never stopped until it had driven the enemy back across the Parallel. But it was hard and bloody fighting all the way, for in those snowy valleys that looked so empty from the air, thousands of Chinese riflemen had been hidden.

Through January and on into February, the attack rolled on. In mid-February the Chinese, side-slipping to the east, struck back in counter-attack, and the 2nd Division took another hard blow. But we quickly contained that break-through, closed up, and the momentum of our forward movement was never stayed thereafter. By the end of March we were crossing the Parallel, and the spirit of the Army was at its peak.

It is hard for me to put into words the magnificent competence, the fierce, combative, aggressive spirit of that force once it had picked itself up off the ground and waded back into the fight. I well remember seeing it at first hand, in the last parachute drop in the valley at Munsan-Ni, a village which, coincidentally, was to become the site of the first peace talks. It was the 24th of March, 1951, a fine clear day, with a little snow still lying in the hollows of the ground. Our plan was to drop a regimental combat team in about twenty miles, then to slam an armored column to them over the roads, hoping to catch a large number of Chinese in the jaws of this nutcracker. As an old paratrooper, I had a tremendous desire to jump in with that airborne unit. As an army commander I knew it would be a damn fool thing to do. I was fifty-six years old. My bones had grown more brittle and my joints had stiffened since I had jumped in Normandy. I could easily crack an ankle or a knee on landing, and I'd have to turn over command of Eighth Army. As much as the idea appealed to me, I could find no justification for it.

I was, however, resolved to be there at the moment of the jump, in a light plane that could land among them, so I could get a close-up look at the fight. George Lynch was my pilot, an old combat infantryman who had switched to air to become one of the most skillful, most courageous, most level-headed light-plane pilots with whom I have ever flown.

We took off early, and alone, hurrying to get there in our slow-flying Cub before the Flying Boxcars, bringing in the first serials, could arrive. We flew at three thousand feet, above the range of small-arms fire. We got there and began to circle just as the first serials came in. It was a good drop. We had improved our techniques some since World War II. We were dropping jeeps now, under big cargo canopies, and 105 howitzers, a heavier gun than we'd been able to take in on the drops in Europe.

As the troopers landed and the fire fight on the ground began, I told George I wanted to land. He picked out a little narrow dirt road, and dropped down to look it over. The chances were good it might be mined and we had no desire to come down on a charge of buried explosives. We saw no signs of mining on either the road or the shoulders, so we pulled up to circle once more and land. By this time, though, the road was full of paratroopers, staring up at us curiously. We swooped over low, waving for them to get the hell out of the way. They didn't move. We tried it again, waving our arms and cussing them in every language we could think of. They merely waved back cheerily. After about five passes, though, when I was beginning to get really provoked with these men, it finally dawned on somebody down there that we wanted to land. So they cleared the road and we came on in. We hit and rolled along this little high-crowned, narrow-shouldered road, across a little culvert, and I got out and told Lynch to park his plane wherever he could. Then, for no particular reason, except an old soldier's wariness, I guess, I stepped off the road and peered into this culvert. There were five Chinese in there, all dead, so recently shot that the blood was still oozing from their head wounds. They had taken cover as the paratroops came down and had been trapped in there. About that time, a little hostile mortar fire began to come in, and I walked back up the road. I heard the bang of an M-1 on the slope above me, and a thrashing in the bushes, and a Chinese came rolling down, looking round and bulky in his padded uniform. He rolled down the hill and hung on the bank above me. He was dead, I guess. He didn't move.

Lynch, my pilot, was having himself a field day. He had grabbed a carbine out of the plane when we landed, and when that dead Chinese came rolling down, all his old infantryman's instincts surged up in him. He was out for bear, and thoroughly enjoying it, as was Walter Winton, my gallant aide, who had landed not far away in another Cub plane.

There was a great deal of sporadic shooting going on, here and there, as the assembling troops hunted the Reds down like rabbits. And I remember feeling that lifting of the spirits, that quickening of the breath and the sudden sharpening of all the senses that comes to a man in the midst of battle. It was good to be in action again, good to be down on the ground with a parachute assault element in a fight. Lynch, I know, enjoyed it as much as I did, the crack of the M-1's, the crump of the incoming mortars—so long, of course, as they didn't get too close.

Months later, when the peace talks had started at Munsan-Ni, I found my tent set up on a familar-looking stretch of road. It was the road where Lynch and I had landed. And just a hundred yards from my door was the culvert where I'd seen the dead Chinese.

It was during our drive to the north that a little thing occurred which I would like to explain. In early March I was up with a forward battalion of the 1st Marine Division, standing on a snowy bank above a muddy road, watching a file of troops move up the road to battle. Just below me a gaunt Marine was trudging by with a heavy radio on his back. One of his boot laces was untied and trailing in the snow, and with every other step he took he stepped on it and stumbled. I knew if he should kneel, to try to tie it, he could not get up again.

He stopped just below me in the road and said something. Later, I was told that he called out to the other Marines:

"Hey, how about one of you sonsabitches tying my shoe?"

I didn't hear him say that, though it would not have made any difference if I had, for in the Marine Corps such an appellation is a term of affection. All I knew was that he needed help. I hesitated just a moment, knowing that what I wanted to do might be misconstrued as showmanship. Then I slid down the bank on my tail, landed right at his feet, knelt down and tied his shoe. Later, when this incident was reported in the States, there were some who did interpret it as a theatrical gesture. This was not true. It was purely an impulse to help a fighting soldier, a man in trouble. I was also told that the grenades I wore on a harness at my chest were worn for picturesque effect, as a trademark like George Patton's pearl-handled pistols. There was no truth in that either. They were purely for self-preservation. I'd learned long before in Europe that a man with a grenade in his hand can often blast his way out of a tight spot. And in Korea I was determined that, in my prowling along the battlefront, I wasn't going to be ambushed and captured without a fight.

The American flag never flew over a prouder, tougher, more spirited and more competent fighting force than was Eighth Army as it drove north beyond the Parallel. It was a magnificent fighting organization, supremely confident that it could take any objective assigned to it.

Military men, and statesmen, too, will long debate the wisdom of stopping that proud Army in its tracks at the first whisper that the Reds might be ready to sue for peace. To my mind it is fruitless to speculate on what might have been. If we had been ordered to fight our way to the Yalu, we could have done it—if our government had been willing to pay the price in dead and wounded that action would have cost. From the purely military standpoint the effort, to my mind, would have not been worth the cost. A drive to the line of the Yalu and the Tumen would have cleared Korea of the Chinese enemy. But he would have still been facing us in great strength beyond those rivers. The seizure of the land between the truce line and the Yalu would have merely meant the seizure of more real estate. It would have greatly shortened the enemy's supply lines by pushing him right up against his main supply bases in Manchuria. It would have greatly lengthened our own supply routes, and widened our battle-front from 110 miles to 420. Would the American people have been willing to support the great army that would have been required to hold that line? Would they have approved our attacking on into Manchuria? On into the heart of the great mainland of Asia, a bottomless pit into which all the armies of the whole free world could be drawn and be ground to bits and destroyed? I doubt it.

I was not privy to the councils that were going on back home. It is clear to me, though, that when all the factors were taken into consideration, it was decided that the political advantage of driving the Chinese back to their lair was not worth the blood it would have cost. I would not quarrel with that decision. We were driving north with half a million men. The Chinese, desperately pouring reinforcements south to bolster their retreating armies, probably numbered three-quarters of a million when the ceasefire came. Knowing the spirit of our Army, I am fully confident we could have kept on driving them back, certainly to the waist of the peninsula. We stopped, instead, on what I believe to be the strongest line in our immediate front —a line I believe the trained ROK armies now can hold.

No thoughts of truce or peace talks, though, were in my mind on the dreary afternoon of April 11, 1951. I was far up front in a hail and snow storm, with Secretary of the Army Frank Pace, who had come out on an inspection trip. A newspaperman, whose face I vividly recall, but whose name I cannot now remember, walked up and put out his hand.

"Well, General," he said, "I guess congratulations are in order."

I looked at him, puzzled.

"What for?" I said.

It was his turn to look puzzled.

"You mean you don't know?" he said.

"Don't know what?" I said. "What's this all about?"

He didn't answer, but turned and walked away. I turned to Mr. Pace. He gave me no sign that he had heard what had been said.

Late that night, back at my command post, an urgent message came for me, over the official radio.

It told me that President Truman had relieved General MacArthur of command and I had been appointed in his place. For several hours, without my knowledge, I had been Supreme Commander in the Far East.

27

☆☆☆☆

Supreme Commander, Far East

AS I left Eighth Army for my new duties in Tokyo, I felt in my heart a tremendous pride and affection for these magnificent fighting men who had come back from the brink of disaster to mold themselves into one of the toughest, most competent, most spirited, and most valiant armies the modern world has ever seen. In every respect, they had fully justified my faith in them.

On the occasion of my taking command on December 26, 1951, I had written and distributed to the troops this brief message:

I have, with little advance notice, assumed heavy responsibilities in battle before, but never with greater opportunities for service to our loved ones and our nation in beating back a world menace which free peoples cannot tolerate.

It is an honored privilege to share this service with you, and with our comrades of the Navy and the Air Force. You will have my utmost. I shall expect yours.

And they had indeed given me, and the land from which they had sprung, their utmost.

Four days later, in a New Year's message, I had said:

Having performed with great gallantry and skill under conditions as adverse as any United States forces have encountered since Valley Forge, there is no shadow of a doubt of the character of this Army's future conduct, teamed as it is with our own great services, and our Allies.

We face severe trials. We shall need dogged determination in attack, and utmost tenacity in defense. We shall need resourcefulness.

The action of one single platoon or squad may vitally affect the whole command.

Never have leaders, in both command and staff, had a greater challenge, or a finer opportunity to show America at its best.

I have complete confidence in our ultimate success.

May God be with you in the coming year.

The severe trials did come, within hours after this message was distributed. Eighth Army did meet them with dogged determination and utmost tenacity and resourcefulness. From top to bottom, its leaders met their challenge, from rifle squad to corps. And God was with Eighth Army as, strong, and proud, and spirited, it fought for General James A. Van Fleet, as valiantly as it had fought under my command.

It was a hot assignment into which I had been thrown on such short notice. As Commanding General of Eighth Army, I had been responsible only for the success of the Allied arms in battle in Korea. Now, as Supreme Commander Allied Powers, Far East, and Commander in Chief of the United Nations Command, I was responsible for one of the great bastions of the free world. Overnight, I had to broaden my horizons to embrace a tremendous defensive theater that swung in a vast arc from the Aleutians to Formosa.

As Commander of Eighth Army my concern was with the day-to-day military operations—the movement of fighting forces forward or back as the tides of battle swung. The greater threat, of what the U.S.S.R. might do, was a worry to rack the minds of men on higher levels than I. There was the possibility that Russia might attack Japan, through northern Hokkaido, which lay well within the range of Russian planes and paratroopers—with only one U.S. division, the 45th, to oppose them there if they should come. To the south, in Honshu, the 40th Division was on guard, but all the land in between, the Kanto plain, had been stripped of U.S. troops.

There was also the possibility that the Russians, if they chose to enter the war, might do it by dropping an atomic bomb on Pusan and Inchon, the Korean harbors through which five-sixths of our supplies were flowing.

All these possibilities up to now had been the responsibility of General MacArthur—along with the problems of administering the domestic affairs of the conquered Japanese and the thorny question of Formosa, where Chiang Kai-shek's troops glowered ominously westward toward the Red mainland.

And now these worries were mine—the full responsibilities mine, in a bigger job by far than any I had ever tackled before.

By noon on the 12th of April I was on my way to Tokyo, for a preliminary conference with General MacArthur. I went directly to his office from Haneda airport, and he received me at once, with the greatest courtesy. I had a natural human curiosity to see how he had been affected by his peremptory removal from his high post. He was entirely himself—composed, quiet, temperate, friendly, and helpful to the man who was to succeed him. He made some allusions to the fact that he had been summarily relieved, but there was no trace of bitterness or anger in his tone. I thought it was a fine tribute to the resilience of this great man that he could accept so calmly, with no outward sign of shock, what must have been a devastating blow to a professional soldier standing at the peak of a great career.

The question as to who was right and who was wrong in that controversy will rage, no doubt, so long as history is written. I have already expressed my views on the point that was at the core of the dispute—the advisability of our driving the Chinese across the Yalu. As a soldier, I do not question the right of the President, as Commander in Chief, to relieve any officer with whose views and actions he disagrees. Out of the great admiration and respect I hold in my heart for General MacArthur, though, I do feel that his dismissal could have been handled with more grace.

In the hours I spent with General MacArthur, we reviewed the whole scope and range of my responsibilities. I then started back from Tokyo to Korea, to wind up my affairs there and turn over my command. We flew by night, in Mr. Pace's Constellation, a far faster and more comfortable plane than my own old war-battered B-17. I was getting on with my paper work, as is my habit when in the air, when sometime after midnight the landing light came on. I had told them to take me to K-2, the main airfield at Taegu. Tired and sleepy, I was glad to get home after a long, hard day. I fastened my belt, leaned back, and thought how good a bed would feel. I felt the wheels touch down, always a happy moment, when suddenly the plane gave a great lurch, and everything banged around inside the ship. There was a great squealing of tires and gravel rattled against the wings like pistol shots.

The crew chief came back with a kind of funny look on his face. "General," he said, "did you want K-37?"

"Hell, no," I said. "I did not want K-37. I wanted K-2."

"Well," he said, shaking his head. "I don't know what happened, but this is K-37."

What had happened was simply this. The pilot had come in radio range, contacted the K-2 tower and gotten clearance to land. But he'd never even seen K-2. He'd spotted K-37, a little light-plane strip that had only recently been lengthened to take twin-engine C-47's. It was never meant to take a big four-engined ship at all. It was five miles or so from K-2, in the same valley, but it lay right up against the flanks of a big mountain, and it was a tricky place to come into, even for a C-47. He told me later that he didn't even see that mountain. He didn't have the faintest idea it was there. So I had to bounce home to Taegu in the dark, in a jeep, to report to Mr. Pace that his beautiful Constellation was trapped, at least for a little while, on a tiny strip five miles away. Later, they got it off all right, but that pilot, I'm sure, took a lot of kidding. I didn't add to his woes. I was too grateful to the good Lord for bringing us safely down.

Within forty-eight hours after I took over as Supreme Commander, Allied Powers, Mr. John Foster Dulles arrived from Washington. He came, quite frankly, to look me over, to assure himself this impetuous combat soldier wouldn't turn out to be a bull in the Japanese china shop. He was the architect of the Japanese peace treaty, and the delicate negotiations leading toward the signing of the peace were then under way.

I was not disturbed by this surveillance. I knew the spot I was in, following in this job a man of the world stature of General MacArthur, who had been dealing with the Japanese government ever since the moment of the surrender. It did not worry me. I didn't pretend to be anything but what I was. All I could do, I figured, was to use the best judgment God gave me. I would call them as I saw them, and I felt supremely confident that if I were given opportunity to analyze the problems that came to me, I could deal with them.

The first hot potato I had to handle was the matter of a huge May Day demonstration by the newly formed labor unions in Japan. Union leaders were insisting that this rally be held on the Imperial Plaza in front of the Emperor's palace. The Japanese government, knowing that the Communists were active in the unions, and fearing a riot, had refused to grant permission. Their ruling was that the unions could hold their rally in Tokyo if they wished but it must be held in another location. To my advisers, this seemed to be a difficult situation. If I failed to back the Japanese government, they said, I would be getting off to a bad start. On the other hand, if I did refuse to permit the rally to be held in the Plaza, British and American union leaders would take offense. It would be interpreted as a slap at the working man. To me there was no problem. The Japanese government had said there would be no rally in the Plaza, and so far as I was concerned, that was that. The rally was not held there, and I never heard a word of protest from the British or American unions.

I received great assistance from Mr. Dulles on his two visits to Tokyo while I was there. He saw the Japanese problem clearly, and saw it whole, and his mature judgment was very helpful to me in forming my own decisions. On his second visit, which came some weeks after I had been in command as SCAP, he told me that he was amazed at the way I had won the confidence of the Japanese government in so short a time.

What degree of confidence I had won was due in large measure to his own help and to the co-operative attitude of the Japanese Prime Minister, Mr. Yoshida. The Prime Minister and I seemed to hit it off well together from the start. I found him frank, courageous, and completely trustworthy. He would come to see me and we would sit for two hours alone, speaking in English, without ever an interpreter present. I would outline to him in my own words the views and wishes of my government as they had been transmitted to me from Washington. He would tell me, with utmost frankness, how he thought these directives would be received by the Japanese people. He never took a note, but he had a photographic memory, for he never failed to carry out in detail everything I asked him to do. At the same time he never failed courageously to present and fight for what he considered Japanese rights. Perhaps the greatest problem was the vital one of reconstituting the Japanese military. It was the firm resolution of both governments to prevent any resurgence of Japanese militarism. At the same time, it was essential to our own defense—and to our finances—that the Japanese reconstitute and support a military force strong enough to defend their own home islands from Russian attack or infiltration. This had to be a ground force sufficiently strong to enable us to withdraw our own troops from Japan in the reasonably early future, together with the necessary air and naval components to provide for minimum needs, with U.S. air and naval strength in reserve, as required.

Here, though, we quickly ran up against the rock of Japanese poverty. The economy of that nation had in great degree been destroyed by the war. Many of her great factories were piles of debris, her huge market in China was lost, and the nation was hard put to support its own people, without taking on the added burden of military expenditures. Throughout our talks, however, I was pressing him hard, urging that the Japanese take on the responsibility for their own defense.

Out of these talks came certain agreements, but with the fall in the political fortunes of Mr. Yoshida, and his departure from the Diet, they have not yet been implemented—at least at anything like the rate he and I together had set as a goal. We had, in principle, agreed that by 1954 the Japanese would field a ground army of 350,000. Toward the end of '55, they had fewer than 120,000 men in uniform, and their air and naval components were equally behind schedule.

It was my belief then, and it is still my belief, that the Japanese economy, weak as it is, could stand a substantially greater military expenditure than her politicians so far have been willing to demand. Before the peace treaty was signed, we could not expect them to do too much. So long as we maintained strong air, naval, and ground forces in their islands, they saw no reason why they should spend heavily for defense. Now that the treaty has been signed and we no longer are there in the capacity of an occupying force, we lack the power to bring pressure upon a nation whose sovereignty has been restored.

My relations with the Emperor were most pleasant. Early in my tour I had conveyed to the Emperor the message that I would be happy to receive him any time he found it convenient to call (I had been advised that under no circumstances should I call on him). He came on a bright May afternoon. I was then living in the Chancery apartment at the foot of the hill on which the Ambassador's residence stands, in an apartment on the second floor. The Emperor arrived, accompanied by a Mr. Matsui, his interpreter. Ambassador Sebald, who was my political adviser, met him on the street level and escorted him up to my apartment, where I met him at the door. I told him, through the interpreter, that it was an honor and a privilege to welcome him here in my temporary home, and expressed the hope that on future occasions we could meet in the Embassy itself, which was then under repair. The Emperor expressed his pleasure at meeting me, and we sat down for our chat. He was, I thought, somewhat tense and nervous to begin with, but when I began a discussion of the war in Korea, some of the tension seemed to go out of his manner and he evinced a great interest. With only his interpreter present, I outlined, from a map I had had prepared, the whole situation on the peninsula. I showed him the dispositions of our troops and of the enemy, going over the situation in considerable detail, giving him our views as to the Red's capability for future offensive actions, as well as our own.

As the talk progressed the Emperor asked questions freely, and seemed to have a very sound grasp of what I was presenting. He was deeply pleased, he said, at my assurance that the war in Korea could, and would, be brought to a satisfactory close, and expressed the hope that relationships between Japan and the Republic of Korea could be worked out satisfactorily.

He expressed his pleasure also at my decision to allow a review of existing directives, imposed by us, which barred certain Japanese from political office who had been active in the war government of Japan. He also said he was pleased at my actions in supporting the Japanese government in opposing the May Day meeting on the Imperial Plaza.

He said he was delighted that the U.S. had seen fit to send troops to protect northern Hokkaido. I told him that we considered the security of Japan intimately related to our own, and that future co-operation between Japan and America was a fundamental in our national policy.

He then said he had heard that Mrs. Ridgway and our little son were to join me soon, a personal query which gratified me, and I asked him if he would like to see pictures of them both. He courteously said he would, and we discussed these small personal family topics for several minutes.

This was the first of several meetings with the Emperor. At each of them, I felt, he grew more at ease, less nervous and self-conscious, and I soon began to feel a sense of friendship for the polite little man who strove so hard to comport himself with dignity in an extremely difficult situation. The thought kept coming back to me that, human pride being what it is, Hirohito handled himself amazingly well in his relationships with the representatives of the nation which had conquered his own country.

We met often again, officially, and also on purely social occasions after Mrs. Ridgway came out to Japan. The Emperor and the Empress invited us to luncheon at the Imperial Palace, a most delicious meal, prepared by a trained French chef and served at tables, Western style. Only the members of his household were present, and it was an extremely pleasant, informal occasion which both Mrs. Ridgway and I thoroughly enjoyed. Again, after the signing of the treaty, just before we were to leave for the States, they invited us to a purely family luncheon in our honor, and we left almost with the feeling that we were saying good-by to an old friend. In my house in Pittsburgh today are four beautiful Japanese vases, two of silver and beaten gold, two of cloisonné, which were personally selected for Mrs. Ridgway by the Emperor's own expert on Japanese art objects.

The signing of the peace treaty with Japan had created something of a domestic problem for the Ridgway family. As Japan became a sovereign nation again, we would, naturally, send out an ambassador and the only proper place for him to live would be in the handsome marble building of the American Embassy, the seat of our diplomats in Japan since long before the war. The arrival of the ambassador would mean we had to move to other quarters.

Other than the inconvenience of moving, and the necessity of furnishing and decorating another house, this did not greatly disturb us. When I went over to Tokyo the first time, immediately following General MacArthur's dismissal, I had expressed the view to our officials there that I did not wish to make my residence in the Embassy. General MacArthur was a figure of world renown, an older officer of great distinction, and I felt that I, as a much younger officer of far less stature and experience, could fittingly choose some other place to live. At first the members of my official family—and even General MacArthur himself—agreed, but when I returned to Tokyo from Korea two days later, to take command, they had completely reversed themselves. The prestige of the United States was at stake, they said, and under no circumstances could I live anywhere else.

So I moved in there, rattling around somewhat in a welter of furniture and bric-a-brac that was considerably dilapidated. The MacArthurs, of course, had taken with them all the beautiful things they had acquired in years of living abroad, and I was left with the basic furnishings of the house, which had been there since before the war.

A few months later, Mrs. Ridgway arrived, bringing out our own furnishings. We had some general painting and refurbishing done, and soon the place again was home, beautifully arranged and decorated with her unerring and exquisite taste.

The signing of the peace treaty meant that all this was to be done over again. So we moved out, to the fine house of Baron Maida, and brightened it up with paint and repairs, and furnished it, and settled down again to make a home.

Our days in Tokyo were considerably brightened by the constant flow of distinguished visitors from the States, many of whom stayed with us, though others preferred to be housed in the fine Chancery apartments at the foot of the hill near the Embassy. General Marshall and Mr. Dulles were the first to come, on brief visits that were official in nature. Others came on a more leisurely schedule which gave them an opportunity to see something of the beauties of Japan. Among these were Senators H. Alexander Smith and John Sparkman and their ladies, Vice President and Mrs. Barkley, and Governor Warren of California, now Chief Justice. Those who were interested—and most were—we sent by car to Nikko and Nara, famous shrines near Tokyo, to see the temples, and the ladies all showed great interest in flower arranging, and the complicated Japanese "tea ceremony." All of them were fascinated by the beautiful silks and brocades to be had in the more expensive shops, and Japanese merchants did a thriving business among our guests.

We lived in the Baron's residence exactly thirty days. Just as the moving and arranging of furniture were done, I received orders to report to Paris. General Eisenhower was returning to the States to enter the Presidential race and I was to take over his duties at SHAPE —Supreme Headquarters Allied Powers Europe.

Many men, even those who fought them so bitterly in the Pacific, have found themselves strangely drawn to the Japanese, and have felt a twinge of deep regret upon leaving those beautiful islands and the friends they made there during occupation days. Mrs. Ridgway and I both felt this emotion deeply. The Prime Minister, Mr. Yoshida, had a farewell dinner for us, a small affair, with perhaps twenty-four guests at table. Toward the end he rose and made a gracious little speech, covering the service he and I had shared together. He showed considerable emotion—remarkable emotion, I thought, for a member of a race which prides itself on concealing its real feelings. At one point, in fact, it seemed to me that he was so deeply moved it would be impossible for him to continue. And I must confess, as I rose to reply, that I felt a great lump in my own throat. We had worked very closely together; we had handled very difficult problems of utmost gravity, and I had come to feel toward him a great warmth, an affection almost, like that which one feels for an old and honored friend.

There was another sentimental moment when the time came to say good-by to the Japanese household staff who had served us so faithfully. They all lined up to say their formal farewells, and then, as we got in the sedan that was to take us to the airport, they reached in through the windows, taking our hands and clinging on, running beside the car until it was going so fast they could keep up no longer.

All the way to the airport, the streets were lined with people waving their good-bys, and I felt that there was more here than mere casual curiosity. There was a palpable warmth of feeling, a sense of good will and friendliness in their presence. It is a happy memory that we still treasure, among the many happy ones we cherish from our days in Japan.

We went to Paris the long way round, via the United States, instead of flying direct from Tokyo. This pleased me, for it would give me a chance to make a brief visit to my mother in San Diego before flying on to Washington. Also, I had been invited to address a joint session of Congress upon my arrival there, a proposal that gave me considerable concern. I worked on an outline of my remarks most of the way across the Pacific, and on reaching San Diego dictated a final draft. My advisers read over what I had prepared and didn't like it. I invited them to produce something better, and they tried their hand. But I didn't like what they had written any more than they liked mine, so I decided to go ahead with my own thoughts, expressed in my own way.

It came off all right. I appeared there before that joint session, and much to my gratification I was not nearly so nervous as I had feared. It was a rare experience. They bring the victim into the Speaker's office, and then lead him in, down the long center aisle, and up to the Speaker's stand. As we walked down my escort remarked that I seemed to be considerably more calm than my predecessor.

"Who was that?" I asked.

"Queen Juliana of the Netherlands," he said.

I must have been more nervous than I realized, of course, for to save my life I cannot now remember that gentleman's name, nor what he looked like.

A few nights earlier, on the long flight over, we had had an experience that was mildly nerve-racking. Our flight plan from Tokyo called for a gas stop at Midway Island, but the pilot had come to me in the middle of the night to say that everything was going fine. We had good winds and plenty of gas, so he planned to go on to Honolulu direct, without stopping for fuel. I told him it was up to him.

Next morning we passed over an island which they said was one of the islands in the Hawaiian group and that we'd land in Honolulu in forty-five minutes. Well, I knew a little about the geography of the Hawaiian Islands, and that didn't look to me like the island they had in mind. So I got out a map and checked, and found that the island we had passed over wasn't the island he said it was at all. We'd been nearly fifteen hours in the air—fourteen and a half or thereabouts—and I knew about how much gas he had. So I went up forward to check. There were three airfields ahead of us—a Navy field at Barber's Point, a Marine field at Ewa, and the big field at Hickam, where we were supposed to land. A decision had to be made fast, whether we'd try for Hickam or touch down at one of the nearer fields. I talked to the flight engineer and could read his very evident concern on his face. I asked the pilot if he'd have to circle, and he said no, the wind was right and we could go straight in. So I said, "All right, I'll make the decision. You go on to Hickam." So we went in there with all four engines leaned down so low they were popping. We had flown nonstop for nearly sixteen hours, and we landed with only about fifteen minutes' worth of gas left in the tanks. It was cutting it a little too thin for my tastes, particularly with my wife and baby aboard. I had at hand the parachute harness for the three of us that I've described before, but jumping out over the ocean, or the rough mountains of Oahu, wouldn't have been a very happy way to end a journey.

28

☆☆☆☆

Supreme Commander, Europe

THE flight from Honolulu to Washington, one of the longest non-stop over-water hops on the world's airways, was made without incident. As I stepped off the plane in Washington, General Bradley met me, and sending Penny and Matty on to the hotel, I went immediately to the White House for a conference with President Truman. The President was gravely concerned about a situation which was also deeply concerning me—the prisoner-of-war riots that had erupted in Korea. He asked me for a briefing on what was happening there, and I detailed for him every step which we had taken. The hard-shelled Communists in the prison camps, I explained, had been growing more and more arrogant and unruly, and this insubordination had reached a climax when General Dodd, the officer in charge of POW enclosures, had been seized and held hostage as he attempted to parley with the prisoners in the camp at Koji-do.

This had happened just a few days before I was to leave the Far East. General Mark Clark had already arrived in Korea to take over from me and the easiest thing would have been just to hand this thing over to him and say: "Here, Mark, it's your baby."

However, I did not wish to hand an old friend such a hot potato, on such short notice. So, on receiving word of General Dodd's capture, I immediately flew to Korea, accompanied by General Clark, to go over the situation on the ground with General Van Fleet, commanding Eighth Army.

In conference with General Van Fleet, I learned that he planned to negotiate with the POW's for General Dodd's release, a procedure which would have taken some forty-eight hours. To me this was unacceptable. However, since any steps we took might affect the peace negotiations at Panmunjom, I felt that I should get the views of Admiral Turner Joy, who was conducting the truce talks for our side. With Clark and Van Fleet I flew to Seoul to see Admiral Joy. He agreed with me completely that we should demand Dodd's release at once, and that we should back up our demands with force.

I then directed Van Fleet, in writing, to establish order in the prison camps immediately and thereafter to maintain it, and to use whatever force was necessary. This order required the movement of a battalion of tanks of the 3rd Division two hundred miles by road from their positions in the north, and their transshipment by LST across to the island. I was determined that if the Red POW's made any resistance, or attempted any delay in carrying out our demands, we would shoot, and I wanted the killing machinery on hand to do a thorough job of it. As it turned out, the use of force was not necessary. Once it became clear to the Communists that we were resolved to back up our demands, General Dodd was released and the situation settled down.

In my view, the whole situation had been ineptly handled by the responsible officers in Korea. The more belligerent Reds in the camps had been arrogant and insubordinate from the beginning, doing all they could to provoke us by singing all night, and crowding against the fences to shout insults at the guards. We should have gone in there immediately and stopped it. There would have been a hell of a bloody howl from Peking, but it would have saved us much trouble and embarrassment thereafter.

Mr. Truman listened with deep attentiveness to my detailed recital and indicated that he fully approved the steps I had taken. Once our official matters had been discussed, the President took General Bradley and me on a tour of the remodeled White House, pointing out the changes that had been made, with the zeal of any proud householder showing off a new home. At the end of the visit he most graciously invited me and Mrs. Ridgway to go with him on the train to West Point a few days later, where he was to deliver the sesquicentennial address, and I accepted gladly. On his own initiative he also arranged to decorate me with the second cluster to the Distinguished Service Medal. The brief ceremony took place before the ten thousand people, including the Corps of Cadets, assembled for the celebration at West Point. His gracious gesture touched me deeply, for it naturally makes a man feel proud to be decorated by his Commander in Chief in the surroundings of his Alma Mater.

During my brief stay in Washington, the Secretary of Defense, Mr. Robert Lovett, gave a luncheon for me in the Defense Department's dining room at the Pentagon. All the top officials of the Department of Defense were there, and a number from State, including Mr. Acheson. The talk was general in nature, ranging the globe in scope, and touching informally on the mutual problems confronting both the military and the diplomats. I was particularly touched by the nice little talk made by Secretary Lovett, who spoke approvingly of my past service in Korea and the Far East, and expressed confidence in my ability to carry out my new responsibilities in Europe.

I had the greatest respect for Mr. Lovett as a dedicated, non-partisan public servant of the ideal type. I had known him first when he came into the Defense Department as Under Secretary, and had come to know him much better when he served as Under Secretary of State under General Marshall. The better I knew him, the more I came to admire his searching powers of analysis. He could listen to the most complex problems and go at once to the heart of the issues involved.

Afterward, when I was Chief of Staff, beset by the many vexations and frustrations which I will discuss in detail later, I thought many times how much happier my service would have been—and how different, perhaps, the course of history—if I had been dealing with Mr. Lovett, instead of Mr. Wilson, as Secretary of Defense. To me Bob Lovett, like General Marshall and Henry L. Stimson, is the highest type of public servant, a man who in the finest tradition of public service rose above all partisanship. I don't believe that anybody could have influenced Bob Lovett to base a decision affecting his country's safety on political motives. I cannot conceive of his ever attempting to force a senior officer to make his reasoned military judgment conform to a political "party line." Though lesser men have made the headlines, history will accord him his proper place.

Shortly before I was to take off for Paris and my new duties as Supreme Commander, Europe, I received a memo from the State Department saying that the French Communists were planning some sort of protest demonstration when I arrived. They intimated that I might want to delay my departure by a few days, to throw these plans out of kilter, and minimize the chance of such an untoward incident occurring at the moment of my arrival. I sent back a message saying that the responsibility for such situations was squarely upon the government of France, and that I had complete confidence in the ability of the French government to handle any incident which might arise. As for myself, I would not change the hour of my arrival by one hour. If the U.S. government wanted to change it, that was its decision to make.

So we flew to Paris on schedule, arriving about eleven o'clock of a fine fair morning. Both General Eisenhower, the Supreme Commander, and his Deputy, Field Marshal Montgomery, were there to meet us, with a guard of honor and many notables. As Penny and I, with Matty right behind us, came down the steps from the plane, General Eisenhower stepped forward, with his usual gracious smile. We would have thought that Matty, even at his age, would have recognized the U.S. Army uniform worn by America's most famous soldier. But evidently he didn't—he trotted right on past General Eisenhower and stuck out his hand to Monty. That pleased the Field Marshal enormously and drew quite a laugh from everybody.

Whatever plans the Communists may have had for giving me a boisterous welcome, they must have abandoned them. As we drove into Paris behind a very impressive motorcycle escort of Metropolitan Police, I saw only one untoward incident. One man broke through a police cordon and started for my car, shouting something unintelligible, but he was quickly collared. In the weeks that followed, we frequently saw signs—"Go Home, Ridgway"—painted on walls, but I did not feel this inhospitable admonition represented the feelings of the French people. One man with a can of paint can attract a lot of attention, and I prefer to remember the warm hospitality, the friendliness that Mrs. Ridgway and I encountered as we traveled, unescorted, about France. We received nothing but courtesy and consideration everywhere, and not the slightest incident occurred throughout our stay except, surprisingly, on our first visit to London, when some "Go Home, Ridgway" leaflets were thrown.

I arrived in Paris on May 26. The following day I met with General Eisenhower, to go over with him the major problems then confronting NATO, and get his views on them. I called on him at his residence, the Villa St. Pierre, a beautiful home into which Mrs. Ridgway and I moved after he and Mrs. Eisenhower had left. It was quite a sumptuous setting for a soldier, for the French government had decorated it for the Supreme Commander with art treasures from the museums. I remember feeling some trepidation that Matty, who was four at the time, and of an exploratory turn of mind, might cause some damage to a piece of priceless bric-a-brac and thus create an international incident.

General Eisenhower was having some sort of very painful and distressing eye trouble, and he received me in his darkened bedroom. He was in bed, propped up on pillows, and wearing dark glasses, but he showed no signs of illness in his manner. He was alert, friendly, and extremely helpful, and it was heartwarming to me to sit there, in the atmosphere of an old friendship that dated back more than thirty years, and hear direct from the distinguished soldier who had guided our armies to victory in World War II his views on how the peace could be won.

The talk, of course, was of the major problems which he must necessarily leave for my decision. Mainly they dealt with command organization—whether there should be one, or two, U.S. commanders; where to fit Greece and Turkey into NATO's territorial organization; the relationship of Admiral Carney, whose command included the U.S. Sixth Fleet, operating in the Mediterranean under the Commander in Chief South, to Lord Mountbatten, when Mountbatten should take over as Commander in Chief Mediterranean.

One big decision which was being left to me was the basic organization of the center, which in the conditions which then existed to me seemed unsound. There was a Commander in Chief, North, and a Commander in Chief, South, but in the most important area, where France would have to be defended—and the defense of France is the key to our whole position in Europe—there were three separate commanders. General Juin, a Frenchman, commanded the ground forces, General Norstad, an American, the Air Forces, and Admiral Joujard, a Frenchman, commanded the Rhine patrol, a naval operation vital to our security.

I immediately raised the question of why this organization existed. To me it seemed cumbersome and unwieldy for the Supreme Commander to have to deal with a triumvirate, when overall command in the center could be vested in one man. General Eisenhower, of course, recognized this weakness in NATO's basic structure. It had grown up, he said, in NATO's earliest days and was a reflection of politics, of national distrust and national pride. Command of NATO, he pointed out, required not only military knowledge, but a great amount of diplomacy, a consummate tact in dealing with touchy problems that had their roots in Europe's ancient hatreds.

This brought us to the discussion of the individuals, both military men and statesmen, with whom I would be dealing. In a masterly series of vignettes he described the character and the attitudes of each, told me the ones I could trust implicitly, and those whom he felt I could not trust. It was an appraisal of men and their motives which proved invaluable to me in the months that followed. In only one case, as I came to know these men, did I feel that his evaluation had been in error. One French statesman whom General Eisenhower felt to be unworthy of trust in all his relationships with me proved forthright, honest, and completely dependable.

In this long informal session I got General Eisenhower's full views. I gave him mine. I left feeling that the burdens falling on my shoulders were heavy, the problems complex. But at least I knew what was facing me.

He turned over command to me ten days later, in a very simple, but to me a very beautiful and impressive ceremony. It was a fine fair day there at SHAPE, with the flags of all the fourteen NATO nations, formed in a great semicircle, snapping in the breeze, and the soldiers, sailors, and airmen of all the Allies drawn up as an honor guard. And it was with a feeling of tremendous pride, tempered with humility, that I took over as SACEUR—Supreme Allied Commander, Europe. The burdens of this command, I knew, would be greater than any I had ever borne, for it was my task to overcome, or at least to abate, somehow, the ancient hatreds and mistrusts that had rent Europe for a thousand years; to mold the fighting forces of thirteen nations—for Iceland had no military—into one great organization for the defense of freedom.

My first task was to tackle the problem of Allied command, to decide whether the Supreme Allied Commander, who was an American, should also be Commander in Chief of the U.S. Armed Forces in Europe, or whether these two posts should be held by different individuals.

Early in June I reported to the Joint Chiefs of Staff that by all means the two posts of highest authority should be vested in the same individual. Though the Supreme Allied Commander was responsible to the North Atlantic Council, the supreme political body of NATO, as the senior U.S. officer in the field he would undeniably be held responsible, by the American people, for whatever happened to American forces in Europe. In case of trouble, the American troops on the ground would be instantly responsive to the orders of the Supreme Commander. There would be no need for "co-ordination," which is often a synonym for red tape and delay. SACEUR, in his other capacity as Commander in Chief United States Forces, could issue direct operational orders to the commanders of all the U.S. Army, Navy, and Air Force elements stationed on the continent of Europe.

This recommendation was approved, and it is the organization which exists today, though there are, and have been, strong arguments advanced for dividing these responsibilities between two individuals.

Another problem dropped in my lap had to do with the organization of the command geographically. As has been pointed out, we had a Commander in Chief, North, a Commander in Chief of the Center, who was the Supreme Commander himself, and a Commander in Chief, South. With the addition of Greece and Turkey to this tremendous organization, our front extended for four thousand miles, from the North Cape in Norway to the Caucasus, where Turkey and the Soviet Union joined. It was too much territory for one command to handle. So I recommended that the Commander in Chief, Land Forces, South, whose headquarters were in Italy, be relieved of responsibility for Greece and Turkey. These two countries could then be placed in a separate command under a three-star general, whose command post would be located either in Greece or Turkey. This raised another problem. Both the Turks and Greeks are a proud people, who do not regard each other with deep affection, and neither wanted the other to be the seat of command. However, the command post had to be located somewhere, so, after considerable deliberation and the making of many surveys, I chose Izmir, in southwest Turkey, on the shores of the Adriatic, and Lieutenant General Wyman was set up there as Commander in Chief, Southeast. To allay the fears of the Greeks, it was also planned, in the event of war, to set up an advanced CP in Salonika.

Less easy to solve was the thorny problem of the unified command in the center. Since the Supreme Commander was an American, this officer had to be either a Frenchman or a Britisher. But the French would not approve a British Commander, nor did the British relish the idea of a Frenchman holding this post. It took me more than a year to work this problem out, and finally get approval of Marshal Juin, of France, as Commander in Chief, Center.

The problem of overall command of NATO's Air Forces was also a difficult one. There were strong arguments for one overall air commander, from one end of the line to the other. Air's great value lay in its mobility, it was pointed out, and to compartment it by assigning air squadrons to separate commands would greatly reduce this mobility. This argument was not convincing to me. I knew this mobility was largely theoretical, for in the nature of things it would have been extremely difficult, if not impossible, to shift a Turkish air squadron to Norway, or vice versa, if Europe was at war. Also, to me it was unthinkable that a modern ground force should not have tactical aviation at its instant call to serve on close-support missions.

My decision was that each Commander in Chief, North, South, and Center, should have certain air units under his control, available for his immediate use in an emergency. I myself assumed the post of Supreme Commander for Air, with a small but extremely able staff of Air advisors.

At about the time I took over, all the problems facing the Supreme Allied Commander in Europe underwent a fundamental alteration. General Eisenhower's job had been primarily a political one. Mine was essentially military. His was the task of using his great powers of charm and persuasion to bring together the nations of free Europe into a coalition for mutual defense—to get them to agree on a common plan of action. Mine was to get them to do what they had promised to do. He was the eloquent salesman who persuaded the housewife to subscribe to the pretty magazines. I was the So-and-So with the derby hat and the cigar, who came around to collect at the first of the month.

When General Eisenhower went to Paris, the free world, and particularly the United States, was rightfully apprehensive that the war raging in Korea was the prelude to World War III. Among all the free nations of the West there was a keen realization of how woefully unprepared we were to defend ourselves if this Korean conflict did spread into global war. The first task facing General Eisenhower, therefore, was to bring the heads of the NATO governments together, to get them to agree to fill without delay the great military vacuum that had been created by our precipitate demobilization and hasty departure from Europe at the end of World War II.

History records how brilliantly he accomplished that mission. He fired their imaginations. He awoke in them a realization of their danger, of the tragic consequences that would surely occur in the event of Russian armed aggression. He brought agreement where there had been no agreement, or at best a hopeless apathy. He got the promise of action.

Now, within a different framework, it was my job to translate promises into deeds, to collect on these I.O.U.'s, these pledges to provide men and guns, planes and tanks, and money, for a European defensive force. When General Eisenhower arrived in Europe, he himself, to all practical purposes, was NATO. There was no supreme political body to which he reported, or from whom he received guidance. But, in February, 1952, three months before my arrival, the NATO nations created the North Atlantic Council, the supreme political body of NATO. And the Allied military commanders in Europe were subordinate to its Military Committee.

Thus, when I took command as SACEUR, the picure had changed completely. There was now a political authority functioning, and the military commanders had reverted to their proper field—the military field.

By the time I arrived, the enthusiasm aroused by the leadership of General Eisenhower had abated somewhat. Time had passed. There was the prospect of a truce in Korea. The threat of global war seemed to have diminished. The full import of the commitments the NATO nations had made was beginning to dawn on them, and they were beginning to wonder whether or not they hadn't been a little too hasty—whether or not they hadn't oversubscribed this bond issue. Maybe they didn't really need, or couldn't afford, to buy these bonds for which they had signed up so willingly.

So, from the very outset of my service there, it became a question of convincing them that they hadn't been too hasty—that it still was vitally necessary to fill that military vacuum in the critical key sector of Central Europe, of which France, by accident of geography, was the keystone. That theme ran all through my period of command,

and continued, of course, into the period of General Gruenther's service.

I feel that we made great progress. In a few short years we built up a tremendous collective potential there. When General Eisenhower went to SHAPE in 1950, there was practically nothing to prevent a Soviet advance overland to the English Channel. When I arrived in 1952, there was the nucleus, but merely the nucleus, of a defensive force. On the continent of Europe we had only the 1st Division, and three mechanized reconnaissance units which could hardly be dignified, even collectively, with the name of an armored division. These were backed up by small British and French contingents, and by inadequate air and naval elements. By the time I left there, three years later, we had fifteen active, D-Day divisions in the field, backed up by a considerable reserve force in varying degrees of battle readiness. Under General Gruenther, at the beginning of his tour, there were some seventeen battle-ready divisions in the field—six U.S. divisions, five French, four British, and two Belgian. Their equipment, with the exception of the British and Canadian units, is practically all first-line U.S. equipment—including atomic weapons. We now have in Seventh Army, the U.S. ground force assigned to NATO, several batteries—some thirty guns in all—of the 280-mm. atomic cannon, plus batteries of the Honest John rocket, and the Corporal guided missile. All of these are capable of delivering an atomic warhead.

That strength is far less, both from the standpoint of quality and quantity, than the responsible commander in the field feels necessary—a view in which I earnestly concur. But it is, nevertheless, a potentially powerful force—a strong deterrent to any aggressive ambitions the Soviet might feel. It could put up a great deal of resistance, and with the support it would get from naval elements, and from the Allied air wings employing their atomic capabilities, it could do great damage to an invader. Recently, of course, the French have found it necessary to transfer several divisions to North Africa, thus greatly weakening our combat strength in the center.

The great weakness in this potentially powerful force lies in the vast front that it must cover, and in the disparity of the number of men under arms as compared with the strength of the Russian forces. The mere addition of men and guns, however, was not the primary problem facing me as I assumed command at SHAPE. The first thing we had to do—and I say *we* because it was the joint and combined effort of all the NATO nations—was to set up the vast and complex logistical structure which would support the forces we had if they should be committed to battle. First, there had to be airfields, and ammunition depots, and supply depots, and pipelines for fuel, and a network of telecommunications, which integrate and bring together in an effective fighting team all the various disparate elements which comprise a military force.

Steady progress was made in this field. Equally great progress, I think, was made in the understanding that grew up between the military staffs of the various governments involved. We came to have a much clearer perception of what our common problems were, our common objectives, our common difficulties—our weakness as well as our strength. We came to have an appreciation of the vital part that training played in bringing a force up to the point where it could be a dependable instrument in war. We all recognized certain tendencies which early began to manifest themselves—tendencies on the part of the political leaders to let down, to slow the pace of the preparations which the military establishments were requiring of their various governments.

Despite this tendency to slow down, I felt greatly encouraged as I came to the end of my service. We had at least started to build and integrate a complex military force within the framework of a great political coalition—the greatest coalition of free nations, perhaps, that ever joined its efforts to put together an organization capable of withstanding the stresses and strains of war.

In my final report to the North Atlantic Council, I tried to analyze and evaluate, as honestly as I could, the capabilities of that fighting force.

The mission of SACEUR, I pointed out, was to defend all of Western Europe, and all the NATO nations, from invasion from the East, whenever and wherever that aggression might come. There was no time table, no period of advance preparation allowed. At any given period, the forces we had on hand were to be a ready force, a D-day force, armed, trained, and equipped for immediate action.

Parenthetically, here, I would like to point out that the D-day divisions in the line *were* and *are* first-class troops. To overrun them in any one area the Russian would have to concentrate his forces, and thereby lay himself open to destruction by atomic weapons, which we most certainly would use. If, however, the Reds should attack in a dispersed line, all the way from Norway to the Caucasus, the problem would be difficult to handle. We could do great damage with conventional weapons, but with his tremendous strength in reserves, breakthroughs would undoubtedly occur. And behind our first-line troops, we have very little in support.

I was acutely aware, I pointed out, that NATO's military needs caused serious political, economic, financial, and social stresses within the member nations. But if NATO's basic objective, the maintenance of a ready force sufficiently strong to deter aggression, was to be attained, these stresses would have to be resolved.

I listed our military assets as follows: There had been a noticeable improvement in the command structure, in planning, and in the combat effectiveness of the troops. Communications had improved. So had the distribution of jet fuel and high-octane gas for planes, and gasoline and other fuels for tanks, vehicles, and self-propelled guns. We could expect that improvement to continue. The growth of the land forces had been encouraging, although not satisfactory. There had been no diminution by the governments in their realization of the theoretical necessity for common defense to meet a common peril. They all officially continued to subscribe to that concept.

Now, our military liabilities: First, the Soviet strength, while not increasing numerically, had increased in quality. The equipment of their ground forces had been modernized, airfields had been lengthened and improved, and many of their air units had been equipped with jets. NATO air power at that time was the weakest link in our defenses. In spite of our progress, our air forces could not adequately carry out their tasks. An increase in air power, therefore, had to receive far greater attention from the NATO nations. There were also great weaknesses in our reserve system. Our operational reserves on the ground were inadequately trained, owing, largely, to the short period of national service required by certain of the NATO countries. It was necessary to revise our mobilization system, in order to provide forces sufficiently well trained to perform effectively against the professional soldiers of the enemy.

My general observations at that time were these, and they are to a great degree applicable today: My overall objectives as the military commander were, first, to attain sufficient strength to deter potential aggressors from breaking the peace, and second, to defend the NATO nations successfully if the peace was broken. The success of NATO military forces in deterring aggression up to that point had tended to reduce the sense of fear and urgency. Nations were beginning to change their planned military programs from rapid rearmament to a longer-term policy, a change that was stimulated, unfortunately, by the actions of our own government, which was beginning a "stretch-out" policy toward Europe.

This, I pointed out, was dangerous. Any real slackening of our collective defense effort might itself open the way to aggression. The build-up of the past two years had resulted only in a *relative* alteration of the military power potential of NATO vis-à-vis the Soviet. The disparity that remained was such that Allied Command Europe was critically weak. It could not adequately carry out its mission in the face of a full Soviet attack. Many gaps still existed in our defensive system that had to be filled without delay. So long as these gaps were permitted to remain, the NATO nations would remain exposed to the peril of decisive military defeat, with all its catastrophic consequences.

We had to increase our active land forces; we had to give higher priority to our air forces; we had to increase our overall supply levels, some items of which were in critical shortage. We had to improve our training, a vital point, for the bravest men in the world, with the best arms and equipment in the world, are mere liabilities unless they are properly trained. Above all, we had to have competent, inspired leadership, for this is the keystone in the military arch.

If I, as an American citizen, had to take stock of the NATO military position in Europe today—two years after that summary given above, that inventory, or appraisal, I would include these points:

In that area of vital importance to the United States—that is, in Western Europe—our reliance must continue to be on collective resistance by all active and readily mobilizable forces available to General Gruenther, the present Supreme Allied Commander. In the event of war anywhere in that region, the forces of all member nations must fight, and fight as one.

That "front" is highly compartmented, and to oppose a Soviet ground offensive in strength, NATO armies would have to fight in their separate compartments: in northern Norway, in the Danish lands of Zeeland and Jutland, in the North German Plain area, in northern Italy, in Greek Macedonia and Thrace, and in Turkish

Thrace and the Anatolian plateau, Turkey's heartland. All these prospective battle zones must be defended, for they carry the hopes of those citizens of NATO to whom they represent inextinguishable human values. They are their immemorial homelands. The defense of each is important to the over-all mission—the defense of NATO territory in Europe—not alone from the tactical standpoint, but from equally important political, psychological, and economic considerations. Major enemy gains in either of the flanking areas—that is, in Scandinavia or the Greek-Turkish areas, would make correspondingly difficult the defense of vital and decisive sectors in the center— the area including France and the Low Countries.

It is the world's longest battle line. No one nation can defend it. Planes alone cannot defend it. Atomic weapons alone cannot defend it, nor can it be defended by men alone. All must be employed, and in strength sufficient to meet the threat. If, in the present state of the world, we should forget this, if we should let our guard down, the Iron Curtain would clang down upon all Europe and that great rampart of the free world would be lost. One example of letting our guard down, to my mind, was the withdrawal of our troops from Austria, a move that hurt the Russians not at all, but greatly weakened us.

29

☆☆☆☆

Monty, Mr. Churchill, and the Queen

As Supreme Commander in Europe, my problems were mainly military, but all of them, I soon found out, had strong political overtones. Shortly after my arrival, I began my formal duty calls on the chiefs of state, the prime ministers, the ministers of defense, and the chiefs of staff of the military services of all the NATO countries. Always, in these talks, the purely military considerations became inextricably entangled with political, economic, and psychological factors, some of which were beyond the ken of a soldier.

I had to study them, analyze them, understand them the best I could, however, for in modern war they are all inseparably related and cannot be ignored. In each of my conversations with the NATO leaders, throughout my tour, these problems came up. We thrashed them out in utter frankness, and with the guidance of my State Department advisers, when political issues were involved, I made my decisions.

I was singularly fortunate throughout my tour at SHAPE in having extremely able men as my political advisers. The first was Douglas MacArthur, a nephew, I believe, of the General. He was thoroughly aware of all those nuances and shades of feeling which motivate the Europeans in their dealings with each other and with us, and I found his wise counsel invaluable. He was a devoted public servant, an indefatigable worker with highly developed powers for analyzing an intricate problem and coming up with a logical conclusion. When he was pulled back to Washington to work with Secretary Dulles in the new administration, I was fortunate in getting Freddy Rinehart, our present ambassador to Indo-China, as his successor. Both were as completely loyal to me as an officer in uniform would have been, and I leaned heavily upon them for advice throughout my tour. When I was in Japan and Korea I depended with equal confidence on Bill Sebald, now Deputy Assistant Secretary of State for the Far East.

Parenthetically, here I would like to condemn as strongly as I can the misguided notion which has been planted in the public mind— that the career State Department officer is a tea-sipping fop in striped pants. I have known many a Foreign Service officer in my day, and I can say without equivocation that, as a body, they are as devoted and as hard-working a group of dedicated public servants as any who serve our government.

I have known and worked with State Department people since I was a young captain, and my respect for them is profound. Since the mid-twenties there has always been some trusted friend in the State Department to whom I could go for counsel and advice, and I have drawn heavily on these sources for thirty years. I strongly deplore the idea that there is an unbridgeable gulf between the diplomat and the military man, that they speak a different language and therefore do not understand each other. In our associations we have worked together only as those who feel a mutual respect for each other can co-operate. My associations with them have been most happy and some of them, such as Bob Murphy, who served so competently in Berlin, I count among my closest friends.

One of the greatest problems facing my political advisers and me was the distrust that many of the smaller nations felt for their larger neighbors. These suspicions were rooted deep in their history and they expressed them freely. They said quite openly that the French had neither the willingness nor the physical resources to defend a smaller neighbor, and that French troops would take refuge behind the Rhine at the first sign of trouble. They also openly expressed the view that the British would run for the Channel ports, and the U.S. would hightail it for the Pyrenees the moment the shooting started.

In Holland and Belgium, the two countries most exposed to Red aggression, there was a particularly well-nourished feeling that we really had no serious intentions of staying to fight if attacked. In an effort to allay these fears, I talked to the Dutch Cabinet for forty-five minutes, in a plain-spoken, informal session at which neither side minced any words. I told them that it was our unalterable decision to defend every foot of European soil that we could defend—subject only to one proviso—that we were not going to throw away any of our troops in a hopeless last-stand defense of a non-defensible position. Our resources in manpower were too meager for that. We would stand and fight as long as we could maintain combat units intact. Then we would pull back to new positions and stand and fight again. Lost territory could be regained later. But the lives of men could never be replaced.

In a spirit of complete frankness, I outlined to the Dutch, the Belgians, the Norwegians, and the Danes our plan of action in the light of enemy capabilities, evaluated our weakness and our strength, and told them what help I required of them. To my great gratification, none of this highly classified information, which was given to large groups of men in closed sessions, ever leaked out to the public. This indicated to me that men in public office in Europe are more close-mouthed than our own statesmen—or that their journalists are less enterprising.

Of all the peoples with whom I conferred, the Danes seemed to feel themselves in the most hopeless position. They felt that NATO's troops were too far away to come to their help in the event the Russians should attack from their zone of Germany. Nor were there any natural terrain obstacles to impede their progress.

I admitted frankly that their position was exposed. I reiterated my determination to defend, with all the strength I could bring to bear, wherever an attack should come. However, I pointed out with equal frankness that the best thing they could do was to make every possible effort to defend their own homes and hearthsides. If they would create that strength to the limit of their ability, it would make our problem that much simpler. The philosophy was accepted as sound, but I don't think the Danes have yet put it in practice. They would not even permit us to put our air squadron on a Danish base, to help in their defense if needed. And so far as I know we have not yet gotten permission to base planes there.

There were many such frustrations throughout my tour. Yet somehow I could not find it in my heart to blame the men in high places whose task it was to guide their nations through the trying postwar years. They were, I knew, merely reflecting the fears, the apathy, and the distrust of their peoples. For many of them I came to have the warmest respect and affection. With Monsieur Pleven of France, for example, I soon was able to work on a most intimate basis of mutual trust and understanding. At any hour, whenever a problem arose, I would call him or he would call me, and we would sit down together, just the two of us, and talk with utmost candor.

I also felt that I had the friendship and support of Mr. Churchill, with whom I had a number of informal meetings at 10 Downing Street. The first of these I well recall. It was about eleven o'clock in the morning, and as I was escorted into the chamber, hung with fine paintings, where the Prime Minister waited, he put out his hand:

"Welcome, General," he said. "Have a Scotch and soda."

It was a little early for that, but I did not make a point of this. So we sat down, each with a glass, and to further put me at my ease he immediately brought up a topic close to my heart—airborne operations during World War II. We talked on this subject for perhaps half an hour, and I was amazed at his detailed knowledge, not only of British airborne exploits, but our own.

My last call, to say farewell when I left to become Chief of Staff, was also in the morning. Again his greeting was the same. This time I refused the proffered glass, explaining that in a few minutes I had to go to pay my respects to Her Majesty the Queen. He said, oh, Her Majesty wouldn't mind. I still refused, however.

"Well, I'll have one," he said, and did.

During the course of our conversation he said he hoped I would not mind his writing direct to me, if occasion arose, during my service as Chief of Staff. I told him that would be fine. Then I did a little fast thinking about what possible reaction there might be if it became known that the Chief of Staff was carrying on a private correspondence with the Prime Minister on military matters. As I was leaving, he walked with me to the entrance and brought up the matter again. This gave me opportunity to express the hope that he would inform President Eisenhower of his intention to write to me. He said of course he would. He never wrote.

I will always remember one small dinner at 10 Downing Street which Mrs. Ridgway and I attended. Present were Field Marshal Sir Harold Alexander and his lady; the Churchills; and General Sir

Bernard Freyberg, the great New Zealand commander who made such a magnificent battle record in two wars.

As we sat down at the round table, a waiter brought a plate of dogfood to the Prime Minister. He rose and took it over to the fireplace where he set it down in front of his poodle. A dog, he pointed out, should always receive his food from the hands of his master.

It was, I am afraid, a fairly dull evening for the ladies, for as Mrs. Ridgway, who was sitting on Mr. Churchill's right, recalls it, the men started talking about war the moment we sat down and continued throughout the evening. And we both remember the great emotion the Prime Minister displayed as he spoke of the wartime years. As he spoke, his eyes filled, his voice shook, tears rolled down his cheeks, which were as pink and smooth and unlined as a baby's.

I was also impressed, on another occasion, with Sir Winston's perfect naturalness, his ability to be himself on all occasions. I had been asked to make the address before the annual meeting of the Pilgrim Society, oldest and most august of the Anglo-American organizations. Mr. Churchill, who also was to speak, was seated at my right. When the main course was served—it was, as I recall it, pheasant under glass—the Prime Minister peered at it for a moment, turned to the waiter and growled,

"Take this back and bring me a plate of roast beef."

At the small dinner at 10 Downing Street, I was much impressed by General Freyberg, whom I had never met. There was an air about him of great serenity, of spiritual strength, of forthrightness. At one moment during the talk I heard him tax the Prime Minister sharply for having sent no message to the troops after their gallant, but ineffective efforts to hold Crete.

"We did the best we could there," he told the P.M. "At least you should have sent me a message."

The Prime Minister did not reply.

As Freyberg spoke, I thought of many of my old comrades of the British service whom I had grown to know and to admire—Monty, Dempsey, "Boy" Browning, General Bols, and Richard Gale, my opposite number when the British Airborne Corps was formed. Great soldiers all, they too had this quality of frankness, of open, plain-spoken honesty. Men of great human qualities, there was none of the stuffiness and pomposity about them with which caricaturists like to portray the British general officer.

One of my more delicate personnel problems at SHAPE, in fact, had to do with the tendency of my old friend, Monty—Viscount Montgomery, my Deputy Commander—to speak his mind at all times. I had served very closely with Field Marshal Montgomery during World War II. I had met him first in the weeks preceding the Normandy invasion, when I was commanding the 82nd Airborne, and the acquaintance begun there had grown into a warm friendship later, when my Corps twice came under his command. In the years after the war we had met and renewed this friendship, for when I was serving on the Military Staff Committee he had come to the U.S. on a visit and had been a guest in my home.

As soon as I took command I asked the Field Marshal to come in and sit down so that we could have a very close and intimate talk. I pointed out to him that I had assumed this command with no option on my part. It was a military assignment which I had not sought. I told him that I was well aware of his great stature as a soldier, and of the world-wide reputation which he so deservedly enjoyed, and that I could well understand that it might be difficult for him to be a deputy to an officer considerably younger in years and experience than he—an officer who once had been his subordinate. Because he knew the great respect and admiration that I had for him, I wanted to be perfectly sure that there was complete understanding between us. His views, I told him, were always welcome. They would always be given attentive consideration. But there was going to be but one commander—and when my decisions were announced, that was it. There wasn't to be any question about them.

He responded as you would expect a great soldier to respond. He pledged his complete loyalty, and that I had, throughout my days with NATO. Monty is a very positive man, however, a free spirit who is accustomed to speak his mind with complete freedom, regardless of the views of anybody else, whether they be held by the officials of his own government, or prime ministers, or military superiors. The result was that certain small difficulties arose at times, when the Deputy Commander, in that amiable offhand way he had, would express views exactly opposite to my own.

Very early in my tour I had laid down a few broad strategic principles, which I had issued for the guidance of my principal commanders. Most important was the basic concept that I have stressed before—that we were here to defend *all* the territory of the European members, not just the parts that were easy to defend. There were many of my staff who held that Greek Thrace and Macedonia, and

Turkish Thrace, were completely indefensible. And I had said, well, maybe so. But the units there were to stand and fight as long as they possibly could without sacrificing themselves. In the event of attack, they were to effect maximum delay consistent with maintaining their major forces intact. The troops, I made clear, were worth more than the real estate, when the chips were down, but we were not going to make a present to the enemy of any territory without a fight.

The Greeks and the Turks understood that, and agreed. Then Monty went off down there on an inspection trip and made some off-hand remarks to the effect that the troops were in the wrong place—they ought to pull back because the area in which they were deployed was indefensible. And that caused a hell of a flap, with the Greek government interpreting his remarks to mean that they should give up some of their own territory. This sort of thing happened several times, but when I spoke to Monty about the possible effect of these off-the-cuff statements, he remained unperturbed.

"Oh, I made it quite clear that those weren't official views," he said. "I was just expressing my own personal opinion."

I'd say to him, "Monty, it's not possible for a man of your world-wide reputation to deliver yourself of any off-the-cuff purely personal views. You are my deputy. Whatever you say is going to be construed as an official SHAPE view despite your disclaimers."

"You're right, Matt," he'd say. "You're quite right."

Then he'd go out and do it again.

Despite these little misunderstandings we got along very well. I could always sit down with Monty and talk things over in a spirit of complete mutual respect and friendliness. And I was always sure that the Field Marshal, for all his penchant for expressing his own views, no matter how they might differ from my own, was always completely loyal.

That area to the southeast—Greek and Turkish Thrace—was of tremendous importance to us strategically, for it represented our anchor to the south, and I spent a great deal of time there, going over the ground held by the troops, and conferring with the prime ministers of the two nations. Menderes of Turkey I found to be a man of sound judgment, a keen analyst of European affairs, and Papagos, his counterpart in Greece, was to my mind a man of great astuteness. I was surprised and pleased to find that neither of them seemed to share the antipathies that affected their people—at least whatever deep-seated animosity Turk might have felt toward Greek, and vice versa, they did not reveal in their conversations with me. Those ancient hatreds are long dying, and I would not be naïve enough to say that they no longer exist. But certainly they were waning then as both nations recognized the threat to their freedom of a greater enemy, the Russians. I pray that they will not be revived. The feeling of animosity toward the Italians is still strong, however. It would be utterly impossible, I think, to get Greek or Turkish troops to serve under an Italian commander, and I strongly doubt that the Italians would be willing to serve under a Greek or a Turk.

The willingness of the Greeks and Turks to co-operate under the NATO organization was also manifested by their military leaders. When I went down to make my first inspection of Greek Thrace, I covered the Struma River front along the Bulgarian border, west to the Albanian frontier, but I was unable, on that trip, to cover a little tongue of Grecian Thrace from Kavala to the east, which borders on Turkish soil. I decided that I would inspect the troops in this area when I came back to finish my inspection of Turkey. So when I came back to Turkey (I had already covered the Caucasus front, where Turkey joins the Soviet Union), I asked General Baransel, commanding all the Turkish land forces, if he would be willing to go into Greek Thrace with me to visit the troops there. He agreed, providing that his government did not object, and the Greek government would agree to his coming. So we sent off a couple of quick messages to both capitals and got an answer back that night. We crossed the border the next morning and were met by General Tsakalotis, the commander of the Greek land forces. We spent the next two days together traveling over Greek Thrace. The two commanders, Baransel and Tsakalotis, took to each other right away. They were both men of great strength of character; each of them was a tough, competent fighting man. We dined that first night in Kavala, a very ancient and very lovely Greek town, near where Philip of Macedon was born. We had a magnificent dinner there that night, and the spirit of friendship was to me remarkable. Both the Greek and Turkish officers commented on it—and on the fact that this was the first time in the memory of either of them that Greek and Turkish officers had sat down to dine together.

This may seem to be a little thing, but it was of great importance to me as Commander of the Allied forces. I had deliberately sought to bring these two together, knowing that if I could get them to co-ordinate their defense planning there, the collective strength in that little critical area would be enormously increased.

My memories of that whole journey are most pleasant. As we rode the border, the people of the little villages along the way came out singing, bringing flowers. The grand old priests, in their flowing robes, with their great beards, would lead the processional, followed by the mayor and the townsfolk. To me it was a moving thing. Their greeting, I knew, had nothing to do with me, a soldier in U.S. uniform. It was a tribute to the country of which that uniform was a symbol, a manifestation of their faith in America as the bulwark of the free world.

As we approached the sizable city of Kavala, I anticipated that my welcome might be something less than warm, for Kavala during the Greek civil war had been a Communist stronghold. There was not the slightest untoward incident. A dozen beautiful girls, wearing the costumes of the different provinces, came out to escort us into the city. I rode in, sitting on the spare tire of an open jeep, through throngs that lined the streets. The only missiles thrown at me were flowers.

My fondest memories of my service as NATO's Supreme Commander, in fact, are the warmth and friendliness I encountered everywhere, from the peasant villages of Greece and Turkey to England's Buckingham Palace. I treasure particularly the memory of those occasions when Mrs. Ridgway and I were received by Her Majesty, the Queen.

We flew to London for our first official call and were lodged in a beautiful apartment in Dorchester House. After weeks of official visits in other countries, where it was often necessary to speak through an interpreter, it was a great relief to us to find ourselves among English-speaking people again. It was somehow like coming home. As we left the plane at the airport and walked down between the ranks of a magnificent honor guard, one small incident took place which is of no importance now, but was a little embarrassing at the moment. Some young Communist among the watching crowd tossed "Go Home, Ridgway" leaflets over the heads of the guard into our path. I took no notice, but the aide who was escorting Mrs. Ridgway did.

"Well," he said, "I suppose you are used to this sort of thing by now."

Mrs. Ridgway assured him that we were not used to it, and that among all the countries we had visited, this was the first time such an incident had occurred.

Whatever unhappiness we might have felt at the rudeness of this welcome was completely dispelled by the warmth and graciousness with which we were greeted by the Queen. We both were anxious, of course, to observe all the court conventions at this meeting, and the day before our call, I asked a senior aide at the Embassy to brief me thoroughly on what was expected of us, asking particularly about the curtsy. He told me that the Queen was very broad-minded about this, and that if an American girl did not choose to curtsy, Her Majesty would not be offended. However, he added, as a mark of respect, it should be done. All I had to do, of course, was bow. So in a few sessions before a mirror there at Dorchester House, Mrs. Ridgway soon had the curtsy down pat. The bow, of course, was no problem, though I do remember thinking it would be a most unfortunate time for my old sacroiliac injury to flare up on me. It would have been most embarrassing if I had found myself unable to bend at the waist, or bending, been unable to straighten up again.

We drove by Embassy car to Buckingham Palace, timing our progress to arrive on the dot of eleven-thirty. We were met by an aide, in naval uniform, as I recall it now, who ushered us through the long corridors to the Queen's reception room, where he announced us and withdrew. The Queen, wearing a simple, long-sleeved black dress, with ropes and ropes of pearls, was standing with the Duke in front of a large fireplace. It was quite a long walk, across that room, and I remember feeling a sense of appreciation that both Her Majesty and the Duke came forward, meeting us halfway. Mrs. Ridgway, I noticed, brought off the curtsy with ease and grace.

The talk was general and light at first, about our trip over, and the other countries we had visited. Her Majesty then asked about the situation in Korea, and the progress of negotiations there, while Mrs. Ridgway at the other side of the fireplace was chatting with the Duke, who was making his first public appearance since suffering an attack of yellow jaundice.

Her Majesty then turned to Mrs. Ridgway and asked: "How is Matty?"

Penny, who was much surprised, as was I, that Her Majesty even knew about our small son, replied that he was fine and much enjoying his life in France.

"I feel as if I know him," said Her Majesty, "I have seen his picture so many times."

She then spoke of Prince Charles and Princess Anne, and of how they loved to play hide and seek in the corridors of the palace, hiding behind the curtains.

The talk then turned to NATO matters, and both the Queen and the Duke seemed most interested in my problems there, and showed complete familiarity with them.

As we were about to take our leave, Her Majesty remarked that the Queen Mother had expressed a hope that she might see us while we were in the palace. So immediately upon leaving Her Majesty's reception room, we were conducted to the Queen Mother's apartments.

She received us alone, just inside the doorway, and both my and Mrs. Ridgway's instant reactions, as we found out later, were the same. Rarely, if ever, have we met so gracious, so charming a lady as the Queen Mother. She was all warmth and interest and invited us to sit there in her lovely apartment, with a profusion of plants and flowers around, while we had a delightful chat for the better part of half an hour, with the usual family subjects coming up for discussion, in addition to her kindly inquiries about my official duties, which I had so recently undertaken.

The coronation was only a few weeks off when we paid our visit to the palace, and Her Majesty most graciously extended us an invitation to attend. My seat was in Westminster Abbey, just above that of General Marshall, and Penny had a wonderful place outside, where from a stand in front of Lancaster House she got a fine view of the processional. So between the two of us we got a good look at that whole magnificent pageant.

I was received again at the Palace just before I relinquished my NATO command, another delightful meeting which Mrs. Ridgway unhappily was forced to miss. I had been notified that I was to come back to the States, and was on my farewell swing around the capitals of Europe, paying my last duty calls on the heads of governments. I had begun this farewell trip at Ankara, in Turkey. We left there at 5:30 A.M. for Athens, where I was to speak at an official luncheon, and then had flown on to Rome for a formal banquet in the evening. The traveling, and the strain of remembering not to say, "I am happy to be in Athens," when I was actually in Rome, had left me bushed. So I told Mrs. Ridgway that we would just have to take a day off and rest. We'd stop off on the Riviera and just lie on the sand all day, soaking up sunshine. Then we would fly on to London for our farewell visit to the Queen. So, with General and Mrs. Tony Biddle, who were accompanying us, we had one beautiful golden day of loafing, the first

I could remember since I had come to Europe. That night, about suppertime, we got a call from Paris. The connection was very bad, and the message was somewhat garbled, but the gist of it was that Matty had a high fever that had come upon him very suddenly and that we should return to Paris at once.

There was nothing to do but worry, for we could not possibly get out of there until morning. It was, of course, a troubled night for both of us, for in every parent's mind there is always the fear of polio. Early the next morning we called again, to learn that Matty's fever was still high and, though the doctors were still there, they had not yet diagnosed the case and could give us no inkling whatever of what the trouble was.

This upset Mrs. Ridgway greatly, of course, and we immediately changed our flight plans. Instead of going direct to London, we flew to Paris, touched down there to drop Mrs. Ridgway off, and I went on to London, deeply troubled, for my meeting with the Queen.

I sent a message ahead to Buckingham Palace, explaining the necessity for Mrs. Ridgway's absence, and as I met Her Majesty I expressed in person my deep regrets.

"Please don't mention it," said Her Majesty. "With two children of my own, I know exactly how she feels. I, too, am distressed."

Her sympathy and understanding touched me deeply; the warm human quality she displayed whenever we met captivated me completely. As I was leaving she gave instructions that she should be informed as soon as word came from Paris reporting on Matty's condition. That word came shortly thereafter, as I was in conference with the British Joint Chiefs of Staff. The fever had gone down. There was no sign of polio. It was just one of those little flare-ups to which young children are subject and from which they so quickly recover.

Another of my happy memories of my service at SHAPE is of a visit to the old battlefields of Normandy, where I had jumped with the 82nd Airborne. Shortly after my arrival in Paris I received an invitation to attend the ceremonies commemorating the eighth anniversary of the Normandy invasion. To my surprise my staff recommended that I should not attend. The day had not been properly planned, they said; the arrangements that had been made did not attach the proper dignity to the attendance by the Supreme Allied Commander. To me this reasoning seemed ill conceived. The question of the dignity, or the honors, to be shown me were of very secondary importance. As one of two airborne commanders who had jumped in

Normandy before H-hour, it was certainly my duty, and my privilege, to pay my undying homage to those brave men who gave their lives in battle there.

I am forever grateful that I made that decision. It was a most inspiring day. We left Paris in the early morning for the invasion beaches, and ended up, just before dark, in Ste.-Mère-Église, the town my paratroopers had captured at dawn of D-day morning. There was a little daylight left, so I told my French escorts that I would like to go out a few kilometers west of the town to see if I could find the place where I'd set up my first command post, after dropping down there in the dark. I didn't have too much hope of finding it, for it is difficult to remember, sometimes, how land looks that you have seen only in the midst of battle. But miraculously we came to a little lane that I recognized, and at the end of this lane was a barred gate, and a little pasture surrounded by high hedgerows. And I looked over these trees into the very pasture I had dropped into on the night before D-day. I let down the bars and walked in there, feeling that strange surge of emotion that comes over an old soldier when he stands on land where he once fought. And bless my soul if the cows didn't converge on me, just as they'd done that night. They moved toward me and stopped about six feet away, staring at me with quizzical looks as if to say: "Well, where the hell have you been all these years?" Mrs. Ridgway followed me down the lane, tripping along in her high-heeled shoes, and I told her of the warm regard I felt for these cows, for their presence there on that night eight years before meant that this field was not mined. While we stood there talking, the old farmer who owned the land came up, with one of his little daughters. We had quite a reunion, for we both well remembered the hours when our para-medics worked over the wounded in his farmhouse, which we had used as an aid station.

It was a moment of deep emotion for me. It was June, and all the hedgerow trees were green with spring, and the ground was deep and soft with grass, and the cattle were fat and sleek. The little girl, who had not been born eight years before, was with us, with not even a memory of what happened there to trouble her dreams at night. Time and the seasons had covered the scars, the grass had done its healing work, life had triumphed over death, and the earth and the people who tilled it lived again in freedom and in peace. And that, I thought, was why we had fought here in these quiet pastures, years before.

30

☆☆☆☆

Chief of Staff

MY FRIEND Omar Bradley was the source of my first information that I was under consideration as Chief of Staff. With his usual consideration for others, he told me that, if I had any very strong feelings one way or another, I could convey my wishes through him. If I wished to stay on as Supreme Commander in Europe, that could no doubt be arranged. If, on the other hand, I did feel inclined to accept as Chief of Staff in the event the office was offered me, he would pass my wishes on to the higher authorities who would make the final decision.

I naturally gave a great deal of thought to this proposal, in full consultation with my wife. We analyzed it from every point of view, and came to the conclusion that if the job were offered me I would accept.

There were several major reasons for this decision, starting with the professional. No higher honor could come to an Army officer than to be chosen for this highest post on the active list. Second, there were purely personal considerations. Both Penny and I were well aware that at a not too distant date I would have to leave the active list. Within two years, which would probably be the length of my service as Chief of Staff, I would have reached the retirement age of sixty. We both agreed that we could not ignore the arithmetic of the years. We were equally agreed that we did not wish to sit down in a rocker and vegetate, once time for retirement had come. We wanted to enter some very active new field, some challenging civilian pursuit, while I was still enjoying the splendid health and vigor with which God had so graciously blessed me. While neither of us knew just when my service would terminate, since that was in the discretion of my military and civilian superiors, we both were firmly resolved that I would not extend my service beyond the normal retirement age. We made our decision then. Whatever happened, short of war, I would retire at the age of sixty.

I go into this somewhat lengthy discussion for a specific purpose. When I did retire at age sixty, there was some public speculation that I was forced into retirement, owing to the fact that my views on military matters did not coincide, in many fields, with those of my civilian superiors. I am well aware that my retirement as Chief of Staff may have been accepted by my superiors with a sense of relief. But I do want to make clear that the decision was my own, made long before any points at issue had arisen between me and the Department of Defense, and with the statutory right to retire at any time of my own choosing well in mind.

There was quite a little delay, back in Washington, in arriving at a decision as to my future. In the spring of 1953, Mr. Wilson, the Secretary of Defense, and Mr. Stevens, the Secretary of the Army, had visited Europe. It was the first time I had met either of these two gentlemen, and I accompanied them on their visit, which started at my headquarters in Paris, and covered all the installations of U.S. Seventh Army, including the American Zone of Germany, a journey on which I had the distinct feeling that both of them were sizing me up. If they were, they gave no indication of their decision, however, and it was not until mid-May that I was informed that Mr. Wilson and Mr. Stevens had finally recommended to the President that I be appointed as Chief of Staff.

It was about this time that I was directed to return to the United States to testify on foreign aid bills—money bills—before committees of Congress. Since I had already paid official calls on all the fourteen members of NATO, except Canada and Iceland, I took this opportunity to pay my respects to the heads of these governments. En route back to Paris, I called on my good friend, Brooke Claxton, the Canadian Defense Minister at that time. We talked NATO business under the most pleasant of circumstances—on a flight into the Canadian woods, where we landed at O'Connell's, a magnificent hunting and fishing lodge 150 miles from Ottawa. We had a fine day's fishing there which both Mrs. Ridgway and I enjoyed to the utmost. We had a fine catch of wall-eyed pike, and I took one northern pike which weighed over eleven pounds.

We flew from Ottawa to Iceland, where I stopped at Reykjavik to pay my devoirs to the President. It was late May by now, a time of variable weather, the long days filled with alternating rain squalls and bright sun. The President was in his lovely country home some distance from the capital, and we fell to talking about the outdoors, and bird life, and that strange bird, the eider duck, whose down is one of Iceland's exports. I found that I was possessed of a great deal of misinformation about the eider duck. I was under the impression that the duck was killed for its down, but the President assured me this was not the case. The mother duck plucks the down from her breast to line her nest, and this down, the eiderdown of commerce, is collected after the young birds have hatched and flown.

The mating season was on at the moment, the President said, and he would be glad to show me the birds in their natural surroundings. We went out in a pouring rain, walking toward the low hills, and had gone little more than two hundred yards when I almost stepped on a nesting duck. She was magnificently camouflaged. Her colors blended perfectly with the local vegetation, a kind of coarse grass, and she was almost invisible except to a trained eye. As soon as I knew what to look for, though, I could pick them out all around me, a dozen or more sitting placidly in the rain. Protected by stringent game laws, they have little fear of man, and they will remain on the nest until you are right up on them.

I had always thought of Iceland as being barren of life, but on the day we were there, it seemed to me to be teeming with birds. Water fowl were everywhere, particularly the greenhead, the mallard duck we know so well in the States. The trout fishing is also excellent in the inland streams, I was told, and the salt-water game fishing is superb. We had no time, however, to enjoy either of these pastimes. Within three hours of our landing, we were on our way back to Paris, to move out from there to make our farewell visits to old friends we had come to know and warmly admire in Oslo, Copenhagen, Lisbon, Brussels, Luxembourg, and The Hague.

As our time came to leave, we cast about for a departure hour that would be of least inconvenience to persons on both ends of the line.

262   SOLDIER: The Memoirs of Matthew B. Ridgway

We did not wish to leave Paris either late Friday or on a Saturday, for
it is the nature of French officialdom to flee Paris Friday afternoon
for a long, relaxing weekend in the country. Neither did we wish to
arrive in Washington on a Sunday, when the Pentagon officials would
also be taking their ease. As things turned out, however, it was necessary to leave on Saturday. I tried to insist to my dear friend, Monsieur
Pleven, the French Defense Minister, with whom I had formed a very
close and warm friendship, that neither he nor any of his top officials
should come out to Orly to see us off. But he insisted, and came out
in person, and we had a very cordial send-off from him and members
of his staff.

Matty, on the occasion of our departure, stole the show as he had
done upon our arrival. General Gruenther, my successor, had given
him a space gun, one of these contrivances which emit a flickering
light when the trigger is pressed, making a sound like a machine gun.
As we walked to the plane, through the lines formed by the formal
guard of honor, I noticed that the cameras were all focused on something that was happening behind me. I turned to see Matty striding
along bringing up the rear. He had his space gun at his shoulder and
he was busily mowing down the guard of honor, all solemnly standing
there at attention. That naturally caused a great deal of laughter,
though I was somewhat apprehensive as to the motives the Communists would attribute to this gesture. They had, I recalled, pointed out
in their publications that the Americans were warmongers—in proof
of which they had published pictures of small boys carrying cap
pistols.

To arrive in Washington on Sunday was bad enough, but to arrive
there early Sunday morning would have been unforgivable. So we
stopped off for a short time in Edinburgh. There I had a chance to see
for the first time that inspiring monument to the Scottish soldier—the
figure of the young rifleman, with the inscription below it which I had
carried in my wallet so long, and which had sustained me in so many
battles:

If it be Life that awaits, I shall live forever unconquered; if Death, I
shall die at last strong in my pride and free.

I had carried that motto with me since the 1920's. Afterward I
had found a picture of the monument and had had it framed, inscription and all, and it now goes with me wherever I go. It is one of the

little things that has meaning to a soldier, and the picture of the monument still has an honored place in my house. Nothing that we possess has attracted more attention than has this little faded picture in its silver frame.

After the trip to the monument, which was truly a sentimental journey for me, we went, in a pouring rain, to see the Memorial Chapel where Scotland honors her warriors. No shrine I have ever seen impressed me more than this little Gothic chapel, where hang the arms and banners of Scotland's famed regiments.

We flew from Scotland to Washington, and arrived without incident, except that provided by Matty. He left the plane first, as a reconnaissance party, armed with his space gun, and immediately mowed down the welcoming committee, headed by General Bradley. He was deeply devoted to this weapon, which had carried him safely through so many tight spots, and it was a great tragedy in the Ridgway household when it was, inevitably, broken.

It was good to be home—to know that barring sudden catastrophe the years of wandering were over. Here I would end my Army career, amid old friends, in the tranquil surroundings of Fort Myer, where with my wife and little son I could find relief from whatever tension and frustrations might await me at the Pentagon.

Quarters One at Fort Myer has been the official residence of the Chief of Staff of the Army for nearly half a century. A big, comfortable, rambling old red brick house, it was built in 1903 by the Quartermaster General of the Army as his own residence, and as is natural with the Quartermaster, he saw to it that nothing but the finest materials went into its construction. As is natural also, the Chief of Staff took note of its superior qualifications as a residence, and took it for himself.

For all its comfort and spaciousness, though, it was not built for the electrical age, and its wiring was totally inadequate to carry the battery of gadgets which modern living requires. General Bradley, who had lived there during his tenure as Chief of Staff, and as Chairman of the Joint Chiefs, told me that every time he left it, he expected to come back and find it a pile of ashes, because of some failure in the overloaded electrical circuits.

Here, as in Panama, Tokyo, and Paris, Mrs. Ridgway carried out one of her superlative jobs of renovation and redecorating. It was her idea that since the house was to be the residence of the Chief of Staff, it should in its decoration reflect the mood and spirit of West Point, which is the repository of the ideals and the ethics, the creed of conduct that guides the members of the Officer Corps whatever their school.

She chose the gold and gray of the Academy colors as her color scheme, therefore, and, with the help of Eastman Kodak laboratories, she covered the walls of the dining room with huge murals—blown-up photographs of scenes at West Point which all graduates treasure in their memory, and which we hope, in years to come, will give pleasure to all those who come to share its hospitality.

Once she had transformed the inside into a wonderfully appropriate, tasteful, and harmonious setting for a soldier's residence, she turned her attention to the lawns and garden. Though the house was most spacious and comfortable inside, there was no private outside sitting space at all. The nice garden plot east of the house was pleasant but small, and it dropped away abruptly down a steep slope to a service yard in the rear. It could not be used for a garden party, for the guests would be clinging to the slope like mountain goats, and ladies in high heels could not move around at all. So she called in the engineers, with a bulldozer, and leveled off that slope, sodded it with grass, and replaced the shabby shrubbery with thriving new plants—little evergreens and Japanese holly. It made a most restful, tranquil spot where we spent many happy hours during the two years we lived there.

I well remember driving from the airport to Fort Myer on the day of our arrival from France. My mind was filled with thoughts of the new and heavy responsibilities I was to assume the next morning— for as has always been my lot when reporting for duty at Washington, I was to set to work immediately—when I happened to notice the sign that marked the entrance to my street. "Hospital," it said. "Fort Myer Chapel," "Arlington Cemetery." I wondered what prophetic significance that might have, in light of the burdens that were about to fall on me. At least I escaped the first two, fortunately, but I soon found myself in Arlington Cemetery, somewhat bewildered, though in good health. I had been at my desk for two or three days and was feeling in need of exercise, when I noticed from the windows of my office in the Pentagon the flag fluttering on the staff at Fort Myer. It seemed to be just a good, leg-stretching walk away, so that afternoon,

filing a few landmarks away in my mind as check points, I set out for
home on foot. I walked for a considerable time, being diverted from
my true course by highways, buildings, and "Keep Off the Grass"
signs, until finally just about dark, I found myself in Arlington
Cemetery. This was quite a distance from where I wanted to be, so I
staked out a new course, much as you will line out a course across
country while riding to hounds, and set out again. My bump of direction seemed to be out of kilter, though, and I ended up at the Lee
Mansion, which was even farther away from home. There wasn't a
soul around to guide me, until finally, at the caretaker's house, I found
a lady who very graciously directed me to the path I should take,
though she did seem a little surprised to see a four-star general in full
uniform wandering around lost. So I started off again and took a few
more wrong turns, and it was full dark before I finally came to one of
the gates at Fort Myer. It was locked. It was also a long walk around
to the main gate, and by now I had had all the exercise I needed.

Looking around, shame-faced, to make sure nobody was observing
the Chief of Staff engaged in such an undignified activity, I scrambled
over the wall and went home.

31

☆☆☆☆

The Statesman versus the Soldier

AT THE special request of President Eisenhower I had returned to Washington a full month before I was to take over my new duties as Chief of Staff. So had Admiral Radford, the new Chairman of the Joint Chiefs, and Admiral Carney, the new Chief of Naval Operations. It was the President's thought that we should take this time to sit down with General Twining of the Air Force, holdover member of the Joint Chiefs, and read ourselves thoroughly into the global situation.

All of us had borne great responsibilities—I as Supreme Commander in the Far East and Europe; Admiral Radford as Commander in Chief, Pacific; Admiral Carney as my Commander in Chief, South, of the NATO Forces in Europe. But our fields of detailed knowledge had been limited to the theaters in which we had served. Now we were to share service together of the broadest scope, and on the highest plane. We must think, now, not in terms merely of the Far East or of Europe, not alone in terms of our own arm of the service. We must broaden our concepts to embrace the defenses of the whole free world, by all the combat elements—land, sea and air.

Shortly after my arrival the President called us in a body to the White House. He looked vigorous and fit, showing no physical sign of the strains of the hard campaign. He was also as warm and friendly as he had been when I last saw him, as he turned over command to me at SHAPE, in Paris. But I knew of course that there had been a subtle change in the old informal "Ike and Matt" relationship that had existed between us when we both were soldiers. I was still "Matt" to him. He now to me was "Mr. President."

The meeting lasted for perhaps half an hour. Succinctly, the President outlined his ideas. He had brought us back a month early, he said, because he thought it was extremely important for us to make a tour together of the major institutions of the armed services, including the great atomic energy plants. He wanted us thoroughly to familiarize ourselves with the entire military establishment. With this background of information, he then wanted us to make a completely new, fresh survey of our military capabilities, in the light of our global commitments.

He stressed the fact that he did not want a long exhaustive staff study. He recognized our great collective experience, he said, and what he wanted from us was our own individual views, honestly and forthrightly stated. As we were leaving he asked each of us, individually, whether there was any reason we could not take this close look at our national policy, and recommend to him the general nature of the military establishment which would be required to support it. I answered, of course there was none.

We spent that month mainly in travel, sometimes together, as on the long trip West to visit the atomic energy plants, at other times separately, as we visited the major installations of our own services. It was almost the last time I had the opportunity to get the "feel" of the situation on the ground, a process of education as valuable to a commander in peacetime as in war. Later, as we became engulfed in the many duties that fell upon us as we took charge of our separate services, such trips were impossible.

The month of travel I think was of value to all of us, not only in giving us the overall picture of our entire military establishment, but in permitting us to get to know each other better. I had met Admiral Radford several times in the Pacific and knew of his great reputation. I had come to know Admiral Carney during his service as C in C South when I was Supreme Allied Commander in Europe. Nate Twining I had known and admired since he was a cadet at West Point, though I had not had the good fortune to serve with him in the intervening years.

The global picture as it unfolded to us during our month of travel and study was fairly clear in outline, though murky in some details.

The Communists had received a bloody nose in Korea. The Korean truce had been signed. Only the most naïve of optimists, however, would assume that the Reds had abandoned one iota of their global plan to harass, and embarrass, and conquer, when they could, the nations that lay beyond the Iron Curtain. Because they had been thwarted in Korea I felt we could expect a shifting of Red forces in the Far East and the application of pressure, perhaps even the outbreak of small wars in that general area, or elsewhere. The flare-up in Indo-China that was to come later, the Quemoy-Matsu situation that was to follow, were the products of the situation that followed the Korean truce.

I was deeply concerned by the fact that the end of hostilities in Korea seemed to have brought with it the hopeful delusion that peace inevitably would follow. There was a definite letting down, not only on our part, but on the part of some of our staunchest allies. There was already a definite tendency in the NATO nations to stretch out their preparations for defense over a far longer period than had been planned. There were signs in the wind that this stretch-out might turn into something more dangerous—an actual renegging on the commitments they had voluntarily made at the Lisbon conference in February of 1952. Unfortunately, in Western Europe, our good friends the British, weary of the austerity that heavy military commitments imposed, were taking the lead in this stretch-out process, which seemed to me to be inviting disaster.

Japan, too, was definitely lagging in carrying out her pledges to prepare for her own defense. And to the south, our Latin-American neighbors, whose friendship and support is so essential to our common security, were growing more and more vocal in their displeasure with our policies. They felt we were focusing far too much attention on other areas of the world, lavishing help on former enemies while ignoring the needs of old friends.

To me, as I took over my duties as Chief of Staff at the end of this month of orientation, some facts were clear. Our national policy was simply this: To keep the peace. To carry out that objective we had made certain commitments to deploy troops or provide matériel support, to more than fifty allied nations around the world. To carry out these commitments would require certain definitely determined forces, some in key areas overseas, and the remainder in the United States. And to support these troops at the minimum level at which they could be expected to carry out their missions would require a certain amount of money.

Appraisals and estimates were based not only on my own observations, but on the considered recommendations of the top commanders in the Army—the men who bore the great responsibility of carrying out these missions with whatever means were given them. They were the honest, forthright judgments of experienced military men, and they were based purely on military considerations.

By that time too there had taken shape in my mind some very definite ideas as to the duties and the functions of the Chief of Staff, as I understood them.

At my swearing-in ceremony in the Pentagon, attended by Secretary Wilson, Mr. Stevens, the members of my staff, Mrs. Ridgway, and Matty, I tried to make my position crystal clear.

I pointed out that when the President had ordered the reorganization of the Defense Department, he had stressed the importance of two main objectives—the maintenance of democratic institutions, and the protection of the integrity of the military profession. The first point, I said—the subordination of the military to the civilian authority—was so universally accepted throughout the officer corps that it needed no elaboration. Since George Washington's time, no top soldier has forgotten that he is a citizen first and a soldier second, and that the troops under his command are an instrument of the people's will. The second point, the protection of the integrity of the military profession, I felt, needed continued explanation to others in government and to the American people.

The "integrity of the military profession," I said, means that we must have an officer corps of such character and competence as will provide the highest professional and spiritual leadership to our citizen armies. It means a non-commissioned-officer corps indoctrinated and inspired by the officer corps, whose precepts are its guides, and whose standards it emulates. This professional, long-term cadre must be adequate both in size and in quality, I pointed out—a great reservoir of character, of devotion to duty, of loyalty, of professional competence. If we are to have this fountainhead of leadership, I added—and without it we do not have an Army—it must truly represent a cross-section of the nation's life—must include a fair share of the best men the country can produce, in character, in intellect, in morality and in culture.

Parenthetically, I would like to say that I have never subscribed to the Air Force and Navy view that they should have the cream of the nation's young men because of the greater complexity of their weapons and machines. There is simply no comparison between the operator of a machine, however intricate its mechanism, and the leader of men in ground battle, each man exposed to every reaction to which flesh is heir, and each dependent for his very life on the character and competence of his leader. At the turn of a wheel, at the captain's direction, a machine, whether it be a ship or a plane, can remain in a fight or at once withdraw. No such mechanical aid is available to a ground-force commander, whether he commands an army or a squad. He can order, but whether his men obey or not depends on the influence which his character, his intelligence, his competence have established over the minds of each individual in his unit. To my mind, therefore, the corporal who leads a rifle squad in battle should, if possible, have every whit as much character, intelligence and competence as the man who flies a plane or mans a ship's gun battery. All branches of the military today require men of the highest type, the Army no less than its sister services.

Finally—and this is the essential point—I said that the civilian authorities must scrupulously respect the integrity, the intellectual honesty, of its officer corps. Any effort to force unanimity of view, to compel adherence to some politico-military "party line" against the honestly expressed views of responsible officers, I pointed out, is a pernicious practice which jeopardizes rather than protects the integrity of the military profession.

From the officer corps, I told my civilian superiors, they could expect fearless and forthright expressions of honest, objective professional opinion up to the moment when they themselves, the civilian commanders, announced their decisions. Thereafter they could expect completely loyal and diligent execution of those decisions.

However, I pointed out, loyalty and complete trust cut both ways. They must flow just as strongly from the top down as from the bottom up. The civilian authorities must give their military services the same unqualified loyalty they receive. And for the Army to function with the deep devotion and the high *esprit* which are its proud traditions, it should know at all times that it has the support, confidence, and understanding of the people it serves.

For a specific reason I set down here in some detail the main points made on that occasion. I want to make it clear that even at that time I was aware of certain trends within the Defense Department, which, if pursued, would work long-range injury to the Army and the nation, the full effects of which would not become manifest until too late to correct them. It was already clear to me that my tour was to be an extremely difficult one—that my time was to be spent in the unhappy task of defending the U.S. Army from actions by my superiors which, to my mind, would weaken it, physically and spiritually.

There was likewise a fundamental difference of opinion as to the proper relationship which should exist between the statesman and the soldier. It was a question to which I had given deep consideration over long years of my service. It was one on which I had written several memoranda, first in War Plans Division when I was a major, then as Deputy Chief of Staff.

The relationship between the statesman and the soldier must be a most intimate and mutually trustful one. It must rest on an almost day-to-day association, a continuing interchange of ideas, a welcoming of considered professional views as the intellectually honest expression of honest opinions.

Boiled down it works like this:

The statesman, the senior civilian authority, says to the soldier (and by "soldier" I mean the professional military man—the Army, the Navy, and the Air Force as represented in the persons of the Chiefs of Staff): "This is our national policy. This is what we wish to accomplish, or would like to do. What military means are required to support it?"

The soldier studies this problem in detail.

"Very well," he says to the statesman. "Here is what your policy will require in men and guns, in ships and planes."

That, in its simplest terms, is the honest and forthright way the statesman and the soldier should work together. If it is an honest and mutually trustful relationship, it produces optimum results in the national interest. For that reason, I say that the professional soldier should never pull his punches, should never let himself for one moment be dissuaded from stating the honest estimates his own military experience and judgment tell him will be needed to do the job required of him. No factor of political motivation could excuse, no reason of "party" or political expediency could explain such an action.

If the objective the statesman wishes to achieve is a costly one, that is not the soldier's business. If it is greater than the political leaders wish to support, or think the economy of the country can bear, that is not his business. It is the constitutional responsibility of the civilian authority to decide these questions. If, of course, on first inspection, the cost is obviously fantastic, the soldier should make that point clear. But within the broad area of reasonable appropriations—within the bracket of what a reasonable man would say the country could afford—he should scrupulously eschew any opinion as to whether the cost is beyond the reach of the national purse or not. He is without competence in that field. If civilian authority finds the cost to be greater than the country can bear, then either the objectives themselves should be modified, or the responsibility for the risks involved should be forthrightly accepted. Under no circumstances, regardless of pressures from whatever source or motive, should the professional military man yield, or compromise his judgment for other than convincing military reasons. To do otherwise would be to destroy his usefulness.

Though the remarks I made at my swearing-in earned the expressed approval of my direct superior, Secretary Stevens, there was little indication thereafter that they had been heard at all by Mr. Wilson, the Secretary of Defense. When I presented my estimates of cost to Mr. Wilson, expressing the view that any lesser budget would dangerously weaken the Army's capability of meeting what I considered its part of United States Government commitments, his answer, in substance, was that he disagreed with my interpretation of what constituted commitments. Subsequently, I was informed that the money available would be reduced by some two billion dollars and the men proportionately.

To me there was no logic in this reasoning. My bewilderment was increased by the fact that at the same time these reductions were being ordered in the Army's budget, economists, with the blessing of the administration, were hailing the country's greatest boom, predicting that within the next five years the national production was going to rise from $360 billion to $500 billion. If that were true, then I was not greatly impressed with the argument that $2 billion more in the Defense Department budget was going to bankrupt the country.

The real situation then dawned on me. This military budget was not based so much on military requirements, or on what the economy of the country could stand, as on political considerations.

The fact that 76 per cent of the proposed reduction was to be made in Army funds indicated to me also that we were in danger of again falling into that serious error that had placed us at such a grave disadvantage against an inferior foe in the first few months of the Korean War. We were subject again to the same dangerous delusion, the misty hope that air power, armed with the fission or fusion bomb, could save us in time of trouble.

To my mind this country could not adopt a more dangerous doctrine, nor one more likely to lead us down the path to war.

32

☆☆☆☆

Indo-China, Quemoy, and Matsu

ALL these actions which in my view were detrimental to the strength and spirit of the Army I protested in meetings with the Joint Chiefs; in my testimony before committees of Congress; and by letter and in personal conferences with the Secretary of Defense. After each exchange of views with Mr. Wilson, I came away convinced that either his mental processes operated on a level of genius so high I could not grasp his meaning, or that considerations beyond the soldier's comprehension were influencing his thinking.

The basic point at issue, I think, lay in differing concepts of how, in the event of war, the doctrine of "massive retaliation" should be applied. My belief was simply this—that we must possess the power of swift and devastating retaliation. At the same time we must possess the capability for *selective* retaliation, the capacity to use one arm, or two, or all three—land, sea, and air combined—to apply whatever degree of force a particular situation demanded. The belief seemed to prevail that it was enough to hold the threat of the A and H bomb over the head of a trembling world.

No thinking soldier can accept this view. No honest student of military history could believe that the nuclear bomb alone was that key to quick and easy victory which mankind has sought since wars began.

Ironically our only potential enemies—the Russians and the Chinese —are not yet sufficiently "advanced" to be truly vulnerable to the nuclear bomb although one, Russia, is now equipped, or soon will be, to retaliate with the H bomb. Their civilization is not based on a complex nerve fabric, a web of interrelated and interdependent functions and services, as is ours. Theirs is a simpler and more primitive society that would be extremely difficult to destroy, just as the turtle and the crocodile are harder to kill than the higher animals. Finally, their two countries are spread out over enormous distances. It is nearly six thousand miles from the Oder-Neisse line to the Sea of Japan, a tremendous area for bombing aircraft to cover.

On this enormous land mass true victory in war could only be obtained by defeating the enemy's armed forces, destroying his hope for victory and his will to resist, and establishing control over his land and people. Mass destruction of his industrial resources is only one way to neutralize his capacity to wage war. Such destruction may not destroy his will to resist; it may strengthen his determination. It may have but little effect initially on his forces in the field. It establishes no ultimate control over his land.

Furthermore, to my mind, such mass destruction is repugnant to the ideals of a Christian nation. It is incompatible with the basic aim of the free world in war, which is to win a just and enduring peace. Lasting peace can only be won by changing the defeated aggressor into a constructive member of the society of free nations.

In the spring of 1954, when the Department of Defense was concentrating its greatest efforts on developing our capability to strike massive atomic blows, we very nearly found ourselves involved in a bloody jungle war in which our nuclear capability would have been almost useless.

It was during the time when a gallant French garrison, made up mainly of mercenaries of the Foreign Legion—for France had lacked the will to draft its own young men for service in Indo-China—was making its brave but futile stand at Dienbienphu. To military men familiar with the maps of Indo-China, the outcome of that siege was a foregone conclusion. The fight could end in but one way—in death or capture for the defenders. The decision to fight at Dienbienphu had not been made on a basis of military considerations. It had been basically political in motive—an effort to stiffen the backbone of shaken Laos, whose boundaries were exposed by the march of the Chinese.

However futile it might have been to stand and fight in that spot, still, the gallantry of the hard-fighting French garrison did capture the imagination of the world. Soon I was deeply concerned to hear individuals of great influence, both in and out of government, raising the cry that now was the time, and here, in Indo-China, was the place to "test the New Look," for us to intervene, to come to the aid of France with arms. At the same time that same old delusive idea was advanced—that we could do things the cheap and easy way, by going into Indo-China with air and naval forces alone. To me this had an ominous ring. For I felt sure that if we committed air and naval power to that area, we would have to follow them immediately with ground forces in support.

I also knew that none of those advocating such a step had any accurate idea what such an operation would cost us in blood and money and national effort. I felt that it was essential therefore that all who had any influence in making the decision on this grave matter should be fully aware of all the factors involved. To provide these facts, I sent out to Indo-China an Army team of experts in every field: engineers, signal and communications specialists, medical officers, and experienced combat leaders who knew how to evaluate terrain in terms of battle tactics. They went out to get the answers to a thousand questions that those who had so blithely recommended that we go to war there had never taken the trouble to ask. How deep was the water over the bar at Saigon? What were the harbor and dock facilities? Where could we store the tons of supplies we would need to support us there? How good was the road net—how could supplies be transported as the fighting forces moved inland, and in what tonnages? What of the climate? The rainfall? What tropical diseases would attack the combat soldier in that jungle land?

Their report was complete. The area, they found, was practically devoid of those facilities which modern forces such as ours find essential to the waging of war. Its telecommunications, highways, railways—all the things that make possible the operation of a modern combat force on land—were almost non-existent. Its port facilities and airfields were totally inadequate, and to provide the facilities we would need would require a tremendous engineering and logistical effort.

The land was a land of rice paddy and jungle—particularly adapted to the guerrilla-type warfare at which the Chinese soldier is a master. This meant that every little detachment, every individual, that tried to move about that country, would have to be protected by riflemen. Every telephone lineman, road repair party every ambulance and every rear-area aid station would have to be under armed guard or they would be shot at around the clock.

If we did go into Indo-China, we would have to win. We would have to go in with a military force adequate in all its branches, and that meant a very strong ground force—an Army that could not only stand the normal attrition of battle, but could absorb heavy casualties from the jungle heat, and the rots and fevers which afflict the white man in the tropics. We could not again afford to accept anything short of decisive military victory.

We could have fought in Indo-China. We could have won, if we had been willing to pay the tremendous cost in men and money that such intervention would have required—a cost that in my opinion would have eventually been as great as, or greater than, that we paid in Korea. In Korea, we had learned that air and naval power alone cannot win a war and that inadequate ground forces cannot win one either. It was incredible to me that we had forgotten that bitter lesson so soon—that we were on the verge of making that same tragic error.

That error, thank God, was not repeated. As soon as the full report was in, I lost no time in having it passed on up the chain of command. It reached President Eisenhower. To a man of his military experience its implications were immediately clear. The idea of intervening was abandoned, and it is my belief that the analysis which the Army made and presented to higher authority played a considerable, perhaps a decisive, part in persuading our government not to embark on that tragic adventure.

It is easy for people to dream up intriguing tactical schemes. It is a pastime in which any high school ROTC cadet can indulge, for it requires only a modicum of military knowledge, and even professionals of long service engage in the same game from time to time. What throws you in combat is rarely the fact that your tactical scheme was wrong—though, of course, history is replete with examples of faulty tactical planning—but that you failed to think through the hard cold facts of logistics. You failed to ask yourself, "How am I going to get Force A from X to Y—and how am I going to supply and sustain it once it gets there?" There is always a great temptation to think only of the objective to be attained, to ignore the basic planning in the hope that in some way the Lord will provide. That sort of wishful thinking prevailed in the early days of the Indo-China discussion—prevailed, in fact, until the Army took the time and trouble painstakingly to survey the ground and then to sit down with paper and pencil and laboriously and unglamorously spell the whole thing out in an analysis that revealed all its costs and implications.

As I have pointed out earlier in this narrative, when the day comes for me to face my Maker and account for my actions, the thing I would be most humbly proud of was the fact that I fought against, and perhaps contributed to preventing, the carrying out of some hare-brained tactical schemes which would have cost the lives of thousands of men. To that list of tragic accidents that fortunately never happened I would add the Indo-China intervention.

Not long after the abortive idea of intervention in Indo-China had been laid to rest, there came the flare-up over Quemoy and Matsu. Again there was strong feeling in high places that here we should take a stand. And again I found myself in disagreement, with the interventionists.

I had studied the maps with care. Quemoy and Matsu were two small islands, occupied by our friends the Nationalist Chinese. They lay within artillery range of the Red Chinese on the mainland. They constituted, to my way of thinking, no more than listening posts on an outpost line of observation. They had little value as offensive bases. Matsu would be useless in this respect, and Quemoy not much better, for there is no major military objective on the mainland that lies within three hundred miles. If we were to go into Red China with ground forces, we certainly would not use Quemoy. Neither do the Reds have to have Quemoy for an invasion of Formosa. It lies along the best and shortest route, but there are many other jumping-off places.

I had also studied the intelligence reports. I had as much information, I suppose, as did anybody else about Red activities on the mainland opposite Matsu and Quemoy. To my mind, what the Chinese were doing there did not justify a conclusion that they were planning an attack on Formosa. Their activities could just as well be defensive as offensive in nature. They were building airfields, and rail lines, which could rush troops to the seacoast in the event of an invasion *from* Formosa. But there was no indication they were concentrating ground troops there, or organizing an invasion force of their own.

These points I made before the Armed Services Committees of Congress while the concern over Matsu and Quemoy was at its height. The decision of the Congress was to leave the matter in the hands of the President. It would be his decision as to when, and where, we would meet force with force in the touchy area where Red and Nationalist China face each other at close quarters.

With this the Quemoy-Matsu issue faded into what seems for the moment to be a mutually satisfactory stalemate. It will, no doubt, flare up again and again. There is no doubt in my mind that we would go to war to defend Formosa or the Pescadores, and we should, for the loss of either of these would make a serious breach in our outermost line of defense in the Pacific, and cause our good friends abroad to doubt our resolution. But the juridical, historical and geographical background of Quemoy and Matsu is radically different. To go to war for Quemoy or Matsu, to me would seem an unwarranted and tragic course to take.

I do not for a moment wish to impugn the intellectual honesty of any others who did not share this view. They sincerely felt, I think, that it were better to face the issue then and there, to make it clear to the Reds that any encroachment on Chinese Nationalist territory, however slight, would mean war.

To me that concept is completely repugnant. I make no pretense to clairvoyance. God alone knows what would happen. But such an action would be almost impossible to limit. It would bring us into direct conflict with the Red Chinese. It could spread to full and all-out war, employing all the terrible weapons at our command.

And we could, by such an all-out effort, conquer China.

But I challenge any thesis that destroying the military might of Red China would be in our own long-range interest. We could create there, by military means, a great power vacuum. Then we would have to go in there with hundreds of thousands of men to fill that vacuum— which would bring us face to face with Russia along a seven thousand-mile frontier. If we failed to go in, then Russia herself would fill it, and the threat to our own security would not have abated one iota.

To my way of thinking the desire to intervene in Indo-China, the willingness to use force in dealing with Quemoy and Matsu reflects a thinking which trends dangerously toward acceptance of the doctrine of "preventive war."

To me nothing could more tragically demonstrate our complete and utter moral bankruptcy than for us deliberately to initiate a "preventive war." Once we take that absolutely fatal step our civilization would be doomed. We would have to rely on conquest for survival from then on, until our society crumbled as the empires of Alexander, and of Rome, crumbled from their own inner decay. In all the history of the world no civilization based on conquest has long endured. America would be no exception.

33

☆☆☆☆

A Day in the Pentagon

MY DAY in the Pentagon began at eight-thirty in the morning. On my desk when I arrived I would find a sheaf of radio messages, already screened and winnowed by my staff. They had come in during the night, and they brought the latest information on the activities— and the problems—of Army units all over the world. Along with them was a summary of key cables which the State Department had received during the past twelve hours, which were passed on for information to all the Chiefs of Staff.

Many of the radio messages posed questions, asked for answers to problems which required my decision. Some could be handled by my excellent staff, with only basic guidance from me, given orally. Matters dealing with operations and administration went to my deputy, Lieutenant General Anthony C. McAuliffe, and later, when Tony McAuliffe left to command Seventh Army in Europe, I reposed the same complete faith and confidence in an old friend and trusted comrade Lieutenant General Walter L. Weible. Matters dealing with plans and research were in the special field of Lieutenant General Lyman L. Lemnitzer, and financial matters affecting the Army were the responsibility of a brilliant fiscal expert, Lieutenant General George H. Decker. In all matters, my Vice Chiefs, first General John E. Hull, and later, General Charles L. Bolté, served as my alter ego, fully authorized to act in my name.

Though authority, in a military command, can and must be delegated, responsibility can never be. It was my duty, therefore, not only to make those decisions which were mine alone to make, but to be fully aware of the actions of my deputies.

The reading of the morning's messages was followed by a series of briefings and conferences based mainly on decisions required by developments of the previous day. These briefings were oral, making as much use of charts and graphs as possible, and they went directly to the point.

Brilliant young officers from the Secretariat, specifically chosen for their ability to grasp complex problems and boil them down to their essentials, conducted these briefings.

"Sir," they would say as they entered, "this is an action briefing. Your decision will be required when it is finished."

Or,

"Sir, this is an information briefing. No decision will be required."

Though concise, these action briefings were complete. They gave the various courses of action open to me and evaluated each. If the opinions of the subordinate officers were unanimous as to which course was the soundest, this point was made. If, on the other hand, the Chief of Engineers, for example, dissented, the reasons for his dissent were given, and were weighed by me.

On the basis of these briefings, out of the knowledge and experience I had gathered in thirty-six years of soldiering, I made my decisions. The big ones, naturally, I made only after consultation with my immediate superior, Secretary Stevens. His office was next to mine. Frequently he would come in to hear the briefings. Often I would step into his office to inform him of some action taken or contemplated. At least once a day he was in my office or I in his. We had no secrets from each other, but worked in the spirit of fullest co-operation. Throughout my tour I felt that I had his complete support. I know he had mine.

So, routinely, went the operation of the office of the Chief of Staff. No matter how carefully I allotted my time, though, nor how well I might have organized my work, each day inevitably brought its crisis —known in Pentagonese as a "flap," which threw us far off schedule. Army garrisons, and our national interests, literally ringed the world. Deployed around the globe were a million and a half men in uniform, and a half a million civilians, for whose actions and welfare, I was, in one way or another, responsible. It was inevitable, therefore, that at least once every twenty-four hours something would erupt which would bring an urgent inquiry from Congress, from the press or the radio people, from my own Secretary, Mr. Stevens, or from Mr. Wilson upstairs.

Most of these queries could be handled fairly expeditiously. As soon as the facts could be assembled, I passed them on, for it was my policy, fully supported by Mr. Stevens, that we should keep the gentlemen on Capitol Hill fully informed on all matters affecting the Army, and that we would give promptly to the press and radio full information on all matters that did not jeopardize the national security.

An inquiry from Mr. Wilson, however, would usually bring all the major activities of the Chief of Staff's office to a grinding halt for a period of two to four hours. In the midst of the morning briefings, with a dozen problems pressing for decision, I would receive a telephone call that Mr. Wilson wished to see me at once. Often, he would require that several key members of my staff be present also. Frequently we were not informed as to what the Secretary wanted to see us about.

So we would file upstairs, where usually we would find our opposite members in the other armed services, for Mr. Wilson was fond of a large audience, and of lengthy, and often rambling discussion of topics having no direct relation to the subject for which we had been assembled.

By contrast, it was a great pleasure to work with his able deputy, Robert Anderson. Bob Anderson was highly intelligent. He was patient. He had tremendous powers of concentration. He would listen, absorb, quickly understand, and promptly decide. And he invariably was sympathetic, friendly, and always warmly courteous.

The long and frequently fruitless sessions with Mr. Wilson often consumed half a working day. I would return to my office to find my desk piled high with work. The result was that rarely did I leave my office for home in the evenings without a full brief case. Yet it always has been my feeling that the man who tries to work at night, at the end of a long and trying day, defeats his own purpose. When bedtime comes he cannot slough off his problems. He carries them to bed with him and turns and tosses half the night, waking the next morning, tired and groggy, to face the decisions of the new day.

For that reason, except in a few cases of the utmost importance, I simply refused to work at night. I much preferred to get up at dawn, and tackle my problems then, when both mind and body were fresh and rested.

My day began, usually, at six o'clock. Before Penny and Matty were awake I'd go into my little upstairs office at my home at Fort Myer, and, still dressed in pajamas and robe, I would set to work. Over a cup of black coffee, brought up by Sergeant Hampton, I would give the more urgent problems the quiet reflection the many interruptions at the office made impossible. I would work from six to eight. Exactly at eight Sergeant Hampton would bring up the breakfast I eat 365 mornings a year—two soft-boiled eggs in the shell, a piece of dry toast, and a pot of black coffee. Five minutes for breakfast, ten minutes more to shower, shave, and dress, a five-minute drive to the Pentagon, and I'd be at my desk before eight-thirty. Borrowing a leaf from the book of General Marshall, I'd leave shortly after noon for lunch at home, taking, on fair days, a little walk in the garden to clear the cobwebs from my brain. By one o'clock, I would be back at my desk, to remain there until six-thirty. Many times, of course, this little midday break was impossible, and I would have a sandwich at my desk. I rarely went to the Secretary's Pentagon dining room for lunch, for here always we would talk shop, and it gave the mind no relief.

One of the great burdens borne by the top staff officer stationed in Washington is that activity referred to by the eminent baseball pitcher Mr. "Satchel" Paige as the "social ramble." There are some sixty diplomatic missions in Washington, and the Chief of Staff is on the guest list of them all. In addition, both Mrs. Ridgway and I had many warm friends from our days in Latin America, Europe, and the Far East, who would invite us for cocktails or for dinner. Many of these old friends we genuinely wanted to see, for they were charming and stimulating people. Soon, though, it was clear that I could not carry my official burdens by day and do much party going at night. Many social obligations, of course, you simply cannot turn down, for various reasons. Finally, though, we had to get pretty ruthless in our refusals. Many times, for example, there would be two or three invitations for one evening, and if we had been so inclined, we could have gone out nearly every night in the year. We made it a rule to limit our social engagements to a maximum of two evenings a week, and even this was a little trying. In fact, my happiest evenings were those when I didn't go out at all, but stayed at home, dining quietly with Penny, playing with Matty until his bedtime, and following him up to bed soon thereafter. This way I could rise refreshed for those early-morning hours of work in the quiet house, face that bulging brief case, full of complex problems, with confidence, and do the work my conscience told me I had to do.

34

☆☆☆☆

Under Pressure

As I said recently in a *Saturday Evening Post* series: "It is not the dangerous days of battle which most strongly test the soldier's resolution, but the years of peace, when many voices, offering many counsels, bewilder and confound him."

Again and again, during my tour as Chief of Staff, pressure was brought on me, in the name of economy, to keep the semblance, but not the reality, of a fighting force overseas.

I well recall one session in the office of Mr. Wilson, when the reductions in the Army budget were under discussion.

"Why don't you reduce the strength of your combat divisions?" he asked me. "Pull them down to 85 per cent. Why don't you inactivate certain units? Just keep them on a cadre basis."

To my mind this would have been a repetition of that tragic policy of retrenchment followed by a former Secretary, Mr. Louis Johnson, when during the Truman administration we so skeletonized our forces in the Far East that we were almost helpless when the crudely armed mass armies of North Korea stormed south across the Parallel. As Mr. Wilson spoke I thought of the brave men who died in those early days in Korea, when the skeleton regiments fought and fell back until they finally stood with their backs to the sea.

And remembering them, I told him that so long as I was Chief of

Staff, I would *not* reduce the strength of combat units who stood face to face with potential enemies overseas, thus exposing them to possible disaster, unless I had clear, specific, and direct orders from him to do so.

Then came the pressure, strongly applied.

This suggestion to reduce our unit strength came directly from the President, Mr. Wilson said. As I was no doubt aware, the President was a man of considerable military experience himself. For me to oppose his wishes, therefore, placed me in the position of taking issue with my Commander in Chief.

"And that," he added bluntly, "would not be good."

I told Mr. Wilson that I had profound respect for the President's military judgment. And I would hope that my views on military matters would always be in accord with his. However, I added, if my deep convictions led me to take an opposite view, I would adhere to that judgment until purely military arguments proved me wrong. I would not be swayed by arguments that what I advocated would be politically unacceptable, or that its cost was greater than the administration felt we could afford.

I learned early in my military career that it is not enough, when great issues are involved, to express your views verbally and let it go at that. It is necessary to put them down in writing, over your signature. In that way they became a part of the historical record.

So I went back to my office and drew up a memorandum, which I signed, and transmitted to the Secretary of Defense through my own immediate superior, Mr. Stevens, the Secretary of the Army. In this report I pointed out that as Chief of Staff of the Army, and as a member of the Joint Chiefs, it was my duty and obligation to advise the Department of Defense, the National Security Council, and the President, on military matters. This advice should be based on my honest, fearless, objective estimate of what the Army needed to serve the national interest, and it should have no reference to the impact my recommendations might have on the national economy, on domestic politics, or on administration policy at any particular time. In this view, I said, I was guided by President Eisenhower himself, who as Chief of Staff in 1947 had told a Congressional appropriations committee:

"I appear before you only as a professional soldier, to give you a soldier's advice regarding the national defense. I am not qualified to proceed beyond that field, and I do not intend to do so. It is my duty to tell you gentlemen what I believe to be necessary for the national security."

Then, as objectively as I could, I gave the Secretary of Defense my best judgment on what Army forces I believed to be necessary for the national security, in the light of our global commitments and the capabilities of the enemy. I also pointed out that the reductions which had been demanded of me—to slash the forces in uniform from 1,500,000 to 1,000,000 by the summer of 1956, to cut Army expenditures from 16.2 billions to 8.9 billions—would so weaken the Army that it could no longer carry out its missions.

I then reiterated my previous stand—that I would not order reductions in Army units in potential combat areas unless I had direct orders to do so.

That Mr. Wilson had the authority to issue such orders I did not question. But the *responsibility* for the consequences, I felt, must also rest on his shoulders. Throughout my tour there was never any lack of willingness on the part of the Defense Department to exercise full authority. Frequently though, this was not accompanied by an equal willingness to assume responsibility for actions taken.

On the other hand there seemed to me to be a deliberate effort to soothe and lull the public by placing responsibility where it did not rest, by conveying the false impression that there was unanimous agreement between the civilian authorities and their military advisers on the form and shape the military establishment should take.

As a combat soldier I have been shot at from ambush, and bombed by planes which I thought to be friendly, both of which are experiences that are momentarily unsettling. I do not recall, however, that I ever felt a greater sense of surprise and shock than when I read in President Eisenhower's State of the Union message in 1954 that:

"The defense program recommended for 1955 . . . is based on a new military program *unanimously recommended* [the italics are mine] by the Joint Chiefs of Staff."

As one member of the Joint Chiefs of Staff who most emphatically had not concurred in the 1955 military program as it was presented to the people, I was nonplused by this statement. The fact is the 1955 budget was a "directed verdict," as were the Army budgets for 1956 and '57. The force levels provided in all three were not primarily based on military needs. They were not based on the freely reached conclusions of the Joint Chiefs of Staff. They were squeezed between the framework of arbitrary manpower and fiscal limits, a complete inversion of the normal process.

It soon became clear to me that the month-long survey which the Joint Chiefs were required to make prior to taking office had been merely an orientation exercise, so far as I was concerned. The recommendations which I later made, partly as a result of that survey, had been given scant consideration in the deliberations which established the force levels for the Army. It seemed likely that the size and strength of the Army—in fact the pattern of the whole military establishment under the new administration—had already been decided upon, in outline at least, long before. In my opinion, which is supported by items appearing recently in the press, this pre-planning took place shortly after the election in 1952, when President-elect Eisenhower met with some of his future key advisers aboard the U.S.S. *Helena,* while en route home from his visit to Korea.

Later, the efforts of the Secretary of Defense and the Chairman of the Joint Chiefs were directed toward securing the unanimous assent of the country's top military men to these pre-set plans.

For example, in the *U.S. News and World Report* of June 3, 1955, there appears this interesting note under the heading "New Chiefs of Staff: More Harmony among the Brass": "Hand picked men who may be more of one mind in backing administration concepts of U.S. defense policy are to make up the Joint Chiefs of Staff, now that President Eisenhower has completed a mid-term shake-up that he deliberately planned two years ago."

And in the Washington *Sunday Star* on December 3, 1954, there appeared this item, referring to the meeting of the President's future inner cabinet with Admiral Radford aboard the *Helena*:

"[There was] developed in these Pacific talks the concept of a hard-hitting, highly mobile force, based in the United States and ready to put out big fires as well as little ones wherever the Communists might set them."

With that concept I have no quarrel whatsoever. But what branch of the service is best equipped to "put out big fires or little ones wherever the Communists might set them"?

That is the role of the foot soldier, the man with the rifle. The great intercontinental bombers cannot do it, even though they may be armed with the fission or the fusion bomb. For who is going to move into the vacuum of chaos and destruction that the bomber creates, to assure that another evil conspiracy does not arise from the ashes of the atomic avalanche? The Navy cannot do it, for modern wars are not won upon the sea, nor beneath the sea. Man is a land animal, his dwelling place is on the earth, and the Navy takes and holds no ground. Despite all the new and terrible techniques of killing that our generation has devised, the foot soldier is still the ultimate weapon. Wars are still fought for little bits of bloody earth, and they are only ended when the enemy's will to resist is broken, and armed men stand victorious on his home soil.

As a nation we are fond of the pat phrase, the comforting cliché. Mr. Johnson assured us that he was merely "trimming the fat" from the military establishment, and the people accepted that assurance until Korea proved our fighting forces had been bled white. Mr. Wilson, the headlines tell us, is giving us "more bang for a buck." By this I presume is meant our concentration on the development of the hydrogen bomb, and of the family of new missiles which carry the atomic warhead. Our efforts in this field have my fullest approval, and throughout my tour as Chief of Staff I did all within my power to further the development of those weapons which had special usefulness to the Army.

However, to me it was specious reasoning to argue, as some of my civilian superiors did argue, that since these new weapons so greatly increased the fire power of a combat unit, we therefore could drastically reduce the number of units in the field.

In the first place, except for atomic weapons deliverable by air, only an extremely limited number of these weapons are available. At this writing (January, 1956) we have in Europe, as the Russians are well aware, only five battalions—a total of thirty guns of the 280-mm. atomic cannon. We have a limited number of Honest John rockets, which carry an atomic warhead, and seven battalions of the Corporal guided missile, which also has recently been deployed overseas. But it should be perfectly obvious to the whole world that the atomic weapons we have in place along a front that stretches four hundred miles from the North Sea to the Alps constitutes an extremely thin line. And these are vulnerable weapons. They are not easy to conceal. They would be the object of the enemy's most intensive intelligence efforts. He would go to any lengths to locate and destroy them, and the destruction of one gun would leave a great gap in our lines that only fighting men could fill.

It was also argued that our new reserve components soon would be of such size and strength that we could afford to cut down the number of men on active duty. But the fact is we simply do not have these reserves in being, ready to move with the speed the next war will demand. In the past it has taken us from ten to thirteen months to convert reserve forces into battle-ready divisions. Under the most optimistic estimates, we cannot hope to have that much time again. The forces that the United States will need in the initial stages—say the first six months—of another war, must be active forces in being on D-day. To say that men who have had one or two years training, and have thereafter taken some forty-eight two-hour drills a year, plus fifteen days in summer camp, can be quickly welded into major units of a combat field army, to me is ridiculous. Nobody who knows anything about getting a unit ready for combat would claim that it could be done.

The third argument for reducing the Army's strength was based on the prospect that a great West German army of half a million men would soon be ready to join with the NATO allies in the defense of Europe. But where are they? We have seen the unfolding of history in regard to those German forces. It was only last July that, after years of effort, authorization was obtained to put in uniform the first increment of six thousand men. Some few have already been sworn in, but by the Germans' own estimate it will be another three years before the whole twelve divisions are under arms.

These three principal reasons given to justify the drastic scope and rapidity of Army cuts do not stand up under impartial analysis. They were specious arguments bound to obscure the true reasons, which were largely political. They were not such as to reassure our allies to whom we had made solemn pledges of military support around the world.

Two years of offering my reasoned judgments, based purely on military considerations, against arguments I knew to be primarily political in nature, created in my mind one strong conviction: The gentlemen who accept the great posts of authority and responsibility in the Defense Department should be as completely divorced from politics as possible. The tendency, which was manifest many times during my tour, of civilian Secretaries making military decisions on a basis of political expediency constitutes a danger to this country. The power that is vested in the civilian Secretaries, particularly in the Secretary of Defense, is so enormous that it could do incalculable harm if applied on a basis of what is good for the party, instead of what is good for the country. They should base their decisions solely on the security interests of the United States, in the light of the best judgment God gave them, free of political considerations.

Nor should they rely for guidance on any one soldier, sailor, or airman, no matter how wide his past experience may have been. Their decisions, on which the fate of this nation depends, *must be made only after full consideration has been given to the views of all the Joint Chiefs.* Certainly they should never be made on the advice of one member only, no matter how closely his views may accord with their wishes, whether he be the Chairman or any other. There is no one human being who knows enough of the detailed conduct of military operations on land, sea, and in the air to be competent to advise the civil authorities on all three.

In that great new field of planning for military operations in a war in which nuclear weapons are used by both sides—all military men are groping for solutions under equal difficulties. No man living has had any experience with that kind of warfare. We have dropped two "small" fission bombs on civilian populations, practically unopposed. But the full and varied use of the atomic device as an instrument of war still lies in the realm of theory and conjecture. Whatever their past experience might have been, therefore, all military men stand today on the threshold of the new and unknown, and no human being can clearly foresee and be sure he foresees, the form the wars of the future will take.

These comments are made without the slightest reference to the qualifications of any particular incumbent of the office of President. Today our President has had as much military experience as any man living. But we may not be blessed with a Commander in Chief with his military experience and his military judgment in our future history. And even if we had such a man he would need advice—the sound objective military advice of not one alone, but *all* the members of the Joint Chiefs of Staff.

It was clear to me throughout my service that if it was our basic mission to keep the peace of the world, to deter aggression wherever it might appear, then it was my duty to create and keep in being combat-ready forces that could in truth "put out big fires or little ones wherever the Communists might set them."

But what deters aggression? First, strength. Strength in being, that is known to the aggressor, who also must know that his prospective victim has the spiritual determination to use his strength if provoked.

And what kind of armed force is required by a nation determined to fight little wars, or big ones, if aggression does occur?

The answer is simple. It must be a properly proportioned force of all arms, so deployed in danger spots around the world that each different component—land, sea, and air—can bring its own special forms of firepower most effectively to bear, as a member of a combined force of all arms. It must be adequately trained, properly armed, highly mobile, and strong in the active elements which can strike back without delay in answer to any armed attack. It must be superbly led.

This was the kind of force which I consistently recommended while I was Chief of Staff. This was the kind of force which Mr. Wilson assured the public he was creating.

As Chief of Staff, it fell to my lot to carry out his will—the will of the administration, perhaps it would be fairer to say, expressed through him.

This I did in travail of spirit. For I say in all earnestness and sincerity that throughout my two years as Chief of Staff I felt I was being called upon to tear down, rather than to build up, the ultimately decisive element in a properly proportioned fighting force on which the world could rest its hopes for maintaining the peace, or, if the catastrophe of war came, for enforcing its will upon those who broke that peace.

Repeatedly, I was called upon to take actions and advocate policies, which, if continued, might eventually so weaken the United States

Army it could no longer stand, strong in its pride and free to fulfill its role as an effective instrument of national policy alongside of its sister services. If these policies were not arrested, it could no longer fulfill its commitments around the world. It might no longer achieve that one thing for which an army exists—victory in war.

35

☆☆☆☆

National Strategy

THERE is one phrase, I think, that should be engraved on the heart of every soldier and every civilian in a position of control over the military.

That phrase is "Success in Battle."

The sole role of any army, the sole criterion by which it will be judged by history, is embodied in these words. An army is one thing only—a fighting organization. And every element which makes up that organization, from the front-line rifle platoon to the great rear-echelon components, must serve one purpose only—the achievement of victory in war.

But what constitutes a winning army?

It is an army which knows that its leadership, its training, and its weapons, are the best the country can produce. It is an army sure of the confidence of the people from which it comes, sure of its place in the nation's heart, proud of its strength, confident of its ability to meet any warlike challenge, small or great, wherever that challenge may arise.

It is an army loyal to its own ideals; an army which resents any disparagement of its leaders, and deplores and opposes the continuing trend to strip from the military career those intangible items of which pride and self-respect and tradition and *esprit* are made.

Throughout my service as Chief of Staff three great tasks confronted me: First, to preserve the spirit and pride of an Army which top-level efforts steadily sought to reduce to a subordinate place among the three great services that make up our country's shield; second, to deploy this waning strength in such a way that ground combat units would be as effective as possible in the event of war; and third, to lay the foundations for a totally different Army than any we have known to date—an Army trained, equipped, and organized to fight and win in an atomic war.

My efforts in this latter task were frequently misinterpreted. And I deeply resented it when I heard, as I did so often hear, prominent Americans who should have known better uttering ill-considered and untrue statements to the effect that the Army was preparing to fight the war of tomorrow with the weapons and the tactics of yesterday. Such assertions are disparaging to the intelligence of the men who lead our Army. There isn't anybody in the United States who has a keener sense of responsibility to his countrymen and his God for the lives of the men who may be entrusted to them than have these commanders. There is nobody who perceives more clearly than they that the new weapons, in our hands and in the hands of the enemy, have rendered obsolete the tactics and the organization of the armies of the past. And it was and is a complete perversion of the facts to say that the Army and its leaders were thinking only in terms of past experience, were planning to use men in the mass, merely because we had said that the Army of the future would require more, not fewer, men.

There are a number of sound and logical reasons why a field army of the atomic age may have to be bigger than its predecessors of the past. The complex new weapons themselves—the atomic cannon, rockets, and guided missiles—require far more men to serve and maintain them than did the simpler field pieces of World War II and Korea. The prospect of sudden and enormous casualties, inflicted by the enemy with his own new weapons, makes necessary the training of replacements in great numbers for the dead, and a medical establishment larger than ever to care for the sick and wounded. In the main, though, the changing shape of the battlefield itself sets the requirements for more men. The battle zones of World War II within which actual ground combat took place were rarely as much as twenty-five miles in depth. Penetrations of armored and airborne forces in the battle areas of the future may well extend two hundred miles or even more in depth, and only by great dispersion, in the wars of the future, will ground elements be able to survive.

To analyze and predict the role the Army should play on this atomic battlefield, I put to work some of the best military brains we could spare. Several senior officers of great experience and judgment, and a number of younger officers of brilliance and imagination, were withdrawn from all other duties to devote all their time and thinking to one question: What should be the form and shape of the Army of the future?

In outlining their mission I stressed to them the importance of mobility—mental mobility—the capacity to move from old, sound, tested attitudes and beliefs into new realms of military thinking. I stressed that they should guard against man's human tendency to resist and avoid change. The Army of the future, I pointed out, inevitably would have to change. Its old organization would have to be drastically altered; its ancient, tested tactics would have to be revamped. Their job was to foresee and suggest the form these changes should take.

I also warned against another disease that afflicts the soldier as it does the layman—the tendency to base all judgment on his own past experience. I reminded them that they were explorers and pioneers, working in a field in which no one living had had any useful experience. We had dropped two atomic bombs in war, though practically under peacetime conditions. From that experience we had learned but little—except the results of an atomic explosion on a densely concentrated civilian population. But what of the effect of an atomic missile on an Army in the field, widely dispersed, adequately trained, and partially sheltered underground? Of that we had nothing but theoretical knowledge, plus the results of some carefully controlled and therefore inconclusive tests.

The first big problem was to decide how far into the future we should try to project our thinking. I chose the decade 1960–1970. If we tried to confine our thinking to two or three years ahead, I felt we should soon become so submerged in the pressures of the present that we could not plan boldly and with sufficient imagination or have time to spread out the tremendous costs within any authorizations we could reasonably anticipate. If we projected our thoughts too far ahead, unforeseen developments in the field of science as applied to weapons, transport, and communications would make our plans obsolete before they could ever begin to go into effect.

That study, begun in 1953, is still going on. It has made great progress. It has found some answers. It has uncovered many new and thorny questions for which answers are still being sought. It has produced some new and forward-looking theories, which are being analyzed in the service schools and tested by the troops in the field.

We do not presume to have final answers to all problems yet. We do not expect the answers we do adopt will ever be final in this fluid art. But we do think we can see, in outline at least, the shape of the future.

In broad terms the Army must be a streamlined, hard-hitting force, armed with a wide variety of nuclear weapons in adequate numbers and with greatly improved non-nuclear weapons. Its basic combat units will probably be aggregations of small "battle groups" of all arms—infantry, armor, artillery, and engineers. The larger units, and to a lesser degree the "battle groups" themselves, will be semi-independent, self-contained, and capable of operating over great distances on a fluid battlefield for long periods of time with a minimum of control and support by higher headquarters. The battle groups, and the higher echelons into which they will be formed, may correspond roughly to the regimental combat teams of our present divisions, and to the divisions themselves, but their number, types, and groupings, and their systems of control, all remain to be determined.

As many elements as practicable of these forces, all except their heaviest ones, must be transportable by air, both between continents and within the confines of the battle zone. Their weapons must be as light and compact and their vehicles as capable of rapid movement over any type of terrain as we can make them without detriment to their capacity to accomplish their missions.

Ground combat will still consist of fire and maneuver, but stylized concepts of battle and formalized battle organizations as we have known them will no longer be employed. The battle commander of the future must possess initiative, self-confidence, daring, and imagination in the highest degree. He must be a man of the greatest mental flexibility, physical stamina, and moral and physical courage.

The nuclear weapon must set the pattern for both offense and defense. The defense must disperse to survive, in staggered tactical formations disposed in great depth, and the composition and dispersion of the larger units must be such as to allow them to absorb an atomic blow without shattering. At the same time they must be capable of moving swiftly to prevent the enemy from exploiting his strikes. This battlefield mobility is also essential in order to maneuver the enemy into forming remunerative targets for our own nuclear weapons.

In the offensive, men and equipment must move from dispersed positions with great speed to the focal point of attack. They must concentrate rapidly, and once the objective is seized, they must disperse with equal speed to avoid a counter-blow. Not only close supporting fire, but guided missiles and rocket firepower, directed from widely separated distant points, must be directed against the objective. Forces must be capable of moving by air into the zone of mass destruction, at such velocity that the enemy in the area will have no time to recover, nor to bring land forces to bear from elsewhere. At the same time, offensive actions by our airborne and armored units must further confuse, disrupt, and paralyze the enemy by hit-and-run hell-raising deep in his rear, on missions similar to, but potentially far more fruitful than, those of cavalry of ages past.

Superior firepower will be absolutely essential to successful operations. It must extend throughout the entire field army. It must be based on a family of weapons capable of delivering nuclear and conventional explosives on any type target anywhere in the combat zone, regardless of weather, visibility or enemy counter-measures.

Superior firepower won't mean much, though, unless the combat units can be fed, supplied, and transported quickly. Fixed land lines of communications will be down-graded in importance and huge supply dumps will be obsolete, for they will be too vulnerable to atomic attack. To a far greater extent than ever before, aircraft must provide the means for troop transport, resupply, evacuation, and communications, and both the supply and transport systems must be flexible enough to adjust to quick changes in task force organization and to swift changes in the location of widely scattered combat units.

It is obvious that the Army described above bears little resemblance to the massed, slow-moving armies of World War II. It is an Army in the process of evolutionary changes—in weapons, tactics, and organization. It is an Army seeking the combinations with which to fight tomorrow's wars with tomorrow's weapons and techniques, and this it will do when tomorrow's weapons are at hand.

No soldier doubts that American inventive genius will provide the tools it needs. But an Army needs more than weapons. It needs the bold and competent leadership of men who are proud of their profession. It must have sufficient numbers of trained, courageous men. For in the last analysis, man is the only ultimate weapon, and upon his determination, his courage, his stamina, and his skill, rests the issue of victory or defeat.

While on the subject of man as a fighter, I would like to speak for a moment about one great problem that faced me throughout my tour of duty as Chief of Staff. That is the problem inherent in training an American Army. The American people, accustomed to ease and luxury in their daily lives, find it hard to appreciate what military training means, and their attitudes are reflected in their sons. There are three essential elements that go to make a force successful in battle. One is arms and equipment, and the American soldier can be confident of having the best that the country can provide. Nothing is more conducive to low spirit among the troops than for them to have the feeling that they are out-gunned, that the other fellow has weapons superior to their own. This feeling may be unjustified, but if it exists it is greatly damaging, for it is of utmost importance that the soldier have full confidence in his weapons.

The second element—actually the first in order of importance—is leadership. For an essentially unwarlike nation, I think we have been singularly blessed in finding among our civilian populace battle leaders of the highest quality. Their competence is a tribute to the blood stock from which they come. It is a tribute, too, to the magnificent system of service schools that has been developed in the U.S. over the past few decades. I speak now not of West Point, for the Academy does not pretend to turn out finished Army officers. Its function in the main is to develop the character of the fledgling officer, to instill in him the ideals, the sense of duty, honor, and patriotism that will sustain him throughout his career. I am speaking instead of the great school system that trains our commissioned and enlisted personnel in the mechanics of war, the techniques of command, from recruit to general, from company officers on up to the highest commanders. These schools are the keystone of our military educational system, and their teaching is superb.

The third element is training. It makes no difference how fine your weapons are, nor how competent your leaders, if the men in the ranks are not physically hardened and highly skilled, you do not have an effective fighting force. Training takes time—not in the use of the individual weapon, but in making the best use possible of all the weapons available, in almost endless combinations. This must be more than theoretical training. It is an easy matter to sit a bunch of battalion commanders down in a classroom and lecture them on firepower, and how to apply all available firepower in a given set of circumstances. It is not enough for them to know that they can call on regiment, division, corps, Army, Air Force—and sometimes the Navy—for supporting fire. To understand firepower and its application you have to use it, actually practice with it and see it work. This means maneuvers in the field, maneuvers that reproduce as realistically as possible, within the bounds of prudence, the actual conditions a soldier will encounter on the battlefield. Only so can you condition, not only the human body, but the human spirit, to face and survive the stresses and strains the soldier will encounter in battle. And in future battle, if it comes, these stresses and strains will be immeasurably greater.

This involves the use of live ammunition. The best cover in the world is afforded by friendly fire. If that fire is of sufficient accuracy and volume, and if it is sufficiently sustained, the combat soldier knows he can get up there to come to grips, hand to hand, with his enemy. At least he can get up there where the enemy was, for if the fire has done its work properly, hand-to-hand combat is rarely necessary. The enemy does not wait for the issue to be settled in that way. He gets out, if he's still alive.

There is, of course, a certain risk to life and limb in training with live ammunition. Despite all our precautions, now and then we do lose a soldier in the execution of these friendly firings during peacetime. This naturally brings strong protest, particularly from mothers of sons in service. I share their deep concern, for I am just as conscious of the preciousness of human life as they, and the Army does all that is reasonably possible to avoid tragic accidents. But I believe that the realistic training that may cost the life of one man may in turn save the lives of thousands of others, once they are subjected to the tests and dangers of actual battle. It is not the conditioned, trained athlete who is most likely to suffer injury in the boxing ring or on the football field. It is rarely the experienced hunter who gets lost in the woods, or shoots himself or somebody else. And in war it is not the veteran, the trained soldier, who loses his life in the first few minutes of combat. Every commander knows one fact to be subject to no challenge—the higher your training level, the lower your casualty rate will be in war. And that is what we strive for in all our training. Whether we send men creeping beneath a curtain of machine-gun fire or place them deep in foxholes while an atom bomb explodes miles away, we are working toward one goal—to find the way to achieve the objectives the nation assigns us, with the lowest possible loss of life.

It is now no longer enough to condition the soldier's body and his spirit by subjecting him to the sights and sounds of simulated battle. Out of the evil brain of Communism has come a new technique of war—the subjection of the captured soldier to mental or physical torture until his spirit breaks.

Men find within themselves the strength to rise to heights of heroism in the brief moments of actual combat. It is a different matter to endure the agony of months and years in prison, the body subjected to gross brutality, the mind besieged by the subtle cruelties of the technique we have come to know as "brain-washing."

There is only one answer the free man can give to this new manifestation of human depravity. He must do his utmost to avoid capture. If captured, he must do all in his power to escape. He must at whatever cost to himself refuse to give information that could be of use to the enemy, for by giving such information, no matter how innocuous it may seem, he jeopardizes the lives of his comrades who are still in battle. If subjected to cruelties, gross or subtle, he must endure to the uttermost. For his duty to his comrades, his loyalty to his country do not end when he becomes a prisoner. He still is an American soldier. Then men who endure in silence, and die, deserve their country's highest tribute. Those who break deserve pity. Whether they deserve punishment as well depends on the degree of their defection. But there is no place in the American Army for the man who, to save himself, will turn against his comrades and his country.

All this means training.

36

☆☆☆☆

The Army's Role

WHEN all my protests against reductions in the combat strength of the Army proved unavailing, there was but one course left open to me—to support completely the course of action prescribed by my civilian superiors, no matter how dangerous it seemed to me.

The Defense Department made known its final decision on force levels just before Christmas of 1953. On January 4 I left Washington by air to visit the commanders of all six continental armies, to tell them exactly what I expected of them. I told them they would carry out the new program vigorously and wholeheartedly, without any foot dragging whatsoever. At the same time my Vice Chief of Staff, General Bolté, left for Europe and the Far East to carry the same instructions to General Gruenther and General Hull.

It was a difficult thing to go to each of these commanders and tell them that the little strength we had was to be further reduced. Each of them, I knew, felt as I did—that this was a dangerous and unwise thing that would jeopardize this nation's security. But their reaction was as I had expected. Each of them, with the incomparable loyalty that is characteristic of the officer corps of the U.S. Army, pledged his utmost effort, and that of his command, in carrying out the decision of civilian authority.

Their deep conviction was the same as my own—that these cuts would leave us dangerously overextended geographically, with a personnel base incapable of supporting the overseas deployment we had considered essential to our safety since the Korean War.

In the light of these facts, there were only two alternatives, as I saw them—partial withdrawal from Europe or from the Far East.

Major withdrawals from Europe to my mind were unthinkable. The whole strength of the great NATO coalition lay in the fact that we were maintaining forces, armed and ready, on the continent of Europe, and had promised to keep them there until the threat of Red aggression had abated or disappeared. To have pulled troops out of Europe would have abrogated these solemn promises to our allies, and even the intimation that such a step was contemplated might have meant the dissolution of NATO.

Withdrawal from Japan, on the other hand, might have a serious effect on the delicately balanced truce situation in Korea, and would leave us in a most difficult position should war break out anew in the Far East. We had hoped that, following the signing of the peace treaty, Japan would rapidly develop ground armies strong enough to protect her home islands, thus enabling us to transfer our own troops elsewhere. This hope grew dimmer day by day as Japan fell further and further behind schedule in the creation of her own defense forces, and there is still no adequate protective force in being there.

Korea presented a somewhat different picture. To my mind we had far too many troops committed to that area, in the light of our overall strength and commitments elsewhere. If grand-scale war should erupt suddenly in other parts of the world, we would find it extremely difficult if not impossible to shift these trained troops to another theater. With 600,000 ROK troops under arms in Korea, I felt that we ran relatively little risk of renewed attack from the Red Chinese in the event our own Army forces were withdrawn. However, the presence of these ROK forces presented another facet to the problem. No one knew what our old, courageous, and belligerent friend, Syngman Rhee, might do if we were not there to restrain him in his determination to drive his country's enemies back across the Yalu. The possibility that President Rhee may send his armies marching north at any moment still exists. And nobody, so far as I am aware, knows exactly what we would do if that should happen. It would be a decision for the President to make, and to my mind a most difficult one, for the flare-up of new war in the Far East might well be the spark that would set the whole world aflame.

There would undoubtedly be strong pressure on us to plunge back into battle on the Korean peninsula. Whether we would do so or not would depend on many cogent factors; whether, for instance, the nations who joined us in repelling that aggression in the first place would join us again, whether in our opinion the Russians would come in, openly, to a new war there. Most mean realize that peace in the world today is almost indivisible. If, tragically, hostilities should be resumed in Korea, nobody could foretell the scope of that conflict and the rapidity with which it might spread. It could easily be the prelude to global war.

For the fact is that Korea is one of those bits of God's earth which has tremendous importance to many powerful nations. On its rugged hills, historically, Japanese, Chinese and Russians have fought their bitter struggles for power. They still regard the government of that country, and the state of friendliness of that government, as of tremendous importance to them. So, too, of course, must the U.S., so long as our interests in the Pacific remain unchanged. If once the power relationships of China, Japan, and the U.S.S.R. were brought into reasonable adjustment, the two parts of Korea, in my belief, would naturally coalesce into an independent buffer state, a Switzerland of the Orient, in which neither Russia, China, nor Japan would exercise control. This, however, must await a new international order, and certainly until Japan finds the strength to reassume her normal place in the power pattern of the Far East—a day which at this moment still seems to be far in the future.

The reductions in force levels which have sorely weakened our power to meet the threat of aggression were accompanied by actions which adversely affected the spirit of the forces that remained. For reasons of economy the Army was repeatedly threatened with the loss of many of those small perquisites which help maintain *esprit,* the soldier's confidence that he has the support of the people at home, that he is not the Tommy Atkins of Kipling's song, idolized in war, ignored and kicked around in peace.

There was, for instance, the attack from civilian authority on the Army's policy regarding the families of personnel serving overseas. In the postwar years, roughly half the career personnel of our active Army has been serving beyond the continental limits of the United States. If present conditions continue, they can expect to spend half their time in the future on foreign duty.

To me it is unrealistic and unreasonable to expect that these men should be denied the right to have their families with them. I well know the evil effects that the separations a military career demands can have upon family life. The separation of a soldier from his family in time of peace impairs his spirit; it breeds social problems of the most pernicious kinds, and gives rise to unfortunate liaisons and all the evils that flow from them. Therefore, I had no patience with the arguments of these civilian gentlemen of the Department of Defense, who, never having been separated from their own loved ones in their lives, except voluntarily, were advocating such separation for other men on the grounds of economy. Certainly it costs a great deal to transport, and house, and provide schools and doctors and other essential facilities and services for the wives and children of service men abroad. But it is small compared to the returns in contentment and satisfaction that are reflected in the re-enlistment rate. And it is infinitesimal compared to the cost of a war that the presence of these soldiers might avert.

Other matters, small in themselves, profoundly affected the spirit of the Army. There was incessant attack on the so-called "fringe benefits"—the little things, such as commissary and post exchange privileges, and medical care for service men's dependents—which help to narrow the gap between a soldier's pay and what he could reasonably expect to earn in civilian life. These small perquisites were protested in the name of economy also, but the basic criticism, I knew, stemmed from local merchants who looked upon the commissary and the PX as a competitor to be destroyed.

There was also a feeling within the service that, as regards tenure, the government was unfairly changing the rules in the middle of the game. Older officers had come into the Army with the tacit understanding that, if they gave competent and faithful service, they could remain on active duty until they were sixty-four. This would give them opportunity to educate their children and see them safely launched on their own careers. And once their children were on their own, it would give them a chance to lay away for themselves some savings for their retired years. In 1947 the retirement age was lowered by law, and now that the law has had time to take full effect, many fine officers are forced into retirement in their middle fifties. This is a personal disaster to them and a loss to the Army of their wide experience and mature judgment. The drastic and rapid reduction in force levels greatly aggravated these basic inequities. Reserve officers on active duty have suffered even greater dislocations. With World War II behind them, and supposedly a long period of peace ahead, they were called back to fight the Korean War. Many remained in service thereafter, their talents desperately needed by an Army deployed around the world. Now, with their lives again adjusted to a military career, they find themselves being forced to return once more to civilian status, at an age when starting anew in their business or profession is not an easy thing.

The policies described above, which in my view were weakening the Army in spirit and in strength, were accompanied by other policies which greatly lessened the overall potential of the Army as a fighting force.

The "potential" of an army may be classified in various ways. One of the simplest is to classify it in terms of, first, its active elements; second, its reserve element; and third, its mobilization potential. I have already pointed out here the lacks and weaknesses in the active elements, and in the reserve setup. The third element, the mobilization potential, is equally vital—and to my mind was correspondingly short of what it should be.

The mobilization potential is the capacity of the country to produce the men and to produce and supply the troops with weapons and equipment. The latter is principally a function of industry, a responsibility of the civilian population.

In all our wars in the past, the mobilization base has been the bottleneck which has slowed the swift entry of the troops into combat. In a few months men can be trained as soldiers, but in the past it has taken us at least two years to supply them with their weapons. In the event of another war, we will not be permitted so lengthy a period of preparation.

The "hot" mobilization base we must have to move swiftly into war in adequate strength did not now exist. Sufficient stockpiles of critical materials did not exist, the "stand-by" factories that can quickly convert from civilian to war production, did not have the requisite capacity. There are bales of dusty blueprints on the government shelves, showing what production facilities would be needed in the event of sudden war, but the facilities themselves fell short of our needs.

Our mobilization base was not only inadequate to our own needs;

it made wholly inadequate provision for the resupply of our allies in a drawn-out war. It must be anticipated that in a general war the allies in whom we place so much dependence would in a very few weeks exhaust their resources in guns, tanks, planes, and the larger types of ammunition through normal battle attrition.

When this happens, we can expect a repetition of those unhappy days we experienced in World War II. As every soldier remembers, there was a time when every rifle in storage in the U.S. had to be taken out and shipped to Europe and the British Isles. Our own armed forces were down to zero in reserve stocks, not only in rifles, but in light field artillery, and many of our units were training with dummy guns. At the time of Rommel's thrust toward Cairo, we had to take the tanks from our armored divisions in training and rush them to Montgomery in Africa. If war should break out tomorrow, we would have to do the same thing. Within a few weeks' time, our troops in Europe and our allies might be fighting with rocks, sticks, and bare fists.

In the last days of my service at the Pentagon another influence, greater perhaps in its ultimate impact upon the Army than the urge to economize, was making itself felt on high levels of civilian authority. I refer to the so-called "peace offensive"—the sudden switch in Russia's diplomatic tactics which cast upon a trusting world a brief effulgent light of hope at the time of the first Geneva conference.

It is not my thought that we should strike down any hand that is offered in genuine friendship. No man would be happier than I to see a genuine easing of the nerve-straining tensions which have gripped mankind in the days since World War II. In that way, and only in that way, can we justifiedly hope that human sanity may yet assert itself, and man can at last begin the long march toward a world free of the frightful scourge of war. We had to go to Geneva. We could not refuse to talk.

But I must confess that from the first I was distrustful of the blandishments of Mr. Bulganin, and the alcoholic amiability of Mr. Khrushchev. For smiles and friendly words are cheap, but the support of great armies in the field is expensive. And I cannot forget that facing NATO's slim divisions in Europe are Soviet and satellite armies ten times as strong. This is no defensive force, but an army organized for attack, deployed and ready astride the old invasion routes that lead to the heart of Europe.

Small as are these NATO forces, it is my belief that it is their presence, plus the threat inherent in our Strategic Air Command, with its encircling bomber bases, that has held the Reds at bay this long. And I think that the dissolution of this force and the abandonment of our bases is still the primary object of Russian diplomacy. Their spurious and short-lived amiability was merely a change of tactics, not of objectives. It was an effort to lull and soothe us, an effort to persuade us to let our guard down. And as I looked at the pictures of Mr. Bulganin and Mr. Khrushchev in the papers, I could not but remember the sage advice of Mr. Kipling, who urged, "Make ye no truce with Adam-zad—the Bear who walks like a Man." Particularly those lines which go:

When he stands up as pleading, in wavering, man-brute guise,
When he veils the hate and cunning in his little, swinish eyes,
When he shows as seeking quarter, with paws like hands in prayer,
That is the time of peril—the time of the Truce of the Bear.

The "Truce of the Bear" did not last long, if the newspaper reports from Geneva were correct. As soon as the meeting descended from the high, hope-inspiring atmosphere of the Summit to the working levels where the prime ministers met to translate good will into good works, the Russians' old intransigence shone through. Mr. Molotov dropped his mask and spoke his mind bluntly on our forces and bases overseas, and on the President's bold proposal—the aerial inspection of atomic facilities.

That proposal, to permit each nation to observe from the air the nuclear facilities which the other possessed, was offered by President Eisenhower in all honesty and sincerity, as earnest proof of our peaceful intent. It was foredoomed from the start. For it must have been obvious to the Russians that such a procedure, if put into effect would have been far more to our advantage than to theirs. They know already, from the information available to anyone who can read, where most of our great atomic and other military installations lie and can estimate with fair accuracy what their capacities are.

They viewed the suggestion with suspicion—and dismissed it bluntly as unworkable. Just as we, for our own protection, must look with suspicion upon the disarmament proposals which from time to time will emanate from the Russians. For no matter in how pretty a package the Reds may wrap their proposals to disarm, their purpose remains unchanging. That purpose is simply this—to bring about such a weakening of our capacity to make war that their own great massed armies will stand supreme in strength and power over all the armies of the world. That was their goal in the years before they had the atomic weapon, when in the councils of the United Nations they urged the outlawing and destruction of the atomic device in all its forms. That is their purpose still.

37

☆☆☆☆

The Army in the Atomic Age

THE position I took consistently throughout my two years as Chief of Staff was based on the simple conviction that when a man is given a job to do, he is entitled to receive the means with which to do it—at least the minimum means with which he can reasonably be expected to accomplish his mission.

As I have tried to make clear in all I have said, I did not feel, during my tour as Chief of Staff, that on the highest civilian levels in the Pentagon there was any real understanding of the Army's needs, or any real recognition of what would be required in men, money, arms, and equipment to carry out the missions the Army was asked to be ready to perform. The Secretary of the Army, Mr. Stevens, understood these needs fully, and supported the Army forthrightly. His splendid under secretaries and assistant secretaries understood them. But on the higher level, where the Secretary of Defense and his assistants sought to evaluate the missions and the needs of all three services, I felt there was a woeful lack of comprehension of the role the foot soldier must play in ensuring the safety of this country. Nor did I feel that any genuine effort was made to remedy this lack of understanding.

Particularly were my views on air power subject to misinterpretation. My attitude toward air power was in no degree whatever a reflection of an old foot soldier's distrust of a new and more glamorous branch of the service. As a paratrooper, I was a hybrid—an infantry soldier who went into battle from the air. In World War II, in the first few hours of an airborne operation, my life, and the lives of the men under my command, literally depended upon fire support delivered from the air, and on aerial resupply of every item a ground-fighting force required. And during my service as Supreme Commander in Europe, I constantly pressed for greater development of the air arm. I believed with complete conviction then, and I still believe, that the airborne principle, when properly employed, can be the keystone of the attack.

My arguments regarding air power, therefore, were in no sense a protest against emphasis on the air arm. They were in protest against what I sincerely believed to be an *over*emphasis on one form of air power, the long-range bomber, to the neglect of other means by which that magnificent weapon, the combat airplane, can be employed.

My strongest arguments, in fact, were for a greater and more varied development of air power. It was clear to me, as to every other even moderately intelligent infantry officer, that the army of the future must be very greatly dependent upon aircraft of one form or another. As I have pointed out in a previous chapter, it must be an air-transportable army, possessed of long- and short-range mobility far beyond anything ever known in war before. To fight the war of the future we must possess the capability not only to transport the nuclear bomb for great distances, and drop it with fine accuracy on a target. We must also possess the capability to lift whole armies, armed with nuclear weapons, and put them down upon any spot on the earth's surface where their tremendous, and selective, firepower will be needed.

We do not possess it, for one reason, because the Army and the Air Force have an entirely different concept of the numbers of planes of the various types we will need to fight the wars of the future. The Air Force thinks mainly in terms of bombers of longer and longer range, for so-called "massive retaliation," and all-weather fighter planes of greater and greater speeds, which can protect this country from the intercontinental bombers of the enemy. These are essential, but they are not enough.

Undeniably, the Air Force with its long-range bombers is capable of wreaking great destruction upon the enemy. Let us assume, even (though this I do not believe), that by aerial bombardment we could achieve such complete destruction that the enemy threat to us has virtually disappeared. This alone would not be enough. Supporting that Air Force must be an Army, ready, armed, trained, and waiting, fully prepared to take over its changeless role—the seizure and occupation of hostile territory as a supreme police authority.

Such an Army must be, first, a highly mobile Army, both between continents and within the battle zone, and it must be an Army equipped to strike devastating blows with its own special type of aircraft.

The Army of the future, therefore, needs long-range transports for intercontinental movement, and a number of different types of specialized aircraft for employment on the battlefield. These latter need not be long-range nor high-speed planes. They are, in essence, aerial trucks and jeeps in the transport field, and as combat aircraft they should be flying gun platforms.

It is difficult to interest the airmen, though, in these specialized needs. We have persistently and consistently importuned the Air Force to provide us with an assault transport to meet the specifications we have laid down. To us, our needs are clear, and the reasons for them plain. As I have pointed out before, our principal potential adversary in the world today is the Soviet Union. It is the greatest land mass on earth, and it possesses the greatest land army on earth. And unless we wish to wait and fight that army at our own front door, we must possess the ability to move our armed forces, by sea and air, to whatever corner of the world we choose to meet their aggression. We can move by sea, as we have always moved, and in great strength, but that is not fast enough. We must possess the mobility to move faster than we have ever moved before, and in greater strength. That means we must have a fleet of global transports capable of ferrying an army halfway across the world and setting it down on rough airfields, in open country where there are no airfields at all, or perhaps even on water.

We do not possess that air armada now, nor do we yet have the prototype planes of which it might be composed. Some steps in that direction have been made. The Fairchild C-123 is now coming into limited production but it is by no means the answer. We need an aircraft that can carry heavy loads, land on very rough fields, or no fields at all, and take off after very short runs. The C-123 can land and take off in distances that are only a fraction of that required by other aircraft, but it still is not the plane we need. The Lockheed 130, nicknamed the Hercules, is a long-range transport capable of carrying heavy loads, but neither does it fully meet the Army's needs, for it, too, is not a cow-pasture airplane. Thus the Army feels that we have nowhere near the capability we should possess, after learning clearly, from World War II and Korea, the type of aircraft we require.

We have even lost a great deal of the capability we possessed in World War II. For all its weaknesses and limitations, the glider did function as a vehicle for transporting troops into the combat zone. We have no gliders today. Nor has the production of helicopters kept pace with the Army's needs. We can take off and land vertically today with loads it was impossible to lift a few years ago, but we have just begun to comprehend the great potential that lies in the principle of the helicopter. The converti-plane is coming along, a hybrid that takes off straight up and then shifts to relatively high forward speeds in horizontal flight. If properly developed, it may be the ultimate answer—a combat aircraft that can work far up in the battle zone, carrying out a multitude of duties for the ground forces without the necessity for any sort of prepared airfield.

There is an understandable opposition in the Air Force to the development of those types and the procurement of those numbers of aircraft for which the Army has so vital a need. The helicopter and the converti-plane do not now fit into the pattern of the Air Force's primary missions, or the limitations of its budget. Nor does the young airman want to fly the close-support and assault aircraft—the dive bombers, cargo ships, the transport planes that carry the paratroopers. He wants to fly jets, for that is where the glamour and the glory lies. And I don't find it in my heart to blame him.

But somebody must man these planes and the Army, of course, has considered seeking to relieve the Air Force of its unwanted burden. Plans have been advanced whereby the Army would develop its own specialized assault aircraft, and recruit and train its own pilots to fly them, and to a slight degree this has been done. If neither manpower nor dollars were to be considered, such an idea would be feasible. Since manpower and dollars both are very much to be considered, the prospect that the Army will be able to develop its own aviation in the near future is highly improbable.

I think perhaps there is a balance to be found somewhere, a reasonable compromise. Of one thing, though, I am sure. To do its job on the battlefield, to gain its objectives in the least time with the least loss of life, the Army must have the support of combat aircraft that can fly in any kind of weather, under all conditions incident to enemy interference, both in the air and from the ground, and deliver its bomb load, or its rockets, on target with the accuracy of a field gun. If the Air Force should develop such planes, we would be deeply pleased. If they continue to ignore our needs in this respect, we eventually will have to develop them ourselves.

The optimum in that close air support which I am describing is now enjoyed by the Marine Corps. In the Corps, each division of infantry has its own "air force" assigned to it, practically as an integral part of it. The result is that each Marine division has more than two hundred combat aircraft devoted exclusively to the support of that division. In its wildest dreams, of course, no organization as big as the Army could ever expect to have any such munificence of combat air support.

The Army's desperate need for close air support, and the Marine Division's opulence in this respect, created a ticklish problem for me in Korea. It was perfectly natural that the Marine commanders there should wish to use all the Marine aircraft for the support of their own troops. I could only say to them: "Gentlemen, we've got nine U.S. divisions here, eight of them Army, one Marine. They are all out here for the same purpose. They are all subject to the same hazards of battle. They all fight a common enemy. I know you would not advocate for a minute that the Marine Air Wing, or even the bulk of it, should be made available solely to the Marine Division."

The Marine commanders over there were big enough men to see that point and there was no open argument. The magnificent Marine airmen served all the divisions, Army and Marine alike, and were as dedicated to the accomplishment of our overall objectives as any element in Eighth Army. Our efforts to speed up and improve the use of Air Force planes in close support met with a less co-operative attitude because of policy decisions made in Washington. Though I strongly advocated that some small part of the combat aviation available be assigned to Headquarters Field Army and its Corps, so that air strikes could be called with a minimum of delay, Air Force adamantly opposed this plan. Requests for air strikes continued to follow the old merry-go-round, up through channels to Army, then to Air Force, and down again. Frequently, as a result of this time-consuming procedure, when the planes got there the enemy had gone.

As I have testified many times before Congress, the present situation is far from satisfactory to us. We do not have the mobility which we require because the Air Force has delayed. We have asked for it time and again. We know it to be perfectly feasible. We know also that it is a very expensive thing. But we must have it—and we must have it *before* we find ourselves in another war.

The public has been led to believe, of course, that the Army does not have to move in a hurry. To the man in the street the Air Force, the Navy, and the Marines are our fire brigades, the forces that would go into action at the first alarm. There is no question that so far as an individual ship is concerned, it could be in action quickly if it were anywhere within cruising range when war broke out. There is no question that the Strategic Air Command could be over enemy territory with its bombs within a few hours. But so far as the commitment of major forces to ground battle overseas is concerned, the most mobile units in existence today are the Army's two airborne divisions. These two divisions can go into ground battle faster than any other major units in the U.S. military establishment, and that includes the Marine divisions. All they need are the planes to carry them.

All the reductions in Army's strength, all the failure to provide for the Army the mobility and the aerial fire support it needs, is merely a reflection of the point of view which I have referred to before—the erroneous attitude that air is all powerful and the foot soldier is obsolete. There are many people, and they have great influence, who continue to shout that a new war would be over very quickly—that air power alone could fight it, and win it, in a matter of weeks, and control the peace thereafter.

Well, as Housman said,

> Hope lies to mortals and men believe her.
> But man's deceiver was never mine. . . .

I wish that I could believe that in air power alone we have found at last the magic formula—the key to quick and easy victory. But I can't. For all our testing and theorizing, no man can know exactly the form and pattern the wars of the future will take. And certainly no one in authority should seize upon the idea of quick and easy victory through air power and make that concept the basis on which a great nation rests its hope for survival.

38

☆☆☆☆

Final Report to Mr. Wilson

IN MY last days as Chief of Staff, I submitted a final report to Secretary Wilson. In it I summarized my concepts regarding the security of our nation, and the dire consequences to that security which I felt in my heart current policies in the Defense Department would entail. I had the statutory right to express these views, and I felt that, as a professional soldier whose life had been dedicated to his country's service, it was my duty to express them. I also feel that I had the duty to set the record straight before the people of America.

On this latter point the Secretary of Defense did not agree. I sent the report up to him as an unclassified document, which meant that it could be disseminated through any medium of public information which might be interested. Acting under a concept which prevailed during most of my tour—that high officers of the Armed Services should not publicly express opinions contrary to those held by the Defense Department—Mr. Wilson sent it back with the request that it be classified. This meant that as a "confidential" document it would be buried in the Pentagon's files and forgotten. And there it stayed, for the few remaining days of my service as Chief of Staff. Some weeks after my retirement, however, by means unknown to me, it came into the possession of the *New York Times*. Shortly thereafter the Secretary himself released it to the press, with the remark that it was "not very important."

Important or not, it was an expression of my heart-felt views, and I set down the highlights here.

Addressing my remarks to the Secretary, I pointed out that, despite recurrent "peace offensives," the United States and its free world allies still are faced by Communist armies, navies, and air forces formidable in size, modern in matériel and techniques, and deployed threateningly along the periphery of the Iron and Bamboo Curtains from the North German plain to the Maritime Provinces of Siberia.

This force, I pointed out, possessed the capability to conduct a nuclear war. Its greatest strength, however, lay in the overwhelming power of its huge land forces, and for this reason it might well refrain from initiating the use of the nuclear weapon. In this event, we would be faced with a decision—whether we should loose the nuclear weapon first, with the moral recrimination which such an act would bring down upon our heads from all the world; or whether we should meet the Soviet on terms of its choosing—with land forces supported by sea and air.

I further pointed out that to meet this threat, whatever the form it might take, the United States has sought and signed compacts with allies around the world. For purposes of the common defense, it has entered into numerous commitments, some vague and some specific, to take action, to deploy forces, or to provide matériel support to Canada, twenty Latin-American countries, Berlin, West Germany, Spain, Yugoslavia, thirteen NATO nations, Libya, Ethiopia, Saudi Arabia, Iran, Australia, New Zealand, seven Manila Pact nations, Korea, Japan, the Republic of China, and the United Nations.

No one, I added, can know when these ominous sight-drafts may be presented for payment. No one can foretell their form and shape. But they obviously may involve action by U.S. military forces in many different types of climate and terrain, from the hills of Greece and Korea to the jungles of Indo-China.

Those are the pledges we have made, the burdens we have chosen to bear. They express our intent to meet force with force, to be prepared to meet and defeat the Soviet bloc, in local or global wars, with or without the use of nuclear weapons.

Then, in all earnestness, I told the Secretary of Defense that, in my view, the present United States military forces are inadequate in strength and improperly proportioned to meet these commitments.

My reasons were these:

1. Sometime between 1958 and 1962 Soviet nuclear development will have reached the capability of inflicting critical damage on the United States's war-making potential. During the same period Soviet air-defense measures against our own nuclear bombers will be greatly improved. When that occurs, the nuclear-air superiority which the United States currently enjoys will have lost its present significance.

2. The military forces of the free world, deployed around the perimeter, other than those in Western Europe, are military detachments only. If they should come under heavy attack they could be destroyed one by one, for they could not support each other, and we lack the truly mobile and adequate reserves with which to reinforce them.

3. While published statements on military policy refer to a "mobile-ready force," no adequate mobile-ready force now is in being and the actual creation of such a force must compete with increasingly emphasized continental defense, and with overemphasized nuclear-air requirements.

These requirements, I pointed out, apply in the main to general war, whereas we are committed not only to general war, but to the stamping out of local, or so-called brush-fire wars. On such commitments to nations both large and small our present diplomacy rests. Yet present forces in being cannot support America's diplomacy fully, for if military power is to be an instrument of diplomacy it must be real, and apparent to all concerned, and it must be capable of being applied promptly, selectively, and with the degree of violence appropriate to the occasion.

Summing up, I said that, in my view, the commitments which the U.S. had pledged to keep created a positive necessity, not for a great standing force of all arms, capable of engaging in global war tomorrow, nor for a force top-heavy with global bombers, but for a fast-moving, hard-hitting, joint force in which the versatility of the whole is emphasized, and the preponderance of any one part is de-emphasized.

In conclusion, I wrote: "Both as Chief of Staff of the Army and as a member of the Joint Chiefs of Staff, it has been my duty to advance the interests of the United States security over and above Service interests. While disavowing any Army claim to an excess of national interest, I would specifically point to the Army's long record in fighting the wars of the United States with all forms of military power. For

180 years it has served to keep America secure. It will continue under new leadership this great tradition of loyal and dependable performance. I am proud to have had the privilege of being a member of that magnificent institution in the profession of arms."

With the transmittal of this final report, my job was over, my work was done. On June 30, 1955, I cleared my desk at the Pentagon and turned over my duties as Chief of Staff to that brave and brilliant officer, General Maxwell D. Taylor. For the first time in seventy-eight years there was no soldier of my name and blood wearing the uniform of my country. My military service and that of my revered father had spanned every conflict in which this nation had been engaged since the Civil War; had required the use or study of every weapon from the horse-drawn gun to the atomic cannon. In command jobs and staff jobs, on school duty and on missions that were both military and diplomatic, in war and troubled peace I had served in thirty countries around the world. Looking back upon it now, I cannot conceive that God has granted any man a richer, fuller, more satisfying life than mine, for it was spent in service with, and for, that finest product of our civilization—the American soldier.

I left bearing no rancor in my heart toward any man who might have differed with me. I left feeling in my heart only the deepest admiration and respect for that magnificent officer corps I left behind —men who loyally and faithfully, with whatever means are granted them, are building the Army of tomorrow.

Today, as a civilian, I still follow with eager interest the fortunes of that Army as it struggles, not against an armed enemy, but against those influences which would, if permitted to go unchallenged, deny it the means of serving our people to the full in future crises. And often my thoughts go back to one wintry night on the battlefield in Korea.

The Eighth Army was withdrawing south across the Han. I had spent the night with one of our Corps commanders at his advanced command post, deep in snow-covered hills up front. I had far to go the next day, and I was up before a trace of dawn.

It was almost zero. The stars snapped and sparkled in the black and moonless sky. Some campfires were burning, casting the leaping shadows of soldiers' silhouettes across the gleaming snow. I stood still and thought:

Here in this bit of far-off earth, cupped in by foreign hills, there burned a warm bright flame, lit and nurtured by free men, whose frigid bodies it warmed and whose spirits it raised and comforted. Beyond its warming miracle, I thought, other millions, silent, hungry and cold, must see its glow and yearn for its warmth. Must wonder, as they yearned: Will these strange, generous men—determined killers in combat, compassionate neighbors in camp—let this fire languish and die. Will they keep faith and fire burning until the sun of freedom rises once more? Or will they, in the hour of decision fail and forsake us?

All over the world, hopeful millions still ask these questions of us. And to me the answer is the same today as it was when we stood and fought in Korea. We shall not forsake those enduring values which free men cherish. Ignoring all lesser considerations of economics, or politics, we must retain the full power to protect them if war again should engulf the world. For we are, in truth, the last best hope of earth, the last great reservoir of strength where freedom dwells. And with all that strength which we possess, on land and sea and in the air, we must stand ready to defend ourselves and all men everywhere who share our dream.

Appendix 1

A LETTER FROM GENERAL RIDGWAY TO THE SECRETARY OF DEFENSE

UNITED STATES ARMY
The Chief of Staff

27 June 1955

Dear Mr. Secretary:

I shall depart from the active ranks of the United States Army on 30 June 1955, thereby vacating the offices I currently hold. Having spent 38 years as a United States soldier on active service around the world, I trust I may be permitted, as I terminate this service, to summarize for you certain of my concepts concerning the security and well-being of the United States, all of which I have expressed, in one form or another and from time to time, as Chief of Staff, United States Army, and as a member of the Joint Chiefs of Staff.

I do so within the statutory provisions of the National Security Act, as amended, which delineate my functions as a military advisor to you, the National Security Council, and the President.

I do so with full awareness of the quickening tempo of international intercourse; of the growing realization among all peoples of what the President brought into such clear focus when he said: ". . . it seems clear that there is no longer any alternative to peace . . ."; of the fateful developments which may have their genesis in the conferences which, beginning in New York and San Francisco, are to continue later in Geneva.

I am mindful of the great responsibilities that continue to devolve upon you as the President's principal assistant for national defense. I would be neglecting my duty if I did not reaffirm prior to my departure my convictions regarding the military defense of the United States. I wish to comment on the general nature of the Soviet threat, the variable strategy permissible to the USSR for general war, the specific United States commitments in reaction to the Soviet threat, the United States strategy to meet these commitments, and a viable United States military strategy for cold war situations. Finally, I will discuss briefly my view of the role of a military advisor in the formulation of national policy.

GENERAL NATURE OF THE THREAT

In today's world power climate, in spite of recurrent peace offensives, the scope and dimensions of the threat which faces America are measurable in terms of the fundamental attitude of hostility by the Soviet regime toward the Free World and especially toward the United States; in terms of the Communist capability for conducting political subversion throughout the world; and principally in terms of the strength of all major components of the continually expanding Soviet Bloc military power.

As a result of this continued increase in Soviet Bloc military strength unmatched by a comparable increase in allied strength, the United States and its Free World allies are faced by Communist armies, navies and air forces formidable in size, modern in materiel and techniques, and deployed threateningly along the periphery of the Iron and Bamboo Curtains from the North German Plain to the maritime provinces of eastern Siberia. The dangers inherent in this situation, and particularly the dangers in the preponderant deployment of land forces, are evident at every significant point of contact between the Western World and the Communist Bloc.

As long as the Soviet Communist Bloc is on the offensive, it is able to retain the initiative in its undertakings; and the centrality of its power base gives it the strategic advantage of being able to concentrate with small risk of detection at any point on its perimeter.

In the nuclear arms race, the day of nuclear plenty for each of the two major world power groups draws nearer; the cost of fabrication drops; and hence the day when even smaller powers may likewise possess such weapons is already foreseeable. Common appreciation of the consequences of unlimited nuclear war may well result in general unwillingness to employ these weapons, in recognition of the mutual disaster which would follow wherein the peoples, property, and institutions of much of the world would vanish.

In a situation of nuclear plenty, mutual cancellation of nuclear advantage can occur in terms of mutual devastation; or, depending on the degree of parity, in terms of mutually limited use; or, finally, in common refusal to use nuclear weapons at all. It seems doubtful that the USSR would initiate employment of nuclear weapons in the face of a preponderance of nuclear weapons possessed by the United States. On the other hand, should the Western nations initiate their use, the USSR would have no choice but to respond in kind, in the hope that the resultant destruction to the West would circumscribe the ability of the United States to continue effective prosecution of such a war. In the light of this major possibility for the future, it is at least debatable whether the United States really has the freedom to rely preponderantly on nuclear weapons to exert its military power.

Moreover, it appears prudent to assume that Soviet strategists are even now giving consideration to a course of action which would put on the

United States the onus of initiating the use of military nuclear fire power, making certain that the United States and its allies know they can reasonably expect retaliation with nuclear weapons by the Soviets, simultaneously with the initial assaults of the Red Armies.

Under these conditions, since national objectives could not be realized solely by the possession of nuclear capabilities, no nation could regard nuclear capabilities alone as sufficient, either to prevent, or to win a war.

VARIABLE STRATEGY PERMISSIBLE TO THE USSR FOR GENERAL WAR

A mere statistical evaluation of the ratio of military power potentials between the Soviet Bloc and the Free World is not sufficient to determine detailed Soviet general war strategy. Instead, Soviet military potentials would first have to be translated into Soviet minimum military capabilities, and thereafter into Soviet general war strategy. For a general war within the next ten years, the Soviets would have to gain their objectives of the defense of the USSR, the control of Eurasia, the severance of lines of communication between the United States and its Allies, and the reduction of the war-making power of the United States and Canada. The attainment of these objectives would have to be integrated in such a manner that the prizes the Soviets would hope to acquire would not be merely the pickings of a vast ash-heap of devastated animal life, or of a human race debilitated by the effects of radiation. On the contrary, the prizes would have to be worth the effort expended and the chances taken to get them; that is, they would have to materially improve the power position and the extension of Soviet dominance.

The Soviet potentiality for gaining these prizes is based on Soviet Bloc military forces, which comprise large ground forces supported by integral tactical air forces, supplemented by air defense forces, and including a minor surface navy, a threatening submarine fleet, and a long-range air force growing in capability.

To use these forces in the attainment of Soviet war aims without modification to or retrenchment from their objectives, the Soviets would have to acknowledge conditions which over the next 10 years could vary from an extreme of clear United States nuclear superiority to full nuclear parity, with vast stockpiles of weapons and of delivery vehicles available to both sides.

Thus the greatest imponderable with respect to probable Soviet strategy concerns the Soviet capabilities and intentions with respect to the use of nuclear weapons. For all practical purposes, nuclear parity between the USSR and the United States will exist when the USSR achieves the ability to deliver critical damage to United States-Allied war-power sources with fusion weapons. In this situation, neither side will have a nuclear advantage, whether the lack of advantage is proven by mutual devastation or mutual withholding of use, or depending on the degree of parity, in terms of limited use. There is little reason to doubt that the USSR, like every other nation, would prefer to avoid the use of nuclear weapons. For these reasons, it is probable that as nuclear plenty is approached and as the relative advantage of United States nuclear superiority diminishes, Soviet strategy will be directed toward the creation of situations which will preclude the use of nuclear weapons on a worldwide basis.

The variable character which general war may assume over the next 10 years, then, makes the best Soviet strategy in each different circumstance the employment in their normal role of conventional Soviet ground forces, supported by the Soviet air force and the Soviet navy. Such a strategy is completely consistent with Soviet war objectives, with Soviet strategic doctrine, with Soviet military potentialities, and with the physical nature of the great land mass it occupies. There is no reasonable basis for expecting Soviet strategy necessarily to duplicate United States-Allied strategy, and thus to gamble on a capability of accomplishing, by a single means, an extremely formidable task. This task, even if successful in accomplishing the reduction of United States war-making power, would attain only one of the major Soviet war objectives. Again it seems logical to expect that all Soviet war objectives would be combined to form an integrated Soviet war aim.

I recognize that the foregoing position is not reflected in current United States strategy with respect to air power. I recognize that, since United States power centers are beyond the effective reach of the Soviet tactical ground-air team, the Soviets, too, have been forced to develop a strategic bombing arm. I am well aware of the requirement for a continuing evaluation of all elements of the Soviet potential. I am also well aware that, in planning for success in war, allowances must be made for special circumstances and unpredictable actions.

My carefully considered position, long advocated, is based realistically on military factors that are consistent with Russian and Soviet history, the tradition of the Soviet offensive-defensive, and the present Soviet military force structure and capabilities. Moreover, it is, I believe, consistent with the entire pattern of recorded military history to date, and, in the light of all human experience, will prove to be consistent with the pattern of the future. These factors must be accorded the full weight they demand by responsible United States planners both within and outside the military services.

UNITED STATES COMMITMENTS IN REACTION
TO THE THREAT

In a world whose determination to combat the Communist menace waxes and wanes, the United States, by example, persuasion, pressure, inducements, assistance, and agreements, has established itself as the leader of Western resistance. The United States has sought and signed allies around the world. For purposes of the common defense, it has entered into numerous commitments, some vague and some specific, to take action, to deploy forces, and to provide material support to Canada, 20 Latin American countries, Berlin, West Germany, Spain, Yugoslavia, 11 NATO nations, Libya, Ethiopia, Saudi Arabia, Iran, the two ANZUS nations, the additional six Manila Pact nations, Korea, Japan, the Republic of China, and to the United Nations organization.

No one knows when those ominous sight drafts may be presented for payment. No one can tell at this time the form or scope of performance these commitments may require of the United States. But they obviously may involve action by U. S. military forces in many different types of climate and terrain, such as the mountains of Greece and Korea or the jungles of Indochina.

UNITED STATES STRATEGY TO MEET COMMITMENTS

In general, the foregoing commitments express the intent of the United States:

a. To meet force with force.

b. To be prepared to meet and defeat limited aggression in small perimeter wars, whether or not nuclear weapons are used.

c. To be capable of defeating Soviet Bloc military forces if general war should occur, whether or not nuclear weapons are used, and in widely varying terrain and climates.

IN MY VIEW, THE PRESENT UNITED STATES MILITARY FORCES ARE INADEQUATE IN STRENGTH AND IMPROPERLY PROPORTIONED TO MEET THE ABOVE COMMITMENTS, SPECIFIC OR IMPLIED, FOR THE FOLLOWING REASONS:

a. The Soviet Communist Bloc has created and is prosecuting a continuous state of conflict as a matter of national policy. They have shown the intention and capability to capitalize on subversion or on local war for military and political advantage in China, Greece, Czechoslovakia, Malaya, Korea, Indochina, and other places, in spite of the superior United States strength in long-range air forces, although this superiority has been obvious to the world since World War II. As the point in time approaches, possibly between 1958 and 1962, when Soviet nuclear weapon and delivery developments will give the Communist Bloc the capability of inflicting critical damage on the United States war-making potential, coupled with a concurrent improvement of Soviet air defense capability, the United States nuclear-air superiority will have lost most of its present significance.

b. The Free World military forces deployed around the perimeter, other than those in Western Europe, are in the position of being military detachments, which are not mutually supporting, which have little or no strategic mobility of their own and which are difficult to reinforce because of the lack of truly mobile and adequate military reserves.

c. Present United States military forces cannot support fully America's diplomacy. If military power is to support diplomacy effectively, it must be real and apparent to all concerned, and it must be capable of being applied promptly, selectively and with the degree of violence appropriate to the occasion.

d. While a "mobile ready force" element is provided for in published policy statements, the actual development of a mobile ready force must compete with increasingly emphasized continental defense, and with, in my opinion, overemphasized nuclear-air requirements; all of which are requirements related primarily to general war.

In view of the Free World's appreciable manpower superiority over the Communist Bloc and of the economic potential of the United States, it is my view that the Free World has ample resources to confront the Soviet Bloc enemy in whatever form of aggression the Soviets choose. The advantage of interior lines on the Communist side can and must be countered by the advantage of strategic mobility on the Free World side. In addition to properly deployed strength, mobile reinforcements are the only effective means of countering the threats growing out of the Soviet ability to concentrate at will, and the United States is the only source of mobile reserves at the present time.

IT IS MY VIEW THAT THE COMMITMENTS WHICH THE UNITED STATES HAS PLEDGED CREATE A POSITIVE REQUIREMENT FOR AN IMMEDIATELY AVAILABLE MOBILE JOINT MILITARY FORCE OF HARD HITTING CHARACTER IN WHICH THE VERSATILITY OF THE WHOLE IS EMPHASIZED AND THE PREPONDERANCE OF ANY ONE PART IS DE-EMPHASIZED.

VIABLE MILITARY STRATEGY FOR COLD WAR SITUATIONS

Currently, the means made available for supporting the United States military strategy for both cold and general war are limited. The present United States preoccupation with preparations for general war has limited the military means available for cold war to those which are essentially by-products or leftovers from the means available for general war.

A wide choice of military means, resulting from properly proportioned, modernized forces, is required to fill the present large gap in effective deterrence resulting from United States preoccupation with long-range bombers as the principal deterrent.

United States strategy, backed by adequate and proper military strength, should make full provision for the following:

a. Every physical action taken in furtherance of the basic United States military strategy should be taken only after considering, individually and in sum, the probable psychological effects of the action on the USSR, United States nationals, United States allies, and neutral nations. Such actions should be designed to counter the Soviet policy of instilling fear with a United States policy of creating confidence.

b. A strong position of tangible Free World strength must be maintained. Continued United States adherence to the concept of collective security is fundamental to the maintenance of Free World strength; coalitions must stand shoulder to shoulder or suffer the danger of disintegration from within.

c. An increase in the readiness and strategic mobility of uncommitted United States and British Commonwealth forces is required to support the strategy, and availability of troops of other key nations for additional deployments in United States and United Kingdom transportation to areas where they are needed is an important aspect.

d. Soviet satellite aggressions should be treated as limited or local wars until the aggressor is defeated or the United States and its allies are prepared for general war.

e. United States reaction to satellite aggression should not be conditioned by a fear of Soviet intervention or unduly prejudiced by a fear of possible maldeployments of United States forces. If sufficient forces are available from the outset such maldeployments could be readily and quickly rectified.

f. The satellite cordon should not be reduced by military force as long as its existence produces advantages for the Free World.

g. The United States should give all practicable assistance to our allies in their efforts to suppress Soviet-Communist-inspired civil disorders.

THE MORAL ASPECT

I should like to add a word on the importance of the moral factor in all human relationships, especially when preparing a strategy to protect America's security. Just as the ultimate and most deadly threat of Communism is the destruction of the religious and moral principles which, imperfectly as they may have been observed, yet have guided man to new heights of dignity and self respect; in seeking to insure America's security, so also we find the same threat in the increasingly significant ignoring by our planners of the consequences of omitting the moral factor in considering the use of the immense destructive capability which now exists in the world. There is a responsibility on everyone of us to evaluate this moral factor, along with all the scientific and other practical factors in seeking solutions to these mammoth problems.

MY VIEW OF THE ROLE OF A MILITARY ADVISOR

In the foregoing pages, I have sought to outline a broad concept of the strategy which, as I see it, is most likely to serve United States interests. In doing so, it has been my intention to discharge my responsibility as a military advisor, from within the field sanctioned by law. In the light of current national military policies, this responsibility is not always clear, even to those to whom the responsibility is assigned.

In closing, I should like, therefore, to outline my view of the proper role of the Chief of Staff, United States Army, as a military advisor.

In March 1953, while still Chairman of the JCS, General Bradley expressed one view of the Joint Chiefs of Staff role as military advisors: "Generally . . . we should confine our part to pointing out the military implications and military capabilities . . . Perhaps some people might feel that the Joint Chiefs of Staff should stand up and resolutely and strongly recommend a national policy which we would prefer, but to date I have not been convinced that this is a proper role for a military leader."

In his message transmitting Reorganization Plan Number 6 on 30 April 1953, President Eisenhower expressed the view that "Professional military leaders must not be thrust into the political arena to become the prey of partisan politics."

Earlier, in 1951, on 26 April to be exact, the Joint Chiefs of Staff were criticized publicly by Senator Robert A. Taft as being "absolutely under the control of the Administration," and that their recommendations were "what the Administration demands they make." During my period of duty as Chief of Staff, events have made it appear that the criticisms once leveled at my predecessors might be better grounded in the future than in the past.

National policy matters which are discussed at the level of the Joint Chiefs of Staff as military advisors to the President, National Security Council, and Secretary of Defense, are seldom, in this day and age, separable into purely military and non-military problems.

I view the military advisory role of a member of the Joint Chiefs of Staff as follows: He should give his competent professional advice on the military aspects of the problems referred to him, based on his fearless, honest, objective estimate of the national interest, and regardless of administration policy at any particular time. He should confine his advice to the essentially military aspects. When testifying as Army Chief of Staff before the Subcommittee of the Committee on Appropriations in the Congress on 28 June 1947, General Eisenhower expressed the following attitude in support of this view:

"I appear before you only as a professional soldier, to give you a soldier's advice regarding the national defense. I am not qualified to proceed beyond that field; and I do not intend to do so. It is my duty as Chief of Staff to tell you gentlemen what I believe to be necessary for national security."

If the military advisor's unrestricted advice is solicited he should give his considered opinion, for in today's climate national security planning is broad and encompasses many aspects. The President, in the message to which I referred earlier, has stated that the nation's military plans "must incorporate the most competent and considered thinking from every point of view—military, scientific, industrial, and economic." However, in my opinion, the military advisor should be neither expected nor required to give public endorsement to military courses of action against which he has previously recommended. His responsibility should be solely that of loyal vigorous execution of decisions by proper authority.

This aspect is perhaps the most difficult one for the military advisor, particularly as he strives to keep himself detached from domestic politics at the time domestic political forces attempt to use him for their own purposes. In his role of advisor, he gives his best advice. In his role as a commander, he implements decisions. Both roles must be respected by civilian officials, as he must respect theirs. In this regard, as the political climate shifts and changes, differing assessments will be made of his proper role; but whatever the situation, he must remain outside the field of partisan politics. It is incumbent upon civilian officials to see that he stays outside, and to protect him from becoming involved.

I am well aware that my remarks here and elsewhere may be taken, indeed, they have been so labeled, as special pleading for out-moded special interests. I have been pictured in some quarters as opposing emphasis on air power. The exact contrary is true. I am opposed to *overemphasis* on air power, as I am opposed to overemphasis on any military force where dependence on that force exceeds its capabilities and impairs the nation's over-all military potential.

As Chief of Staff, United States Army, it has been my duty to seek to maintain the capability of the Army to fulfil the Army's assigned commitments. However, both as Chief of Staff of the Army and as a member of the Joint Chiefs of Staff, it has also been my duty to advance the primary interests of United States security over and above Service interests. While disavowing any Army claim to an excess of national interest, I would specifically point to the Army's long experience, past success, and tested judgment in fighting the wars of the United States with all forms of military power.

The Army has no wish to scrap its previous experience in favor of unproven doctrine, or in order to accommodate enthusiastic theorists having little or no responsibility for the consequences of following the courses of action they advocate. While the Army is adapting itself readily to the employment of new weapons and new techniques, nothing currently available or foreseeable in war reduces the essentiality of mobile, powerful ground forces, the only forces which can seize the enemy's land and the people living thereon, and exercise control of both thereafter.

The United States Army has for 180 years served America's security. It will continue under new leadership its proud tradition of loyal and dependable service.

It has been my proud privilege to have been a member of that magnificent institution in the profession of arms—the United States Army.

Respectfully,
/s/ M. B. RIDGWAY
General, United States Army
Chief of Staff

The Honorable
The Secretary of Defense

Appendix 2

CITATIONS FOR UNITED STATES AWARDS TO MATTHEW B. RIDGWAY

HEADQUARTERS SEVENTH ARMY
APO #758   U. S. Army

GENERAL ORDERS)
                    :   11 September 1943
NUMBER   24   )

II—*AWARD OF THE DISTINGUISHED SERVICE CROSS*

Under the provisions of Army Regulations 600-45, as amended, a Distinguished Service Cross is awarded to the following named individual:

MATTHEW B. RIDGWAY, 0-5264, Major General, United States Army, for extraordinary heroism in action. From the earliest moments of the Sicilian invasion, as Commander of the 82nd Airborne Division, Major General Ridgway displayed an uncanny ability for appearing during crucial moments in the advance, and by his compelling leadership and inspiring presence helped his command to hurdle their obstacles and once more to continue the victorious advance. The morning of D-Day found him ashore making personal reconnaissance, while exposed to enemy action, in an effort to locate the 505th Combat Team which had landed by air the night of 9-10 July. Again, during an opposed movement of the Division from Agrigento to the valley of the Verdura River; and on the 23rd before Trapani—fearlessly exposing himself—accompanying his advance guard—and by undaunted behavior in the face of hostile fire, inspiring sorely beset gun crews into renewed resistance. Always to the fore, helping, encouraging, driving continually on, his dynamic energy, fearless leadership and steadfast devotion to duty were leading factors in an onslaught which ended in complete defeat of the enemy. Entered the United States Military Academy from Virginia.

By command of Lieutenant General PATTON:

OFFICIAL:

W. G. CALDWELL,
Lt Col, AGD,
Adjutant General

HOBART R. GAY,
Brigadier General, GSC,
Chief of Staff

HEADQUARTERS
NORTH AFRICAN THEATER OF OPERATIONS
UNITED STATES ARMY
APO 534

GENERAL ORDERS)
:   2 December 1943
NUMBER   152)

AWARD OF LEGION OF MERIT

Under authority contained in Section IV, War Department Circular Number 131, dated 3 June 1943, a Legion of Merit Medal is awarded in the name of the President, to each of the following named individuals:

MATTHEW B. RIDGWAY, 05264, Major General, United States Army, for exceptionally meritorious conduct in the performance of outstanding services from August 1942 to October 1948, as Commanding General of the 82d Airborne Division. General Ridgway has intensively trained his division developing a high degree of individual all-around proficiency among his troops, and forging each unit into a self-sufficient organization, well versed in administration, movement and tactics. The notable success of the division in the landing operations against Sicily and the mainland of Italy, achieved despite the handicaps of widely separated bivouac areas, restricted transportation, suddenly changed directives, and the novelty of the types of equipment, movement and tactics, were a tribute to the great leadership and tactical skill of General Ridgway.

By command of General EISENHOWER:

OFFICIAL: E. L. FORD
                                        Brigadier General, GSC,
                                                Chief of Staff
H. V. ROBERTS,
Colonel, AGD
Adjutant General

The President of the United States of America, authorized by Act of Congress July 9, 1918, has awarded the Distinguished Service Medal to

MAJOR GENERAL MATTHEW B. RIDGWAY
UNITED STATES ARMY

for exceptionally meritorious service in a duty of great responsibility:

Major General Matthew B. Ridgway, 05264, United States Army. For exceptionally meritorious service to the government in a position of great responsibility from 15 August 1942 to 27 August 1944, as Commanding General of the 82d Airborne Division. General Ridgway directed the planning, training, and operation of the first major night airborne operation ever attempted by any army, the invasion of Sicily. Based upon this experience he originated and put into practice new operational techniques, the soundness of which was evidenced in the decisive contribution of the division to the consolidation of the beachheads in Italy. General Ridgway's brilliant and comprehensive conception of coordinated tactics and logistics were well demonstrated in the mounting of the two American Airborne Divisions for the assault on Normandy. The effective commitment to action of the 82d and 101st Airborne Division on 6 June 1944 was due in large measure to his contributions to the coordination of the Air, Ground, Naval, and Troop Carrier Commands involved. Major General Ridgway has perseveringly directed the force of his keen intellect and professional skill to the ultimate perfection of principles and techniques of the employment of airborne forces. General Ridgway realized the inherent potentialities of airborne troops as a decisive influence in war and his determination, pioneer spirit, and masterful command on the field of battle proved the soundness of his concepts.

HEADQUARTERS
FIRST UNITED STATES ARMY
APO 230

GENERAL ORDERS)

:

No. 35)

19 July 1944

SECTION

Award of Bronze Oak-Leaf Cluster to the Distinguished Service Cross—I

I-AWARD OF OAK-LEAF CLUSTER TO DISTINGUISHED SERVICE CROSS—Under the provisions of AR 600–45, 22 September

1943, and pursuant to authority contained in paragraph 3c, Section I, Circular No. 32, Hq ETOUSA, 20 March 1944, as amended, in addition to the Distinguished Service Cross previously awarded, a Bronze Oak-Leaf Cluster is awarded to the following officer:

Major General *Matthew B. Ridgway*, 05264, 82nd Airborne Division, United States Army, for extraordinary heroism in action against the enemy from 6 June 1944 to 9 June 1944, in France. Major General *Ridgway* jumped by parachute at approximately 0200 prior to dawn of "D" Day and landed about ¾ mile northeast of Ste Mere Eglise, France, to spearhead the parachute landing assault of his Airborne Division on the Cotentin Peninsula. Throughout "D" Day, he visited every point in the then surrounded area in order to evaluate the opposition and to encourage his men. He penetrated to the front of every active sector without thought of the personal danger involved. He exposed himself continuously to small arms, mortar and artillery fire; as, by his presence and through words of encouragement, he greatly assisted and personally directed the operations of one of his battalions in the important task of securing the bridgehead across the Merderet River, which required a frontal assault against strongly entrenched enemy positions. His personal bravery and his heroism were deciding factors in the success of his unit in France.

By command of the ARMY COMMANDER:

OFFICIAL: W. B. KEAN,
                                                     Major General, G.S.C.,
                                                     Chief of Staff.

R. S. NOURSE,
Colonel, AGD,
Adjutant General

———

GENERAL ORDERS)   HQ FIRST ALLIED AIRBORNE ARMY
                  :   APO 740, U. S. Army
No. 22   )   13 March   1945

AWARD OF SILVER STAR MEDAL

Auth: Under the provisions of Executive Order Number 9419, 4 Feb 44, (Sec II, Bull 3, WD 1944) and pursuant to authority contained in AR 600–45, and Cir 32, Hq European TO US Army, dated 20 Mar 44, as amended by Cir 56, Hq European TO US Army, dated 27 May 44, the following officer is awarded medal indicated.

By direction of the President, the SILVER STAR MEDAL is awarded to MAJOR GENERAL MATTHEW B RIDGWAY, 05264, United States Army, Commanding xviii Corps (Airborne), for gallantry in action in the vicinity of Eindhoven, Holland, during the period 17–18 September 1944. On 17 September, MAJOR GENERAL MATTHEW B RIDGWAY flew with the assault echelon of the airborne invasion of Holland. On September 18–19 he proceeded by air and land through territory in imminent danger of seizure by the enemy. Despite the fact that the road to Eindhoven was reported cut, MAJOR GENERAL RIDGWAY moved forward to join the troops in operation. His presence with the assault echelons of the airborne divisions encouraged and inspired the troops at critical moments and contributed materially to the shattering of enemy attempts to destroy the airborne effort. MAJOR GENERAL RIDGWAY's courage and inspiring leadership were in keeping with the highest traditions of the United States Army.

By command of Lieutenant General BRERETON:

OFFICIAL:

                                              F. L. PARKS,
                                              Brigadier General, GSC,
                                              Chief of Staff.

W. F. SMITH,
Lt Col, AGD,
Adjutant General.

The President of the United States of America, authorized by Executive Order, February 4, 1944, has awarded the Bronze Star Medal to

             MAJOR GENERAL MATTHEW B. RIDGWAY
                     UNITED STATES ARMY

for heroic achievement:

For heroic achievement in connection with military operations against the enemy as Commanding General, xviii Corps (Airborne), United States Army, from 18 December 1944 to 8 January 1945, in Belgium.

The President of the United States of America, authorized by Act of Congress July 9, 1918, has awarded the Distinguished Service Medal, First Oak Leaf Cluster, to

LIEUTENANT GENERAL MATTHEW B. RIDGWAY
UNITED STATES ARMY

for exceptionally meritorious service in a duty of great responsibility:

General Ridgway performed exceptionally meritorious service from 18 December 1944 to 8 May 1945, as Commanding General, XVIII Corps (Airborne). Given the mission of blocking the German Ardennes attempt to break through to the North, with only a few hours warning, he concentrated his command, attacked, established contact with our isolated troops and, relieving these forces, disposed them in an integrated position. Engaging in an active defense against a determined enemy, he subsequently passed to the offensive and launched a series of attacks which culminated in an advance to and the breaching of the Siegfried Line. Subsequently in airborne operations across the Rhine in support of the Second British Army, he seized key terrain in the vicinity of Wesel on 24 March 1944, disrupted enemy defenses and exploited the gap in the enemy positions. He then participated in the reduction of the Ruhr pocket. Later, following the concentration of his command, south of the Elbe, he forced a passage of the river in late April, protected the east flank of the Second British Army, completed the elimination of enemy resistance in a rapid drive to the Baltic and made contact with Russian forces. His decisive actions and unrelenting pressure were distinct contributions to brilliant victories over the enemy.

———

The President of the United States of America, authorized by Act of Congress July 9, 1918, has awarded the Silver Star, First Oak Leaf Cluster, to

MAJOR GENERAL MATTHEW B. RIDGWAY
UNITED STATES ARMY

for gallantry in action:

For gallantry in action in Germany on 30 April 1945. When heavy artillery concentration forced the suspension of work on a pontoon bridge being constructed across the Elbe River, General Ridgway proceeded to the site where, despite the falling artillery, he moved among the dug-in troops and encouraged them to proceed with their work. Inspired and encouraged by his presence the troops resumed construction and completed the bridge in record time. The gallantry and courage of General Ridgway reflect great credit upon himself and are in keeping with the highest traditions of the military service.

HEADQUARTERS
U.S. FORCES EUROPEAN THEATER

GO 16   17 Jan 1946

EXTRACT

Bronze Star Medal I
Bronze Star Medal (Oak Leaf Cluster) II
Medal of Freedom III

II—*BRONZE STAR MEDAL (OAK LEAF CLUSTER)*. 1. By direction of the President, under the provisions of AR 600–45, 22 September 1943, as amended, in addition to the Bronze Star Medal previously awarded, a bronze Oak-Leaf Cluster is awarded, to:

Lieutenant General *Matthew B. Ridgway* (then Major General), 05264, United States Army, for heroic achievement in connection with military operations as the Commanding General, xviii Corps (Airborne), on 25 March 1945, in the Wesel-Hamminkeln area, Germany. With disregard for his personal safety, Lieutenant General *Ridgway* proceeded through territory which had not yet been cleared of the enemy in order to establish contact with the two airborne divisions of his command and coordinate their operations. He found that communications with the 6th British Airborne Division had not been established and could only be made possible by courier through enemy territory. Without regard for his personal safety Lieutenant General *Ridgway* proceeded on this dangerous mission. While enroute to the Command Post of the 6th British Airborne Division, his party of two jeeps was ambushed by a German patrol of thirty men. The patrol was dispersed and routed after brisk fire fights, during which Lieutenant General *Ridgway* was wounded by a German hand grenade. His courage and disregard for personal safety on this mission contributed materially to the final success of the airborne operations, reflecting great credit upon Lieutenant General *Ridgway* and the armed forces of the United States.

BY COMMAND OF GENERAL McNARNEY:

OFFICIAL:

                                         H. R. BULL,
                              Major General, GSC, Chief of Staff.
        L. S. OSTRANDER,
Brigadier General, USA, Adjutant General.

The President of the United States of America, authorized by Act of Congress July 9, 1918, has awarded the Distinguished Service Medal, Second Oak Leaf Cluster, to

GENERAL MATTHEW B. RIDGWAY
UNITED STATES ARMY

for exceptionally meritorious service in a duty of great responsibility:

General Ridgway has distinguished himself by exceptionally meritorious service to the United States and to the free people of the world in positions of great responsibility. At an extremely critical period, he assumed command of the United States Eighth Army and of United Nations Forces in Korea and through magnificent personal leadership led these forces in a counter-offensive which crushed the Communist advance and drove the enemy north of the 38th parallel. In April 1951 General Ridgway became Commander-in-Chief of United States Forces in the Far East and Supreme Commander, Allied Powers in Japan. In addition to directing United Nations strategy and guiding the armistice negotiations in Korea with skill and firm forbearance, he supervised, on behalf of the Allied Powers, the final stages of the rebirth of the Japanese people as an independent nation. In these grave responsibilities he displayed the highest order of physical and moral courage, skilful leadership, and broad understanding. General Ridgway's extraordinary service merits the gratitude not only of the American people but of free peoples everywhere.

The President of the United States of America, authorized by Act of Congress July 9, 1918, has awarded the Distinguished Service Medal (Third Oak Leaf Cluster) to

GENERAL MATTHEW B. RIDGWAY, UNITED STATES ARMY

for exceptionally meritorious service in positions of great responsibility from 30 May 1952 to 30 June 1955:

As Supreme Allied Commander, Europe, General Ridgway was charged with the responsibility of welding an effective military structure for the defense of Western Europe. Through dynamic leadership, he furthered the development of the elements of the North Atlantic Treaty Organization into an alert, efficient, fighting team. He advanced the prestige of the Allied Forces and strengthened the bonds of friendship and cooperation among the many nations serving together in the common defense of democratic principles. In discharging this grave responsibility, he displayed indomitable spirit, inspirational application of military skills, and a sincere concern for the furtherance of the causes of freedom. As Chief of Staff of the United States Army he continually demonstrated the highest order of leadership, professional competence, astute judgment, and devotion to duty. Under his brilliant direction, the Army was maintained in a state of combat readiness, and fulfilled its world-wide commitments in a manner which contributed significantly to the advancement of the foreign policies of the United States. Ever mindful of the well-being and dignity of the individual soldier, he constantly worked to improve the welfare of the men entrusted to his care. His keen professional ability and great strength of character, displayed in his every action, have been an inspiration to the entire Army. His selfless dedication to the service of his country represents the highest form of patriotism, and merits the gratitude of not only the American people but of free peoples everywhere.

Appendix 3

THE CHIEF OF STAFF'S INTRODUCTION OF, AND ADDRESS TO, HIS PRINCIPAL AIDES UPON ASSUMING OFFICE

On assuming any post of responsibility, the incumbent is at once and primarily concerned with the qualifications of the key men to whom he must delegate great authority, and in whom he must repose complete confidence.

I was singularly fortunate in that officers occupying the four top posts on the executive level as I assumed my duties as Chief of Staff were men I had known for practically all my service. Their characters and conspicuously superior records ensured the kind of performances required— the highest.

The Vice Chief of Staff was General John E. Hull. The two Deputy Chiefs of Staff were Lieutenant Generals Anthony C. MacAuliffe, in charge of operations and administration, and Lyman L. Lemnitzer, the head of Plans and Research. The Comptroller was Lieutenant General George H. Decker.

Any of these gentlemen would perform superbly in any post, and it was a source of deep gratification to start my tour as Chief of Staff with such a team at the top. Yet change is the law of life, and nowhere is that truer than in a military organization, the personnel of which is constantly changing.

Throughout World War II General Hull had carried especially heavy responsibilities in the Army's top staff under General of the Army George C. Marshall. So essential were his abilities that, like many another officer of like character and competence, he was fated to see his dreams of combat command service evaporate in the mephitic atmosphere of the Pentagon. Following the war, he had been selected to head the newly created and very important Armed Forces Special Weapons Evaluation Group, and then successively as Deputy Chief of Staff, Operations and Administration, and finally a Vice Chief of Staff with promotion to full general.

This prolonged period of continuous service in Washington had, I know, served only to stimulate his desire for a field command. So it was with considerable apprehension that I asked him if he would be willing to remain on as Vice Chief, knowing the complete confidence and trust I had in him and in his abilities. Characteristically he stated he would do whatever the Chief of Staff wanted, but, he added, he did still hope for command duty in his final active duty years.

I then asked him to stay on for the first few months of my incumbency, at the end of which period I would do all in my power to see that he got either the European or Far East command. General Hull at once agreed.

This then soon presented a major problem—the choice of a new Vice Chief. As my alter ego, this selection was of the utmost importance. In my view, the criteria included absolute integrity, uncompromising refusal to yield to political pressures, the highest degree of professional competence proven in combat as well as in peacetime service, the right personality, and such seniority as would make this assignment his final one on the active list.

General Charles L. Bolté met all these requirements pre-eminently. I had known, respected and admired him for thirty-odd years. We had also a warm personal friendship which was now to be really tested, for Charlie was at last in the post of his dreams—Commanding General, United States Army Forces in Europe, with station in the beautiful country of Hesse.

I wrote him frankly that I felt in the hard days ahead he was pre-eminently qualified for this vitally important post; that I realized full well what it meant to take him away from a command for which he was so ideally suited, in which he had made so splendid an impact on the German people, and to which he was himself so fully devoted. I could only say, I told him, that only my earnest conviction that the overall best interests of the United States Army absolutely required him in that assignment would induce me to ask his return. As heart-wrenching as it was to him, and I have no doubt scarcely less so to his family, he came with a smile and a cheerful willingness, and his magnificent service was of incomparable assistance to me and of benefit to the Army.

To succeed General MacAuliffe, on his departure for a field command in Europe—the Seventh Army—I reached out for my old schoolmate of Staff College Days, and of service shared in the Far East, Lieutenant General Walter L. Weible.

General Weible had had rare opportunities to display his rare abilities in a great variety of highly responsible posts. He had been Chief of the Operations and Training Division of the Army Service Forces and also of the Army Ground Forces in World War II; had served with great distinction at the head of the Japan Logistical Command, responsible for the supply of all our forces and of the United Nations in Korea from the very beginning of that conflict; and had then joined me at my request to help me with the great logistical problems pertaining to Allied Command Europe—most of those problems of unprecedented difficulty. He brought a wealth of experience, energy and sound judgment to his difficult post and relieved me of a large share of my burdens.

Lieutenant General George H. Decker had followed that splendid citizen-soldier, Lieutenant General Raymond S. McLain, into the post of Comptroller, during the time I was serving as Deputy Chief of Staff, Operations and Administration. I knew his sterling worth and outstanding record, attested to by the high tributes paid him by members of the House Appropriations Committee, as he was leaving his post of Comptroller last spring, to receive at long last a field command—an Army corps in our forces in Europe.

So with these officers in the top executive spots—Bolté, Lemnitzer, Weible, and Decker—and with a superior group as chiefs of staff divisions and as commanders of the continental armies, I could be sure that all that integrity, vision, devotion, loyalty, and zeal could accomplish would be forthcoming. It was.

In my first meeting with the officers of my staff, I tried to put into words a distillation of all I had learned, in thirty years of service, of the duties and the responsibilities of the career officer to his country, to the men who serve under him, to his equals and superiors, and to his own ideals.

This first meeting upon assumption of a new assignment is of the utmost importance. It deserves the most careful, painstaking thought of which the individual is capable, because it represents the first impression you make upon the senior officers with whom you are going to work, and upon whom you must depend for success—for success in any post of high command is always a collective, never an individual, effort. Here, at this first meeting, you establish your leadership. You gain their confidence, you stimulate the desire to work as a team. Or you fail to do these things.

The higher you go up the ladder of command, of course, the more transcendently important this first meeting becomes, for you are dealing with men of wide experience, of great maturity, who by reason of their years have crystallized many of their views. They are not as easily swayed as youngsters. They are not impressionable. The extent to which this first meeting does or does not accomplish this purpose of establishing leadership is of vital importance. If you succeed, your path will be smooth. If you fail you have failed entirely.

For that reason, I put hours of thought and study into the remarks I was to make as, in the assembly room across from my office, I brought together the top staff officers of the Army.

I began with what I believe to be a fundamental truth.

"The one point uppermost in my mind today," I told them, "is the opportunity that here is offered us—the limitless opportunity for purposeful service. I believe every one of you subscribes to the criterion that there is some purpose beyond the power of humans to discern for which we are put here on this earth. For my part, I subscribe to that fully, and I believe that the greatest purpose which we are allowed to see is to serve others. I believe that never has a higher form of service been demanded of mortal men than that which is demanded of us—the service of those principles for which the Founding Fathers established this nation. And I believe that never has this nation, and the cause of freedom which it supports around the world, been in greater need of the loyal and devoted service of men and women of principle and integrity.

"Each of us has been rendering, I am sure, the best service of which each is capable. You have been doing so as a closely integrated team concerned with the whole range of global problems confronting our Army and military establishment. I have likewise been doing my utmost, but in distant fields. I am well aware, therefore, that however broad my responsibilities seemed, and were, they were but regional, compared to yours.

"Now we join to share service together of the broadest scope and on the highest plane, and as I join you I want you to know of my profound respect for the service you have been rendering, and to express the earnest hope that together we can render still better service. I have known each of you for years, some more intimately than others, but all with a sufficient knowledge of your conspicuously superior records to appreciate them fully. Some of the things I shall say will touch upon matters which at this initial stage of our teamwork I think are of sufficient importance, either as basic principles, or as indications of my working methods and line of thinking, to bring to your attention.

"In the first approach to any job, regardless of magnitude, my mind follows a certain sequence of steps.

"First there is a mission. Second, this mission breaks down into certain functions to be performed, in order to accomplish the mission. Third, there must be a sound, a simple, positive, workable organization for the performance of these functions. Fourth, men of the proper caliber must be selected and assigned, each in his proper place, to this organization. Fifth, the organization as a team must then perform its functions and accomplish its assigned mission; and

"Finally, the execution of performance must have that vital essential at all times and at all stages—the element of command supervision.

"Now I have been here in Washington for thirty days. Little of that time has been available for me to go through this mental process, and even less was available before I relinquished command to Al Gruenther four hours before departure from France. I therefore am just starting to follow through this pattern of thinking, and it occurs to me that while, of course, I will receive the major benefit, you, too, may perhaps glean an idea or two of value.

"I shall not try on this occasion to state the Army's missions in detailed form, but I do wish to recall to your mind that however you word the Army's mission, there is but one final criterion by which to judge what the mission was and the manner of its performance. That criterion, gentlemen, is success in battle. The modern state and its government, particularly our own, is about the most complex organization yet developed on earth. In the formulation of its policies, and in their execution, the political, economic, financial, social and military elements are inseparably interdependent. No one field can any longer be isolated, and major decisions in it made without regard to one or more of the others.

"Yet, and I think this is basic—at least it is in my way of thinking—the responsibility of the professional military man lies in the professional military field. His over-riding responsibility is to give his honest, objective, professional military advice to those civilians who, by our constitution, are his commanders. It is not his responsibility to decide whether the military means which he determines are essential to accomplish the military task assigned him will cost more than the nation can afford. He has not been trained for that. He must, of course, as every senior commander is today, be aware of the major factors in these other major fields. He must recognize as every senior commander does today the imperative necessity of maximum economy and efficiency in the utilization of whatever military means his government may make available to him. There is no question of this any more than there is any question of the loyalty of these senior officers in carrying out the decisions announced to them by proper civilian authorities.

"The point I wish to make here, and I repeat it for emphasis, is that the professional military man has three primary responsibilities:

"First, to give his honest, fearless, objective, professional military opinion of what he needs to do the job the nation gives him.

"Second, if what he is given is less than the minimum he regards as essential, to give his superiors an honest, fearless, objective opinion of the consequence of these shortages as he sees them from the military viewpoint.

"Third and finally, he has the duty, whatever be the final decision, to do the utmost with whatever he is furnished.

"Now let me return to what I was talking about a minute ago, namely, our overriding mission.

"The Army's peacetime successes, however numerous, are secondary in importance to this one overriding vital requirement. It must win in war.

"Now there are certain simple essentials by which it can and will win in war.

"In simplest terms these are: Men, money and morale. But, since we don't control the acquisition of money, these essentials are:

"First, arms and equipment; second, training; third, leadership.

"None of these needs much explanation to you and the first doesn't need much explanation to the American people. I think they recognize pretty well that the days of club and sling and spear and axe have passed, and that no army or military force today can expect success in battle if insufficiently or inadequately armed, no matter how well trained or how well led.

"The other two basic elements need a lot of continuing explanation to our people and one of them at least—leadership—needs a lot of continuing study by ourselves.

"In training and leadership, two basic requirements stand out.

"First, foremost and always, we must have an officer corps comprising a professional long-term cadre, adequate both in size and in quality. This is the heart and soul of any military organization. None will ever be better, or even quite as good, as its officer corps. This is the great reservoir of character, of devotion to duty, of loyalty, of professional competence, the fountainhead by which tradition is planted and nourished.

"If we are to have this—and without it we do not have an Army—we must have represented in our professional officer cadre a cross-section of the nation's life, a fair share of the best the nation produces, in character, in intellect, and in culture. If we do not, if it is not representative of the cross-section of America, it will not in the long run have that support of the American people which it must have to accomplish its ultimate mission.

"Next and closely after the officer corps is the requirement for the non-commissioned officer corps with its professional cadre of career personnel, inspired by the precepts of the officer corps whose standards it emulates.

"These, gentlemen, are the essentials with which leadership can accomplish the seemingly impossible. These are the essentials without which ultimate success is impossible. These are the elements to which I invite your attention and which I suggest we, all of us, keep before our eyes, however numerous the distractions of our day-to-day concerns.

"With these two instruments with which to work—an officer and a non-commissioned officer corps of proper quality and adequate size—we can then be confident that the young men and women of America turned over to us to train will receive the best in professional, physical and spiritual education that it is possible to provide.

"This brings me to the last of the major generalizations which I wish to make in this talk this morning. That is the officer and enlisted man relationship.

"I was struck during the first twenty-four hours of my return to Washington by two incidents which highlighted this topic in my mind. One was the case of a non-commissioned officer driver of an official car. I asked him at which of several Pentagon entrances it would be better for me to get out in order to go to an office which I named.

" 'Well,' he replied, 'I usually drop my Old Man off at the River entrance.'

"That was the last time that driver drove for me and the reason was duly communicated to his superior.

"The second case occurred on a Sunday afternoon when a non-commissioned officer in charge of several men was manhandling some of the baggage which accompanied my party in the flight from Paris that day. At the conclusion of the work, one of my officers thanked this non-commissioned officer.

"The reply was, 'Oh, think nothing of it. We enjoy working on Sunday afternoon.'

"Now it seems curious to me that two such incidents so indicative of exactly the wrong spirit which should animate the officer-enlisted man relationship should have come to my attention so quickly, unless there is widespread need of basic training in our officer corps, and right here in Washington.

"When we were young officers we served a long apprenticeship, during which our primary concern was the care, training, and welfare, professionally, physically, and morally, of the men under our command. We had on the average between fifteen and twenty years to learn those lessons. They became ingrained. We recognized a responsibility for these men, twenty-four hours a day, seven days a week, and however provoked we became at times, we knew affection for them in our hearts; we knew their unfailing response to real leadership. They were American soldiers and there weren't any finer ones.

"Today it seems we have not fully kept our trust. We have not passed on to the younger officers the know-how of handling the American soldier. We have not taught the young officer what to us became second nature—the responsibility of the officer for his men. We have that responsibility here in Washington equally with our brother officers in the field.

"We exist here in the Pentagon for one primary purpose, and that is to ascertain, evaluate, and to the limit of our ability to meet, the requirements of the commanders in the field who are charged with the execution of decisions made here. I shall expect that no matter how engrossed we become in the complexities of staff procedure here, we remember these basic elements for which we, individually and collectively, are responsible.

"I have a few other topics on which I wish to dwell, unrelated for the most part but deserving, I think, of being brought to your attention.

"We face a situation unparalleled in the history of our or any other country. We are in the presence of evolving social and scientific forces of which we can perceive only the general trends at this time.

"The more confused we may tend to become, the more imperative is it, therefore, that in our thinking we keep simple, basic principles and objectives before our minds.

"One of these basic principles is the necessity for the maintenance of democratic institutions. This point is illustrated by a reiteration of a principle to which America has been unfailingly dedicated, the principle of civilian control of the military.

"The command channels by which that control is to be exercised have been made unmistakably clear. The channel goes from the constitutional Commander in Chief to the Secretary of Defense and through him to the Service Secretaries. In my own case my commander is Secretary Stevens. I had not known him until last April when he first visited my command in Europe. I want to say to you gentlemen without reservation that the Army has as its civilian commander as high-principled a man as the nation can produce.

"We have a new team of civilian commanders. Each of them has a new team of civilian assistants. It is natural for us to regard with some apprehension the development of staff procedures whereby these civilian assistants might begin to operate on their own, outside of the clearly defined command channel from the Secretary of Defense to the Service Department Secretaries, thence down the military chain of command. In fact there have been incidents in your experiences of Assistant Secretaries of Defense giving 'orders,' to someone in the Department of the Army. These are not 'orders,' in my view. Proper orders are issued by, or in the name of the Secretary of Defense. And they come from him to the service Secretary involved, and from him to the Chief of Staff.

"I want to say to you that I know of no one more aware of this situation than the Service Department Secretaries themselves. I want you to know that these gentlemen have fearlessly and forthrightly expressed to the Secretary of Defense himself their apprehension lest any such development as that which I have described might occur, and their strong disapproval if it did occur. I want you to know that the Secretary of Defense has himself expressed his strong disapproval of the development of any such practices and his determination to see that it does not occur.

"Now I assign to you senior responsible members of the Staff the responsibility for proper indoctrination of all the personnel in your respective divisions, to the end that our teamwork and the mutual respect and understanding essential to teamwork be steadily strengthened and broadened. I shall look to you for the exercise of patience and discretion in handling any such cases as may come to your notice.

"Finally I invite you, at any time you think it proper, to bring such occurrences as the kind to which I have been referring to the attention of General Lemnitzer, General McAuliffe, General Hull or me. We cannot expect perfection. However, with good will, with patience and determination such occurrences will, I hope, approach the vanishing point.

"Please remember in this as in everything else I have presented today, there is a responsibility on each of us to educate others. Actually everything in life can be translated into some form or other of educative process, or, if you like, of training, and the requirements for training and for leadership are just as active and just as necessary in this great staff as they are in any field command anywhere in the Army. It plays just as vital a part right here as in the Seventh Army in Europe, Eighth Army in the Far East, or anywhere in the Continental United States.

"Now a few points secondary in importance to what I have already said, but still worth while because they represent some of my own idiosyncrasies as applied to the tasks we must work out together.

"General Hull, the Vice Chief of Staff, stands in essentially the same relation to me as does the Chief of Staff to the commander of a major unit. It has always been my principle and practice in high command that there are no official secrets of any kind between me and my Chief of Staff. He and I together are a dual personality; my responsibility cannot be delegated, but my authority can be and must be. Therefore, the decisions and directives you will receive from the Vice Chief of Staff, General Hull, will in every sense be my decisions and my directives. My confidence in him is complete.

"The duties of the Deputy Chiefs of Staff General McAuliffe and General Lemnitzer, are clearly defined in current regulations. They, too, must have broad delegation of authority.

"The Assistant Chiefs of Staff, and in fact, each Chief of a Staff Division, has, I trust, adequate, proper, delegated authority for the operation of his division and the discharge of his functions within the prescribed staff procedure. If anyone feels he has not, he should raise the issue.

"Now loyalty—loyalty is a state or condition, like pregnancy. It either does or does not exist, and sometimes determination is difficult. It is particularly vital today in this period when we cannot see very far beyond the horizons and when the utterances of senior officers, whether made publicly or in private groups, assume ever-increasing significance.

"I shall expect the officers of this Staff to present their own honest views fearlessly, forthrightly, but objectively in the light of their own conclusions as to what best serves the Army's overall interests. The most dangerous advisor to have around is the yes-man, and the most useless is one who thinks of self instead of service. I shall also expect, at all levels, that having once expressed his opinions and having heard the decision, the officer's entire support will then be put behind the execution of that decision regardless of what his views had been.

"Cliques. I have not the slightest knowledge of the existence of any cliques within this Headquarters. I pray there are none, but I want to say in unequivocal terms that I will not tolerate such vicious elements if it is within my power to eliminate them.

"Criticism. Indulgence in criticism is an ever-present temptation. If yielded to it can quickly become a vice difficult to break. In the civilian fields, it is of lesser importance. In military organizations it is of vital importance. It tends to corrode, and corrosion produces friction and friction generates heat and eventually spoils any machine if uncorrected. I am not talking of honest difference of opinion, least of all at those times when issues are being debated. I am talking of the practice of vicious crabbing about the official actions of proper authority.

"Briefing. It is of the highest importance. It will be impossible for me to read the masses of paper which my conscience might dictate that I should read and the only alternative is oral presentation. I expect only matters of major importance, generally speaking those requiring basic decisions, or providing basic information which I should have, to reach me. When they do I want, in general, an oral presentation by an officer thoroughly familiar with the major points on each side of every issue involved. These presentations will be arranged for by the Secretary of the General Staff.

"When there are issues which are not clear, or when the matter is too involved for the presentation to be made by a member of the Secretariat, I shall expect the Chief of the Staff Division involved, or his Deputy, to present it in person. I do not want him accompanied by a whole array of assistants, advisors and counselors. If the problem is big enough to come to the Chief of Staff, and for him to have to understand the facts of the issue, then it was big enough to go to the Chief of the Division for like action.

"I want no ex-parte presentations at any time. If unresolved issues are presented to me, the views of the principal advocates of alternative courses of action must likewise be presented. Where the matter involves execution by a principal subordinate command, I want in advance, wherever practicable, the views of the commander who is to be charged with the responsibility for execution.

"High-type briefing requires high type thinking, a mastery of the facts, and the ability to summarize these facts with maximum effect in minimum words.

"Now, as to the work load. I think it is excessive. I think it must be and can be reduced. I shall seek the full co-operation of Secretary Stevens and the Under and Assistant Secretary, but within our own resources I think we can do much by better organization. More of the spoken than the written word; less attention to the written record for alibi purposes; and more efficient and adequate delegation of authority to subordinates.

"Now I have covered a good many things, all of them in my opinion of substantial and some of essential importance. There are many others. I don't pretend to know the answers yet. I have a lot to learn from you before I can expect to know the answers, but with your full help, on which I count, I am confident we shall find them. We shall meet together like this from time to time but not so often as to trespass unduly upon your busy days. I shall visit each of you in your domains in the near future.

"I have one note on which I want to close this first meeting. . . . I shall have in all matters that come before us but one criterion—the overall good of the United States Army—in the light of the counsel which you and our field commanders give me and then of the best judgment I am capable of exercising.

"I am convinced that whatever specters appear to some to lie ahead on close or distant horizons are the visionary imaginings of timid minds. Decisions that will try the soul may well lie ahead, but the strength of the people is found in its energies, its capabilities and above all in its character and moral principles. I think we have those in abundant measure.

"I believe we were put on earth for a high purpose. I believe the American people have a reservoir of material and spiritual strength amply adequate to fulfill that purpose.

"I am utterly confident in America's future, in the capacity of its leadership to meet the future and in the ability of the Army to contribute to that leadership in fullest measure."

Appendix 4

EXTRACTS DEFINING THE DUTIES OF THE CHIEF OF STAFF OF THE UNITED STATES ARMY

EXTRACT

(PUBLIC LAW 581—81st CONGRESS)
(CHAPTER 383—2d SESSION)
(H. R. 8198)

AN ACT

To provide for the organization of the Army and the Department of the Army, and for other purposes.

TITLE II—CHIEF OF STAFF AND THE ARMY STAFF

DUTIES OF CHIEF OF STAFF

Sec. 204. (a) The Chief of Staff shall have supervision of all members and organizations of the Army, shall perform the duties prescribed for him by the National Security Act of 1947, as amended, by this Act, and by other laws, and shall perform such other military duties not otherwise assigned by law as may be assigned to him by the President.

(b) The Chief of Staff shall preside over the Army Staff. Subject to the provisions of section 101 of this Act,* and of subsection (c) of this section, he shall be directly responsible to the Secretary of the Army for the efficiency of the Army, its state of preparation for military operations, and plans therefor. He shall transmit to the Secretary of the Army the plans and recommendations of the Army Staff, shall advise him in regard thereto, and, upon the approval of such plans or recommendations by the Secretary of the Army, he shall act as the agent of the Secretary of the Army in carrying the same into effect.

(c) Except as otherwise prescribed by law, the Chief of Staff shall perform his duties under the direction of the Secretary of the Army.

* Prescribes the powers and duties of the Secretary of the Army.

EXTRACT

SPECIAL REGULATIONS)   DEPARTMENT OF THE ARMY
No. 10-5-1   )   Washington, 25, D. C., 11 April 1950

ORGANIZATION AND FUNCTIONS

DEPARTMENT OF THE ARMY

26. Chief of Staff.—a. The Chief of Staff is the principal military adviser of the Secretary of the Army and is charged by him with the planning, development, and execution of the Army program.

b. The Chief of Staff, under the direction of the Secretary of the Army, supervises all members and organizations of the Army, performs the duties prescribed for him by the National Security Act of 1947 * and other laws, and performs such other military duties not otherwise assigned by law as may be assigned to him by the President or by the Secretary of the Army. Except as otherwise prescribed by law, by the President, or by the Secretary of Defense, the Chief of Staff performs his duties under the direction of the Secretary of the Army. The Chief of Staff, by virtue of his position, takes rank above all officers on the active list of the Army, Navy, and Air Force, except the Chairman of the Joint Chiefs of Staff and except the Chief of Naval Operations and the Chief of Staff, United States Air Force, if those latter two officers' appointments, as such, antedate his.

c. The Chief of Staff presides over the Army Staff, transmits to the Secretary of the Army plans and recommendations prepared by the Army Staff, advises him in regard thereto, and, upon the approval of plans or recommendations by the Secretary of the Army, acts as the agent of the Secretary of the Army in carrying the same into effect.

* These are duties of the Chief of Staff as a member of the JCS.

Appendix 5

ADDRESS BY GENERAL RIDGWAY BEFORE A JOINT SESSION OF CONGRESS MAY 22, 1952

Address by
General Matthew B. Ridgway
Before a Joint Session of Congress
May 22, 1952, 12:30 PM (EDT)

MR. PRESIDENT, MR. SPEAKER, DISTINGUISHED MEMBERS OF THE CONGRESS.

To be here, before the members of the Congress of my country, is the greatest honor. To the Senate and The House of Representatives, from whence came the invitation, and to the President, who gave his sanction, I express my profound and respectful thanks. Absorbed as you are with a multitude of problems, domestic and foreign, I hesitate to trespass upon your crowded hours. However, having just returned to this country, after nearly a year and a half in the Far East, the last thirteen months of which I served there as Commander-in-Chief, I feel you would wish me to report briefly on major problems encountered there, and to touch on a few of those matters which seem to me to be of substantial importance in our relations with the peoples of that region.

In outline, the matters I shall cover will be three: the conduct of military operations in Korea, the armistic negotiations, and our relations with the Japanese Government and its people. The first two pertain primarily to the Military Missions assigned me; the third, to my responsibilities as Supreme Commander for the Allied Powers, in which role, acting of course under the policy directives of superior authorities, I had overall responsibility for all acts of the Japanese Government, as well as for the relations of all Americans and allied personnel in Japan, both military and civilian, with the Japanese people.

I shall first discuss the conduct of military operations in Korea, from Christmas of 1950, the day of my arrival in the Far East, to date.

Assuming command of the Eighth Army on 26 December 1950, I found but three of its seven United States Divisions, and these badly depleted in strength, in the combat zone.

Three of the other four had been only recently evacuated from the Hungnam area and of these only the First Marine Division was again ashore in the southern tip of the peninsula. The Third and Seventh Divisions were still aboard ship, while the Second Division was reorganizing and re-equipping as a result of its severe battle losses in the Far North.

Thus, on a 135-mile front, only two United States Divisions were on the line of contact, the Third in blocking position to the rear. The remainder of this extended front was covered by the Republic of Korea Army, one British, and one Turkish regiment. The Korean Divisions were likewise at reduced strength in men and equipment, each with an exceedingly meagre artillery component, and all still suffering from the grievous blows they had sustained in the preceding six months.

Little time was granted before the first major hostile offensive struck. That time was used for personal visits to all Corps and Division Commanders in their own battle sectors, in order to obtain on the ground, as is possible in no other way, a personal estimate of the character and competence of the Commanders and of the problems and conditions confronting them. Based on those visits, decision was made that in the event of major hostile attack, the Army would delay in successive positions. With the instant cooperation of President Rhee, tens of thousands of indigenous laborers were put to work digging trenches and gun emplacements north of Seoul, South Korea's capital.

On New Year's eve the hostile attack was launched. It came shortly after dark on that winter evening, with its main effort a converging attack straight south—objective Seoul. By the afternoon of 3 January the situation of our troops on the north bank of the partly frozen Han, with its few bridges within range of enemy guns, became precarious and withdrawals to a secondary delaying position were directed. The withdrawal and establishment of the secondary line south of the Han was accomplished with only light losses in personnel and equipment.

The hostile follow-up was unaggressive, and within a few days the Army was realigned intact on its new position. Intelligence had earlier reported an unconfirmed mass of 174,000 Chinese troops within easy striking distance in the West alone, excluding the North Korean forces to the East. To check on this intelligence, aggressive reconnaissance was begun at once and steadily increased in strength.

Based on the combat intelligence so secured, the Eighth Army, with all of its United Nations and Republic of Korea contingents, was launched on 25 January 1951, into a slow, thoroughly coordinated offensive, so designed as to preclude large scale enemy penetrations and the by-passing of substantial enemy forces which might have been a menace to the Army in its then weakened condition. The results of this general offensive action are a matter of historical record. In February and March of 1951, we repulsed two strong hostile counter-thrusts, inflicting upon the enemy many times the losses we ourselves suffered.

I wish I could pay proper tribute to the magnificent conduct of United Nations troops throughout these operations. It is difficult to single out any one unit or the forces of any one nation, but to illustrate, I shall speak briefly of the 23d United States Infantry Regiment, Colonel Paul L. Freeman, Commanding, with the French Battalion and the normal components of artillery, engineer and medical personnel from the United States 2d Infantry Division. These troops in early February of 1951 sustained two of the severest attacks experienced during the entire Korean campaign. Twice isolated far in advance of the general battle line, twice completely surrounded, in near zero weather they repelled repeated assaults by day and night by vastly superior numbers of Chinese Infantry. They were finally relieved by an armored column from the United States 1st Cavalry Division in as daring and dramatic an operation as the war provided.

I personally visited these magnificent men during both operations and personally directed the attack of the relieving armored column which finally broke through and contributed to the utter and final rout of the enemy forces. I want to record here my conviction that these American fighting men with their French comrades-in-arms measured up in every way to the battle conduct of the finest troops America or France has produced throughout their national existence.

By late March a year ago the Eighth Army knew it had control of the situation. With few checks and with scrupulous concern for the conserving of every possible United Nations life, the Eighth Army with its magnificent Naval and Air support, moved steadily forward until by mid-April it stood again, with fighting heart, on or north of the 38th parallel almost entirely across the peninsula, imbued with unshakeable belief in its ability to destroy the enemy whenever and wherever met.

In no way could its splendid spirit have been better displayed than in the next succeeding six weeks, when under the conspicuous battlefield leadership of General Van Fleet, the Eighth Army met, checked and destroyed two more major enemy attacks. Both of these had gained considerable ground and had penetrated deeply into United Nations territory.

Subsequently, the entire Army, again with magnificent support of the air and sea arms, passed to the counter-offensive and continued its advance until by November last it stood approximately where now it stands—proud, defiant and confident of its capability for accomplishing any mission it might be assigned.

In a scant eighteen months, beginning with that early July day in 1950, when those first few immortal riflemen and airmen saw the Communist aggressors over their gun and bomb sights, the Eighth Army, comprising our own forces and those of the Republic of Korea, the British Commonwealth, Turkey, Greece, India, France, Ethiopia, Belgium, The

Netherlands, Luxemburg, The Philippines, Thailand, Denmark, Sweden, Norway, Colombia and Italy, has left a record of fidelity, valor and co-operation unsurpassed in all military history.

I pass now to the second of my three topics, the armistice negotiations.

For more than ten months, a group of men representative of the United Nations Command, and individually and collectively of as high principled integrity, fidelity, courage and vision, as any group ever assembled for any similar purpose has sought with full faith and loyalty to achieve an honorable armistice in accordance with the instructions of competent authority. That these gentlemen have so far been unsuccessful is no slightest mark of failure, but rather, in my opinion, a monumental tribute to their strict adherence to United Nations' concepts of human dignity and human rights and to their efforts in the cause of peace. As the military arm of a great Democracy, where that arm is completely, and under all conditions and circumstances, wholly subordinate and responsive to civil authority, they have served well.

Day after day, week after week, month after month, these splendid American soldiers, sailors, airmen and marines, with their colleagues of the Republic of Korea, acting on behalf of the United Nations, have striven with logic and reason, with patience and restraint, and above all with principle and truth, to overcome the blind hatred, the vituperative venom, the vicious falsehoods, deliberately employed, which are all inseparable elements of the technique of Communist negotiation.

I am constrained at this point to refer again to the officially propagated allegations of Communist leaders that the United Nations Command in Korea has employed both germ and gas warfare. I wish to reiterate what I have repeatedly stated publicly, that these allegations are false in their entirety; that no element of the United Nations Command has employed either germ or gas warfare in any form at any time.

In the whole black record of false propaganda, these charges should stand out as a monumental warning to the American people and to the Free World—a warning as menacing and as urgent as a forest fire bearing down upon a wooden village. The extent to which Communist leaders world wide have gone in fabricating, disseminating and persistently pursuing these false charges should impress upon the brains of those who yet fail or refuse to see the purpose of Communism, the deadly danger with which it confronts us and the Free World.

Today there rests in the Communists' hands a logical, reasonable, and honorable proposal for the settlement on equitable terms of the three remaining major unresolved issues—airfield construction, the Communist proposal for membership of the Soviet Union on the Neutral Nations

Supervisory Commission, and the Communist demand for forcible repatriation of prisoners of war.

The United Nations Command Delegation, under Vice Admiral C. Turner Joy, that sterling American who has presided over it with such distinction through these ten months, still stands ready to remove by explanation and clarification, any honest doubts or misunderstandings of the meaning of this proposal which the opposing delegation may harbor. It does not intend to bargain on those issues, the logic of which and the reasons for which have been repeatedly and exhaustively debated.

Acceptance or rejection, cessation or continuance of hostilities in Korea, is now the responsibility of the Communist leaders.

My third and final topic pertains to our relations with Japan.

This relation is of incalculable value and importance to this nation. Whether Japan grows in strength and resilience sufficient to withstand the impact of the inevitable blows of accidental and deliberate origin, or whether it declines in strength until circumstances or hostile powers succeed in effect in abrogating it, only history will tell. But if I may be pardoned expressing before this august body a personal conviction in a field of responsibility which was formerly mine, I would say the continuance, in fact the strengthening of the bonds which today make of America and Japan mutually understanding, mutually respecting, and cooperative friends, each confident of the support of the other, is of vital importance to the national welfare of both nations and to the peace of the world. The Japanese are a proud, sensitive, diligent and homogeneous people. They have given much to world culture. They have achieved much with little in a brief time. They are capable of far greater contributions within the society of free nations.

In Japan where the basic essentials of life—food, shelter, clothing and fuel—are in chronic short supply; where past mistakes, which no one recognized better than do the Japanese as both tragic and lamentable; these people face obstacles in number and magnitude which might make the stoutest hearts quail, but theirs do not. With vision, with resolution, with courage, and with high principle, they propose to build a new Japan, to set before their people a picture of their goal, and to choose a path to take them there. They are asking no charity but understanding, and the minimum reasonable help which will permit them to reassume in self-respecting dignity the responsibilities which sovereignty, now restored to them by the Japanese peace treaty, confers upon them as their own inherent right.

In this presentation I must express other convictions which to me have the stature of mountains viewed from the plain.

Underlying all major problems is Japan's vital need for the creation of a healthy and viable economy. Her present standard of living should be raised. Were it to be depressed, resulting conditions could have potentially grave consequences, for us as well as for them. The nourishing of her population, its employment in gainful occupation, its relations with neighbors both friendly and hostile, its ability to control the small but ever-dangerous Communist threat within her shores, all affect directly the extent to which she can stabilize a basic economy essential to her continued existence as a free and independent nation. In simple sequence, she must have access to raw materials which her industry can convert into products which she can sell in markets in which she must give and receive fair treatment in order to gain the foreign exchange to buy and import the food, fuel, and cloth she herself cannot produce.

The complexity of each of these problems will tax the best in intellect and integrity. That we can find mutually acceptable solutions to these problems is with me a matter of faith. I am convinced we can. I am convinced that if responsible, reasonable men will meet and sit down with a common purpose of finding a common solution, that the Creator of the world will endow their efforts with success. I am convinced that in no other way can success be achieved.

Included among these many problems are ones of singular political difficulty for the present, or any other Japanese government. Her military power having been destroyed, her merchant marine, vital to an island people, having been drastically reduced in tonnage, her constitutional limitations against maintaining ground, sea and air forces now having rendered her incapable of preserving unaided the independence recently restored to her, any government in Japan, the present included, is vulnerable to a degree to all manner of attack by both well and ill intentioned opposition.

Despite all this, the overwhelming attitude of the Japanese people toward us today is one of gratitude for the past, of hopefulness for sympathetic consideration in the future, and of great friendliness.

The unfortunate occurrences on the first of May last were reported with accuracy and objectivity from the scene. I believe, however, they received a misleading interpretation in the United States.

Throughout Japan as a whole, that day passed in a generally quiet and orderly manner. The few disorders which occurred, other than in Tokyo, were relatively minor in character. Had they occurred in the United States, they would have excited little, or no comment.

The disorders in Tokyo were of a different character. They bore the unmistakable stamp of deliberate communist design, the target of which would, of course, have been America and all the principles for which she stands. Such was the case. It was marked, however, and I believe the facts will sustain this opinion, by an absolute minimum either of anti-foreignism or anti-Americanism. The individual Americans who suffered bodily injury or indignity and the foreign property damaged or destroyed, the latter almost exclusively limited to a few automobiles, happened to be among or in the direct path of the rioting demonstrators. The results could have happened anywhere, and they have, on other occasions, even in our own land.

It would be a grave injustice to both Japanese and Americans to accord to this incident an exaggerated importance. That it revealed to the Japanese people the character and objective of Communist designs is a beneficial by-product. The overwhelming majority of responsible Japanese opinion has already repudiated these acts in no unmistakable terms. The Japanese government is alive to the Communist threat and resolved adequately to control it. The full influence of the Emperor, the Prime Minister, and of all responsible members of the present government will be employed to solve this problem in a manner to bring this situation under adequate control with the least practicable delay, and to keep it there.

In short, the Japanese are at our side. Their gaze is lifted to see the same objective we see. They are presently walking with us. Whether they continue or not is a responsibility which rests rather more on us in the immediate future than on them, for our strength is superior, our resources immeasurably greater, and ours is the role of leadership.

In all these great problems, which though lightly touched upon, have such profound significance for us and the future of our country, we can, I think we must, look for strength to solve them upon that greatest reservoir of America's strength—faith in principle and trust in God. If we draw upon this reservoir with resolution and courage, it will meet all our needs.

I have been greatly privileged to have had the responsibilities which I recently relinquished. I shortly assume new ones. With full reliance on this same reservoir and on the cooperation of all those engaged in our great crusade for peace and security, I approach our tasks with confidence higher than ever.

Index

SOLDIER:

The Memoirs of Matthew B. Ridgway

By General Matthew B. Ridgway, U.S.A., Ret.

As told to Harold H. Martin

Illustrated with 16 pages of photographs.

THE Ridgway memoir is the story of a second-generation professional soldier—a hawk-nosed hard-eyed battle commander whose sense of dedication has brought him both glory and anguish, but never deprived him of his essential humanity.

It's the story of a man with the range of mind to grasp a complex battle situation and plan an operation vast in scope—but who, when things got hot, was likely to (and did) grab an old-fashioned Springfield and fight like a platoon leader.

And of a man who became one of the leaders of the free world in the hazardous postwar years, taking his place beside (though not always in agreement with) Churchill and Truman, MacArthur and Montgomery, Eisenhower and Eden—and all the various statesmen and soldiers of East and West who have had to contribute to the vital decisions of peace or war. Do we fight for Quemoy and Matsu? For Korea and Formosa and Indo-China? For all of Western Europe and the Middle East? How do we match our strength to our mission?

It's about a man who could send his nearly shattered division into one last big fight, though he knew that it would bring his losses up to nearly 50 per cent—and who would fight like hell against his superiors when he thought they were sending his men into an operation that was beyond their strength and capabilities to perform.

The story traces the influences that made him—the early life on lonely Army posts in the West—the camping, the hiking, the pack trips that prepared him for life in the open. It takes him on through West Point, where he received a back injury which he was afraid to report and which has